THE SECRET SERVICE OF THE CONFEDERATE STATES IN EUROPE

Volume I

James D. Bulloch *(Century Magazine)*

The Secret Service of the Confederate States in Europe

or

How the Confederate Cruisers Were Equipped

by

JAMES D. BULLOCH

Volume I

With a New Introduction by

Philip Van Doren Stern

NEW YORK • THOMAS YOSELOFF • LONDON

Library of Congress Catalogue Card Number: 59-6863

Thomas Yoseloff, *Publisher*
11 East 36th Street
New York 16, N. Y.

Thomas Yoseloff Ltd.
123 New Bond Street
London W. 1, England

MANUFACTURED IN THE UNITED STATES OF AMERICA

INTRODUCTION TO NEW EDITION

TO UNDERSTAND the American Civil War one must go far beyond the military maneuvers, the political disputes, and the social history of the period. The sectional conflict was a major event in international affairs, and its great drama was played out not only on American battlegrounds but in Europe and on four of the world's five oceans. In fact, the shooting war began on the Atlantic Ocean when the Confederates drove away the steamer *Star of the West* on January 9, 1861, while she was trying to bring provisions to Major Anderson's garrison in Fort Sumter. And it ended on June 28, 1865, long after Appomattox, when the Confederate cruiser *Shenandoah* captured ten Yankee whaling vessels in the Bering Sea near the Arctic Circle.

Yet the naval phase of the Civil War has been neglected. The battle between the *Merrimac* and the *Monitor* has been well publicized, although it proved nothing more than the obvious fact that iron is harder to penetrate with shot and shell than wood. The sinking of the *Alabama* by the *Kearsarge* is fairly well known; so is Cushing's extraordinary exploit in blowing up the *Albemarle*. And there has been a spate of books about blockade running — the most picturesque and glamorized aspect of Civil War naval history. But that is about all. Aficianados who can give a day-by-day account of the movements of the Army of Northern Virginia, who know what Grant had for breakfast on the morning of the surrender of Vicksburg, or who can describe in detail what various cavalry commanders did as they dashed around the country, are strangely ignorant about what happened in Europe or on the high seas.

Yet it was there that the fate of the Confederacy was determined. Not Antietam or Gettysburg or Vicksburg decided the destiny of the United States as a nation. The decision was made in the chancellories of Europe, and, except for a few major battles, the outcome was influenced more by what happened on the sea than on the land. The United States and England nearly went to war over the seizure of the Confederate Commissioners Mason and Slidell on the open ocean. Had Brazil been more powerful, she might very well have terminated friendly relations with the United States when the U.S.S. *Wachusett* recklessly disregarded international law and rammed and captured the Confederate raider *Florida* in the neutral harbor of Bahia in 1864. Such far-flung ports as Melbourne, Cape Town, Halifax, Bermuda, Nassau, Havana, Matamoras, Lisbon, Gibraltar, Brest, Calais, Liverpool, Terceira, and Funchal all played parts in this mighty drama of world-wide significance. And, most important of all, was the deadly effect of the Federal blockade which slowly strangled the Confederacy by cutting it off from the rest of the world.

Since the Confederates did not win a single major battle on the high seas, even Confederate historians have tended to underplay naval affairs. Bulloch himself was apologetic when he said: "The officers of the Confederate Navy had so few opportunities to manifest their professional acquirements and personal qualities — indeed, so few of them were employed in strictly naval operations at all — that scarcely more than some half-dozen will find their names recorded in any future history, and the Confederate Navy as a corps will hardly appear as a factor in the Civil War." Yet a brief outline of the influence of this neglected aspect of Civil War history will show how important the sea was in shaping the final outcome of events.

On April 15 (the day after Fort Sumter was evacuated), President Lincoln called for 75,000 volunteers. Reaction was swift and retaliatory in the South. Virginia seceded from the Union on April 17; on the same day, Jefferson Davis, president of the provisional Confederate government in Montgomery, Alabama, issued a proclamation offering letters of marque and reprisal to owners of private vessels who would arm their ships and attack Yankee commerce. The Northern government promptly countered on April 19 by proclaiming a blockade of all Southern ports from South Carolina to Texas. On the 27th the blockade was extended to include North Carolina and Virginia.

Secretary of State Seward, who was known for his impetuous action at the beginning of the war, is generally blamed for two grievous technical errors involved in the Northern government's move. North Carolina had not yet seceded at this time, and did not actually leave the Union until May 20. Her decision to secede was doubtless accelerated by this too-hasty blockade of her ports.

Even more serious, however, was the use of the word blockade, for, as critics of the Lincoln administration quickly pointed out, a nation *blockades* an enemy's ports but *closes* its own in time of insurrection. This was a major blunder. It paved the way to foreign recognition of the Confederacy as a belligerent and would have led to full recognition of Southern independence if the coolly calculating men who were running the governments of Europe thought the Confederate States of America had a better-than-even chance of winning the war.

Both Northern and Southern governments blundered in their handling of naval and diplomatic affairs at the beginning of the war. The United States had refused to adopt the principles of international maritime law established on April 16, 1856, by the Declaration of Paris. Americans then believed that a nation with a small navy had nothing to gain by subscribing to the declaration. The four principles of international maritime law established by the Paris Convention were: 1. Privateering is and remains abolished; 2. The neutral flag covers enemy's goods, with the exception of contraband of war; 3. Neutral goods, with the exception of contraband of war, are not liable to capture under the enemy's flag; 4. Blockades . . .

must be effective, that is to say, maintained by a force sufficient really to prevent access to the coast of the enemy.

In 1861, just five years after the unfortunate American decision of 1856, Secretary of State Seward tried to repair the damage. It was to his country's advantage at this time to subscribe to the Paris convention because such a move would outlaw the Confederate privateers in the eyes of the world. He threw out tentative feelers to determine how his offer would be taken.

The discreet answer indicated that, although the United States would undoubtedly be welcomed to the convention, the offer would be received favorably only if it came from a united nation, North and South alike. Seward's counter-reply that the Confederate states in rebellion against the authority of the central government could not be considered an independent nation met with the answer that if the Confederate States of America was not independent then the United States could not impose a blockade of her ports. The full effect of the misuse of the word blockade was now felt.

The Confederates, however, were also in trouble. Since the Declaration of Paris outlawed privateering, the sending to sea of armed vessels of non-governmental origin (whose owners were out to make a profit) was naturally frowned upon by the powerful nations which had subscribed to the convention.

When news of the firing on Fort Sumter reached Europe, Proclamations of Neutrality were issued by England on May 13, and by France on June 10. These moves temporarily discouraged the Confederacy's hope for foreign intervention, but at no time did the South entirely abandon the effort to win active support from abroad. Even while her Army of Northern Virginia was marching to Appomattox in April, 1865, at least two "unofficial" Confederate agents were at work in Europe trying to persuade Napoleon III to aid the dying Confederacy.

At the opening of the war, the South had very few ships and even fewer yards or materials for building them.

Hasty but not very effective efforts were made to purchase ships in the North and Canada. Half a dozen small Federal revenue cutters were seized and sent out as armed vessels. A few vessels of various origin which were lying in Southern ports were acquired and outfitted.

But the agrarian Confederacy could not arm her soldiers or build an adequate navy without obtaining supplies and ships from abroad. Hardly more than three weeks after the provisional Confederate government had been formed at Montgomery, its new president named three commissioners to go to Europe. In addition to them, Major Caleb Huse was sent to England to buy arms and ammunition; credit was established in London with Fraser, Trenholm and Company, and James Dunwody Bulloch was summoned to Montgomery to be given *carte blanche* to buy and arm ships in Europe for the Confederate Navy. Since Great Britain was then regarded as "the arsenal, treasury, and dockyard of the greater part of the world," Bulloch naturally went there first.

The Confederacy was fortunate in obtaining the services of a man with Bulloch's wide experience in naval affairs, merchant shipping, shipbuilding, and naval armament. He was also trained in the ways of business, had many contacts abroad, and, above all, was the soul of integrity. His forthright honesty in insisting on returning the ship he was commanding at the outbreak of the war to her Northern owners may have irritated some of the Southern fire-eaters, but it established Bulloch's reputation for fair dealing beyond dispute.

To his work he brought superb competence, much ingenuity in solving ever-changing problems, and cool courage in the face of danger. It is doubtful whether anyone in the entire Western hemisphere was as well fitted for his special job as Bulloch was. The Confederate government had such faith in him that it entrusted millions of dollars to his care and abided by his decisions in matters which required huge investments and great discretion in negotiating on an international level. His efforts far outshone the combined accomplishments of the better known diplomatic commissioners Mason and Slidell. Yet everything Bulloch tried to do ended in failure, for he had bound his fate to the Confederacy's and had to see his hopes dashed with the downfall of the nation he had pledged himself to serve.

Bulloch's story is the story of the failure of a mission, but that does not detract from its interest. All Confederate missions eventually proved to be failures no matter how brilliantly successful they may have seemed at the time. A hundred successes will not save a war that is going to be lost. Yet Lee and Jackson and many lesser figures who fought for a lost cause are not forgotten. The men who worked to build the Confederate Navy are.

The expert in naval affairs whom fate had endowed with such potentialities for success — and then cruelly doomed to failure in the greatest enterprise of his life — was born near Savannah, Georgia, on June 25, 1823. He came from distinguished Scotch ancestors, one of whom settled in South Carolina in 1729. His great-grandfather, Archibald Bulloch, helped found the American nation, for he took an active part in the Revolution and fought in its wars. And James Dunwody Bulloch's father* was among the far-thinking men who backed the *Savannah* on her history-making voyage in 1819 as the first steamship to cross the Atlantic Ocean.

Salt water played an important part in Bulloch's life. At sixteen, six years before the Naval Academy at Annapolis was established in 1845, he became a midshipman in the United States Navy. For more than ten years, he slowly worked his way up in a branch of the services that had hardly changed since the Revolution and the War of 1812. Wooden ships and clumsy, heavy guns were operated by hard-driven men under a system of such brutal tyranny

* Bulloch's father, Major James Stephens Bulloch, married twice, in 1817 and 1832. Bulloch was the only child of the first marriage. Children of the second marriage were: Anna Bulloch (Mrs. James K. Gracie); Martha Bulloch (Mrs. Theodore Roosevelt, Sr.); and Irvine S. Bulloch, who was on the *Alabama* and the *Shenandoah*. In 1840 Major Bulloch built a pleasant Greek Revival house on the

that mutiny was not unknown. During Bulloch's training he came in contact with some of the officers who were to command the Federal fleets during the Civil War. He was on the *Decatur* under Farragut and succeeded David Dixon Porter to the command of the *Georgia.*

This steamer was the first one subsidized by the United States to carry mail to California when that new state became prosperous as a result of the large deposits of gold discovered there. Bulloch also commanded government mail steamers in the Gulf. Then he resigned from government service in 1853 to devote all his time to private shipping interests in New York.

At the outbreak of the war, he was in command of the steamer *Bienville,* plying between New York and various Southern ports. He was in New Orleans when word of the firing on Fort Sumter arrived. He immediately proffered his services to the Confederate government but explained that he was honor bound to take the *Bienville* to New York to turn her over to her owners there. Refusing all local efforts to buy the ship, he sailed for New York, found a letter summoning him to Montgomery, Alabama, and promptly hurried South.

The Confederacy appreciated his value. He was sent abroad forthwith and given almost limitless powers to buy ships and arm them. The story of his four-year long struggle with the governments of England and France is told here by Bulloch himself. This record of his efforts is one of the key books of the Civil War, fit to rank in importance with those written by the leading commanders on both sides. And his is a little-known but fascinating tale, involving, as it does, all sorts of cloak-and-dagger operations and behind-the-scenes negotiations carried on on a grand scale.

His account, however, is strictly a personal and partisan one. He does not attempt to write the history of the Con-

western edge of Roswell, nineteen miles north of Atlanta, Georgia. James D. must have visited there occasionally, but since he was away at sea after 1839, his connection with this place cannot have been close. His half-sister Martha was married there on December 22, 1853; her son was Theodore Roosevelt, President of the United States, who visited the house in 1905. Although no longer owned by the family, the old building, called Bulloch Hall, still stands.

federate Navy. His book contains practically nothing about naval warfare along the coasts and rivers of the North American continent. It is the report of a mission, addressed to the people of the former Confederate states who had never been told the whole truth about the secret efforts to build a navy overseas. One can only wish that all reports of secret missions were as well and as honestly written.

It is seldom that the top man in any major enterprise writes the history of the undertaking that was under his direction. On the Confederate side, Lee planned to write such a history and even began to gather material for it, but apparently did not put down a word. Jefferson Davis wrote a two-volume work which is really an apologia for his administration. Curiously enough, he practically ignored the naval aspect of the war, perhaps because (as Bulloch charitably explains, II, 51-52) he felt it unnecessary to mention disappointed hopes for a navy that never materialized in any great force.

The privateers which put to sea so hopefully as early as May, 1861, soon proved to be of little value because the increasingly vigilant Union blockading fleet made it nearly impossible for them to bring a captured prize of war into a Southern port. And most privateersmen were interested only in capture and sale, for profit was their primary motive. Only government-owned ships could afford to seek out and destroy, ruthlessly burning their captures at sea even though they were sometimes worth hundreds of thousands of dollars. Many of the people who directed this wholesale destruction and sent hundreds of fine ships to the bottom disliked having to do what they did even as a necessity of war. Bulloch explains his own feeling about this and indicates that he was not alone in his attitude (II, 112-13).

But the three Confederate commerce-raiders which Bulloch managed to get to sea were so effective in harassing Yankee shipping that American vessels either stayed in port, were sold to the Federal government to be armed and become part of the Navy, or were transferred to the flags of other nations. By March, 1864, the much-feared Confederate raiders had swept the oceans of the world so thoroughly of American merchant ships that the commander of the Confederate *Tuscaloosa* reported that out of more than a hundred vessels seen by him in the South Atlantic only one was of American origin. The depredations of the cruisers cost the North untold millions of dollars not only for the actual value of ships destroyed but for the potential value of trade that was lost.

The story of the Confederate commerce-raiders is confusing because the ships often changed names several times or bred new cruisers at sea by arming the vessels they captured. And ships under construction sometimes had to be sold under pressure to other governments. The exploits of the raiders of American origin, like the *Retribution,* the *Nashville,* and Raphael Semmes' first wartime command, the *Sumter,* are fairly easy to follow. But the foreign-built ships had much more complicated histories. The chart (which appears after the Introduction), summarizing what happened to the various Confederate raiders of foreign origin, will help to guide the reader through their tangled careers.

A study of the chart will show that of the nineteen commerce-raiders ordered abroad, only three — the *Florida,* the *Alabama,* and the *Shenandoah* — can be said to have had truly successful careers. (So did the five ships they captured, armed, and commissioned at sea: the *Lapwing* (rechristened the *Oreto*), the *Clarence,* the *Tacony,* the *Archer,* and the *Tuscaloosa.* Three other ships did some damage. These were: the *Georgia,* which ranged far and wide during her thirteen months at sea, but she was an unlucky vessel from the start; and the two British-built but American-based cruisers, the *Tallahassee* and the *Chickamauga,* which dashed out of Wilmington, N.C., to make many captures along the Atlantic coast, but they spent little time as active cruisers. The *Georgiana* never got to Charleston where she was to be armed, for she was wrecked while trying to enter the harbor. The *Rappahannock* was sealed up in Calais, and the *Stonewall* put to sea only a few days before Appomattox. The other ten ships contracted for in Europe never reached Confederate hands.

The failure to obtain possession of the ironclads (except the *Stonewall,* which was acquired too late in the war to be of any use) was most disappointing of all, for Bulloch had ambitious plans for them. The French-built rams were purposely planned to be short in length and shallow in draught so they could be maneuvered in the Mississippi River to defend that essential waterway for the Confederacy. The Laird rams were larger, but the French rams were more heavily armed and armored. Bulloch wanted to run them into Wilmington to recruit full crews there and then terrorize the Atlantic coast. He hoped to run them up the Potomac, make Washington untenable, and then steam north to Portsmouth, New Hampshire, spouting shot and shell, burn the important navy yard there, and demand a million dollars in gold as ransom for sparing the city from destruction. Boston and New York would also probably have come under the threat of the two ironclads' mighty guns.

These plans are not so far-fetched as they may seem. The *Tallahassee's* captain planned to take his far less formidable wooden cruiser "up the East River, setting fire to the shipping on both sides, and when abreast of the (Brooklyn) navy-yard to open fire, hoping some of our shells might set fire to the buildings and any vessels that might be at the docks." And he might have done so if he had been able to capture a local pilot who knew the treacherous waters around Hell Gate. Lt. Charles W. Read, whom Maffitt, commander of the *Florida,* had authorized to arm and commission a series of small Yankee ships as cruisers, boldly entered the harbor of Portland, Maine, to capture the U.S. Revenue Cutter *Caleb Cushing.* Only a dead calm prevented him from running away with his prize during the night.

Even though Bulloch considered his mission a failure, the tiny Confederate Navy inflicted so much damage on Northern commerce that the United States government demanded enormous reparations from Great Britain after the war. These were the famous *Alabama* Claims, which, after protracted correspondence and several meetings, were finally settled by arbitration in Geneva by an International Tribunal that (on September 14, 1872) awarded the United States $15,500,000 in gold as damages. By an odd coincidence this was almost exactly the same amount raised by the Confederate (Erlanger) bond issue of March, 1863.

When the war ended in April, 1865, the Confederate Navy still had two cruisers at sea. One was the armored ram *Stonewall* which entered Nassau on May 6 only to find that the Confederate States of America had ceased to exist as a government. This heavily armed and armored ram might very well have made a difference in the outcome of the war if it had arrived earlier, for no ship — or combination of ships in the United States Navy — could have stood up against it. The Union also was building a super-ram, the giant *Dunderberg,* which was under construction in New York. But this powerful ironclad, nearly 400 feet long with a 50-foot ram, was not ready for launching until July 22, 1865, and therefore could have been of no help.

Far out in the North Pacific, near the Arctic Circle, the *Shenandoah,* cut off from all communication from Richmond, went on burning Yankee whalers until June 28, 1865. Her mass capture of ten ships on that day was the last offensive act of the already extinct Confederacy. Bulloch had notified the *Shenandoah's* commander on June 19 that Jefferson Davis had been taken prisoner and that the war was over, but copies of his letter, which were sent by Earl Russell to various British consuls in the Pacific, never reached the *Shenandoah.* Her commander hailed the British ship *Barracouta* on August 2, and on being informed that the war had ended, dismantled her guns, and made a 17,000-mile run to Liverpool, where he turned his ship over to the British authorities on November 6, 1865. That day marks the true end of the Confederate States of America as a fighting nation.

Besides building and buying vessels intended to be armed

and used as commerce-raiders, Bulloch also obtained a number of fast blockade runners for the Confederate government. Some of them were still on the ways in various British yards when the war ended; others got to sea. One of them was the *Bat* which was captured late in 1864, and which Admiral David Dixon Porter then used as his flagship. During the Appomattox Campaign, President Lincoln slept on this ship several times, and it carried General Sherman back to New Bern after the historic council of war at City Point on March 27-28, 1865.

After the end of the war, the United States government tried to seize all Confederate assets in Europe. Years of litigation brought ruin to the house of Fraser, Trenholm and Company, which had handled Confederate funds and credits. As so often happened in governmental financial transactions of this kind during the postwar era, fraud and chicanery drained off the greater part of the money that was obtained, so the American taxpayer gained very little from the long-continued effort to obtain what was left of the Confederate funds in Europe.

Bulloch was embittered by his experiences. Since it seemed unlikely that amnesty and pardon would be extended to him as one of the chief agents of the former Confederate government, he decided to remain in Liverpool permanently. He entered the shipping business there, specializing in the cotton trade, and although he prospered in his new enterprise, he dropped so far out of the public's eye that his postwar career would be practically unknown if it were not for his close connection with the Roosevelt family.

Young Theodore, not quite eleven, first met "Uncle Jimmie" when he went with his family to visit the Bullochs in England in 1867. He was there again in 1872 and also in 1881, when the aspiring twenty-three-year-old author got some help from his uncle on certain nautical problems involved in the history of the War of 1812 which he was then writing.

Bulloch had been married twice — in 1851 and in 1857. He had five children, three boys and two girls. As he grew older, the conservative Southern gentleman became a British Tory with Gladstone (who had succeeded Lord Russell in 1867 as leader of the Liberal Party) as his special *bête noire.*

He sometimes traveled to other countries on business, but he apparently never revisited his native land. He lived on until the twentieth century, and was well spoken of by those who knew him as a kind, affable, and distinguished elderly gentleman who could seldom be persuaded to talk about his wartime experiences. His book is his testament, his autobiography, and his personal account of the secret operation he had masterminded for the Confederacy. Evidently he said in it all that he intended to say. It was published in England in a small edition from which a few hundred sets of sheets were imported into the United States to be published in New York in 1884. Since then the book has become so exceedingly rare that copies of it are seldom offered for sale.

Its author died in England on January 7, 1901. His gravestone, now reportedly overgrown and neglected, should have borne an inscription more impressive than the simple dates of birth and death. A suitable epitaph for the man who tried so hard to build a Confederate Navy would be Seneca's words: "Admire those who attempt great things, even though they fail."

PHILIP VAN DOREN STERN

A CHART OF THE NAVAL HISTORIES OF THE CONFEDERATE CRUISERS OF EUROPEAN ORIGIN

Name by which ship is best known. Names of Commanders.	*Dockyard or first name.*	*Date started to build or acquired. Place of origin.*	*Contract negotiated by —*	*First sailing date. Names of supply vessels.*	*Captured ships armed and commissioned at sea.*	*Eventual fate*
Florida J. N. Maffitt J. N. Barney C. M. Morris	*Manassas* and *Oreto*	Built at Liverpool by W. C. Miller & Sons. Work started in June, 1861.	J. D. Bulloch	From Liverpool, Mar. 22, 1862. *Bahama* and *Prince Alfred*	*Lapwig (Oreto)*, Mar. 28, 1863. com. S. W. Averett; com. R. S. Floyd. *Clarence*, May 6; *Tacony*, May 10; *Archer*, June 15; com. Charles W. Read	Captured by U.S.S. *Wachusett* at Bahia, Brazil Oct. 7, 1864. Sunk at Hampton Roads, Va., Nov. 28, 1864.
Alabama Raphael Semmes	No. 290 and *Enrica*	Built at Birkenhead by the Lairds. Work started August, 1861.	J. D. Bulloch	From Liverpool, July 29, 1862. *Aggripina*	*Tuscaloosa*, June 21, 1863. (origin. the *Conrad*). com. John Low	Sunk by U.S.S. *Kearsarge* off the coast of France, June 19, 1864.
Georgiana Geo. T. Sinclair	?	Construction ordered in the spring of 1862	J. D. Bulloch	From Liverpool, Jan. 21, 1863.		Wrecked Mar. 19, 1863, trying to enter Charleston.
"Lt. North's ironclad"	?	Built at Glasgow by G. and J. Thompson May, 1862.	Lt. James H. North			Sold to Denmark
Pampero	*Canton*	Glasgow July, 1862	George T. Sinclair			Detained by British, Nov. 1863; then retained by builders.
Two Laird ironclad rams	No. 294, No. 295 Temporary names during Egyptian deal: *El Tousson* *El Mounassir*	Birkenhead, July, 1862	J. D. Bulloch	Seized by British, Oct. 1863. Bought for their navy.		Became part of British Navy, (May 20, 1864) under names *Scorpion* and *Wivern.*
Georgia Wm. L. Maury	*Japan* *Virginia*	Dumbarton. Launched Jan. 10, 1863.	M. F. Maury	From Greenock, Scotland Apr. 2, 1863. *Alar*		Armament dismantled in Liverpool, May 2, 1864. Ostensibly sold and sent to Lisbon, Aug. 8, 1864. Captured Aug. 15 by U.S.S. *Niagara.*
Alexandra	?	Built at Liverpool by W. C. Miller. Launched Mar. 7, 1863.	Built for Fraser, Trenholm who intended to present her to Confederacy. Though small, Bulloch admits she could have been armed (I, 338-39).	Seized by British Apr. 5, 1863. Released Apr. 1864.		Name changed to *Mary.* Sailed for Bermuda, etc.; again seized in Nassau, Dec. 13, 1864. Held for trial until end of war.

Four French-built wooden corvettes	Bordeaux corvettes: *Yeddo, Osacca* Nantes corvettes: Names: ?	Two in Bordeaux Two in Nantes, May, 1863	J. D. Bulloch	Two (Bordeaux) sold to Prussia. Two (Nantes) sold to Peru. May, 1864.	Remained in Prussian and Peruvian Navies.
2 French-built rams. Prussian ram sold to Prussia.	?	Bordeaux July, 1863	J. D. Bulloch		Sold by the French to Prussia.
Danish ram, later *Stonewall* (CSN). Thos. J. Page	*Sphinx* *Stoerkodder* *Olinde*			Sold to Denmark, May 1864. Resold to C.S.A. Dec. 1864; renamed *Stonewall;* sailed from Copenhagen Jan. 6, 1865. Supply ship: *City of Richmond*	In Ferrol, Spain, Feb. 2 to Mar. 24 for repair. Arrived Nassau May 6 to find war over. Surrendered to U.S. May 19, 1865. Later sold to Japan.
Rappahannock Samuel Barron C. M. Fauntleroy	*Victor* *Scylla*	Purchased as former dispatch boat from British Navy, Sept. 14, 1863.	M. F. Maury	From Sheerness Nov. 24, 1863.	Laid up in Calais from Nov. 1863 to Mar. 1865; claimed by U.S. Govt. at end of war.
Tallahassee John T. Wood Wm. H. Ward J. Wilkinson	*Atlanta* *Olustee*	Built at "Millwall below London." Made two trips as blockade runner in spring 1864 between Bermuda and Wilmington, N.C. Fitted out in Wilmington and commissioned as cruiser July 20, 1864.	?	From Wilmington, Aug. 6-25, and Oct. 29-Nov. 7, 1864, to raid Atlantic coast. Transformed into blockade runner *Chameleon.*	Ran to Liverpool near end of war. Claimed there by U.S. and sold to Japan.
Shenandoah J. I. Waddell	*Sea King*	Purchased Sept. 20, 1864. Had made one voyage to Bombay.	J. D. Bulloch	From London Oct. 8, 1864. *Laurel*	Turned over to British at Liverpool, Nov. 6, 1865. Surrendered to U.S. and sold to Sultan of Zanzibar. Sank in storm in Indian Ocean, 1879.
Chickamauga J. Wilkinson	*Edith*	Built in England as blockade runner, and made several trips in spring of 1864. Acted as cruiser from Oct. 29 to Nov. 19, 1864.	?	From Wilmington, Oct. 29, 1864.	Burned after fall of Ft. Fisher in 1865.

CHRONOLOGY

1860	
Nov. 6	Lincoln is elected President of the United States.
Dec. 20	South Carolina secedes.
1861	
Jan. 9	Mississippi secedes.
Jan. 9	*The Star of the West* is fired on when it attempts to provision Fort Sumter.
Jan. 10	Florida secedes.
Jan. 11	Alabama secedes.
Jan. 19	Georgia secedes.
Jan. 26	Louisiana secedes.
Feb. 1	Texas secedes.
Feb. 4	Delegates from the first six states to secede meet at Montgomery, Ala., to form a provisional Confederate government.
Feb. 9	Jefferson Davis is named president of the provisional Confederate government.
Feb. 18	Davis is inaugurated.
Feb. 27	Davis names three Confederate Commissioners to Europe: William L. Yancey, Pierre A. Rost, and A. Dudley Mann. Yancey and Rost sail on March 16.
Mar. 4	Abraham Lincoln is inaugurated President of the U.S.A.
Mar.	Bulloch's ship, the *Bienville,* is seized in New York. He goes to Washington to see the Secretary of the Treasury, Salmon P. Chase.

1861	
Apr. 12	The Confederates fire on Fort Sumter at 4:30 A.M.
Apr. 13	Gen. Anderson hauls down the flag at Fort Sumter at 1:30 P.M.
Apr. 13	Word of the firing on Fort Sumter reaches New Orleans by telegraph while Bulloch is in port with the *Bienville*. He offers his services to the Confederate government. Confederate officials try to purchase the *Bienville*, but Bulloch refuses to sell.
Apr. 14	The *Bienville* sails from New Orleans at 8 A.M. Fort Sumter is evacuated.
Apr. 15	Lincoln calls for 75,000 3-month volunteers.
Apr. 17	Virginia secedes.
Apr. 17	Davis issues a proclamation offering letters of marque to privateers who will capture or destroy Union shipping.
Apr. 18	The U.S. arsenal at Harpers Ferry is burned and abandoned to prevent it from falling into Confederate hands.
Apr. 19	Lincoln proclaims blockade of the Southern coast from Texas to South Carolina. The Sixth Massachusetts Regiment is attacked as it passes through Baltimore to defend Washington.
Apr. 20	The Norfolk (Va.) Navy Yard is burned and abandoned.
Apr. 20	Robert E. Lee resigns from the U.S. Army and offers his services to his native Virginia.
Apr. 22	Bulloch arrives in New York on the*Bienville*, turns the ship back to her owners, and finds a letter from Judah P. Benjamin summoning him to Montgomery.
Apr. 22-25	Washington, D.C., is cut off from communication with the Northern states.
Apr. 27	The Union blockade is extended to North Carolina and Virginia.
Apr. 29	Confederate Commissioners Yancey and Rost arrive in London.
May 1 (?)	Bulloch leaves for the South.

1861	
May 3	Lincoln calls for 42,000 3-year volunteers.
May 3	News of the Proclamation of Blockade is published in the London papers.
May 5	Bulloch arrives in Nashville, Tenn.
May 6	Arkansas secedes.
May 7	Bulloch arrives in Montgomery, Ala.
May 8	He sees Benjamin, who asks him to go to Europe.
May 9	He leaves Montgomery by train, goes to Detroit, and takes a steamship from Montreal to Liverpool.
May 13	The British issue a Proclamation of Neutrality.
May 13	Charles Francis Adams, the new American Minister to England, arrives in Liverpool, and goes to London on May 14.
May 16	At noon, Adams takes full charge of the American Legation in London.
May 20	North Carolina secedes.
May 29	Richmond becomes the capital of the Confederacy.
June 4	Bulloch arrives in Liverpool.
June	Construction of the *Oreto* (later the *Florida*) begun.
June 10	The French issue a Proclamation of Neutrality. They are followed on June 16 by the Netherlands; on June 17 by Spain; and on August 1 by Brazil.
June 24	Tennessee secedes.
June 30	Raphael Semmes takes the *Sumter*, the first Confederate warship, out of the Mississippi River and escapes the Union blockading fleet.
July 3	Semmes captures his first prize, the *Golden Rocket* of Maine, and burns her at sea off the coast of Cuba.
July 21	The Battle of Bull Run (First Manassas) is a Confederate victory.
July 27	McClellan replaces McDowell.
July 27	The first remittance for the Confederate Navy reaches England.

1861

Aug. 1 — A contract for the construction of No. 290 (later the *Alabama*) is signed.

Oct. 15 — Bulloch leaves Holyhead in the newly purchased blockade runner, the *Fingal.* The ship, loaded with arms, ammunition, and supplies, heads for Savannah, Ga.

Nov. 2 — After leaving Terceira (in the Azores) the *Fingal* arrives in Bermuda.

Nov. 7 — The *Fingal* leaves Bermuda.

Nov. 8 — Confederate Commissioners Mason and Slidell are taken from the British steamer *Trent* by Captain Charles Wilkes of the U.S.S. *San Jacinto.*

Nov. 12 — The *Fingal* arrives in Savannah.

Nov. 14 — Bulloch goes to Richmond to report to the Confederate Navy Department.

Nov. 23 — He returns to Savannah.

Nov. 30 — Bulloch is ordered to take command of the first cruiser to leave England.

Dec. 24 — For the next few weeks Bulloch tries to take the *Fingal* back to England, but Savannah is so closely patroled by the Federal blockading fleet that he has to give up the attempt.

Dec. 26 — The State Department admits that the seizure of Mason and Slidell was illegal and allows them to proceed to Europe.

1862

Jan. 1 — Mason and Slidell embark on a British gunboat in the harbor of Provincetown, Mass.

Jan. 13 — E. M. Stanton replaces Simon Cameron as U.S. Secretary of War.

Jan. 24 — Bulloch arrives in Wilmington, N.C., to sail for England.

Feb. 5 — He runs the blockade as a passenger in the *Annie Childs.*

Mar. 9 — Battle of the *Monitor* and the *Merrimac* at Hampton Roads, Va.

Mar. 10 — Bulloch arrives in Liverpool.

Mar. 14 — Federals capture New Bern, N.C.

1862	
Mar. 21	Bulloch notifies the Confederate Navy Department that he is investigating the possibility of having ironclad ships built in England.
Mar. 22	The *Florida* sails from Liverpool.
Apr. 6-7	The Battle of Shiloh (Pittsburgh Landing).
Apr. 11	Fort Pulaski, commanding the approaches to Savannah, Ga., is surrendered to the Federals after a heavy bombardment.
Apr. 28	The *Florida* arrives in Nassau.
Apr. 29	Farragut runs his fleet past the Mississippi River forts and occupies New Orleans on April 29.
May 4	Maffitt takes command of the *Florida.*
May 11	The Confederates evacuate Norfolk, Va.
May 15	The *Alabama* is launched.
May and June	The Peninsular Campaign to take Richmond is unsuccessful.
June 15	The *Florida* is seized by the British when her supply ship, the *Bahama,* arrives in Nassau.
July	Work on the two Laird ironclad rams is begun in England.
July 20	Yellow fever strikes the *Florida* in Nassau.
July 29	The *Alabama* sails from Liverpool.
Aug. 2	The British release the *Florida.* She leaves Nassau the next day and goes to Green Cay, about 75 miles south of Nassau, to be armed and fitted out.
Aug. 16	With yellow fever still raging on board, the *Florida* begins her career as a Confederate raider.
Aug. 19	The *Florida* enters the port of Cardenas, Cuba, with nearly everyone on board prostrated by yellow fever.
Aug. 24	The *Alabama* is commissioned at sea.
Aug. 27	The Battle of Second Manassas is a Confederate victory.
Sept. 4	The *Florida* enters Mobile Bay under fire. She remains there, undergoing repair, until January, 1863.

1862	
Sept. 16-17	Battle of Antietam (Sharpsburg).
Sept. 20	Bulloch is notified that Commander M. F. Maury is being sent to England on special service.
Sept. 22	Lincoln releases his Emancipation Proclamation to the press.
Nov. 5	McClellan is relieved from command and is replaced by Burnside.
Dec. 13	The Battle of Fredericksburg is lost by Burnside.
Dec. 28	Bravay and Company of Paris start negotiations to purchase the two Laird rams, ostensibly for Egypt.
1863	
Jan. 16	The *Florida* runs out of Mobile Bay and escapes the Federal fleet.
Jan. 25	Hooker replaces Burnside.
Jan. 29	A European loan of $15,000,000 is authorized by the Confederate Congress.
Jan. 31	The Confederate ironclads *Chicora* and *Palmetto State* make an unsuccessful attempt to raise the Federal blockade of Charleston.
Mar.	Maury buys the *Japan* (the *Georgia*) to be used as a Confederate cruiser.
Mar. 7	The *Alexandra* is launched.
Mar. 19	Confederate bonds offered for sale in Europe. The issue is oversubscribed.
Apr. 5	The *Alexandra* is seized by the British.
Apr. 11	Mallory directs Bulloch to employ European mechanics and experts for work in Confederacy.
May 2-4	The Battle of Chancellorsville is lost by Gen. Hooker.
May 6	The *Florida* captures the *Clarence* and converts her into a Confederate raider, Lt. C. W. Read commanding.
May 22	The *Alabama* leaves Bahia, Brazil.
June 17	The *Atlanta* is captured by the *Weehawken* near Savannah.

1863

June 20	The *Alabama* captures the U.S. bark *Conrad* and converts her into a Confederate raider under the name *Tuscaloosa,* John Low commanding.
July 1-3	Battle of Gettysburg. After it, Lee retreats to Virginia.
July 4	Vicksburg, Miss., surrenders; on July 8, Port Hudson, La., also surrenders, thus closing the Mississippi River to the Confederacy.
July 13-16	Draft riots in New York.
July 16	Bulloch signs a contract for two ironclad ships to be built in France.
Aug. 16-29	The *Georgia* at Simon's Bay, Cape of Good Hope.
Aug. and Sept.	The Union fleet makes an unsuccessful attempt to take Charleston Harbor.
Sept. 19-20	The Battle of Chickamauga, Ga., except for Thomas's firm stand, is a Union defeat.
Sept. 24	The Russian Atlantic fleet visits New York as a gesture of friendship. On Oct. 12, the Russian Pacific fleet enters San Francisco Bay. The ships remain in American waters for the next seven months.
Oct. 1	Bulloch reports "disappointment in all our British undertakings."
Oct. 9	The British plan to seize the two Laird ironclads before they are completed.
Oct. 27	The British seize the two Laird ironclads and put a marine guard on them.
Oct. 28	The *Georgia* arrives in Cherbourg.
Nov. 23-25	Battles of Chattanooga and Missionary Ridge are Union victories.
Nov. 24	The *Victor* is commissioned at sea as the *Rappahannock.*
Nov. 26	Bulloch begins to doubt that the two ironclad rams being built in France will be permitted to go to sea.
Dec. 27	The Confederate raider *Tuscaloosa* is seized by the British at Simon's Bay, Cape of Good Hope.

1864

Jan. 27	Bulloch goes to France to try to persuade Napoleon III to buy the two Laird rams but is advised that such an appeal would be hopeless.
Feb. 18	Bulloch notifies the Confederate Navy Department that the ships ordered in France have been forbidden to sail.
Mar. 10	U. S. Grant is placed in command of all Union armies.
May	The *Alexandra* is released by the British; her name is changed to the *Mary;* and she sails for Bermuda and Halifax.
May and June	Wilderness, Spottsylvania, and Cold Harbor campaigns.
May 2	The *Georgia* reaches Liverpool, is sold to new owners there, sails for Lisbon on August 8, and is seized by the U.S.S. *Niagara.*
May 20	Preliminary terms for the two Laird ironclad rams (Nos. 294 and 295) to be sold to the British Navy are settled.
June	Bulloch goes to Paris to consult with Slidell on the disappointing status of the French-built rams.
June 7	Lincoln is nominated for President by the Republican (Union) Party.
June 11	The *Alabama* arrives in Cherbourg to refit.
June 14	The U.S.S. *Kearsarge* arrives off the coast of France and watches the port of Cherbourg to prevent the *Alabama* from leaving.
June 19	The *Alabama* leaves Cherbourg and is sunk at sea by the *Kearsarge.*
Aug. 1	Bulloch gives up hope of getting any ships built in France.
Aug. 5	Farragut captures Mobile.
Aug. 31	McClellan is nominated for President by the Democratic Party.
Sept. 2	Sherman takes Atlanta.
Sept. 16	Bulloch tells Richmond he has bought the *Shenandoah,* then named the *Sea King.*

1864

Oct. 7	The *Florida* is captured at Bahia, Brazil, by the U.S.S. *Wachusett*.
Oct. 8	The *Shenandoah* sails from London, while her supply ship, the *Laurel*, sails from Liverpool to meet her.
Oct. 20	The *Shenandoah*, outfitted at sea, goes into action.
Nov. 8	Lincoln is elected President for a second term.
Nov. 15	Leaving Atlanta burning, Sherman marches across Georgia toward the sea.
Nov. 28	The *Florida* is sunk at Hampton Roads, Va.
Dec. 1	William L. Dayton, American Minister to France, dies in Paris; John Bigelow succeeds him.
Dec. 13	The *Alexandra* (now the *Mary*) is again seized by the British, this time in Nassau, and is held under trial until after the end of the war.
Dec. 16	The details of buying the ram *Stonewall* from Denmark are settled.
Dec. 21	Sherman takes Savannah.

1865

Jan. 6	The *Stonewall* sails from Copenhagen.
Jan. 8	The *Stonewall* arrives at Elsinore.
Jan. 15	Fort Fisher is taken by Union assault, closing Wilmington, N.C., the last major Confederate port.
Jan. 24	The *Stonewall* meets the *City of Richmond* at sea to take on crew.
Jan. 25	The *Shenandoah* arrives in Melbourne, Australia.
Jan. 31	The House of Representatives passes the Thirteenth Amendment abolishing slavery.
Feb. 1	No new contracts made in Europe by the Confederate Navy Department after this date.
Feb. 2	The *Stonewall* puts into Ferrol, Spain.
Feb. 3	Lincoln holds a peace conference with the Confederates at Hampton Roads, but it comes to nothing.
Feb. 18	Sherman takes Columbia, S.C.; Charleston, S.C., surrenders to the Federal fleet.

1865

Feb. 18	The *Shenandoah* leaves Melbourne.
Mar. 24	The *Stonewall* sails from Ferrol.
Mar. 29	Grant begins the Appomattox Campaign.
Apr. 1	The Battle of Five Forks. The *Stonewall* sails from Teneriffe (Canary Islands) to attack Sherman's bases in the Carolinas.
Apr. 2	Richmond and Petersburg are evacuated.
Apr. 9	Lee surrenders the Army of Northern Virginia to Grant at Appomattox Court House.
Apr. 14	Lincoln is assassinated and dies the next morning.
Apr. 26	Surrender of Joseph E. Johnston's army.
May 6	The *Stonewall* arrives in Nassau to find that the war is over.
May 10	Jefferson Davis is taken prisoner near Irwinville, Ga.
May 11	The *Stonewall* arrives in Havana and is surrendered there.
May 21	The *Shenandoah* enters the Okhotsk Sea; she leaves there June 13 and sails north.
May 26	Kirby Smith surrenders all the Confederate troops west of the Mississippi River.
June 28	The *Shenandoah,* on the edge of the Arctic Circle, makes her last capture.
Aug. 2	The *Shenandoah,* off the coast of Mexico, learns from the captain of H.M.S. *Barracouta* that the war has ended.
Nov. 6	The *Shenandoah* arrives in Liverpool and is turned over to the British authorities there.

1871

May 8	The Treaty of Washington is signed to arbitrate the *Alabama* Claims.
Dec. 15	An International Tribunal meets in Geneva, Switzerland, to decide the *Alabama* Claims.

1872

June 15 to Sept. 14	The Geneva Tribunal settles the *Alabama* Claims and awards the United States government $15,500,000 in gold as damages.

PREFACE.

THE American Civil War of 1861-65 will always remain a notable event in history; and its effects upon the character of the American people and the political institutions of the country are questions which have not yet received a final solution. Thus it is probable that every addition to the history of that great struggle which is founded upon facts not hitherto known, will be received with some favour by those who were actors in the events, or who, from their position as statesmen, are led to observe and to carefully note the political disasters which periodically disturb contemporary nations.

But it is, nevertheless, manifest that the subject has already lost its interest with the general public, who are mostly absorbed in practical affairs of present importance, or who seek amusement in literature of a wholly different kind. This work has not, therefore, been written with the expectation of supplying a public demand, but from a sense of duty, and in compliance with the urgent request of many persons who took opposite sides in the Civil War, and who have thought that the future historian should be furnished with the facts relating to the foreign-built navy of the Confederate States.

Many unavoidable hindrances have prevented the steady, continuous completion of the work; and the necessity of reading a very large mass of diplomatic correspondence, official reports, and legal proceedings, not always readily accessible, has added to the difficulty and delay. The Introduction and Chapter I. were written in the autumn of 1881; the greater portion of the remainder was written from April to August, 1882; and two chapters not until April-May, 1883. As it has been impossible to revise the manuscript critically, the foregoing explanation is necessary to account for the apparent discrepancy in the illustrations taken from current events, which, upon the supposition that the whole work was written at about the date of the opening chapter, would place some of the incidents in the anomalous position of being used for demonstration before they happened. The events thus used had very lately or just occurred, at the time when the chapters in which they appear were in course of composition; and it is hoped that the context will sufficiently mark the time when they transpired, even if the date has not been altered.

A thorough revision of the whole work would have made it necessary to rewrite a large portion of several chapters and to abridge others, in order to bring them all into precise harmony in respect to the dates of those incidental and transitory occurrences which have been chosen for illustrations, and also to avoid the appearance of unnecessary repetition in applying the principles of law and the actions of public officials to the case of each separate ship.

But while the want of a careful revision has left many defects which mar the excellence of the narrative as a literary production, it does not in any way affect the historical accuracy of the statements, and I have had no other purpose than to furnish a truthful record of the efforts made by the Confederate Government to organize a naval force during the Civil War.

The facts connected with the building and equipping of the ships are stated upon my own knowledge. Such incidents in their cruises as involved questions of belligerent or neutral rights and duties are taken from the letters of their commanding officers to me at the time of the occurrences, or have been epitomized from subsequent conversations with them. All that has reference to the origin, armament, and commissioning of the ships has been stated specifically and without reserve.

Their adventures afterwards have not been told with much particularity, because special histories of their cruises have already been published, and because the chief purpose of this work is to explain the naval policy of the Confederate Government, and the controversies which that policy provoked between the United States and some of the neutral Powers.

I would have gladly avoided any allusion to the causes of the war, and criticism of the diplomatic and other correspondence of United States officials on the subject of the Confederate cruisers, but that correspondence was not confined to complaints and remonstrances against the alleged encouragement and facilities granted to the Confederate States by the neutral Powers. It was made the medium for prejudicing those Powers against the South by *ex parte* statements in reference to the causes of the war, and of disseminating charges and insinuations wholly unsupported by evidence, whose manifest purpose was not only to discredit the policy, but the honour of the Confederate Government.

To have pointed out the inaccuracies of the statements affecting the conduct of neutrals, and of those which specifically referred to the equipment of the ships, and to have omitted all reference to the political disquisitions and allegations contained in the same despatches, would have borne the appearance of tacitly admitting their truth and the justice of their application.

I hope it will be understood that the names of official persons are mentioned historically, and that the criticisms are directed against the contents of the documents and not against the writers.

LIVERPOOL, *June*, 1883.

CONTENTS OF VOL. I.

CHAPTER III.

CHAPTER IV.

CHAPTER VII.

ILLUSTRATIONS — VOLUME I

THE SECRET SERVICE OF THE CONFEDERATE STATES IN EUROPE

Volume I

THE SECRET SERVICE

OF THE

CONFEDERATE STATES IN EUROPE.

INTRODUCTION.

SINCE the end of the great Civil War which convulsed the States of the American Union during the years 1861-5, many partial histories of the causes which produced the struggle, and the events which marked its progress, have been published.

Some of these were written under the influence of the heat and passion aroused and fostered by the magnitude and bitterness of the contest, and cannot therefore be received with the confidence which every narrative must inspire in order to win and to maintain that worthy and lasting credit which distinguishes history from fiction.

Others have been published to defend the writers from charges of neglect or incapacity in military or civil offices, and are too personal and controversial to interest the general reader.

Lastly, there have been many accounts of events both in the field and in the Cabinet which the writers themselves took part in, and they have narrated the incidents with the clearness and precision which are always manifest in the evidence of an eye-witness.

It is now well known that the Confederate Government made great efforts to organize a naval force abroad during the Civil War, and that a few armed cruisers were got afloat, which destroyed many American ships and well-nigh drove the American commercial flag from the high seas.

The almost romantic cruise of the *Alabama*, and the account of her tragic burial in the stormy Norman Sea off Cherbourg, have been graphically narrated by the late Admiral Semmes, who commanded her during her short career; and there have been brief histories of the cruises of the *Florida*, *Shenandoah*, and other Confederate ships, so that their performances afloat are familiar to all who feel interested in such adventures.

No account, however, has yet been published which even approaches to a correct statement of the building and equipment of those vessels, nor were the real facts brought out in the well-known suit of the Attorney-General *v.* Sillem and others (commonly called the *Alexandra* Case), tried before the Lord Chief Baron of her Majesty's Court of Exchequer in London, nor yet in that of the *Oreto* (*Florida*) in the Vice-Admiralty Court of Nassau.

When the time comes for some wholly independent and impartial historian to write a full and complete record of the great Civil War, he will perceive that the naval operations of the Confederate States, which were organized abroad, possess an importance and attraction greater than their relative effect upon the issue of the struggle, as compared with the stupendous military movements and the gigantic campaigns which were carried on within the contending States.

He will perceive that they gave rise to many important legal and diplomatic questions, that they gave much occupation to her Majesty's Courts, and employment to many barristers who occupied the very highest positions at the English bar, a list of whose names would include two who have since been Lord Chancellors of England, one a Lord Justice of Appeal, and one a Vice-Chancellor. He will learn that they were the subject of much negotiation and some rather acrimonious correspondence between her Majesty's Secretary of State for Foreign Affairs and the United States Minister; that they created the necessity of a special mission to Washington, and the negotiation of a special treaty between Great Britain and the United States, by which a material change was made in the rules defining the obligations of neutrals; and finally, that they were the cause of that great international suit known as the Geneva Arbitration, by whose judgment the British taxpayer was unhappily mulcted in damages to the substantial amount of £3,000,000 sterling.

When the future historian contemplates these results, he will naturally look for the facts relating to them, and he will look in vain among the records thus far published to the world.

Much misapprehension has heretofore prevailed in reference to the acts of the Confederate Government in the effort to organize a naval force abroad.

The allegations and affidavits collected by the American Consul at Liverpool, upon which the United States Minister founded his complaints, were in almost every particular either inaccurate or greatly exaggerated; and the 'Case of the United States' presented to the Arbitrators at Geneva was full of errors and misstatements, many of which could have been disproved by very direct and positive evidence if her Majesty's representatives had called upon the parties concerned for the real facts.

It surely is not to the interest nor to the permanent advantage of the people of this or any other country to form a conclusion or shape a policy upon a hasty consideration or misapprehension of facts; and the time has arrived when it would seem to be advisable for anyone who is in possession of the authentic records to make them public, both as an act of justice to those whose conduct has been misrepresented, and as a trustworthy historical record.

I was the agent selected by the Confederate Government to manage and direct the general naval operations in Europe, and I was the chief representative of the Navy Department abroad, during the whole period of the war. All of the ships that got to sea, except the *Georgia*, were despatched and equipped under my instructions; and all the documents pertaining to their origin and the means adopted to get them to sea as cruising ships are in my possession.

It would be difficult for anyone not personally conversant with every incident to decipher and arrange the documents, or to edit a narrative of the transactions, which extended throughout a period of four years, and were attended with many complications and perplexities, and not a few disappointments.

Often since the end of the war I have been urged to write an account of those interesting adventures, but have heretofore been unwilling to do so, for the following reasons, among others not necessary to mention:

First, it was necessary to have important dealings with a great many persons—shipbuilders, tradesmen, and manufacturers—who probably would not have liked to see their names put in print while the animosities and ill-will aroused by the war continued. I made it a rule never to deal with any but people of the highest character and credit in their respective branches of business. They were never asked, nor did they offer, to do anything inconsistent with the strictest principles of commercial honour ; and I have the happiness to feel conscious that every contract I made in England was fulfilled by the contractor with scrupulous fidelity, although it was often quite impossible for me to supervise the work while in progress, or even to inspect the materials before shipment.

In recurring now, after the lapse of sixteen years, to those literally vast transactions, it is a consolatory and satisfactory conviction to feel that the good understanding between us was never once disturbed by doubt or suspicion ; and if any of them happens to see his name mentioned in these pages, he will find no record of anything to his discredit, and I pray him to accept my apology for naming him at all without his leave, which I could not very well get.

The second reason for my reticence up to the present time arose from the reluctance most men feel to write of events which must necessarily appear to be largely of the character of personal adventures, and therefore require the frequent and embarrassing use and repetition of the personal pronoun

I have got over this difficulty by reflecting that every business or enterprise must have an active agent to manage and direct it ; and if it is meet and right to publish a history of these naval affairs at all, no mere squeamishness should deter me from giving them publicity, and furnishing the future historian with the facts pertaining to an interesting episode in that great Civil War which set the Western World in painful commotion, and disturbed the repose of Europe as well.

No one who is attracted by the title, and feels disposed to read this book, need be deterred by the fear of being drawn into an exposition of the causes of the war, or the right of secession; nor will he be asked to join in a wail over the mortification of defeat, or the agonies of 'Reconstruction.' Whatever opinions may now prevail in regard to the constitutional right or expediency of secession, hostile and depreciatory criticism of the Southern people has long ceased to have any influence.

It is admitted that they fought gallantly, and exhibited admirable qualities in attack and defence, in victory and defeat. When the last hope of success was extinguished; when the drain of battle and the combined forces of hunger, toil, and exposure had consumed their energies and exhausted the power of resistance, the remnant laid down their arms, and took to the plough and the pruning-hook with as little murmuring as any reasonable critic could expect.

It was, literally, beginning a new life from the very start. The whole land was impoverished. Towns had been burned and fields devastated. Throughout large districts every corn-mill and implement of husbandry had been destroyed. There was scarcely food for the people to eat, and the only currency in the country was the paper promises of the dead Confederacy.

Sixteen years have passed, and the South is again in blossom. Railways have been reconstructed and towns rebuilt. Milk and honey, corn and wine, can be had in plenteous profusion, and there is money to buy them; and, lastly, in this year of grace 1881, 6,700,000 bales of cotton have been grown on Southern soil, picked and baled by Southern hands, and there is cheery music among the spindles of Lancashire, in place of the silence and gloom which overshadowed them while the people who grow the fleecy staple were fighting for their cotton-fields. Men who can refer to such a record in the past, and point to such a position to-day, need make no plaintive appeals for pity. They had much sympathy during the struggle, and many kind things were said of them. These served to cheer and inspirit them in the day of adversity, and are gratefully remembered now. Those in England and elsewhere who predicted that the South would win, have failed in their prophecy, but they can at least feel that their sympathies were given to no mean people. The South was defeated, and secession from the Federal Union was shown to be inadmissible. That is all that has been determined by the appeal to arms. Wars do not define principles. They neither analyze nor solve political problems. The sword cuts the knot, and does not unravel it. No Southern man can efface from his mind the conviction that among the reserved rights of the States was that of withdrawing from the Union, and to deny that he held that opinion in the year 1861, and to shrink from confessing it to have been an article of his political faith at that time, would prove that with the loss of his cause he had also been bereft of his honour, and he would be without excuse for the part he took in resisting the authority of the United States Government at the bidding of his own State. When the Southern leaders laid down their arms, they admitted the supremacy of the Federal Congress, and surrendered the right of separate State action ; but they did not renounce their belief that the Constitution as it stood at, and previous to, 1861, was an agreement between Sovereign States, and that each State had the first claim to the allegiance and service of her citizens. But the South has 'accepted the situation,' and as a condition of restoration to the political privileges common to all the States, she has relinquished her own interpretation of the Constitution, and has agreed to accept that of the majority. Every Southerner is bound by that compact, and there is no evidence that a single sane or reasonable man wishes to break, to evade, or to modify it. In fact, causes are already at work in the Southern States which are likely to effect very important and notable changes in the political principles of the people. The large increase in the number of cotton mills in the South since the war, and the tendency to embark in other mechanical industries, will probably ere long attach the capitalists of that section to the Union, and its fostering system of protective tariffs, with the same ardour which has in these latter years distinguished the national affinities of the manufacturing States of the North.

Secession was not indigenous to the South. The doctrine was broached in the early days of the Republic by Massachusetts and other New England States, and was very clearly and forcibly enunciated by a Convention of those States which met at Hartford in 1814-15, as the following extract from the Journal of the Convention will prove:

'That Acts of Congress in violation of the Constitution are absolutely void, is an undeniable position. . . . In cases of deliberate, dangerous, and palpable infractions of the Constitution, affecting the *sovereignty* of the State and *liberties* of *the people*, it is not only the right, but the duty of such State to interpose its authority for their protection, in the manner best calculated to secure that end. When emergencies occur which are either beyond the reach of judicial tribunals, or too pressing to admit of delay incident to their forms, *States which have no common umpire* must be their own judges, and execute their own decisions.'

Anyone at all familiar with the political history of the United States from the adoption of the Constitution to the year 1815, must admit that the right of secession was a doctrine which did not originate at the South, and was not peculiar to Southern men. After the purchase of Louisiana in 1803, the Legislature of Massachusetts passed the following resolution: 'Resolved, that the annexation of Louisiana to the Union transcends the Constitutional power of the United States. It formed a new *Confederacy*, to which *the States united* by the *former compact* are not bound to adhere.'

The speech of the Hon. Josiah Quincy, of Massachusetts, delivered in the Congress of the United States, January 14, 1811, in opposition to the Bill for the admission of Louisiana into the Union as a State, has been often quoted. He said, 'If this Bill passes, it is my deliberate opinion that it is virtually a dissolution of the Union; and as it will be *the right of all*, so it *will be the duty of some, definitely to prepare for separation—amicably if they can, violently if they must.*'

The States which withdrew from the Union in 1860-61 merely exercised a prerogative which had been previously claimed as an inherent 'State right' by Massachusetts and other New England States, and which had been asserted and defended by many prominent Northern men.* Georgia, the Carolinas, and Virginia made

* I might fill pages with extracts from the Journal of the Hartford Convention, the writings and speeches of eminent Northern politicians before the secession of the Southern States, and leading articles from Northern papers published at or about the time of the secession, in support of this statement. But I have no wish to recriminate, or to even approach controversial topics, except in so far as may be necessary to repudiate the crime of 'treason' which has been so recklessly alleged against the South. Those who wish to test the accuracy of the statement may refer to the following American works: 'Is Davis a

common cause with the Northern Provinces, and were loyal to the Confederation during the trying times of the

---

Traitor?' by Professor Bledsoe; 'The Rise and Fall of the Confederate Government,' by Mr. Jefferson Davis; and 'Buchanan's Administration;' in all of which will be found copious extracts from the speeches and writings of Northern men who occupied high and influential positions, with particular references to the original sources from which the quotations are taken.

I mention the above works, not with the purpose of directing attention to the arguments of the authors in support of 'State rights,' but solely because they contain indisputable proof that the assumption was not a new doctrine in 1861, but that it was co-existent with the Union itself, and had some of its staunchest supporters among Northern statesmen and expounders of Constitutional law.

It is a just subject for surprise, and is equally a matter of regret, that two such eminent men as Mr. John Lothrop Motley and the late Mr. Alexander Everett, when writing and delivering public addresses during the Civil War, with the purpose to enlighten public opinion at home and abroad in respect to the action of the Southern States, should have suppressed, or at least omitted to mention, those facts which would have tended to diminish the alleged criminal culpability of the Southern people, and a knowledge of which was absolutely necessary to a fair, impartial judgment. No cause is ever benefited in the long run by an over-statement of its merits, or by exaggerated depreciation of the opposite side; and when public opinion has been influenced by appeals founded upon insufficient evidence, whether by assertion of what is false, or by the suppression of essential facts, there is always a reaction in the opposite direction. This has been notably manifest in regard to foreign opinion in the matter of secession. It is now quite exceptional to meet a European among the reading class who does not believe that the Southern States acted within their constitutional rights.

For the opinion of intelligent foreigners in regard to the right of secession, I may refer to De Tocqueville's 'Democracy in America' and 'The American Union,' by Mr. James Spence, published by Richard Bentley, London, 1861. The allusions in 'Buchanan's Administration' to the 'View of the Constitution of the United States,' by William Rawle of Philadelphia, are much to the point; and the extracts from a correspondence between Mr. John Quincy

Revolution, though they had far less cause for complaint against the mother country.

Again, the Southern States were loyal to the Union in the war of 1812-15, although their special interests had not been hurt or interfered with by Great Britain.

When Massachusetts and other Eastern States, through the action of the Hartford Convention, manifested their purpose to dissolve the Union, the country was engaged in a foreign war—namely, in defence of New England commerce, and for the protection of New England seamen.

The right which Great Britain affirmed to the

Adams and Mr. Harrison Gray Otis, both of Massachusetts, are worthy of especial notice. Mr. Adams charges the Federal Party in New England with a deliberate purpose to dissolve the Union. He says, 'I had no doubt in 1808 and 1809, and have no doubt at this time (December 30, 1828), that it is the key of all the great movements of the Federal Party in New England from that time forward until its final catastrophe in the Hartford Convention.' Mr. John Quincy Adams's opinion in respect to the right of secession is very clearly set out in an address before the New York Historical Society in 1839. A very full quotation from that address will be found in 'The Rise and Fall of the Confederate Government,' p. 190, etc.; and the following extract from a leading article in the *New York Tribune* of November 9, 1860, manifests not the isolated feeling and opinion of Mr. Horace Greeley, its editor and proprietor, but the views and sentiments of a large number of Northern men at that time:

'The right to secede may be a revolutionary right, but it exists, nevertheless; and we do not see how one party can have a right to do what another party has a right to prevent. We must ever resist the asserted right of any State to remain in the Union and nullify or resist the laws thereof; to withdraw from the Union is quite another matter. And whenever a considerable section of our Union shall deliberately resolve to go out, we will resist all coercive measures designed to keep her in.

'We hope never to live in a Republic whereof one section is pinned to the other by bayonets.'

perpetual unalienable allegiance of all natural-born subjects, the repeated and vexatious vindication of that right by the stoppage of American ships on the high seas, and the violent removal of alleged British subjects from them, were the chief causes of that war. The South had neither ships nor seamen, and there was nothing to arouse the interest of the Southern people, or to bind them to a participation in the contest, but the sense of loyal obligation to the Union.

When the Southern States seceded in 1861, the country was vexed by no foreign complications, and their action did not add to any existing troubles. This difference in the conditions under which Massachusetts threatened to secede and the Southern States actually did secede, should, in common fairness, be borne in mind by those who extol the loyalty of New England and have so vehemently denounced the Southern people as traitors and rebels.

But the result of the Civil War has been to produce a general disavowal of the principles so emphatically laid down by the Hartford Convention. The New England States helped with all their energies to force a contrary admission from the South, and the authority of the Federal Congress has now been made paramount from Maine to Texas, from New York to California, by the compulsory, but still by the unanimous, consent of the people of all the States.

The bitterness and the passionate heat of family quarrels are proverbial, and many unhappy incidents of the war between the States of the American Union have confirmed the experience upon which the proverb is based. But old associations and the memory of past troubles, tribulations, and triumphs, shared in common, are drawing the people again together ; and it will be well for them earnestly to reflect upon the causes of the estrangement, and to devise the means of preventing their repetition, in a spirit of fraternal regard alike for the common welfare and the separate, if not conflicting, interests of the various communities embraced in the vast domain of the Union. Americans have learned from the sad experience of the Civil War that Democratic institutions are not exempt from the dangers which beset other forms of government. History furnishes no record of any people who have been fused into one cohesive and durable nationality without much internal commotion and many internecine struggles.

It is eight hundred years since the last foreign conquest of England; but since the battle of Hastings there have been the bloody Wars of the Roses and the fierce contest between Cavalier and Roundhead, besides lesser revolutions and much border strife. Only within the present century have the three kingdoms been brought into willing union, and even now the unhappy condition of Ireland excites fears for the peace and quiet of the realm.

The United States could not have reasonably hoped to escape the political afflictions which other people have had to suffer, nor could they have expected to grow from their birth into the family of independent Powers to the full maturity of national life without passing through some political convulsions. The territory is vast, and even at the present rate of increase in population it will be many years before the people are brought into as close contact as in the countries of Europe.

Celt and Saxon, Teuton and Scandinavian, are flowing in a seemingly exhaustless stream towards the great prairies of the West, and the problem of amalgamating those divers races with the descendants of the original colonists, and fusing them into one nation, with language, feeling, tastes, and interests in common, must be left for its solution to those laws of nature or of Providence which have united equally variable materials to form the existing European types.

The theory that the late Civil War was a mere insurrectionary movement can deceive no one now. The fact that the secession of the Southern States divided the American Union into two separate Federal Republics, cannot be destroyed by the counter-fact that the Union has been restored. The judgment of every foreign power declared that there was for four years a *de facto* Government at Richmond, which was wholly independent of the power and control of the Congress at Washington, and every department of the United States Government confirmed that judgment by practical acts of recognition.

The Union founded by Washington, Adams, Jefferson, Hamilton, Madison, and the other 'Fathers,' was a Federal Republic, that is to say, it was a Government constituted of several Constituent Republics, which were united by an agreement or compact between themselves as distinct and separate States. That Union proved to be inadequate to the exigencies of the conflicting forces to which it was exposed. It resisted several severe strains, and was maintained by one or more compromises, which served to demonstrate its imperfection and its inherent weakness.

In 1861 the disintegrating forces prevailed, and eleven of the Constituent Republics withdrew from the Union on the plea that the original conditions of Union had been broken by the others, and they formed a fresh confederation among themselves.

The remaining States or Republics resisted that act of separation, and affirmed that the people of the whole

United States were, or should be fused into, one nation, and that the division of the Union into States had, or should hereafter have, no greater political significance than the division of the several States into counties.

The States which remained in the original Union, and supported the foregoing dogma, proved to be stronger than those which clung to the opinions of the 'Fathers,' and they succeeded, after a long and bloody war, in compelling the latter to admit that 'the people of the United States' meant the aggregate population of all the States, and that the majority, as represented in the Congress at Washington, was the true and only Sovereign of the whole country, irrespective of geographical State lines or separate State Constitutions. I am broaching no theory, but am simply stating facts. And they are facts which it behoves every American who wishes to practise a broad and comprehensive patriotism, and hopes to maintain a hearty and brotherly union among the reunited States, to admit and to thoughtfully consider in the future arrangement and policy of political parties. It is folly and ruin for men in trade to act without reference to the clear manifestations of supply and demand; it is equally unwise and disastrous for politicians and statesmen to deny or to take no account of the difference between theories for which it has been thought necessary to strive even to the shedding of blood, and principles which are fundamental and unchangeable.

The Union of 1787 was dissolved in 1861 by the action of ten of the constituent republics. A new Union was formed in 1865 by the military power of the majority of the States, compelling the minority to accept their view of the national compact. The former Union was a confederation of States, and was of course a Federal Republic ; the latter Union is founded upon a fusion of the people into one nation, with a supreme centralized executive and administrative Government at Washington, and can no longer be called a Federal Republic ; it has become an Imperial Republic. The latter name gives some promise of greater strength and cohesion than the former, but the duration of the restored Union will depend very much upon whether the people of the whole country fully realize, and are really reconciled to, the new dogma that each State is only an aggregate of counties, and that its political functions are only to consist in regulating such purely domestic concerns as the central authority at Washington may leave to its discretion. The principle upon which the new Union is founded may or may not be sound in theory, but there can be no doubt that the increased influence and power granted to the national executive and legislative authorities will make it more than ever necessary for the educated classes in the United States to interest themselves in politics, and to see that the representatives sent to Washington are not the mere creatures of the corrupt organizations commonly known as the 'Machine.' If the majority who have effected the change in the conditions of the American Union are content to leave the management of public affairs to the professional politicians, the 'caucuses,' and the 'wire-pullers,' they will have fought in vain, and will find that to secure the semblance of a strictly national Union they have sacrificed the substance of individual liberty.

Those who are accustomed to closely scrutinize current political events, must perceive the tendency of both North and South towards a re-assertion of the doctrine of State rights, and a tacit admission of that claim by the Federal Government.

A specific manifestation of the revival of the principle may be seen in the action of California with reference to Chinese immigration, and the cautious conciliatory treatment of the subject by Congress and the executive authorities at Washington. It is hardly possible to doubt that the pretension of each State to regulate its own affairs without the intervention of any other authority will, before many years, be as rampant as ever, and unless the statesmen and political leaders have the wisdom and prudence necessary to keep national party lines distinct from geographical boundaries, the danger of another secession will be imminent.

It is earnestly to be hoped that the reunion of the States may be cemented and perpetuated; that bickerings and recriminations may cease; that nothing further may be done or spoken on either side through strife or vain-glory, and that neither diversity of interests, discriminating tariffs, nor State jealousies, will again set the hearts of the people against each other. But, whatever may happen in the distant and inscrutable future, it may be safely predicted, that if there should be a second violent struggle for 'State rights,' the issue will be fought on very different geographical lines from those which separated the contending parties in the Civil War of 1861.

CHAPTER I.

Sketch of the anomalous condition of the whole country, North and South, during the period between the election of Mr. Abraham Lincoln as President of the United States and the beginning of hostilities, in theory an undivided Republic, in fact two separate Governments: one at Washington, one at Montgomery.—The organization of the Confederate Navy Department.—The poverty of the South with respect to naval resources.—The naval policy of the Confederate Government.—The necessity of looking abroad for the means to carry on naval operations.—The commencement of hostilities.—The Louisiana 'Board of War' and the Bienville.—Personal incidents.—Journey South.—Blocking the Mississippi.

SOUTH CAROLINA was the first of the Southern States to secede from the American Union. Her 'Ordinance of Secession' was passed on the 20th of December, 1860, about one month after the election of Mr. Abraham Lincoln to the Presidency of the United States. Mississippi, Florida, Alabama, Georgia, and Louisiana soon followed. Delegates from those States met at Montgomery in February, 1861, organized a Legislative Assembly, and formed a Provisional Government, with Mr. Jefferson Davis, of Mississippi, as President.

Arkansas, Texas, and North Carolina followed at short intervals, and were not long in joining the Confederacy. Tennessee, with Maryland, and the great border States of Missouri, Kentucky, and Virginia, still faltered, not from want of sympathy with the movement,

Jefferson Davis, President of the Confederate States of America.
(National Archives)

Stephen R. Mallory, Secretary of the Confederate Navy.
(National Archives)

but because they hoped to act as a barrier between the two sections, and to secure a peaceful separation by negotiation. Events moved rapidly. Tennessee and Virginia withdrew in time to save serious complications; but while Maryland, Kentucky, and Missouri hesitated, the 'Union men' within their borders, aided by active partizans from without, got partial control of affairs, and the United States authorities were able to arrest the leading Secessionists, to disperse the local Legislatures, and to maintain possession of those States during the war. By withdrawing from the Federal Union in this irregular way, the South demonstrated that there was no concert of action, and no premeditated purpose to break up the Federal Government. The political organization of the seceded States remained intact, although the Union between them had been dissolved. Each preserved its complete autonomy as a Commonwealth, with Executive Judiciary and Legislative Departments unbroken, and there was, therefore, no confusion and no disturbance of the ordinary routine of civil government. The delegates at Montgomery had no difficulty in settling the terms of a fresh compact between the States represented by them, and the Provisional Government was soon in working order. The chief and most urgent business of the newly created Executive was to prepare for the great struggle which was becoming more and more imminent day by day. The lack of military resources, and the efforts which were made to organize an army, have been described by many previous writers, and especially with much minuteness and effect by ex-President Jefferson Davis in his great exposition of the 'Rise and Fall of the Confederate Government,' a work which may be called his 'Apologia.'

My business is with the concerns of the Navy alone. When President Davis arranged his Cabinet, the Navy Department was assigned to the Hon. Stephen R. Mallory, of Florida. Mr. Mallory had much experience in the management of public business.

He had been a Senator in the Congress of the United States, and had served as a Member of the Committee on Naval Affairs in that branch of the National Legislature.

He was well versed in naval usage and naval law, and had a thorough knowledge of the organization, equipment, and general disciplinary rules of the United States Navy. If he had been placed at the head of that service, he would have been a popular and efficient administrator, but at Montgomery he was like a chieftain without a clan, or an artizan without the tools of his art. It would have been comparatively easy to organize and administer, but the task before him was to create, and the means for constructing and equipping a naval force for offensive warfare, or even for a vigorous resistance, were practically *nil.* The pine belts of Georgia and the Carolinas, the live oak groves of Florida, and the forests of other States, contained inexhaustible supplies of what are called 'naval stores' and materials for ship-building of the old wooden type, but they were still in the raw state. The masts and frames of navies were there, but they were sprouting and blooming in the green-tree, and there was great lack of skilled workmen to fell and fashion them. Iron, so indispensable in the equipment of ships of war, even at that time, was scarce to the degree of poverty, and before the end there was a famine. Between March, 1861, and January, 1865, the price of iron advanced from $25 to $1,300 per ton, and although this extreme advance was not wholly due to the scarcity of the article, but arose to some extent from the depreciation of the paper currency, yet it is well known that the home product was never equal to the ordinary wants of the country, and during the Civil War the supply could only be supplemented by driblets through the blockade.

At the beginning of the war there was not a mill in the whole country which could roll a 2½-inch plate, and in the entire Confederacy there was but one shop capable of turning out a first-class marine engine. There was pressing need of everything required to build, equip, and maintain a ship of war. Ordnance and ordnance stores, even medical supplies, provisions, and clothing, were scarce from the very outset; and the Tredegar Iron Works, at Richmond, Virginia, was the only establishment south of the Potomac where a gun of large calibre could be cast or wrought; and Virginia, when Mr. Davis and his Cabinet began their labours, was not among the Confederate States.

Norfolk, in Virginia, and Pensacola, in Florida, contained the only public dockyards within the limits of the Confederacy. The Navy-yard at Norfolk before the war was an extensive and efficient establishment. It contained a dry dock, foundry and machine shops, and a fair supply of materials had generally been kept there. But just at the time when Virginia was in the throes of secession, before there was any organized force at Norfolk capable of effective resistance, the United States naval officers were ordered to evacuate the dockyard, which they did hastily, taking ship to Hampton Roads, after setting fire to and scuttling the vessels that could not be carried off, and destroying as much of the property on shore as possible. (See Note, p. 49.)

Pensacola was in an isolated position, and its dockyard was not one of construction, but only of shelter and repair.

But even if these two naval arsenals had been complete in every particular, and there had been no want of material, machinery, and skilled workmen, they would still have been well nigh useless as places of outfit for vessels suited to cruise at sea, because the Federal Government held the fortifications at their entrances, and there was safe and ample anchorage within reach of the guns on shore, so that a thorough and efficient blockade could be, and indeed was, maintained at those points during the whole war, by a powerful combination of ships and land batteries.

If the Confederate Government had been able to build and equip cruisers at Norfolk, they could not have got to sea, unless they had been strong enough in number and armament to defeat the blockading squadron in Hampton Roads, and had remained after their victory in condition to engage and pass the forts.

There was equal deficiency and want in respect to private ship-yards. The conditions of labour, soil, and climate which prevailed in the South had made the people agricultural and not commercial. They produced valuable and bulky staples, and ships chiefly from the Northern States and from England performed the carrying trade. The merchants who lived and did business at the Southern ports owned few if any ships, and as there was no home want for large shipping, there had been no demand for architects to design and build them.

It is quite safe for me to state that at the beginning of the year 1861 there was not, within the whole boundary of the Confederacy, a single private yard having the plant necessary to build and equip a cruising ship of the most moderate offensive power.

When President Davis and his Cabinet contemplated this paucity of supply and poverty of home resources, they did not renounce the purpose or abandon the hope to harass the enemy's commerce, to interrupt his lines of maritime communication, and to break through his blockading fleets, but they perceived that an effective effort to accomplish all or either of those aims must of necessity be made abroad; and as early as April, 1861, it was determined to send an agent to England to set on foot and direct such naval operations as it might be possible to organize beyond the limits of the Confederate States.

At a very early period of the war it became a matter of common conjecture that ships were building in England for the service of the Confederate States, and it was not many months before the depredations of the *Alabama* and *Florida* confirmed those suspicions. To build or even to buy ships suitable for either attack or defence, to get them out of English ports, and then to equip and arm them, were undertakings requiring the utmost secrecy and reserve, the success of every effort depending upon the fidelity and discretion of many subordinate agents, and the precise correspondence of many complicated arrangements. It was necessary, first, to build or buy a ship, and to disguise or omit the semblance of equipment for purposes of war; to obtain the guns from one maker, and often their carriages and gear from another; to get the shot and shells from a third, and the small arms and ammunition from at least two other parties. The large quantity of stores, clothing, hammocks, etc., etc., required for a cruising-ship could not, with prudence, be obtained from one dealer, and a tender was needed to receive and carry abroad the whole of those essential effects, which it was necessary to forward to the port of shipment with quick despatch and at short notice.

When everything was ready, it was no easy matter to so combine movements that ship and tender, sailing from different ports, should meet at the appointed rendezvous; and then, after the meeting, there was always much difficulty and many obstacles to the safe and speedy transfer of stores and the completion of the armament. The necessity for these perplexing and intricate proceedings arose not from the fact that there was the slightest degree of moral criminality in their performance, but because there is in England, as there is in other countries, a statute known as the Foreign Enlistment Act, or other cognate title, which forbids either of two belligerents to equip, furnish, fit out, or arm any vessel within the realm, for the purpose of making war upon the other. A violation of that statute involved the forfeiture of the whole of the property; and, as the Act might also be so interpreted as to bring the parties concerned under its penal provisions, every detail in the fitting of a ship, which could by any possible construction of the law be considered 'equipment,' was of necessity dispensed with.

During the war, when the partizans of both sides were irritated and excited, and each spoke and wrote about the other with heat and passion, it was common to denounce the secession of the Southern States as an act of criminal rebellion, and the efforts made by their agents to obtain abroad the supplies which the resources of the country at home could not furnish, were condemned in rather strong language.

That view of the subject has been almost universally discarded in Europe, and even in the Northern States there are now but a scant minority, chiefly of the professional politician class, who affect to regard the late Civil War in any other light than that of a revolution justified by innumerable precedents in history. If the Confederate army had been defeated at Bull Run, and General McDowell, by a rapid pursuit, had captured President Davis, with Johnston and Beauregard red-handed from the fight, those gentlemen would probably have been summarily tried, and possibly executed, as traitors.

With equal probability that would have been the fate of Washington, Hancock, and Adams if General Gage had been able to disperse the 'Continental forces' at Cambridge, Massachusetts, at the beginning of the War of Independence, and to obtain possession of their persons. The vicissitudes of the late war often gave to the Confederacy a preponderance of advantage, both as regards success in the field, and the number of prisoners.

Under those conditions it was manifestly impossible to treat the captive Confederates as traitors, and since the two opposing parties negotiated with each other for years upon equal terms, arranged conditions of surrender, and exchanged prisoners in accordance with the universally admitted rules of war, sensible men everywhere have perceived the irrelevancy of such expressions as 'treason' and 'traitor.' They have ceased to be used in dignified and grave discussions, and will not probably be revived in any fair and impartial history which may be written in the future.

It will be my effort in the following pages to demonstrate that nothing was done by the agents of the Confederate Government in Great Britain which was not justified by the rules of fair and honourable warfare, nothing contrary to English law as construed by English jurists, and confirmed by the judgment of English courts, and nothing in abuse of the hospitality and refuge England has ever offered to the exiled and oppressed. But it will be necessary, or at least it will be convenient and proper, to give a brief account of the condition of the country during the period between the election of Mr. Abraham Lincoln to the Presidency of the United States and the beginning of hostilities, and to describe the manner in which the agent was selected, and with what instructions he was sent to Europe.

The personal incidents are neither important nor peculiar. Adventures similar in kind, and involving greater personal risk to the actors, are without doubt preserved in the memories of many, but they have not been narrated in connection with the general course of events.

It is my wish and purpose to mention no circumstance whose interest is of a purely personal character, but only such as may help to illustrate the very peculiar condition of affairs during those eventful months which immediately preceded the great Civil War.

From the date of the formation of the Provisional Government at Montgomery to the beginning of hostilities, the political condition of the country had been anomalous.

There were two Presidents, two Cabinets, two Congresses. The Government at Washington retained all the regalia and prestige of the supreme power. It controlled the army and navy, and held the national treasury and the national domain. The foreign Diplomatic Corps still recognised it as the only national authority, and no foreign Power had yet questioned Mr. Abraham Lincoln's title to be the President of the

The inauguration of President Jefferson Davis at Montgomery, Alabama, February 18, 1861. *(Harper's Weekly)*

The *Lady Davis*, one of the first government-owned ships of the Confederacy. *(Harper's Weekly)*

Bulloch's former command, the *Bienville*, used as a transport for Rhode Island artillery at the Washington Arsenal on April 25, 1861. *(Harper's Weekly)*

whole Union in its entirety, both by privilege of law and by right of possession. Notwithstanding all this, there had been for several months a rival Executive and a rival Congress at Montgomery, to whom at least six States had given their adherence, and within the limits of those States no United States writ could run, and no United States soldier could remain.

The Government at Montgomery had, moreover, assumed control of the postal routes within the seceded States, and the Custom Houses throughout their coasts were administered under the same authority.

By a law of the United States, a vessel sailing from one home port to another was required to have a regular Custom House clearance, under penalty of seizure and forfeiture. The authorities at Washington did not, of course, recognise those at Montgomery, and a certificate of clearance from New Orleans, verified by a Collector of Customs appointed by the Confederate Treasury Department, was not admissible at any port in the United States. In spite of this embarrassing condition of affairs, the coasting trade and the postal intercourse between the North and South were not for some months interrupted or seriously disarranged. The Customs officers at New York and elsewhere made some seizures of vessels arriving with irregular Confederate Custom House clearances, but they were released by orders from Washington. As a test case, the mail-steamship *Bienville*, under my command, was seized at New York in March, 1861, for alleged violation of the United States revenue laws, and I was requested to go to Washington, where I had an official interview with the Secretary of the Treasury, the Hon. Salmon P. Chase, on the subject. I pointed out that there was no United States official of any kind at New Orleans, and that I was compelled either to take a clearance from the *de facto* authority or to remain at that port indefinitely.

Mr. Chase perceived the peculiarities and perplexities of the situation, and released the ship from all liability, but he was manifestly puzzled, and asked me if it was the intention of the Company to send the ship back to New Orleans. I replied that it was.

He then said that the right of the so-called Confederate Government to assume control of the Custom Houses at the Southern ports could not be admitted even by implication; but still it was obvious that for the moment those who had usurped the legitimate authority had the power to enforce it against private persons, and he directed me on the next occasion of applying for a clearance to make a formal notarial protest setting forth the precise circumstances. Before the *Bienville* returned again to New York, hostilities had begun, and questions of civil jurisdiction had been silenced by the clamour of war. All thinking men perceived that this dual authority, and this conflict of prerogative, could not continue for an indefinite time. Virginia was still mediating, and a 'peace commission' was sent from the South to Washington to treat for a friendly separation. But neither intercession nor negotiation could effect that purpose. The South wanted to withdraw from the Union, peaceably, if possible. The North wished to preserve it, peaceably if possible. The South urged the distinct autonomy and the complete individual sovereignty of each State. The North saw in that doctrine an indefinite extension of the secession movement and a final dissolution of the whole Union.

That was the real issue. None other could have united the Southern people or have nerved them to suffer as they did; none other could have overcome the repugnance of many in the North to engage in a war of conquest against their brethren of the South. The charge often made, that the North fought for empire in the sense of coveting more territory, appears to me to have been as unfounded as the counter-allegation that the South took up arms to extend the area of slavery, or even to preserve that institution in perpetuity.

Political parties had ceased to be divided upon principles and interests common to both sections of the country, and had come to be separated by a geographical line. Thus had arisen a condition which the Fathers of the Republic foresaw might happen, and which they had predicted would be dangerous, if not destructive, to the Union.

There were, unhappily, many men of extreme views in the dominant party at the North who had got control of the party machinery. They appeared determined to force upon the country measures which would have placed the South at the mercy of a sectional majority. But I believe that the great mass of the people on both sides were very desirous to find a peaceful solution of the difficulties. The principles at issue were, however, too antagonistic to be reconciled, and the tension was approaching nearer day by day to the breaking strain. The fuel was laid in order, the kindling materials were abundant. A spark might at any moment light a conflagration, and the spark soon fell. When Louisiana seceded, the Governor of that State, the Hon. Thos. O. Moore, appointed a committee of experienced and influential men to advise and help him to put the State in a condition to meet any emergency that might arise. Among the members were General Braxton Bragg and Colonel J. K. Duncan, both of whom were ex-artillery officers of the United States army, and the committee was called the 'Board of War.' The board had been sitting for some time at New Orleans, and State troops had occupied the old forts, built many years before for the protection of the river approaches, and had put them in habitable and fairly defensible condition against a sudden attack. These circumstances had somewhat accustomed the people of New Orleans to the prospect of a possible conflict. During the early days of April, 1861, there was a general feeling that affairs could not be peaceably arranged, and there appeared to be a nervous solicitude, and a seeming impatience of further delay, together with a suppressed inclination to precipitate a direct and immediate issue.

On the 13th day of April, 1861, I was in New Orleans in command of the United States mail steamer *Bienville*. The ship was appointed to sail on the following morning, and a large number of passengers had booked for the voyage, some for their customary migration during the hot months, and some to escape the danger and privations of battle and siege, which they already scented in the air.

Early in the morning of that day there were flying rumours that fighting had begun somewhere, and about ten o'clock it was known with certainty that Beauregard had opened fire at Charleston upon Fort Sumter.

The tidings soon spread, and the whole city was alert to learn the particulars and to discuss the consequences. There was no excitement. Groups of men collected about the street corners, at the hotels, and other places of public resort, and talked earnestly, but gravely, about the possibilities of the future.

Every man who has had to face extreme danger

probably remembers ever afterwards his feelings on the first occasion. There was a tingling of the flesh, a chilliness of the scalp, and a sensation as if each hair was slowly lifting itself on end. It was not fear, because the bravest of the brave are thus affected. It was only the keen consciousness of peril.

It is narrated of the great Henri Quatre, that once, at the beginning of a battle, he felt this premonitory shiver creeping over him, and looking down at his knees, which appeared to be shaking, he addressed them thus: 'Ah! you tremble. You would tremble much more if you knew where I am going to take you.' New Orleans seemed to be in that sort of tremor.

There was no appearance of bravado, which is never the mark of true self-reliant courage, neither were there any signs of despondency or distrust. There was an effervescence among the younger men, and a few talked of arming and marching to the frontier without waiting for a call; but the majority of the people spoke and acted like men who were conscious that a great crisis had arisen, and they were ready to meet it.

The Southern officers of the United States army and navy had, with remarkably few exceptions, resigned their commissions when their respective States seceded, and the Confederate Congress very soon passed an Act to incorporate them into the new service with the same relative rank which they had held in the old. I was one of a small number of lieutenants in the United States navy who had been detailed by the Government to go into the Mail Service some years before the war, with the object to enlarge the school for experience in steam. The Steam Packet and Mail Service increased, and there was a demand for commanders. In the navy promotion was slow, and the certainty of remaining in a subordinate position until age had sapped the energies and ambition had ceased to inspire was depressing.

Private companies offered good positions and satisfactory emolument, and several lieutenants resigned their naval commissions and remained in the private Mail Service. I was one of those who retired, and when Georgia seceded I was only a private individual engaged in the ordinary business of life. I had become completely identified with the shipping enterprises of New York. I had no property of any kind at the South, nor any pecuniary interests whatever in that part of the country.

Many persons thought to the very last that somehow or other an agreement would be come to, and there would be no war, and I did not feel that there was either a necessity or obligation requiring me to give up my occupation and business connections prematurely. All to whom my opinions were of any interest or importance knew what they were. I had never concealed or even disguised the fact that in respect to the issues at stake my heart and my head were with the South. My sympathies and convictions were both on that side, although my personal interests were wholly, and my personal friendships were chiefly, in the North. Whatever had happened, neither friend nor foe could have said with truth that I was not ready to act in harmony with my convictions at the proper time. When Beauregard fired the first shot at Fort Sumter in the early dawn of April 13th, 1861, he sounded a call which summoned every man to fall into line on his own side, and there could no longer be either hesitation or delay. Those officers who had retired from the United States navy to enter the Mail Service, and who still remained in it, were now drawn by a natural law to their own side of the dividing line. Those from the Northern States thought it their duty to offer their services to the Government at Washington, and were restored to their former positions in the United States Navy. Those from the Southern States were impelled by corresponding motives to offer their services to the Government at Montgomery, and were incorporated into the Confederate Navy. At 10 a.m. on the 13th of April, 1861, all doubt in regard to the condition of affairs at Charleston had vanished, and I wrote a letter to the Hon. J. P. Benjamin, who was then the Attorney-General of the Confederate States, requesting him to offer my services to the Government.

Some members of the Cabinet knew of my naval education and employment in the Mail Service, and I explained to Mr. Benjamin, that being in command of the steamship *Bienville*, it was necessary for me to take her back to New York, and return her to those to whom she belonged, but that on arrival in New York I would be ready for any service. After posting that letter I went on board ship, to hasten the preparations for sailing on the next morning.

In the course of the afternoon two members of the 'Board of War' came to the ship with the company's agent, and informed me that it had been thought important to secure the *Bienville* for the naval service of the Confederate States, and if I would name a price, the Governor would order the amount to be paid.

I replied that I had no authority to sell the ship, and therefore could not fix a price, nor could I make any arrangements for transferring her to the Confederate States. We had some further conversation on the subject, the members of the Board urging me to accept the Governor's offer, and I repeating, in substance, what I had said at first. Finally, they told me that if I did not accept the terms offered, it would probably be necessary to take the ship by force, but they would inform me of the Governor's decision at a later hour.

The Governor of the State and the members of the Board of War knew precisely my position, and the proposal for the purchase of the ship was made in a very friendly way to me personally. I felt assured that nothing would be done in a harsh or violent manner, but still I felt that I could neither sell the ship nor give her up without resistance, and it was inexpressibly painful to contemplate the possibility that I might be forced into collision with the Government I was willing and had just offered to serve.

Late in the afternoon, one of the gentlemen who had previously called came again to the ship, and told me that the Governor had decided to refer the matter to the authorities at Montgomery, and he had telegraphed for instructions. The agent of the Mail Steamship Company, Mr. John Fox, spent the evening on board with me. He was a Southern man, and a Secessionist, and, I believe, in his heart hoped that the ship would be seized; but he was loyal to me and to the New York owners, and said I was quite right in refusing to give her up on any terms.

I told him I could not, of course, fight, but I could run, and I meant to. To that end I had the mooring lines shifted, so that they could be slipped from on board, and I directed the engineer to get up steam. My purpose was to swing off from the pier, or 'levee,' at the first show of force, and 'skedaddle' down the river. There was a good four or five knot current, for the Mississippi was in the spring freshets, and I had no fear of being stopped by the forts ; but I felt both grieved and annoyed at the prospect of having to run from my friends, to save the property of those who were constructively my enemies.*

Happily, the necessity for the race did not arise. At about 10 p.m. I had the pleasure to receive a message from the Governor to the effect that the offer for the purchase of the ship was still open, but that nothing would be done to prevent my departure with her in the morning. The two gentlemen who brought me this very agreeable assurance were authorized by the Governor to show me the reply which had been received from Montgomery to his own despatch about the purchase or seizure of the ship.

The reply was from President Davis. I believe I remember the very words. 'Do not detain the *Bienville* ; we do not wish to interfere in any way with private property.' These personal incidents are of no importance in themselves, but they may be of some interest as demonstrating the comparatively trivial circumstances which mark the beginning of great events, and they manifest the purpose of the Confederate authorities to act with prudence, and without the heat and passion which commonly mark the conduct of men when driven into revolutionary enterprises. At 8 a.m., April 14, the

* The question of the ability of the forts to stop an ascending fleet by their fire, independently of an artificial obstruction in the river, had been frequently discussed in New Orleans after the secession of the State. On the previous voyage of the *Bienville*, I had noted the time required to pass from a position in which the first gun could be brought to bear upon the ship, until she reached a point at which the curve of the river interposed the protection of the shore. I had found it to be fifteen minutes when descending, and twenty-five minutes when ascending, and I had furnished the Board of War with a memorandum to that effect.

Bienville sailed from New Orleans for Havana *en route* for New York. As the ship neared the forts, every one on board came on deck to look at them. We saw the sentinels standing at ease on the parapets. At our peak flew the United States ensign. The flag at the staff on Fort Jackson bore the familiar red and white stripes, with blue Union in the corner, but the stars representing the States which still remained in the Union had been erased. The Confederacy had not yet adopted an entirely distinctive flag. The *Bienville* carried, I believe, the first report to Havana that hostilities had begun, and there was much excitement there in consequence. The United States steamer *Corwin* was in port, and two transports *en route* for New York with a dismounted regiment of United States cavalry on board. The troops had been serving on the frontier of Texas, and when that State seceded, they had been called upon to surrender the public property to the State authorities and to evacuate the State.

Many officers came on board the *Bienville* to learn the news. The officers of neither army nor navy had been fired with the war-fever at that early date, and all expressed regret at the unhappy turn of affairs. They were nevertheless Northern men, who meant to retain their commissions, and fight it out on that side, and I listened to their comments, but maintained a prudent reserve.

In due course the *Bienville* sailed for New York, and arrived there on the evening of April 22. Off the bar we met two outward-bound steamers, standing to the southward. Both were crowded with troops. One of them hailed in passing, and reported that she was bound for Washington.

It was about 9 p.m. when the *Bienville* reached her

berth. Off the pierhead there was lying at anchor a large Long Island Sound steamer. She loomed up grandly in the thin mist that lay upon the river. Her lofty tiers of saloons were brilliantly lighted, and she appeared to be swarming with passengers.

As soon as the *Bienville* was berthed, one of the managing directors of the company came on board. The information he had to give was important. 'There had been fears that the Confederates would make a sudden dash and seize Washington, and troops were hurrying forward for its protection. There had been a collision between a regiment of United States volunteers and a mob in Baltimore, and some lives had been lost. The steamer off the pierhead was the *Empire State*, with a regiment from Rhode Island on board.

'The Government had chartered the *Bienville* to take troops to Washington, and the Rhode Island regiment must embark as soon as possible.'

Of course, I could not go on that enterprise, and I told the director so.

Fortunately I was not pressed for reasons. The directors of the company were friendly to me, and another commander was appointed in such a way that no especial attention was attracted to my retirement. Very shortly afterwards the steamers belonging to the company were bought by the United States Government, and they were soon armed and sent to blockade the Southern ports.

At a later period of the war I recognised the *Bienville* off the port of Savannah, where she formed a part of Admiral Dupont's fleet.

It was only nine days since Beauregard's guns had opened fire upon Fort Sumter, but their echoes had already reached the farthest limits of the country. They had lighted a conflagration which spread with electric speed and burned with consuming energy for four years.

On the morning after the arrival of the *Bienville* at New York, I went at an early hour to the office of the Steamship Company.

I was in some doubt how to act, because I had received no reply to the letter I had written to the Hon. J. P. Benjamin from New Orleans, and it was manifest that postal and telegraphic intercourse between the North and South would not be kept open, even if it had been safe or prudent to communicate by those means. My embarrassment was happily relieved by finding a letter from Mr. Benjamin awaiting me. It must have been among the last to come through the regular United States mail. The letter was brief, but to the point.

'Department of Justice, C.S.A.
Montgomery, Alabama.

'The Secretary of the Navy desires you to come to Montgomery without delay.

'Yours, etc.,

'(Signed) J. P. BENJAMIN.'

The document was too compromising to be retained about me, and I destroyed it at once. It was necessary to wind up my affairs with the company, and to settle other matters of business, and safety required that I should act without precipitancy. It is probable that my return to New York with the *Bienville* had removed any suspicion of my 'loyalty' which the public authorities might have had, and my friends either thought that I intended at least to remain neutral, or else they were too considerate to ask questions or to suggest doubts. I was detained about ten days in New York, and the com-

Judah P. Benjamin, Attorney-General of the Confederacy, February, 1861 – September, 1861; Secretary of War, September, 1861 – February, 1862; Secretary of State, February, 1862 – April, 1865. *(National Archives)*

William L. Yancey, Commissioner for the Confederate government in England and France, March, 1861 – February, 1862.
(Library of Congress)

pulsory sojourn there at that time was not agreeable. Subsequent information has assured me that if I had shown any haste in my movements, I should have been arrested. I mentioned to a few personal friends that I purposed going to Philadelphia, and possibly to Cincinnati, and in the early days of May I started southward with light luggage, as if for a short journey.

In the train to Philadelphia I met a commander in the United States navy, an old shipmate of former days. The war was uppermost in our minds, and we could talk of nothing else. My friend knew that I was a Southerner, and he had the tact and prudence not to ask any embarrassing questions, but he told me that he was going to Washington to apply for a command in the East Indies, and said that he wanted to get on foreign service, where he could not be employed against the South, and wished no professional honour or preferment which might be gained in such a struggle.

This feeling was common to the majority of the regular officers of the United States army and navy whom I met during the memorable period between the election of Mr. Abraham Lincoln and the attack upon Fort Sumter, and there is no doubt that many took up arms, if not with reluctance, at least with the feeling that they were performing a painful duty.

I stopped one night in Philadelphia. In the public squares and parks large bodies of men were drilling, and the streets were thronged with detachments of troops. Everywhere the din and bustle of preparation. I hurried on *viâ* Pittsburgh to Cincinnati, arriving at the latter place at six o'clock in the morning.

Here it was necessary to take steamer for Louisville, and the boat did not start until 4 p.m. I walked down to the steamboat landing and looked across the Ohio river at the Kentucky hills beyond. Kentucky was still 'in the Union,' but I knew that the feeling of the people was with the South, and once across the border I should be free from the danger of being asked at any moment to stop and give an account of myself. At the steamboat landing there were a military guard, and two civil officers who examined the packages of freight, and I learned that passengers and their luggage would be searched. When I went to embark in the afternoon, the guards were examining and questioning passengers at the ship's side, but a local gentleman whom I accidentally met told them I was a friend of his, who was going to Louisville on business, and I was permitted to pass without question and without search. There were a number of Kentucky people on board the boat. The elder were grave and silent, but some of the younger men were loud and vehement in denouncing the examination of their luggage. It was a relief to me when the lines were cast off and we moved swiftly down the river. I took the first train after my arrival at Louisville for Nashville, Tennessee, and arrived there at mid-day, May 5th. Tennessee had not yet seceded, but the Convention elected especially to determine the important question of secession was sitting in the State Capitol, and the town was full of volunteer corps and people from the country. There was no doubt about the feeling here ; it was intensely Southern, and everyone with whom I spoke, at the hotel and elsewhere, expressed both the hope and belief that the Convention would 'vote the State out of the Union.' The telegraph was working to Montgomery, and as it was quite safe to communicate, I telegraphed Mr. Benjamin that I was in Nashville *en route* for the Confederate capital.

While waiting for the departure of a train for the

South, I walked to the building in which the Convention was sitting, and saw there General Barrow, a prominent citizen, who had been in the diplomatic service of the United States. General Barrow was a member of the Convention. I mentioned to him that I was on my way to Montgomery to report for duty, and he requested me to say to President Davis, confidentially, that although the vote might not be taken for several days, he might feel confident that Tennessee would secede.

In due time the train started, and I got on rapidly through Chatanooga, Atlanta, etc., to Montgomery. It was nearly midnight, May 7th, when I reached the hotel at Montgomery, but no one seemed to think or care about sleeping. Everywhere on the journey from New York I had heard but one topic of conversation, and everywhere I beheld the same feverish excitement, the same hastening to prepare for the now inevitable conflict.

At an early hour next morning I called at Mr. Benjamin's office. He said the Secretary of the Navy had been expecting me from day to day, and would be desirous to see me as soon as possible. He took me at once to the Navy Department, and introduced me to its chief.

Mr. Benjamin was a busy man at that time, and so were all the members of that hastily constructed Provisional Government at Montgomery. No useless phrases were employed in the presentation.

'Mr. Secretary, here is Captain Bulloch.'

'I am glad to see you: I want you to go to Europe. When can you start?'

'I have no impedimenta, and can start as soon as you explain what I am to do.'

The announcement of this foreign mission took me aback, to use a nautical phrase. I had somehow become possessed with the expectation that I would be sent to New Orleans.

The insufficiency of the forts to prevent the passing of a hostile fleet up the Mississippi had been a frequent subject of discussion by the 'Board of War,' and among the leading citizens of New Orleans there had been much argument and many suggestions as to the best means of obstructing the channel. The difficulties to be met were the depth and volume of water, the great strength of the current, especially during the spring-freshets, when the Mississippi flows to the sea with the velocity of a mill-race, and the quantity of drift wood and timber which are borne along by the stream.

The question was thought to lie within the scope of nautical experience, and I had been drawn into the discussion and asked as a naval man to give an opinion. It was manifest, I thought, that no permanent immovable obstruction could stand the strain of flood and drift-wood, and I suggested the following plan :

'Float down to the bight, between Forts Jackson and St. Philip, a large number of logs from 60 to 100 feet long, some with the stumps of the branches remaining. Bore large auger holes through the butts of the logs, reeve chains through the holes, and toggel or staple the ends. Anchor a line of the logs a short distance below Fort Jackson, say 20 feet apart, using for this line logs with the stumps of their branches remaining, to form a sort of marine *chevaux de frise*. Anchor a second line a short distance above the first, with about half of each log trailing in the space between two logs of the first line; and a third line trailing in like manner between the openings in the second line, etc., etc. Multiply the lines to any extent that may be thought necessary. Anchors being scarce, stones of suitable weight, which would soon sink in the soft muddy bottom and hold well, can be used, and timber being abundant, the cost of such an obstruction will be moderate, and it will offer no impediment to the current, while the drift timber will cant and pass between the logs. When the attacking fleet enters the lower reaches of the river and appears to be preparing to force a passage, make fast to the ends of the lower line of logs 6 or 8-inch hawsers, so that they will trail down the river. Between the forts the river takes a great curve, and the action of the current will keep the logs constantly sheering from starboard to port, and they will thus be so completely interlaced as soon to bring up ships attempting to force through them, and the hawsers will foul the screws. While the ships are clearing their screws, and trying to drift out of the obstructions, the fire of the forts can be directed upon them with deliberation, and therefore with precision.'

I proposed that field-pieces or howitzers, covered by a protecting force, should be masked on the river-banks opposite the lower line of logs, to prevent the enemy sending boats to cut the hawsers and the log chains. I am not at all sure that the foregoing plan was ever formally submitted to the Governor in Council—indeed, I suspect it was not; but it was unofficially discussed with me by one or two members of the Board, and when I was in New Orleans with the steamship *Bienville* in March, 1861, I was asked to put the suggestion in writing, and would have done so on my next return in April, but the suddenness of the crisis at that time, the rapidity with which events then moved, and my necessary departure from New Orleans, either prevented my doing so, or other pressing questions took precedence.

The military men on the Board probably thought the

plan too simple; at any rate, it was not adopted. When Admiral Farragut attempted to pass the forts on the night of April 23-24, 1862, just one year afterwards, he found the passage obstructed by 'a chain which crossed the river, and was supported by eight hulks strongly moored.'*

Parties were sent in advance to blow up the hulks and break the chain. 'This duty was not thoroughly performed, in consequence of the failure to ignite the petards with the galvanic battery, and the great strength of the current.' 'The vessel boarded by Lieutenant-Commanding Caldwell appears to have had her chains so secured that they could be cast loose, which was done by that officer, thereby making an opening sufficiently large for the ships to pass through.'

The fleet does not appear to have been delayed by the obstructions, for Admiral Farragut says, 'We soon passed the barrier chains,' and the forts could only therefore get flying shots at the ships as they steamed up the river. From Confederate accounts it appears that the obstruction was a raft, the logs and hulks composing it being held together by chains, and the whole kept in position by numerous anchors.

This stationary and rigid structure could not resist the strain of flood and drift-wood, and was frequently broken. Its condition excited both interest and fears at Richmond. A few days before Admiral Farragut's attack, Mr. Secretary Mallory telegraphed to the officer commanding the naval defences at New Orleans, 'Is the boom, or raft, below the forts in order to resist the enemy, or has any part of it given way? State condition.' Captain Whittle replied (April 18), 'I hear the

* Admiral Farragut's report, dated May 6, 1862, in his 'Life' by his son, p. 243, etc.

raft below the forts is not in best condition They are strengthening it by additional lines. I have furnished anchors.' The Commanding General at New Orleans had exclusive charge of the construction of the raft, or obstruction, and the Naval Commander was simply required to supply anchors and assistance when asked.

Discussions in respect to the best mode of obstructing the river channel are useless at this late date, and conjectures whether any other mode than the one adopted would have been effectual in stopping the attacking fleet, would seem to imply some reproach upon the defenders, who doubtless did their best with the materials at hand.

Remembering the discussions on the subject at New Orleans, I got the impression, when summoned to Montgomery, that I was wanted about the Mississippi river defences, and the Secretary of the Navy's laconic query, when could I start for Europe, rather surprised me. There was, however, no time for parley. The Confederate Government had been scarcely three months in existence, and yet it was pressed by the requirements of a great emergency.

The South was outnumbered in population at least five to one. In military and naval resources the disproportion was many times greater. The only hope of success lay in the prompt and energetic use of her whole strength, and it was the bounden duty of everyone to accept the position and employment allotted to him without cavil or remonstrance.

Many of the Southern officers were on foreign stations when their States seceded. They had not only to return to the United States by long routes, but, after arrival, they were compelled to find their way to the South through the Northern States, whose people were daily becoming more and more hostile. They had often to take circuitous and expensive routes, and hence most of them reached their homes with pecuniary resources exhausted, and they had nothing to offer to their country 'but their patriotism and their swords.' Even their experience and their technical knowledge were at first of little profit, because the Confederacy had no ships for them to serve in, and no seamen to be organized and drilled.

Mr. Mallory briefly touched upon the condition of his Department. Very few of the naval officers who had resigned from the United States Service had found their way to Montgomery, and not many had yet come into direct communication with him. He had been able to buy one small steamer at New Orleans, and Commander Semmes had been ordered to fit her out for a cruise.

A committee of naval officers were examining the few vessels at the different Southern ports, but up to that date had found only the one Semmes had in hand which could be converted into a ship-of-war.

There were no machine shops, nor yards, no shipwrights, and no collection of material for ship-building. It was thought to be of prime importance to get cruisers at sea as soon as possible, to harass the enemy's commerce, and to compel him to send his own ships-of-war in pursuit, which might otherwise be employed in blockading the Southern ports. These were the chief points of Mr. Mallory's explanatory remarks. He then discussed the description of vessel best suited to the requirements of the service, and the possibility of being able to buy or build them in England, and finally he told me to go to my hotel, turn the whole subject over in my mind, and make such notes of the conversation as might be necessary to impress the substance on my memory, and to call on him again the next day. Even at that early date, the blockade of the chief Southern ports had been established more or less rigidly, and it was thought better that I should find my way into Canada through the Western States, and from thence to Europe, than to attempt an exit from one of the home ports in a sailing vessel, the only description of craft then available; besides which, the route *viâ* Canada promised quicker transit, and time was of the essence of the enterprise. This mode of departure manifestly prohibited the carrying of any documents, or even memoranda, which could betray the object of my mission in case of capture; hence the necessity for committing the chief points of the instructions to memory.

In compliance with Mr. Mallory's request I called at the Navy Department on the following morning, May 9. He examined my notes of the previous day's conversation, and enlarged upon the various subjects. He dwelt especially upon the probable course of the European Powers, and expressed the belief that they would recognise the *de facto* Government at Montgomery, and would grant to the commissioned cruisers of the Confederate States the shelter and privileges conceded to all belligerents by the comity of nations. He did not expect a formal recognition of the Confederate Government as an independent Power until the probability of success had been demonstrated by some substantial victories in the field. He warned me to be prudent and heedful, so as not to involve the diplomatic agents of the Confederate States in embarrassing complaints for alleged violation of neutral law or obligation, and he directed me to acquaint myself, as soon as possible after my arrival in England, with the nature and scope of the Foreign Enlistment Act, and the Queen's Proclamation of Neutrality, if one should be issued. Reverting to the special objects of my mission, he impressed upon me the wish of the Government to get cruising ships of suitable type afloat with the quickest possible despatch, and urged me to buy and forward naval supplies of all kinds without delay. He authorised me to practise a wide discretionary power within the limits of his general instructions, and discussed at some length the financial question, and the mode of placing funds in Europe. He informed me that Messrs. Fraser, Trenholm and Co., of Liverpool, would be the bankers or 'depositaries' of the Confederate Government, and directed me to communicate with them, and with the Hon. W. L. Yancey and the Hon. Dudley Mann, the Confederate Commissioners, immediately upon my arrival in England. Finally, he requested me to start as soon as possible, and said that written instructions, with anything further he might wish to communicate, would be sent me by the first opportunity through one of the seaports.

I left Montgomery by that night's train. Before reaching the Kentucky line I destroyed all notes and memoranda, and from Louisville I proceeded, without let or hindrance, to Detroit, Michigan.

The whole North appeared to be in military commotion. Volunteer corps in uniform, and large detachments of men without uniform, were seen drilling in every town through which I passed, and 'the war' was the one absorbing topic of conversation among the passengers in the trains, and the crowds assembled at the railway stations.

Crossing from Detroit to the Canada side of Lake Erie, I took the Grand Trunk Railway to Montreal, and the Allan Line steamer *North American* to Liverpool, arriving at that port on the 4th of June, 1861.

The burning of the Norfolk Navy Yard on April 20, 1861. *(Harper's Weekly)*

The Washington Navy Yard as it looked in 1861.
(Harper's Weekly)

The burning of the *Merrimac* at the Norfolk Navy Yard.
(Century Magazine)

NOTE TO PAGE 21.

The dockyard at Norfolk was at that time under the command of Commodore C. S. McCauley, U.S.N. He had not sufficient force on shore to have held possession of the dockyard if an attack had been made upon it from the land side. But such an attempt was not contemplated by the local authorities—indeed, it was not possible. The *Cumberland*, a powerful sailing corvette, with a crew of 300 men, had lately arrived from sea, and was lying close at hand. Her batteries commanded the neighbouring town, and not only afforded ample protection to the dockyard, but in fact made Commodore McCauley master of the situation. Virginia had not yet seceded, but the Convention to determine that important question was in session at Richmond, and the signs pointed to the expectation that she would soon cast in her lot with the States which had already withdrawn from the Union. General Taliaferro had been appointed to the local military command at Norfolk on behalf of the State of Virginia, but he had no organized force under his control. Confederate accounts state that he had carried on some negotiations with Commodore McCauley in respect to the dockyard, and that it had been agreed that 'none of the vessels should be removed, nor a shot fired, except in self-defence.' During the night of April 20th the ship-houses in the yard were set on fire, one of which contained the frame of a line-of-battle ship. These, with a long line of store-houses and offices adjoining them, were soon enveloped in flames, and were burned. The ships afloat, including the sailing line-of-battle ships *Pennsylvania* and *Delaware*, the frigates *Raritan* and *Columbus*, and the corvettes *Plymouth* and *Germantown*, were set on fire and scuttled. The above-named vessels were completely destroyed. The screw-frigate *Merrimac* was burned nearly to the water's edge, but the fire was extinguished after the United States forces had evacuated the yard, and she afterwards became famous as the Confederate ironclad ram *Virginia*. While Commodore McCauley was preparing for the work of destroying the dockyard and its contents, Commodore Paulding arrived with the screw-corvette *Pawnee*, having a detachment of troops on board, and the further operations were carried on under his orders. The greater portion of the guns in the parks were spiked, the machinery in the shops was broken, and an attempt was made to blow up the graving-dock, but this failed. Finally Commodore McCauley, with the officers, embarked; and the *Pawnee*, with the *Cumberland* in tow, proceeded down the river. As much of the naval stores as could be got on board the *Cumberland* was carried off; the remainder was either destroyed or greatly damaged. No effort was made by the Virginia State authorities to stop the ships, for the simple reason that there was no military or naval force capable of opposing them.

It will thus be manifest that when Virginia joined the Confederacy she could offer but a small contribution to the naval resources of her allies—only the wreck of her great dockyard.

CHAPTER II.

Messrs. Fraser, Trenholm and Co.—The Confederate Commissioners.—Major Huse, the Military Agent.—Early operations.—Restrictions of the Proclamations of Neutrality.—Their effects upon United States and Confederate Cruisers.—The *Oreto* (*Florida*).—Messrs. Laird and the *Alabama*.—The Equipment of the *Alabama*.—Counsel's Opinion on the Foreign Enlistment Act.—Despatch of the *Bermuda* with supplies for the Confederate Army.—Second Voyage and Capture of the *Bermuda*.—The Trial at Philadelphia.—The United States and belligerent rights.—Decree of Court in the *Bermuda* case.—Contrast between the action of the United States as a belligerent and as a neutral concerning belligerent rights.—The United States and neutral vessels during the Crimean War.—The Bahama Islands 'Regulations' of the British Government.—Reasons for the seeming indifference of the British Government.—Precedents established by the United States favourable to Great Britain.—European Naval Armaments.—British Shipbuilding.—Importance of British Mercantile Marine.—Weakness of the United States as a Naval Power.—Former efficiency of the American Navy.—Seamanship in the Past and the Present.

My first duty after arrival at Liverpool was to communicate with the financial agents of the Confederate Government, but it was already late in the day, and places of business were for the most part closed. At an early hour on the next morning I called at the counting-house of Messrs. Fraser, Trenholm and Co., and went up to London the same afternoon, to see the Confederate Commissioners, who at that time were the Hon. William L. Yancey and the Hon. Dudley Mann.

I had no credentials, and nothing to prove my personal identity, or the nature of my mission ; but when men are moved by a common sympathy, and their minds are earnestly set upon the same object, the powers of discerning seem to be quickened, and they recognise each other by intuitive perception. At any rate, the Commissioners gave me a cordial welcome, and we were soon deep in Confederate affairs. They explained the diplomatic situation. They had not been officially received by Her Majesty's Secretary of State for Foreign Affairs, and did not think the Confederate States would be recognised until they had demonstrated their ability to win and to maintain their independence ; nevertheless, the chief European Powers had admitted that there was a *de facto* Government at Montgomery, with power to raise armies and to levy war, and they thought we would be permitted to obtain supplies in England upon the same conditions as any other belligerent, and they encouraged me to set to work with due precaution, but with alacrity, promising their hearty support whenever I might need their intervention.

Messrs. Fraser, Trenholm and Co. received me with equal cordiality and equal trust. No funds had yet reached them, and they had no advice of remittances on behalf of my mission ; but Mr. Charles K. Prioleau, the resident partner, perceiving the necessity of prompt action, authorized me to give out such orders as were of pressing importance, and to refer to his firm for the financial arrangements. Captain, afterwards Major Caleb Huse, of the Confederate Army, had preceded me to England, and had already made some large purchases of arms, and still larger contracts, upon the credit of Messrs. Fraser, Trenholm and Co.

Major Huse was a graduate of the Military Academy

at West Point, and after serving a number of years in the United States artillery, had retired from active service, and when the Southern States seceded he was superintendent of the Alabama State Military Academy. When the Provisional Government at Montgomery was formed, Major Huse was sent to Europe to buy arms and other ordnance supplies for the army, and he represented the War Department, and especially the Ordnance Bureau, during the whole war. This officer was a man of ability, and of unusual energy, but his services were scarcely known beyond the office of his departmental chief. I have always felt that the safety of Richmond at the time of General McClellan's advance from Yorktown up the peninsula, in the spring of 1862, was largely due to the efforts of Mr. Charles K. Prioleau and Major Huse, because the former furnished the credits, and the latter bought and forwarded the rifles and field artillery without which the great battles of Seven Pines and the Chickahominy, could not have been successfully fought.

It is an unquestionable fact that the Confederate Government had great financial difficulties to meet, and the 'depositaries' in England were often under heavy advances to the various Bureaux of the War Department, and on one or two important occasions to the Navy Department also. Major Huse showed both skill and energy in pressing the credit of the Government, and he often made large contracts, and even got delivery of arms and other ordnance stores, when there were no public funds at all in England.

My early operations were greatly helped by the generous confidence of Messrs. Fraser, Trenholm and Co. Within a month after my arrival, I had not only been able to buy a fair quantity of naval supplies on their credit, but had laid the keel of the first foreign-built Confederate cruiser, and she was partly in frame before the Navy Department had found it possible to place any funds in Europe. The vessel thus early begun (June, 1861), was the *Oreto*, afterwards *Florida*.

As it is the purpose of this narrative not only to show that a Confederate naval force was organized abroad during the Civil War, but that the operations were carried on with strict regard to local law, I feel the necessity of being somewhat minute in describing the manner in which all contracts for ships were made.

The great Maritime Powers in Europe issued proclamations of neutrality* at a very early date after the beginning of hostilities, and these proclamations were supplemented from time to time by Admiralty orders and regulations defining the conditions upon which the ships of both belligerents would be allowed refuge in the neutral ports, to make repairs and to obtain supplies. The chief restrictions specified in those orders were, that no ship should reinforce her crew, or make greater alterations and repairs than were necessary to ensure her safety; that the armament should not be changed or increased, and that no ordnance or other description of stores classed as 'contraband of war' should be taken on board; that the quantity of coal to be taken should be no more than enough to carry her to the nearest port of her own country, and after receiving that quantity she should not enter any harbour of the same neutral power for another supply until the expiration of three months, except by special permission.

The example of England and France was followed by the minor Powers. Spain and Portugal proclaimed their neutrality, and announced the conditions upon

* Proclamation of Her Britannic Majesty dated May 13, 1861.

which their ports might be used by the two belligerents. Even Brazil and the South American Republics soon fell to defining their views, and swelled the general chorus of 'impartial neutrality' in the great struggle between the North and South which the easterly trade-winds wafted over to them from Europe. If the restrictions thus imposed upon the cruisers of both parties in the Civil War were vexatious and inconvenient to the Federal Government, they were manifestly more burdensome and perplexing to that of the Confederacy.

The United States had four ample and well-found dockyards on the Atlantic coast (Portsmouth, Boston, New York and Philadelphia), at which their ships could be efficiently and completely equipped. In addition to this advantage, the home ports were always open to them for shelter, repair and supply, and everywhere abroad there were diplomatic and consular agents to appeal to for aid in case of difficulty or undue exactions on the part of local authorities. Besides this, the United States Navy Department could furnish each cruising ship with ample credits through bankers whose financial position had long been assured the world over. A Confederate cruiser, on the contrary, had no home port for outfit or retreat. She was compelled to be as nearly as possible self-supporting. Her flag was tolerated only, not recognised. Once upon the seas, she could never hope to re-supply the continual waste of her powers of offence or defence, and could obtain but a grudging allowance of the merest necessaries. Her 'military chest' was the paymaster's safe, and her financial resources were the moderate supply of sovereigns with which she began her cruise. In case of difficulty, there was no resident Minister to whom the captain could refer for counsel or support, no consular representative who could set his case before the authorities in the neutral ports.

In the home ports of England and France the Confederate cruisers were fairly and courteously treated—at any rate, the treatment was uniform and consistent—but in the distant colonies, and at the ports of other less powerful and independent countries, the manner in which they were received, and the spirit in which the neutrality regulations were enforced, depended very much upon the individual sympathies and opinions of the local Governor, or the amount of influence the resident United States Consul could exert.

I believe this to be a very moderate statement of the contrast between the conditions under which the United States and Confederate cruisers were kept at sea during the war.

If it had not been for the limitations and restrictions of the 'Admiralty orders' previously referred to, many more vessels might have been got to sea under the Confederate flag; but it would have been manifestly improvident, and a purposeless waste of the limited resources of the Navy Department, to commission ships for distant and continuous cruising, unless they could carry ample supplies of all necessaries, especially of ordnance stores, and could sail as well as steam at a good rate of speed. A vessel without good sailing qualities, and without the arrangement and means for lifting her screw, would have been practically useless as a Confederate cruiser. She could only have made passages from one coaling station to another; and as she could only coal at a port of the same country once in three months, her career would soon have been brought to an untimely and not very creditable end.

The necessities of the case, then, dictated the type of

the Confederate ship, and the *Oreto* (*Florida*) and the *Alabama* were especially designed to meet those requirements.*

The *Florida* was a wooden vessel. Messrs. William C. Miller and Sons were the builders, and she was built at their yard in Liverpool. That firm was selected to build the hull of the ship, and to supply the masts, rigging, boats, and general sea-outfit, because the senior of the firm had been in the Royal Navy as a shipwright, and had served in her Majesty's dockyards as a naval constructor. He had therefore much experience in the construction of wooden ships designed to carry heavy weights on deck and to berth large crews. Messrs. Miller and Sons were not engineers, and, as it was advisable, for many reasons, that ship and engines should be as near together as possible, Messrs. Fawcett, Preston and Co., of Liverpool, were chosen to design and build the engines. The financial arrangements were made with Messrs. Fawcett, Preston and Co. exclusively. They took the whole contract for both ship and engines, and the preliminary discussions were of the ordinary business character.

Mr. W. C. Miller had a scale drawing of one of her Majesty's gunboats, which we adopted as a base to start from. She was drawn out in the midship section, and the floor was flattened to get greater carrying capacity. The increased length thus obtained admitted of finer entrance and clearance lines, which secured higher speed.

* The two vessels built at Liverpool, and which were afterwards commissioned abroad as Confederate cruisers, are generally mentioned in this narrative as the *Florida* and *Alabama*, to avoid frequent explanation. It will, however, be understood that they were never known by those names in the port of their construction, and were never alluded to in the arrangements with the builders, except as the *Oreto* and *No.* 290.

The rigging scale was also largely increased, so as to get a good spread of canvas, especially when close hauled, or with the wind a-beam. The type and rig of ship being satisfactorily adjusted, Messrs. Fawcett, Preston and Co. designed the engines, which were carefully discussed. The contract was made with me as a private person, nothing whatever being said about the ultimate destination of the ship, or the object for which she was intended. It is not usual for building firms to ask questions, or to express opinions as to the motives or purposes of those from whom they take orders. Before the completion of the ship, Messrs. Fawcett, Preston and Co. and the Messrs. Miller may both have had a tolerably clear notion that she would at some future time, and by some subsequent arrangement, pass into the possession of the Confederate Government; but they never mentioned their suspicions, and they undertook nothing more than to build and deliver in Liverpool a screw-steamer, according to certain specified plans and conditions, fitted for sea in every respect, but without armament or equipment for fighting of any kind whatever. To provide an answer in advance for any inquisitive comments or surmises, *Oreto* was chosen as the dockyard name for the ship. It was incidentally mentioned among the workpeople that she would probably be sent to a mercantile firm doing business in Palermo, and a local representative of that firm undertook the details of supervising and despatching her.

While the negotiations for the *Oreto* (*Florida*) were in progress, I went with a friend to visit the Birkenhead Ironworks, and was introduced to the Messrs. Laird. After an interesting examination of their extensive establishment, I led the conversation to the subject of wooden despatch vessels, and described with some minuteness the type which appeared most desirable in my judgment. The subject was naturally of interest to the Messrs. Laird, and they gave me their opinions and the result of their experience with freedom. A few days after, I called again, re-opened the conversation about a screw despatch vessel, discussed the matter somewhat more in detail, and finally told them that I wished to build such a ship, and asked if they would be willing to go into the necessary calculations, draw up specifications, and make drawings and a model, upon my assurance that I meant business and was ready to give them the necessary financial guarantee. They were satisfied with my proposals, and in a very short time all the details of the *Alabama* were settled to our common satisfaction.

The origin of the *Alabama*, her departure from England, and her career afloat, have been much discussed. Probably no single ship has ever given occasion for so much diplomatic correspondence, or has furnished the grounds for so many complaints, and the foundation for so great an alleged international grievance. She has been called a 'British pirate;' many persons believed that she was paid for by a subscription among English merchants. The builders were often accused of risking the peace of the realm by supplying a vessel of war to cruise against the commerce of the United States, and they have been openly charged with committing a flagrant breach of the Queen's proclamation of neutrality for their own selfish profit—bartering, as it were, their loyalty as subjects, and their duty as citizens, for a pecuniary consideration, which it has been erroneously alleged they received in an extravagant price for the ship.

The great Commonwealth which forms one of the

mighty union of States across the Atlantic is scarcely known in Europe except as the producer of some half-million bales of cotton per annum ; but her little name-sake of a thousand tons, in a lifetime of barely two years, has spread the name to the uttermost parts of the earth, and has made it familiar to thousands who know nothing of geographical State lines, and at the mention of it now would probably think of the '*Alabama* Claims,' and not of the ' Alabama State.'

This notoriety of the ship, and the long-current mis-statements affecting her builders and all who were in any way concerned with her origin, seem to impose upon me the duty of dwelling upon the purely business arrangements with the Messrs. Laird more particularly than would be at all necessary, or even expedient, under ordinary circumstances.

The contract for the vessel afterwards called the *Alabama* was made in my own name as a private individual, and the negotiations were carried on between the members of the firm and myself, without the inter-vention of any other parties whatever. The Messrs. Laird very properly looked first to the financial security. I did not leave them a moment in doubt on that point, and being fully satisfied that the proposed transaction was in every particular safe and regular, they took it in hand as a part of their ordinary business.

At that time, wood had almost entirely gone out of use as a material for ship-building in Great Britain, and it was suggested, and as readily admitted, that there would be some difficulty in getting suitable timber for the heavy scantling, such, to wit, as the stem, keelson, and especially the sternpost, which would require to be bored to receive the screw shaft. These facts were mentioned and discussed with reference to the cost and time necessary to build the ship, and it was perceived that both would considerably exceed the estimate for an iron vessel.

The general dimensions and other particulars of the *Alabama* were: length 220 feet; breadth, 32 feet; draft, with all weights on board, 15 feet; tonnage, 1040; engines, two horizontal, of 300 horse-power nominal, but on trial trip indicated 1,000 horse-power. She was barque-rigged, with very long lower masts, to get large fore and aft sails. Her sails, carried at will, were as follows: fore, fore-topmast staysail and jib; two large trysails, the usual square sails on fore and main masts, with the exception of the main course, which was set flying; spanker and gaff-topsails; all standing rigging wire. She was admirably fitted in every respect: engines equal to Admiralty standard; brass screw, Griffith's pattern, with lifting apparatus, and stowage in iron bunkers for 350 tons of coal. She was provided with a double suit of sails and the usual outfit for an East India voyage. She had five boats, including launch, cutter and whale-boat, and ample ground-tackle. She was well supplied with hawsers, and had spare blocks, running gear, etc., to meet all requirements for at least a year. The engineer's stores and spare engine-gear were on the scale supplied to ships of the Royal Navy intended for long and distant voyages, and she was provided with condensing apparatus and cooling tank to supply fresh water. She was built of the very best materials, copper-fastened and coppered, and was finished in every respect as a first-class ship. I was satisfied in every particular with the manner in which the builders fulfilled their contract, and I believe she was as fine a vessel, and as well-found, as could have been turned out of any dockyard in the kingdom, equal to any of her Majesty's ships of corresponding class in structure and finish, and superior to any vessel of her date in fitness for the purposes of a sea rover, with no home but the sea, and no reliable source of supply but the prizes she might make.

The price paid to the Messrs. Laird, including the outfit, was £47,500, payable by the terms of the contract in five equal payments of £9,500 each ; and the last instalment was made payable after satisfactory trial and delivery to me on the Mersey in the *port of Liverpool.* Everyone who has had experience in the cost of ships will admit that the price named was not in the least degree excessive or unreasonable. I had previously superintended the construction of vessels of varying types, and I thought at the time, and am of the opinion now, that the contract price for the *Alabama* afforded only a fair commercial profit to the builders.

The foregoing statement will, I trust, be accepted as a complete and final refutation of the charge often made, that the Messrs. Laird were paid a high price for undertaking the exceptional risk of building a vessel of war, and delivering her to an agent of the Confederate Government beyond British jurisdiction. In point of fact, they delivered to me an unarmed ship in the port of Liverpool. As another simple matter of fact, they did not know for what purpose the ship was intended when they agreed to build her. They were not informed of anything which had reference to the armament, and are to this day ignorant of the manner and place of equipment, excepting in so far as the movements and performances of the ship, after she passed out of their hands, are known to the general public. (See p. 96.)

I feel that I owe to the memory of the late Mr. John Laird, M.P., an explicit and unequivocal denial of the charge so often made that he was concerned in the building and equipment of the ship afterwards called the *Alabama*, a statement which many persons have thought to be confirmed by some inadvertent expressions in Admiral Semmes' narrative of her cruise under his command. At the time when I was negotiating for the *Alabama*, Mr. John Laird had retired from the firm which bore his name, and he was shortly afterwards elected to serve in Parliament as the first member for Birkenhead. My business arrangements, and all the discussions about the design and cost of the ship, were carried on with Messrs. William and John Laird, junr. Mr. John Laird, the subsequent member for Birkenhead, had nothing whatever to do with the transaction, and I am quite sure that he was never even present at any of my interviews with the firm in reference to that subject.

After Mr. Laird took his seat in Parliament, I understood and appreciated his position, and was rigidly reticent about Confederate affairs. Our acquaintance ripened into friendship, and I was his debtor for many acts of kindly social courtesy, but never, in the freedom of friendly and familiar conversation, was the subject of the *Alabama* discussed or even alluded to until she was afloat as a Confederate cruiser, and her acts had become matters of common knowledge, and topics of general comment.

In May, 1874, I had occasion to go to the Brazils on business, and I called to bid Mr. Laird good-bye, and to get a number of letters of introduction which he had kindly obtained for me. We were talking about the Amazon, and a steamship company formed by the Baron de Maua to navigate that mighty river. The conversation turned upon ships in general, and the *Alabama* was incidentally mentioned. I told him how her battery and ordnance stores were shipped from London, and gave him an account of our adventures at the island of Terceira, where she was armed and equipped. He was much interested, and remarked that he had always thought it most fortunate that I had never mentioned the circumstances to him during the war, because his ignorance of them enabled him to say, when attacked in Parliament, without the least mental reservation, that he was not only free from all complicity in the equipment of the ship, but that he knew nothing about her, except what had been revealed to the general public.

Mr. Laird's statements in the House of Commons that he had nothing to do with the building or equipment of the *Alabama* were frequently spoken of with distrust by other members who were ardent partisans of the United States, and the newspapers which adopted and defended the same cause persisted in repeating the original charge, in face of the most distinct and unequivocal denials ; but he had the satisfaction to know that her Majesty's Government implicitly believed his disavowal, and he came to feel at last that the repetition of the charges was merely intended for party purposes, and hence he ceased to give much heed to them.

At this late date, when time has softened the resentful temper and the sharp antagonism which seem always to warp the judgment and embitter criticism during periods of great political excitement, I may indulge the hope that my testimony in regard to the building and equipping of Confederate ships abroad will be received without distrust. I can conscientiously say that I have neither the purpose nor the wish to conceal a single fact ; indeed, my only fear is that anxiety to tell the whole truth may lead me into the error of too great minuteness of detail, and that I may be seduced into the expectation that incidents and adventures which force of circumstances strongly impressed upon my own mind may be of corresponding interest to others.

The chief object of this narrative is to demonstrate, by a plain statement of facts, that the Confederate Government, through their agents, did nothing more than all other belligerents have heretofore done in time of need—namely, tried to obtain from every possible source the means necessary to carry on the war in which they were engaged, and that in doing so they took particular pains to understand the municipal laws of those countries in which they sought to supply their wants, and were especially careful to keep within the statutes.

The Foreign Enlistment Act, and its bearing upon the naval operations of the Confederate States in England, will be fully explained and discussed in a subsequent chapter; but to preserve a due and relevant connection of subjects, and to keep the record in appropriate relation to the order of events, it seems fitting to mention that at a very early day after my arrival in England I took legal advice.

The object of the Confederate Government was not merely to buy or build a single ship, but it was to maintain a permanent representative of the Navy Department abroad, and to get ships and naval supplies without hindrance as long as the war lasted. To effect this purpose it was manifestly necessary to act with prudence and caution, and to do nothing in violation of the municipal law, because a single conviction would both expose the object and defeat its aim. A fortunate circumstance led me to consult the late Mr. F. S. Hull, a member of a leading firm of solicitors in Liverpool, and he continued to act as my solicitor during the whole period of the war. Mr. Hull was a prudent, cautious, conscientious adviser, and throughout all those troublous times I found him a watchful and safe mentor. I kept him informed of all important transactions, and consulted him with reference to all contracts.

There were many complications, and perplexing questions were constantly cropping up. These he faced with coolness, judgment, and good temper, and never once led me astray or encouraged me to undertake the impracticable. He piloted me safely through the mazes of the Foreign Enlistment Act, in spite of the perplexing ambiguity of its 7th Section, and the bewildering iterations and reiterations of the precept not to 'equip, furnish, fit out, or arm' any ship with intent, etc., etc.

Generally Mr. Hull felt and proved himself competent to deal with the legal questions as they arose, without referring to any other authority; but at the time of making the contracts for the *Alabama* and *Florida*, no case involving the forfeiture of a ship had ever been brought to trial under the Foreign Enlistment Act,* and there had therefore been no judicial decision as to its interpretation. If the Act prohibited the building of a ship for a belligerent under all circumstances, and imposed upon the builder the onus of proving that there was no intent to arm her beyond British jurisdiction, it was important to know it, because if that was the law, merely concealing the ultimate purpose from the builder would not protect the property from seizure and forfeiture. Mr. Hull therefore drew up a case for counsel's opinion, and submitted it to two eminent barristers, both of whom have since filled the highest judicial positions. The case submitted was a general and not a specific proposition. It was not intimated for what

* '*Alexandra* Case,' speeches of the Attorney-General and Sir Hugh Cairns.

purpose or on whose behalf the opinion was asked, and the reply was therefore wholly without bias, and embraced a full exposition of the Act in its bearing upon the question of building and equipping ships in her Majesty's dominions.

The inferences drawn from the investigation of the Act by counsel were put into the following form by my solicitor:

'1. It is no offence (under the Act) for British subjects to equip, etc., a ship at some country *without* her Majesty's dominions, though the intent be to cruise against a friendly State.

'2. It is no offence for *any* person (subject or no subject) to *equip* a ship *within* her Majesty's dominions, if it be *not* done with the intent to cruise against a friendly State.

'3. The mere building of a ship *within* her Majesty's dominions by any person (subject or no subject) is no offence, *whatever may be the intent of the parties*, because the offence is not the *building* but the *equipping*.

'Therefore any shipbuilder may build any ship in her Majesty's dominions, provided he does not equip her within her Majesty's dominions, and he has nothing to do with the acts of the purchasers done *within* her Majesty's dominions without his concurrence, nor *without* her Majesty's dominions even with his concurrence.'

The foregoing deductions from the terms of the Act were kept rigidly in view in all contracts for ships in England, and every possible precaution was practised both for the protection of the builders against criminal prosecutions under the Act, and for that of the ships against forfeiture. In no case was any builder or vendor informed what was the purpose of the purchaser. No ship was ever supplied with any portion of her equipment *within* her Majesty's dominions, nor was the builder or vendor of any ship employed to assist in the equipment *without* her Majesty's dominions.

On the 27th of July, 1861, the first remittance on account of the Confederate Navy Department reached England. The *Oreto* (*Florida*) was then partly in frame, and the plans and specifications of the ship afterwards called the *Alabama* being complete, the contract with the Messrs. Laird was closed on the first day of August.

It is very seldom that a particular name is given to a ship until at or about the time of her launch, but a dockyard number is assigned to her, for convenience of reference, and for specification in the accounts of expenditure. The number given to the ship contracted for with Messrs. Laird was '290,' which, it will be perceived, had none of the mysterious signification so often ascribed to it, but meant simply that she was the 290th ship built by them.

It was often alleged, after the departure of the *Alabama* from Liverpool, that a peculiar and mysterious secrecy was practised in respect to her, and that no one was permitted to examine her, or even to go into Messrs. Laird's yard while she was building, without a special permit. This is quite a mistake. My intercourse with the builders was only so far secret that I kept my own counsel, and did not communicate to them the purpose for which the ship was intended. They, on their part, asked no questions, and, so far as I know, they adopted no special restrictions with regard to visitors to the works while she was in their hands. Official documents, long since published, have proved beyond doubt that the officers of Her Majesty's Customs had free and unopposed access to her at all times, and the general public were not excluded in a greater degree, nor under more stringent conditions than are commonly enforced in all well-regulated manufacturing establishments.*

When the United States Minister was clamouring at the door of the Foreign Office, and pressing Her Majesty's Government to seize, or at least to detain, the *Florida* and *Alabama*, the Consul at Liverpool supplied him with numerous 'affidavits' of persons who subscribed the usual form of oath that they had seen me on board giving instructions and describing the type, arrangements, and ultimate destination of the ships. Either those affidavits were 'made to order,' or else it was not difficult to get a view of both the ships. By-and-by it will be shown that many of the affidavits were prepared with little regard to actual facts, and that they were generally made either by hired 'private detectives,' whose chief aim was to earn their pay, or at least to give something in return for it, by self-appointed spies, who found a ready market for their tales, or by that class of persons who are possessed

* See report of Mr. Morgan, Surveyor of Her Majesty's Customs, Liverpool, dated 28th June, 1862:

'The officers have at all times free access to the building yards of the Messrs. Laird at Birkenhead, where the said vessel is now lying; and there has been no attempt on the part of the builders to disguise what is now apparent to all, that she is intended for a ship-of-war.'—'*Alabama* Papers,' 24th March, 1863.

That the *Alabama* subsequently left Liverpool unarmed is proved by the official report of the Surveyor of Customs, dated 30th July, 1862:

'I have only to add that your directions to keep a strict watch on the said vessel have been carried out, and I write in the fullest confidence that she left this port without any part of her armament on board. She had not as much as a signal-gun or musket.'—'*Alabama* Papers,' 24th March, 1863.

with a mania to spring at a leap to convictions which may or may not prove to be right in the end, but who, unwilling to await the natural and regular fulfilment of events, are impelled by a restless impatience to manufacture the intermediate facts or to mould and distort them so as to confirm their preconceived opinions.

None but an unsophisticated or very impertinent person would think of walking into any business premises and asking the owners what they were doing, and who for. Such inquirers get either evasive replies, or rebuffs more or less courteously expressed. It is probable that the Messrs. Laird had frequently to meet such contingencies, and I have no doubt that they invariably 'rose to the occasion,' and knew when to be courteously equivocal, and when to maintain a frigid reserve.

About the month of August, 1861, Messrs. Fraser, Trenholm and Co. determined to send a steamer to one of the Southern ports with a cargo, not wholly of arms, but of general supplies suited to the wants of the armies in the field, and their Charleston house, Messrs. John Fraser and Co., had sent over an experienced coast pilot to take her in. Mr. Prioleau told me of this purpose, and informed me that while his firm expected to realize a fair commercial profit from the undertaking, their chief object was to demonstrate that the blockade was inefficient, and thus they hoped to encourage others to embark in like enterprises, by which means the pressing wants of the South could be supplied with more or less certainty.

It was important to keep the destination of the ship secret, but Mr. Prioleau told me of his purpose, as he said, to advise me about the adventure, and also to offer me the opportunity to ship such arms and ordnance stores as Major Huse and I might have ready to forward. The steamer engaged for the purpose was the *Bermuda*. She was fitted out and loaded at West Hartlepool, and I went to that port with Mr. Prioleau to superintend the shipment of the goods especially intended for the Confederate War and Navy Departments, while Major Huse looked after their despatch to the shipping port.

The *Bermuda* was commanded by Captain Eugene Tessier, who had long been employed by the firm in the Charleston trade; and his pilot was Captain Peck, well known on the coast from Charleston to St. Augustine. She sailed from West Hartlepool in August, 1861; got safely into Savannah, September 18th; and ran out again with a large cargo of cotton, which she brought to Liverpool.

Mr. Edwin Haigh, of Liverpool, the registered owner of the ship, in an affidavit presented to the United States District Court of Pennsylvania in October, 1862,* said as follows: 'I am informed and believe that the said steamship (*Bermuda*), in the prosecution of her voyage, was not warned off by any of the blockading cruisers; and that she entered the port of Savannah without meeting with any of such cruisers, or having the opportunity of ascertaining whether the said blockade was still in force, and there discharged her cargo.'

It will thus be seen that Messrs. Fraser, Trenholm and Co. accomplished their purpose of demonstrating that the blockade of the Southern coast, at the time of the *Bermuda's* voyage (August and September, 1861), was inefficient; and it is probable that their expectation of realizing a commercial profit by the adventure was

* See 'Report of Proceedings in Admiralty, U.S. *v.* SS. *Bermuda* and Cargo, Philadelphia, August, 1862,' p. 448.

also fulfilled. Their example undoubtedly stimulated the trade, but the United States soon strengthened and increased the blockading force, and during the last two years of the war the difficulty of getting in and out of the Southern ports was made greater and greater, until only the swiftest vessels stood any chance of success, and they only when favoured by dark nights and suitable weather.

In February, 1862, the *Bermuda* was despatched again from England, but the greater efficiency of the blockade at that time, together with the fear that she was both too large and too slow to promise success, caused the owner to abandon the purpose or attempt to run her into a Southern port. The cargo, laden in England, was intended to be discharged at Bermuda or Nassau, and a return cargo for Liverpool had actually been provided by her consignees at Nassau.

This voyage of the *Bermuda* is interesting and important, because it affords a typical example of the manner in which the United States dealt with neutral vessels captured for real or alleged violation of the blockade, and furnishes also a fitting occasion for some remarks upon the general conduct of the United States towards neutrals during the war, and the precedents that Government persistently laboured to establish.

In pursuance of the owner's purpose, the *Bermuda* sailed from Liverpool, touched at the island of Bermuda, and in due course proceeded towards Nassau, her final port of destination. On the morning of April 27th, 1862, being off the southern point of Great Abaco Island, the Hole-in-the-Wall Light bearing south-west, distant, according to the varying testimony of witnesses, from less than three to over seven miles, the *Bermuda* was stopped by a shot fired across her bows from the United States steamer *Mercedita*, a prize crew was put on board, and she was taken into Philadelphia.

There was some delay in bringing her case to trial; but finally she was arraigned before Judge Cadwalader, of the United States District Court sitting in Admiralty at Philadelphia. The proceedings began August 12th, 1862, and the arguments *pro* and *con* were closed on the 16th of the same month. 'At the conclusion of the argument, the judge remarked that he would consider the case very carefully, and deliver his opinion at as early a day as practicable.'* The outline of the case cannot be better stated than in the words of Mr. George M. Wharton, counsel for the owners, or the 'claimants,' as they are designated in the legal proceedings. Mr. Wharton said: 'It is the case of a British vessel, owned by a British subject, laden at Liverpool by British merchants, and bound for Bermuda, a British colony. After arriving at Bermuda, the ship has directions from those who have the right to control, so far, her movements, to go from Bermuda to Nassau, another British colonial port; and while navigating in the direct line from Bermuda to Nassau, and at the distance of about 415 miles from that portion of the American coast the blockade of which she is alleged to have violated, while sailing among these British islands in a direct line toward her place of destination, she is overhauled by a cruiser of the United States Government, captured, and brought here for trial and consequent condemnation.'

The contention of the United States Attorney was to this effect. The voyage to Bermuda and Nassau was only a colourable pretext. The cargo was either

* See 'Report of Proceedings,' p. 397.

enemy's property, or was shipped with the intent to be forwarded to an enemy's port through the blockade, and that even though the *Bermuda* might break bulk at Nassau and land the whole of her cargo there, the purpose was to reship it for Charleston, or some other blockaded port. He furthermore urged the plea that a vessel bound in point of fact from London to Charleston, could not plead in defence an original design to stop at Nassau during the voyage, and that she was sailing at the moment of capture for or in the direction of the intermediate port. In their arguments the counsel for the United States also contended that if the original intention was to run the blockade, and merely to make Nassau a place of call for any purpose whatever, the vessel was liable to capture the moment she got beyond the limit of British jurisdiction, which they specified to be any distance beyond three miles outside of the port of Liverpool.

International law is not an exact science. The highest authorities differ in the construction of its rules, and the most learned judges have variously interpreted its provisions. It is a code which has never received the willing or unanimous consent of all nations, but bears upon its face the impress of having been forced by the stronger upon the weaker, and history furnishes many instances in which during times of war belligerents have set aside or acted in defiance of its apparent and commonly received conditions, whenever their interests required, and their power was sufficient to enforce their purpose. Interference with trade between neutrals and either of two belligerents has always been considered oppressive, and in derogation of a natural right. By the declaration of Paris of 1856, the principle that the neutral flag covered the goods and protected the ship also from search, when on the high sea, was agreed to, and the rules which prohibited a neutral from carrying the goods of a belligerent, or compelled the neutral to submit to 'the right of search,' were done away with, as between the Great Powers who were parties to that declaration. This did not, of course, abolish the right of blockade.

It is not my purpose to argue or even to comment upon the law points involved in the case of the *Bermuda*. The whole of the proceedings have been published, and have been no doubt carefully examined by the interested parties. The present object is merely to set out the circumstances of the capture, and the facts appertaining to the disposal of the ship and cargo, and thus to demonstrate the manner in which the United States enforced their belligerent rights, and the broad scope they claimed and practised in the exercise of them. It is manifestly difficult to prove an intent, and in the case of the *Bermuda* the only evidence on the part of the United States was purely circumstantial; on the other hand, a number of persons in Liverpool were interested in the shipments by her, and the particulars of the voyage were known to many persons, and were much discussed. It was well understood among the shippers of goods that the vessel would go only to Bermuda and Nassau, and among the documents laid before the Prize Court,* there appears an affidavit by one of the Liverpool agents of the ship, in which there is set out, among others, the following declaration: 'That the cargo laden here' (Liverpool) 'was intended to be discharged at Bermuda or Nassau, and that a return cargo for this port' (Liverpool) 'had been provided by her consignees at Nassau.'

* See 'Report of Proceedings,' p. 424.

The *Bermuda* was no doubt tainted by the alleged previous violation of the blockade, but it has been shown that she was not warned off, nor did she even see a blockading vessel when she entered the port of Savannah in September, 1861, and it is therefore questionable whether that voyage was in reality a breach of blockade. The captain, too, seems to have lost his head, or to have been over-confident in the protecting influence of his flag and register. He should either have got his ship clearly and indisputably within the marine league, and held on to all of his papers, or destroyed every document except his manifest, letter of instruction, and register, or he should have beached the ship and thus have prevented her capture. He did neither, but stopped at the first shot, and then destroyed only the papers in his personal charge, containing those which demonstrated that the ship was to go no further than Nassau, and left on board the private correspondence, for the nature of which neither the owners nor the agents were responsible.

However, the name and previous history of the ship, the nature of the cargo, and the particulars of the voyage, could neither of them have been known without forcible stoppage and search, and the fact remains that the commander of the *Mercedita* enforced an extreme and unusual belligerent pretension against a neutral ship proceeding to a colonial port of her own country, when steering towards that port, and on a course away from, and 415 miles distant from the nearest part of the coast the blockade of which she was alleged to have violated.

Although the arguments in the Prize Court were concluded on the 16th of August, 1862, and the judge announced his purpose to render judgment 'as soon as practicable,'* no decision was given up to December 19th, 1862, and the further proceedings in the case may be briefly stated as follows :

December 19th, 1862, the 'Attorney of the United States' petitioned the Court for an order directing the Marshal to deliver to any authorized agent of the Navy Department of the United States the said steamer (*Bermuda*), on the payment by the United States into the Registry of the Court of the amount of her appraised value.† The petition showed that the ship had been appraised at the sum of $120,000, that the United States wished to employ her in the naval service of the United States, and had deposited the full amount of the appraisement with the United States Marshal for that district (Philadelphia) ; that the steamer had been brought to the port of Philadelphia, *May 3rd*, 1862, and had remained there from that time at heavy charges consequent upon her detention ; that besides the official compensation allowed the Marshal for the custody of said steamer, special expenses had been incurred in the employment of means necessary for the preservation of the engines, boilers, and other parts of the ship, 'and that the expenses incident to said detention which have accrued, and are continually accruing, render the said steamer in a relative sense perishable,' etc.

On the same date (December 19th, 1862) counsel for the owners filed protest against the foregoing in due form.‡ *December 23rd* the Court ordered survey and appraisement. Appraisers reported, *December 30th* :§ 'The said steamship (*Bermuda*) has deteriorated in value since the 12*th day* of *September last* at the rate of $800 *per month*, exclusive of interest . . . caused

* 'Report of Proceedings,' p. 397. † Ibid. p. 458.
‡ Ibid. p. 459. § Ibid. p. 461.

mainly by a want of the care and attention of proper officers and crew;' and they fix the value at $120,000. *March* 5*th*, 1863, the Court decreed as follows:* 'It appearing to the Court that the said steamer was, at the time of capture, the property of enemies of the United States, or otherwise confiscable as prize-of-war, it is ordered, adjudged and decreed that the said steamer, her tackle, apparel and appurtenances be, and the same are, condemned as good and lawful prize.' In a sort of preamble to the foregoing decree, the judge stated that he was not prepared to give judgment in respect to the cargo, and would therefore defer his 'reasons in detail as to the vessel until a decision as to the cargo.' On the same day counsel for the owners gave notice of appeal, and the Attorney for the United States moved for delivery of the ship to the United States;† and it was ordered 'that, on the deposit of the said sum of $120,000 in the registry of the Court, the said steamer be delivered to the Navy Department of the United States.' *March* 6*th*, 1863, counsel for the owners prayed an appeal in due form,‡ which was allowed; but, nevertheless, the ship was delivered to the United States Navy Department. She was quickly armed and equipped as a vessel-of-war, and was cruising off the Southern coast under the flag of her captors before the appeal was heard.

It can hardly be the deliberate purpose of any Government to exercise its belligerent rights with vexatious stringency as regards neutrals; and when vessels are captured or detained on suspicion of an intent to violate a blockade, or of carrying enemies' property, the least forbearance that can be claimed is that the case should

* 'Report of Proceedings,' p. 462. † Ibid. p. 463.
‡ Ibid. p. 463.

be promptly dealt with, and that the property should be carefully protected from injury pending the judicial proceedings. But a very brief summary will demonstrate that, if the United States were severe in the practice of their rights on the high seas, they were none the less rigorous and unyielding in the treatment of those whose commercial interests were involved in the captures made by their cruisers. The *Bermuda* was captured April 27th, 1862, and reached Philadelphia May 3rd, 1862, where she was suffered to remain until August 12th, deteriorating 'at the rate of $800 per month, exclusive of interest, for want of care and attention.' Then, when the hearing of the case was concluded, no judgment was rendered for seven months, the deterioration going on at, or in excess of, the above rate; and finally she was handed over to her captors, upon their application, in spite of the owners' protest, and pending an appeal.

It will be perceived from the statement of this case —and many others of like particulars might be mentioned—that the United States asserted and practised the right to stop any neutral vessel anywhere exceeding three miles from her own coast, to take her to a United States port, and there to determine whether there was circumstantial evidence of a purpose or intent to proceed herself, or to re-ship her cargo, to a blockaded port. Manifestly this pretension was a virtual denial of the doctrine that 'the flag covers the goods,' a principle for which the United States had contended previously to the Civil War, although they had not formally assented to the agreement of the Great Powers at Paris. It was also an assertion of the 'right of search,' a doctrine which the United States had ever before resisted with vehement earnestness, carrying the opposition so far, in

1812, as to face the cost and peril of a war with Great Britain rather than submit to it.

The commonly admitted principle that there could be no such thing as contraband goods in a neutral vessel bound from one neutral port to another was wholly abolished by the United States during the Civil War, although no country had so strongly contended for its maintenance in regard to its own commerce in past times.

These statements are not now made as matters of complaint or reproach against the United States, but they serve to confirm the truth of the old and somewhat homely phrase, 'circumstances alter cases.' They demonstrate the fact that when nations are at war they act upon the principle that the end justifies the means, and although the laws of humanity in reference to the treatment of persons are not often violated in these latter days, yet the 'sacred rights of property' are seldom treated with reverence, and belligerents limit their encroachments upon the privileges of neutrals, not by abstract principles of law and justice, by respect for treaty stipulations, or sentimental regard for international comity, but by considerations of policy and self-interest. They press their rights and use their privileges to the full measure of forbearance on the part of neutral states, or their own power to enforce and maintain them.

The bitter complaints of the United States Minister against Her Majesty's Government for alleged neglect in permitting the Confederate agents to get a few unarmed ships in England, the querulous despatches of Mr. Secretary Seward on the same subject, and the harsh epithets which were freely showered upon the persons concerned in those undertakings, appear almost ludicrous when the acts of those agents are contrasted with what was done by the American commissioners to France during the War of Independence, the equipment of Paul Jones's ships *within* the French dominions, the capture of the *Florida* by the United States ship *Wachusett* in the neutral port of Bahia; the seizure and search of numerous vessels sailing under neutral flags, and passing on their course many miles away from the blockaded coast during the Civil War of 1861-65, and the enlistment of thousands of men in Europe, and their shipment from Liverpool and elsewhere for service in the United States army, under the thin disguise of labourers for American railways, or an ordinary exodus of emigrants. If there was any blockade-running under the French or Spanish flags, the attempts were too few to attract public notice, and I have no record of any official remonstrances from either Paris or Madrid against the interference of the United States with the commerce of those countries.

It will scarcely be pretended that French or Spanish subjects refrained from engaging in the prohibited trade with the South because they thought the traffic wrong in itself, or because of any high notions of duty or favour to the United States as a friendly power. The Confederate Government confined their operations chiefly to the better and cheaper markets in Great Britain, and the purchases made in France were for the most part sent first to England, or to the Havana, Bermuda and Nassau, from whence they were transhipped to a Confederate port. Moreover, maritime adventure of that kind has always been peculiarly attractive to the Anglo-Saxon race, and during the American Civil War many British subjects embarked in the contraband traffic, stimulated alike by the prospect of large profits and the exhilarating effects of the risk and uncertainty. Besides this, all shipments on account of the Confederate Government were made chiefly in English vessels, because it was soon perceived that no vessel under the Confederate flag could load in a British port and hope to escape interference, detention, and perhaps seizure, on suspicion that she was intended for armament as a cruiser.

The United States Government knew that England was the source and fountain of supply for the Confederate States, and that English bottoms were the means of conveyance. They looked with suspicion upon every British ship which ventured to approach the Western World. Their men-of-war policed the waters adjacent to Mexico and the Spanish as well as the English West Indies, and were not particular as to the course a vessel was steering, or the port to which she was bound. A British register, and a British flag, were assumed to be *prima facie* evidence of an 'intent' to run the blockade, and many steamers, and even one sailing vessel, the *Springbok*, were captured when bound from Europe, chiefly from England, to a British Colonial port, or to Cuban and Mexican ports. Many of the vessels employed by the United States in blockading the Southern ports during the war were captured blockade-runners, and it has always seemed strange that no fast steamers were built at the North for that special purpose.

A United States naval officer, who was a long time on blockade service, has told me that few of the original blockaders could steam over eight to nine knots, and it is a fact that very few blockade-runners were caught in an open chase with ample sea-room.

During the Anglo-French War with Russia, commonly called the Crimean War, the Russian Government made a large contract with Colonel Samuel Colt for repeating arms of his patent. The arms were chiefly manufactured at Colonel Colt's works, near Hartford, in the State of Connecticut, and they were shipped together with other goods, contraband of war, in large quantities from the United States in American and other neutral vessels to the Prussian port of Memel, on the Baltic, from which they were forwarded to Russia, probably in great part overland.* The British and French Governments either admitted the legality of this traffic between neutral ports in articles contraband of war, and manifestly intended for their enemy, or else they did not care to involve themselves in controversy with the neutral Powers who were engaged in it.

In the same way the Confederate agents and private commercial parties also shipped goods of all kinds from England to English colonial ports, to Havana and to Matamoras during the Civil War. The general purpose was no doubt to use those ports as *entrepots*, and to tranship the goods not intended for *bonâ fide* delivery by steamers especially designed to run the blockade. The ships actually engaged in running the blockade were liable to capture whenever they approached the blockaded coast or were in proximity to it, and were legitimate prize-of-war when thus caught. But neutral vessels on voyages, say from England to Nassau, Havana, and Matamoras, and steering the direct course for those ports, were surely within their rights, and were or should have been as free from interference by either belligerent as American ships trading to the Baltic at the time of

* Besides the taking of arms to Memel on behalf of Russia, many American ships were chartered by the French Government, and were employed as transports during the Crimean War.

the Crimean War were exempt from interference by the cruisers of France and England.

The United States would have complained most bitterly, and would probably have done something more than remonstrate, if those Powers had so stretched their belligerent rights as to use the Swedish and Danish bays along the shores of the Cattegat as points of observation from which to watch and interrupt American trade with the neutral ports in the Baltic.

It is on record, however, that United States ships kept up a *quasi* blockade of Nassau during the years 1861-65, and that British vessels bound to that port were chased and captured within the Bahama Channels. The British steamer *Margaret Jessie* * was chased off the island of Eleuthera by the United States steamer *Rhode Island*, but escaped, though repeatedly fired at with shot and shell when so close to the shore that some of the shell fell upon the land, cut down trees, and did other damage. In fact, the United States Government attempted to establish coal-depôts at both Bermuda and Nassau, and kept cruisers at or in the near neighbourhood of the latter port, especially to intercept vessels, whether inward bound from Europe or outward bound in the direction of the southern coast.†

To prevent this use of the Bahama Islands, and to prevent also the possible collision of United States and Confederate ships within British waters, her Majesty's Government were induced to issue 'regulations,' in January, 1862, forbidding the vessels of both belligerents alike to enter the port of Nassau except by permission of the Governor or in stress of weather. The United States paid but little heed to the spirit of those regulations. 'There were no less than thirty-four visits of

* '*Margaret Jessie* Debate.' † See 'British Counter-Case,' pp. 63—65.

United States ships-of-war to the Bahama Islands during the time that the regulations were in force.* On four occasions, at least, vessels of the United States exceeded the twenty-four hours' limit, and took in coal by permission ; one of them also received permission to repair. Several were engaged in pursuit of vessels suspected of being blockade-runners, and did not in every instance relinquish the chase within British limits. Two prizes appear, indeed, to have been captured by them, one within a mile of the shore, the other almost in port.'†

'The use made of the waters of the Bahamas by Federal cruisers, for the purpose of watching and intercepting vessels supposed to be freighted with cargoes for Confederate ports, was so persistent as to induce the Governor on one occasion, when granting permission to coal to the commander of the *Dacotah*, to accompany it with the condition that the vessel should not, within the next ten days, be cruising within five miles of any of the Bahama Islands.'

It will be perceived that the United States adopted the most rigorous means to repress the trade in neutral ships between England and the British and Spanish West Indian Islands ; and they did finally almost entirely suppress it by a strict and severe extension of the belligerent rights of visit, search, and capture—an extension previously unknown to International Law.

Before the American Civil War, it had been commonly assumed that a neutral vessel bound to a neutral port was free from capture, and that a prize court would not inquire into the destination of her cargo. The American Courts introduced the principle that if sufficient evidence could be discovered of an intent to tranship the

* See 'British Counter-Case,' Geneva Arbitration, pp. 109—110.

† 'Appendix to British Case,' vol. v., p. 224, for particulars.

cargo for delivery at a port of the belligerent, the cargo itself, and in some cases the ship also, became, as Judge Cadwalader expressed it *in re Bermuda*, 'confiscable.' The United States Government acted upon the above interpretation of international law. During the Civil War many neutral vessels were captured by their cruisers on the high seas, when bound from one neutral port to another, and were condemned upon evidence of an intended breach of blockade which was often very slight, and, from the nature of the cases, purely inferential.

The course pursued by the United States cruisers among the Bahama Islands, to which her Britannic Majesty's Government opposed no effectual prohibition, and the decisions of the United States Prize Courts, to which no formal objection seems to have been offered, destroyed in a great degree the advantage which the proximity of Nassau to the southern coast afforded to the Confederate Government, because the risk of capture extended over the whole voyage from England, and was not limited to the comparatively short run from the Bahama banks to the blockaded ports; and the only benefit left was that of transferring the cargoes to lighter and swifter vessels at Nassau.

The United States Secretary of State, Mr. Seward, often complained of and denounced the use which the Confederates made of Nassau, and the trade which grew up at that port, in language not always suited to the courtesy of diplomatic correspondence or the dignity of State Papers, and the United States cruisers continued to chase and often to capture the neutral ships within the waters of the Bahamas and Spanish West Indies, or when approaching them from Europe. England, the Power chiefly concerned, submitted, or at least made no effectual protest, and it is both interesting and important to investigate the reasons for her seeming indifference.

No one who remembers the promptness and spirit with which Lord Palmerston's Government resented the taking of the Confederate Commissioners from the Royal Mail steamship *Trent* by Captain Wilkes, and the alacrity with which preparations were made to forward troops to Canada, and to prepare a fleet for offensive operations if the said Commissioners were not given up, can suppose that her Majesty's Government were deterred from protecting British ships engaged in trade between England and the West Indian Colonies, or between the several islands on that side of the Atlantic, from lack of spirit to uphold the national honour, or from a conviction that the trade was in itself contrary to either Municipal or International Law. In the 'counter-case' presented on the part of her Britannic Majesty's Government to the Tribunal of Arbitration at Geneva, it is correctly stated that Havana and Cardenas, in the Spanish island of Cuba, were made use of for the same purpose as Nassau, and that Confederate agents were maintained at those ports, and it is then remarked (p. 58): 'In this there was nothing that the British Government was bound or legally empowered to prohibit, nor was any such obligation incumbent on the Government of Spain. Persons trading either with the Southern States or with those which adhered to the Union were free to use Nassau, as they were free to use any other port in the British dominions convenient for their purpose.' Clearly, then, according to the views of her Majesty's Government, the Confederate transactions at Nassau, so far at least as regarded its use for the purpose of an *entrepot*, were unobjectionable both in equity and law.

I would not venture to say that the British Ministry of that day seriously discussed the conduct of the United States Government in Cabinet Council, and determined to submit to the interruption of British trade, and to the violation of the British flag, with the intent to confirm a new interpretation of International Law and to establish precedents against the United States; but there can be no doubt that a broad construction of belligerent maritime rights would be especially and peculiarly favourable to Great Britain and the other Great Maritime Powers of Europe whenever they may be again engaged in war, and the course pursued by the United States towards neutral ships during the years 1861-65 and tacitly acquiesced in by the European Powers, will at some future day involve the former Government in a dilemma.

It is manifest to those who are acquainted with the British steamship trade at this time, and the class of vessels engaged in it, that at very short notice—say two months after a declaration of war—England could have at sea not less than one hundred steamers taken from the merchant service capable of carrying heavy guns, ample supplies of stores and fuel, and with an average speed of thirteen knots, a good many with much higher speed. So large a marine police, in addition to the powerful fleet of the Royal Navy, would render the transfer of contraband goods across the seas impossible, and it can scarcely be doubted that, if England were engaged in war, she would act upon the example of the United States, and would stop the conveyance of such goods to ports adjacent to those of her enemy, even though covered by the American flag. What would the successor of Mr. Secretary Seward say to that? He could not deny or explain away the precedents. Submission to such an interruption of their trade would not be long borne by the people of the United States. The alternative would be war, probably at a time when the country would be unprepared with ships either for active cruising or for a vigorous defence of the coasting trade.

All the European Powers are steadily increasing their naval forces. They are not only building armour-cased ships and torpedo vessels, but others especially designed to cruise into distant seas. France, Germany, and even Austria and Italy, have dockyard accommodation and stores of material which would enable them to add quickly to their present force of cruising ships. Steamers taken from the British or Continental merchant services would be more vulnerable than vessels constructed especially for war, but at the beginning of hostilities they would be greatly superior in speed, power, and in number to the opposing ships the United States could quickly put afloat—strikingly superior to those commissioned by the United States during the Civil War. It is well known that many British commercial steamers built of late years have been constructed with special reference to future conversion into cruisers or torpedo vessels, under arrangements with the Admiralty, and the great building-yards of the Clyde, Mersey, Thames, Tyne, etc., could turn out any description of vessels with great rapidity.

The aggregate of tonnage built in Great Britain during the year 1881 was not less than a million tons, the Clyde alone having completed 269 vessels, representing a tonnage of 340,823 tons. There was one firm on the Tyne—Messrs. Palmer—who turned out no less an output than 50,492 tons of iron shipping in that year. In reference to the advance which has been made in speed, it is only necessary to mention such ships as the *Britannic*, *Germanic*, *Servia*, *City of Rome*, *Arizona*, *Alaska*, all of which have crossed the Atlantic between New York and Queenstown at a speed of not less than 15 knots for every hour they were at sea; and the steamship *Stirling Castle* has actually performed, at sea, with a dead weight of 3,000 tons, 18½ knots in an hour. There would be no insurmountable obstacle in converting the majority of modern steam vessels of the British mercantile marine to war purposes. The chief and most important alterations would be to remove deck-houses, increase pumping power, place additional water-tight compartments, and perhaps protect exposed parts of engines. Such alterations as the foregoing would enable most modern British steamers not only to carry batteries sufficient to defend their own cargoes, but would fit them to cruise against commerce and to make raids upon an enemy's coast. The *Hecla*, a private steamship, was bought by the Admiralty in 1878. She has been armed with five 64-pounders and one 40-pounder gun, and without any structural strengthening has proved a decided success.

The figures in respect to increase of tonnage, performance of steamship *Stirling Castle*, and success of *Hecla* are taken from the address of the President of the 'Institution of Naval Architects,' and from the paper read by Mr. John Dunn 'On Modern Merchant Ships,' at the Session, March 29th, 1882. The logs of the Liverpool and New York packets have been published, and their performances are well known to the travelling public and to all who take an interest in steam shipping.

During the Crimean War, and on other occasions of need, the ability of the private shipbuilders of Great Britain to supplement the efforts of her Majesty's dockyards has been fully and satisfactorily demonstrated, and some of the Continental Powers have in late years largely increased their building capacity. American naval officers, and probably the executive naval authorities also, are conscious of the continuous increase of maritime strength abroad, and contemplate with painful misgivings the apathy that prevails at home. The United States do not appear to have any fixed policy in reference to the national armaments or the efficiency of the naval service. Congress doles out a few millions of dollars from year to year, which barely suffices to keep the public dockyards in repair and a few ships of a bygone type at sea, and allows nothing for steady continuous enlargement of the cruising and fighting fleet proportionate to the increasing extent and growing requirements of the country, or the progress and development of naval efficiency abroad.

There is an admirable naval school at Annapolis ; the course of study and the scientific training of young officers for the United States Navy is very thorough, and embraces a large range of subjects. Some may and do think that both the education and the training are too strictly theoretical, and too purely military, and that too little attention is now paid to practical seamanship. Some critics also say that the cadet midshipmen are kept so long and so exclusively employed at the pure mathematics, in the study of law, and at artillery and infantry drill, that they are too old when sent afloat for regular cruising to acquire the constitutional aptitude for the sea, and the smart active habit of handling ships, which the officers bred, say, thirty years ago possessed.

This impression is strengthened by the appearance and manœuvring of the United States ships I have seen abroad since the war. In the year 1841-42, I was serving on board the United States sailing sloop-of-war *Decatur*, on the Brazil Station. She was a model man-of-war. Some of her performances would almost seem incredible to the officers brought up in these days of steam. We used to furl sails from a bowline in thirty-five seconds, and shift courses, when at sea with all sail set, in nine minutes from the time the first order was given to 'up courses' until the tacks were on board again. Once, while cruising with a squadron of five other ships, off Cape Frio (the late Commodore Charles Morris being in command), the flagship made signal to 'shift main topmasts.' The squadron, all sailing ships, was standing by the wind in two columns with top-gallant sails set, and the spare main-topmasts were lashed in cranes outside and abreast of the main-chains, and in tidy ships like the *Decatur* were covered with canvas laced tightly round the spar and painted black. The *Decatur* had her spare spar aloft and on end, rigging all set up, and the main top-gallant sail set again, in fifty-two minutes from the time the signal was hauled down on board the flagship. The times of performing all evolutions were entered in the log-books, and I took notes of them in my journal.

The foregoing may be considered fancy performances, when everything was ready, or at least in expectation; but the smart, well-trained crew of the *Decatur* were equal to any emergency. On one notable occasion the ship was lying off Buenos Ayres. She was moored for the winter gales with seventy-five fathoms of chain on the port bower, and one hundred and five on the starboard, the latter backed by the stream-anchor. The top-gallant masts, top-gallant and royal rigging were on deck, the topmasts were housed, the topsail-yards were down from aloft, and the lower yards were lashed across the rails. While in this condition, the captain received orders very unexpectedly to proceed without delay to Montevideo, and in two hours and forty-two minutes the ship was standing down the river La Plata, under top-gallant sails, jib, and spanker, with both bower-anchors fished and the stream-anchor in the fore-hatch. I ought to mention that at the time referred to the *Decatur* was commanded by the late Commander Henry W. Ogden, and her first-lieutenant was John H. Marshall, who was unsurpassed in his day as an executive officer. Before the end of the cruise, Commander Ogden was invalided, and was relieved in the command by the late Admiral David G. Farragut, who did not permit the *Decatur* to fall off in smartness; indeed, while the latter officer was in command, he once, as an experiment, put the ship through the evolution of reefing topsails in stays, a manœuvre immortalized in nautical song and naval poetry, but which I never saw performed except on that single occasion.

Such performances would not be possible with the heavy ironclads of the present day, and as all men-of-war appear now to enter and leave port under steam, and use canvas only with leading winds, or when they can make nearly the desired course, officers and men have but little practice in manœuvring under sail, and it is not surprising that smart handy seamanship should have declined since the universal application of steam-power to men-of-war. This lack of smartness is apparent in the ships of all the Maritime Powers. I stood at the George's Pierhead in Liverpool, and saw her Majesty's ship *Defence* man yards on the occasion of the visit of his Royal Highness the Prince of Wales to open the New North Docks in 1881, and such first-lieutenants as used to handle the British frigates and corvettes in olden times would have nearly gone out of their minds to see the slow cautious way in which the men laid out on the yards, and the prudent deliberation with which they clung to the ratlins when laying down from aloft.

Officers of the American navy are now probably, as a class, more carefully and thoroughly educated than those of any other national marine, at least in the theory of their profession, but there is great scarcity of native seamen, and it is not too much to say that there is not now a single ship on the United States Navy List which would be classed at all among the effective naval forces of any European Power, and the United States could not send a squadron to sea upon a sudden emergency equal in the character of the ships to the fleet which even the little Republic of Chili had in commission during the late war with Peru.

In fact, the United States appear to have voluntarily abandoned their claim to be included among the naval, or even the maritime, Powers. The military marine has been suffered to fall below that of almost every other country; and such is the lack of mercantile ships, that the great staples produced in such prolific abundance in the vast territory of the Union would never reach a foreign market if dependent upon American vessels alone for transportation. England has, in fact, appropriated almost the entire carrying trade of the United States; and the splendid steamships which issue from English ports, and the wealth of British steamship companies, furnish a measure of Britain's profit and America's loss from the apathy of the United States Government in respect to its maritime interests.

If this indifference to naval equality with other

countries was the result of a well-considered policy of economy, or arose from confidence in the ability to make good the deficiency by a great effort in case of need, it would be intelligible, although of doubtful wisdom; but ships fit to meet the requirements of modern warfare cannot be built hurriedly, and hasty preparation always involves waste of material and extravagant expenditure.

The United States Government, through a combative but indiscreet Secretary of State, has quite lately re-announced its purpose to insist upon the application of the 'Monroe doctrine,' with special reference to the Panama Canal and the Chileno-Peruvian embroglio. To make remonstrances effective, either at the Isthmus of Darien or on the coast of Chili, would require the presence of a strong fleet of ships fully up to the modern type; and the United States have none of that kind. Governments who persistently keep their naval and military forces at a low point of strength and efficiency should also practise a modest and inoffensive diplomacy, because otherwise their declarations will either be treated with indifference, or they are liable at any time to receive a rebuff which would wound the national pride and bring upon the responsible Ministry the indignant reproaches of the people.

The 'Monroe doctrine' as lately enunciated would surprise its author, who probably never dreamed of so broad an application of its meaning. But if the United States seriously purpose to undertake the sole guarantee of the highway between the two great oceans, and aspire to be the only arbiters in matters affecting the interests of the numerous American States, it is indispensable that they be able to place a powerful fleet at the required spot and at the critical moment.

England's right of way through the Suez Canal would not be worth the value of her shares in the capital stock of the company, if it was not thought that she could hold the two ends of the canal against all comers. A British Minister will probably never issue a circular manifesto to inform Europe that no one must attempt to block the way, but the Admiralty continue to lay down and to launch such vessels as the *Northampton*, *Thunderer*, *Polyphemus*, *Dreadnought*, *Edinburgh*, *Ajax*, *Colossus*, *Majestic*, etc., and everyone understands that to interfere would involve the absolute consequence of a hard struggle, to say the least.

In these times of great armaments, nations who wish to advance their influence, maintain their prestige or even to take part in international discussions with the expectation of being listened to with respect, must demonstrate that they are prepared for attack as well as for defence, that they can strike as well as parry. Those who are content to make peaceful progress in wealth and domestic comfort, may possibly be left to enjoy their freedom and their gains ; but then they must not attempt the *rôle* of dictators, nor challenge attack by a pretence of aggressive strength which they take no pains to develop, and which all the world knows they do not possess.

Note to Page 62.

After the departure of the *Alabama* from Liverpool and her equipment as a Confederate vessel-of-war was publicly known, it was often stated that the Messrs. Laird had been guilty of a violation of law in building her. In consequence of such reports, those gentlemen published a letter in the *Times*, dated 25th of May, 1869, which contained copies of the following documents and opinions of counsel:

"I am of opinion that Messrs. Laird had a right to build the ship which has since been called the *Alabama* in the manner they did, and that they committed no offence against either the common law or the Foreign Enlistment Act, with reference to that ship. I am of opinion that the simple building of a ship, even although the ship be of a kind apparently adapted for warlike purposes, and delivering such ship to a purchaser in an English port, even although the purchaser is suspected or known to be the agent of a foreign belligerent Power, does not constitute an offence against the Foreign Enlistment Act (59 Geo. III., c. 60, s. 7) on the part of the builder, unless the builder makes himself a party to the equipping of the vessel for warlike purposes. The *Alabama*, indeed, appears to me to have been equipped at the Azores, and not in England at all.

'GEORGE MELLISH.

'3, Harcourt Buildings, 6th February, 1863.

'We entirely concur in the opinion given by Mr. Mellish on the statements laid before him, and our opinion would not be altered if the fact were that Messrs. Laird Brothers knew they were building the *Alabama* for an agent of the Confederate Government.

'(Signed) H. M. CAIRNS.
'JAMES KEMPLAY.

'17th April, 1863.'

Opinion of Lord Chief Baron Pollock on the trial of the *Alexandra*, June, 1863:

'Many allusions in the course of this case had been made to the *Alabama;* but he held that as that vessel left Liverpool unarmed, and as a simple ship, she committed no unlawful act; and we had nothing to do with the fact that at a subsequent period she was armed and converted into a vessel-of-war at Terceira.'

Letter from Lord Clarendon to Mr. Adams, 2nd December, 1865, quoted by Earl Russell in his speech, 27th March, 1868:

'It is nevertheless my duty, in closing this correspondence, to observe that no armed vessel departed during the war from a British port to cruise against the commerce of the United States.'

Sir Roundel Palmer, Solicitor General, speech in the House of Commons, 27th March, 1863:

'It was not till the *Alabama* reached the Azores that she received her stores, her captain, or her papers, and that she hoisted the Confederate flag. It is not true that she departed from the shores of this country as a ship-of-war.'

It will be perceived from the foregoing that Messrs. Laird were well supported in the view that they were acting in strict conformity with law when they built the ship afterwards called the *Alabama*, but this whole subject is dealt with in another chapter.

Mr. George Mellish, Sir Hugh Cairns, and Mr. James Kemplay, are well known to have been leaders of great eminence at the English Bar, and Sir Hugh Cairns (now Earl Cairns) has since been Lord Chancellor of England.

CHAPTER III.

Financial embarrassments of the Confederate Agents.—Incomplete organization of the Confederate Executive at this period.—The financial arrangements of the Confederate States in Europe.—Incompleteness of the instructions of the Naval Representative, and insufficiency of the arrangements to meet financial requirements.—Purchase and equipment of the *Fingal*, afterwards the *Atlanta.*—Shipment of war material.—Mr. Low, second officer of the *Fingal.*—An unfortunate start.—The island of Terceira.—The crew agree to run the blockade.—Arrival in the Savannah river. The state of the Southern forces.—Correspondence concerning the future operations of the *Fingal.*—Enlargement of powers as Naval Representative in Europe.—Flag-officer Josiah Tattnall.—Conversion of the *Fingal* into the armour-clad *Atlanta.*—Her engagement with and capture by two United States 'Monitors.'—Return to England.

THE narrative of the *Bermuda's* * second voyage, the account of her capture and condemnation by the Prize Court at Philadelphia, and the remarks upon the general policy of the United States in the practice of their maritime rights as a belligerent, which occupy much of the last chapter, have somewhat anticipated the precise order of events. But the naval operations of the Confederate States in Europe were full of complications,

* Captain Tessier, who commanded the *Bermuda* on the occasion of her successful voyage to Savannah in 1861, was not in her at the time of her capture, or the result would probably have been less disastrous.

and gave rise to many questions affecting international duties, as well as international comity, and it will save both time and space, and will, I think, be more impressive, and also more systematic and instructive, to treat such questions, as a general rule, subjectively, and to explain and discuss them when they appear to have a natural connection with a special event in the narrative, than to postpone them for more formal and exclusive treatment in separate chapters.

The *Bermuda* made her first and only voyage to a Confederate port in August—September, 1861, and she took to Savannah the first shipment of war material from Europe on behalf of the Confederate Government. I reported to the Secretary of the Navy by that vessel the particulars of the *Alabama* and *Florida*, advised him of the contracts which had been made for general naval supplies, called attention to the financial difficulties, and informed him that it would probably be necessary to buy a steamer and return to the Confederate States in her myself, with military stores, as well as for further consultation and reconsideration of my instructions. There were at that early date numerous agents of the United States in England, who seemed in no way desirous to conceal their operations. They went about their business with the air of men who were sure of their position, and who neither anticipated nor feared interference or opposition. They were well provided with money, or satisfactory bank-credits, and they rapidly swept the gun market of well-nigh every weapon, whether good or bad. The Confederate agents were forced from want of means to be content with moderate purchases; but they made large contracts for forward delivery, at first on the credit of Messrs. Fraser, Trenholm and Co., and then, when remittances began to arrive, upon the confidence they had already won by prompt payment, and the assurance they were able to give that the Government had made suitable arrangements to meet all liabilities, and to place their bankers in funds. There was always, however, much perplexity and embarrassment from lack of ready money. At one time, in September, 1863, I was forced to report to the Navy Department that the outstanding contracts would require £700,000 in excess of the amount held at that date by the financial agents, and the War Department was rarely, if ever, able to keep pace with its requirements. The compulsory sale of ships that could not be got to sea because of the prohibition of her Majesty's Government more than once supplied the means of continuing purchases and shipments of war material which otherwise could not have been bought.

The home authorities pressed us to hurry forward supplies, and I was urged to place and to keep cruisers at sea, but they appreciated the difficulties, and in looking over the correspondence now, I can find no unreasonable complaints, and no insinuations even, that more could have been effected than was being done.

It has been said that the first remittance from the Navy Department was received July 27, 1861. The funds were forwarded in the form of sterling bills and bank-credits, but the aggregate amount was not sufficient to cover the orders for naval stores already placed, and the price of the two ships (*Alabama* and *Florida*), and no additional funds were received, nor any advices on the subject, until October, hence no further contracts could be made at that time. Meanwhile the work upon the ships was progressing rapidly. It was estimated that the *Florida* would be finished in February—March and the *Alabama* in June, 1862, and such arrangements had been made with the builders that my personal supervision was not necessary, and, moreover, frequent personal attendance at the building yards was not prudent.

The Consular agents of the United States had already begun to practise an inquisitive system of espionage, and it was soon manifest that the movements of those who were supposed to be agents of the Confederate Government were closely and vigilantly watched. Men known to be private detectives in the employ of the United States Consul were often seen prowling about the dockyards, and questioning the *employés* of Messrs. Laird and Miller in reference to the two vessels, whose somewhat peculiar type had attracted notice, and at a very early date it became manifest that her Majesty's Government would take a rigid view of the Foreign Enlistment Act, and that there would be very great difficulty and expense in getting ships to sea especially adapted in their construction and general outfit for purposes of war. The financial question was, however, the greatest cause of perplexity at that time. The rapidly advancing rate of exchange clearly indicated that the Confederate Government would soon be compelled to resort to some other mode of placing funds in Europe than by sterling bills. There was also much delay in communicating by letter, and the danger of miscarriage or capture made it hazardous to write fully and clearly upon subjects it was vitally important to explain and discuss without reserve.

Very soon after the beginning of hostilities the policy of buying up the whole of the cotton at the South, on account of the Government, and forwarding it as quickly as possible to Europe, was suggested to the executive authorities, and was no doubt earnestly considered by them. If 200,000 bales of cotton could have been shipped to Liverpool during the first year of the war, the financial position of the Confederate States would no doubt have been infinitely strengthened, and the first levies might have been put into the field in such a state of efficiency, as regards clothing and equipment, as to have greatly affected the results of the struggle. There have been many persons in the South who have severely criticized the Confederate Government for not adopting the above policy at the beginning; but those who were early employed in important offices connected with the supply of the military and naval wants of the country, and whose faculties were keenly aroused and directed to the consideration of the ways and means, are conscious that there were great, if not insurmountable obstacles to the fulfilment of that policy when it was first suggested. During the greater part of the time which intervened from the secession of South Carolina to the beginning of hostilities, not quite five months, there was no general Executive Government at all. The several States withdrew from the Union at different periods. Each in turn was fully occupied with her own internal affairs, and none were at all sure which, if any, of the neighbouring States would secede, or whether after seceding they would be willing to unite in a joint Confederacy for a common purpose. The Provisional Government was not formed at Montgomery until February, 1861.

On the 13th of April, barely two months after, when the Executive Departments were still in the very throes of organization, with the whole machinery of Government new and untried, without a single shipyard or military arsenal in working order, and with no military forces except the State volunteer corps, and those not yet regularly enrolled into the general service, hostilities were precipitated by the events at Charleston.

While affairs were thus coming to a crisis, the ships lying in the cotton ports took in full cargoes and sailed; but they were of course loaded on private account, and when they left, few, if any, came in their places. The mercantile world, more astute than the politicians, foresaw the coming storm, and did not care to expose their ships to its fury; hence the vessels that came to Southern ports immediately before the attack upon Fort Sumter made haste to load and get away.

The authorities at Montgomery did not prevent their departure, and the United States granted some respite before closing the ports by a declaration of blockade. There were several lines of steamers plying between Boston, New York, Philadelphia, and Southern ports, both on the Atlantic coast and the Gulf of Mexico; but their movements were so arranged that at the critical moment they were almost to a ship either at the Northern ports or *en route* for them, and at the time when actual hostilities began, there was scarcely an available ship of any description in Southern waters. It has already been mentioned that the steamship *Bienville* was permitted to leave New Orleans on the day after the attack upon Fort Sumter, and I know of only three regular sea-going steamships which were still at Southern ports a month after that event. One of the number was bought by the Confederate Government, and was commissioned by the late Admiral Semmes as the *Sumter*; a second, the *Nashville*, was also bought by the Government, and made a short cruise to England *viâ* Bermuda, and back to a Confederate port, under the command of Captain R. B. Pegram, and the third was bought by Messrs. John Fraser and Co., of Charleston, and sailed from Wilmington, North Carolina, for Liverpool, with a cargo of cotton, rosin, etc., on their account. There were two or three paddle-steamers at Richmond, suited to the coasting trade, but not for foreign voyages, and they were taken up by the Navy Department.

I do not state positively that the above were the only steamers remaining in Southern ports at the time mentioned, but I think that if there had been any others suitable for deep-sea voyages, the fact would not be forgotten by me now, and I feel sure that they would have been promptly and eagerly appropriated by the Confederate Navy Department. Whether, therefore, the Provisional Government at Montgomery approved of the proposition to buy and ship the cotton still remaining at the plantations and other interior points or not, there can be no doubt that the means for shipping it in large quantities were wholly wanting. Private persons and several mercantile firms made many ventures to the Bahamas and Havana during the first six months of the war with no better craft than the ordinary river steamer, but undertakings quite in keeping with mercantile usage, and justified by the ordinary commercial considerations of profit and loss, are inadmissible—indeed, they are impracticable—as State enterprises, for the sufficient reason that the public Departments are enveloped in legal as well as traditional routine. National funds can only be applied in accordance with legislative appropriation, and therefore schemes which may be put in course of effectual progress at the moment of suggestion by a private firm or corporation, can only be executed by the State after due consideration by two or more branches of the Government, which necessarily involves delay, and often such modifications of the original project as to lessen the chances of success, or at least to increase the difficulties to be overcome. Many persons will remember how quickly, and on what a stupendous scale, the

Government at Washington hastened to prepare for the invasion of the Confederate States when the surrender of Fort Sumter ended the period of suspense and the state of war began.

The so-called Democratic Party at the North had been generally favourable to the Southern view of 'State rights,' and was strongly opposed to that party which, by a division among its opponents, had succeeded in electing Mr. Abraham Lincoln to the Presidency. There had been also a strong minority of the dominant or Republican Party, who, while reprobating the action of the South, and denouncing the principle of secession as revolutionary and unauthorized, were yet opposed to the exercise of any coercive measures for the maintenance of the Union.

The Cabinet at Washington, the party leaders and the party press, combined to arouse and direct public sentiment, and to bring the people of the North to the conviction that the right of secession, if once admitted, would logically and inevitably tend to complete dissolution. They addressed themselves to the fears, the prejudices, and the patriotism of the North, and with such success that, when President Lincoln issued his proclamation calling for troops to 'avenge the insult to the national flag at Charleston,' and to 'restore the Union' (to use the phraseology of the period), there was a prompt and ample response. Party distinctions and party principles ceased to restrain men from joining together for the common purpose of restoring and maintaining the Union, and large masses of troops were soon gathering around Washington, along the Potomac and the northern frontier of Virginia. To prepare for the threatened attack, and to provide the means for an adequate resistance, must have strained the resources and taxed the administrative faculties of the Provisional Government of the Confederate States to the fullest tension.

Those who wish to form just and impartial opinions of public men, and who aspire to write the history of great public events, must first look for the facts ; then they must give a fair, judicial consideration to all the circumstances. They must be careful not to infer that a course of action which commends itself when viewed in the light of accomplished events was practicable ; or, if practicable when first suggested, whether something else of more pressing and essential importance did not necessarily demand precedence. The people of the South will probably admit that it was of more vital consequence to keep the Federal armies out of Richmond in 1861 than to effect even the important purpose of transferring the cotton crop to Europe. An equitable investigation of the facts, and due consideration of all the circumstances, the insufficient means of transport by land, and the still greater lack of means of transport by sea—will demonstrate that both enterprises could not have been accomplished at the same time, and the project of perfecting the financial arrangements abroad was unavoidably delayed. At a later period of the war the Government made great efforts to forward cotton and other products of the south to Europe. The Confederate Congress passed an Act authorizing the Treasury Department to buy and ship whatever staples were readily convertible into money in the European markets, and agents were sent into the interior, and were stationed at the seaports to carry out that purpose. A special agent of the Treasury was sent to Europe, with power to make contracts with banking or commercial houses to supply the money necessary to build steamers suitable for blockade running ; and he brought over orders from the Navy Department directing me to look after the designing and construction of the ships, and to see that they were properly fitted for the proposed work. The Treasury agent was Mr. Colin J. McRae, and he made capital contracts with two or more firms, who agreed to advance the money for a commission of ten per cent., and to be recouped from the proceeds of the cotton or other products brought out by the ships themselves. The precise arrangement was that the ships were to be employed in running the blockade, the inward cargoes to be exclusively on Government account, and the outward cargoes half for the Government, and half to go towards payment of the ships, until the whole amount advanced, together with the stipulated commission, was cleared off. Until paid for in full, each steamer was to be registered in the name of a nominee of the firm who had advanced the money, and then she was to become the property of the Confederate Government. Time being of incalculable importance, four paddle-steamers, the best that could be found, were bought to begin with; and ten were laid down, carefully designed to get high speed on a light draft of water. Afterwards several larger and powerful screw-steamers were designed, but these latter were not finished in time to perform any service. One of the smaller class of paddle-steamers brought out on her first voyage 700 bales of unpressed cotton, on a draft of six feet, which was a very satisfactory performance, with cotton at two shillings and sixpence per pound.

Those who have most sharply criticized the Executive Departments of the Confederate Government, and have especially charged them with want of foresight and promptness in the management of the finances, are chiefly Southerners, who must have been impelled by their impatience to expect striking results without taking due heed of the pressure upon the several Departments, and the extreme efforts they were so suddenly called upon to make. Although the Confederate Government was never recognised by any foreign Power, yet when the Treasury Department made a bid in Europe for a loan of £3,000,000, five times that amount was subscribed. There was for a short time what is called a 'spurt' in Confederate Bonds, and they actually rose to a premium of five per cent. upon the price at which the loan was placed, and they stood for several months at a higher figure than the bonds of the United States. This is an interesting fact, although it is of no financial importance now; at any rate, it may be fairly taken as an offset to the allegations of the grumblers. Reverting now to the actual state of the finances at the beginning of the operations in Europe, it is proper to remark, *en passant*, that before I was sent from Montgomery the difficulties were foreseen in kind, but not in degree, and it soon became evident that the full purposes contemplated in my original instructions could not be accomplished without a modification of plans and a well-arranged system for providing funds with certainty and regularity. After considering all the circumstances as they were at the time when the first remittance arrived (July, 1861), and taking also into account the fact that personal supervision of the ships under construction was neither necessary nor advisable, it was thought that I should communicate personally with the Government at Richmond, and in September, 1861, I submitted a proposal to the officers representing the War Office, that we should contribute equally from the funds of the two Departments, buy a fast steamer, and that I should go into a Confederate port with her myself, in order to report the precise condition of affairs, as well as to take in the war supplies which were then ready for delivery, and which we knew were greatly needed. We had a consultation with the financial agents, and the proposal was not only approved, but I was urged to carry it out at once. Going upon such an expedition was a deviation from my instructions, and it was also a diversion of a considerable sum of money from the original purpose to which it had been appropriated; but the position of affairs was critical, and I had been authorized to exercise a wide discretion when it appeared necessary to effect an important purpose. However, before taking any decisive course, the proposition was referred to the Commissioners, who expressed their full concurrence, and one of them, the Hon. Dudley Mann, wrote me spontaneously an official letter, virtually offering to assume the responsibility, so far as he could. I immediately bought the screw-steamship *Fingal*, built on the Clyde for the Highland trade. She was a new ship, had made but one or two trips to the North of Scotland, was in good order, well found, and her log gave her speed as thirteen knots in good steaming weather. I had to take her as she stood, with all outfit on board, and was amused to find, in the inventory of cabin-stores, six dozen toddy glasses, with ladles to match. Each glass had the capacity of about a half-pint, and they were hard and thick and heavy enough to serve for grape-shot, in case of need. The ship was placed on a loading-berth at Greenock, and the goods were forwarded to her as rapidly as possible, partly by rail, and partly by a steamer from London. It was necessary to act with caution and secrecy, because the impression had already got abroad that the Confederate Government was trying to fit out ships in England to cruise against American commerce, and during the whole period of the war all vessels taking arms on board, or cases supposed to contain arms or ammunition, were closely watched by agents and spies of the United States Consuls, who frequently sent affidavits to the Customs authorities, affirming the belief that the ships receiving such materials were intended to be armed, and thus often effected their detention, and on several occasions their seizure.

Colonel Edward C. Anderson, of the Confederate army, had been sent to England in July, 1861, to communicate with Major Huse, and to look generally into the affairs of the War Department. Colonel Anderson was directed to remain in Europe if his services seemed to be necessary; but he found that Major Huse had everything in good working train, and was manifestly capable of conducting the operations alone, so he determined to return to the Confederate States, and the *Fingal* expedition afforded a favourable opportunity. Two Charleston gentlemen (Messrs. Charles Foster and Moffat), detained in Europe at the beginning of the war, and unable to return through the United States, had consulted me about the best means of getting to their homes, and I arranged to take them in the *Fingal;* and Dr. Holland, a spirited Texan, who had served in the United States army during the Mexican War, and wished to go to Richmond, was notified to be ready for a move at short notice, and was requested to prepare a big medicine-chest and a case of surgical instruments to take with him. As the *Fingal* was the first ship that ran the blockade solely on Government account, and her subsequent fate as the Confederate ironclad *Atlanta* gives her some historical importance, the particulars of her cargo, and the incidents of her voyage, will probably be of some interest. In 1861 the English army weapon was still the muzzle-loading Enfield rifle. Prussia was adopting the needle-gun, and France was preparing to exchange her old arm for the *chassepot*, but no breech-loaders could be got either in England or on the Continent, except as samples, and the purchases for the Confederate States were of the muzzle-loading type.

The shipment *per Fingal* was:

On account of the War Department—10,000 Enfield rifles, 1,000,000 ball cartridges, and 2,000,000 percussion caps; 3,000 cavalry sabres, with suitable accoutrements, a large quantity of material for clothing, and a large supply of medical stores.

On account of the Navy Department—1,000 short rifles, with cutlass bayonets, and 1,000 rounds of ammunition per rifle; 500 revolvers, with suitable ammunition; two 4½-inch muzzle-loading rifled guns, with traversing carriages, all necessary gear, and 200 made-up cartridges, shot and shell, per gun; two breech-loading 2½-inch steel-rifled guns for boats or field service, with 200 rounds of ammunition per gun; 400 barrels of coarse cannon-powder, and a large quantity of made-up clothing for seamen.

For the State of Georgia—3,000 Enfield rifles.

For the State of Lousiana—1,000 Enfield rifles.

No single ship ever took into the Confederacy a cargo so entirely composed of military and naval supplies, and the pressing need of them made it necessary to get the *Fingal* off with quick despatch, and to use every possible effort to get her into a port having railway communication through to Virginia, because the Confederate army, then covering Richmond, was very poorly armed, and was distressingly deficient in all field necessaries.

Shortly before the *Fingal* was ready for sea, I was

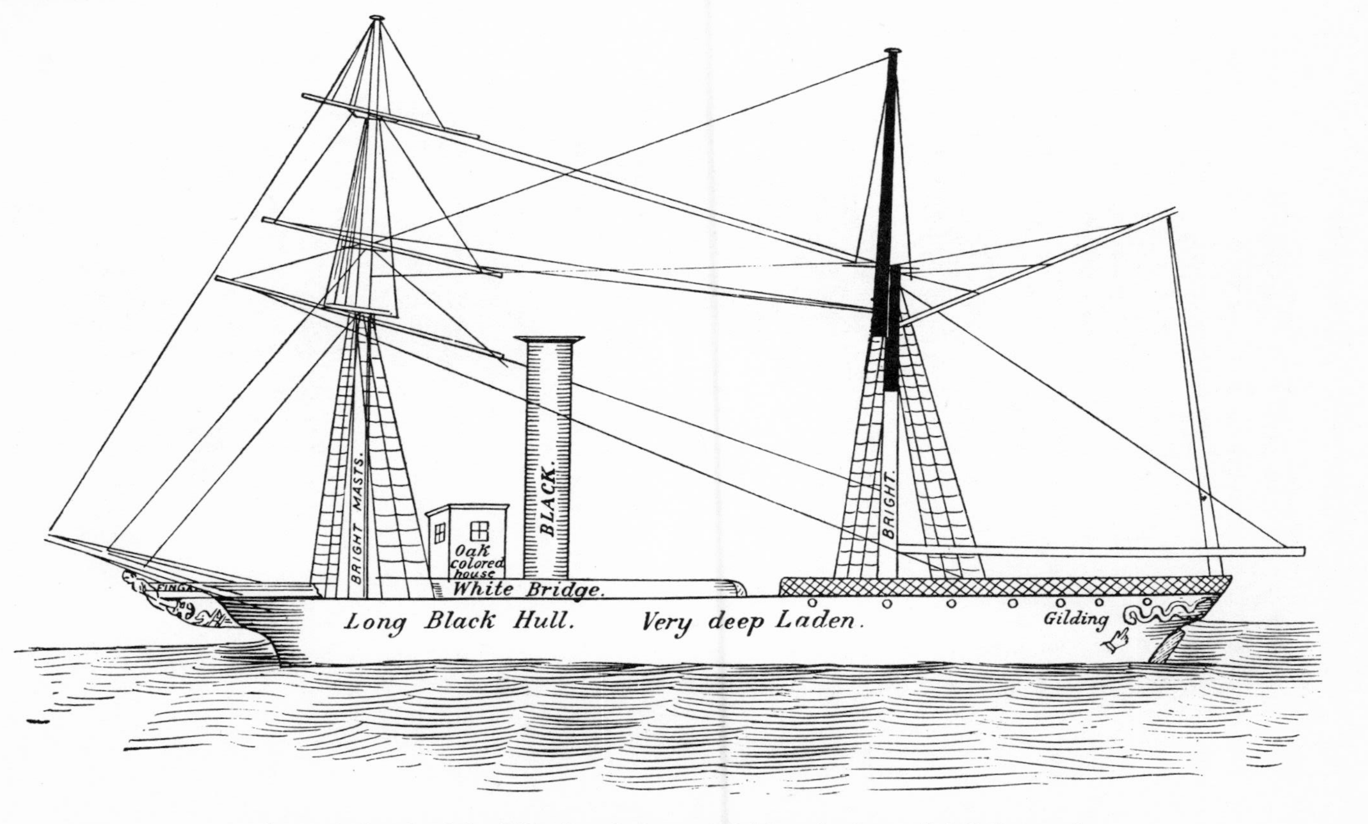

A rough sketch of the *Fingal* made by one of Adams' spies as it left Greenock.
(Official Records of the Union and Confederate Navies)

Capture of the Confederate ironclad *Atlanta* by the Monitor *Weehawken. (Harper's Weekly)*

joined by Mr. John Low, who was a Liverpool man by birth, but he had lived several years in Savannah, and was there at the beginning of the war. His purpose at that time was to remain permanently in Savannah; he was ardently attached to the South, and at the beginning of hostilities he went to Virginia in a cavalry corps from Georgia, but subsequently came over to England to join me for special service. Mr. Low had been bred to the sea in the British mercantile marine, and as he arrived at a very opportune time, I sent him instanter to Greenock to ship as second officer of the *Fingal*.

The *Fingal* was kept under the British flag for obvious reasons, and it was therefore necessary to employ a captain holding a Board of Trade certificate to clear her outward, and to ship the crew in accordance with the Merchant Shipping Act. Some pains were taken to engage good engineers and a few leading men, but no hint was given that the ship would go further than Bermuda and Nassau. Mr. Low proved to be an able seaman, a reliable and useful officer in every situation. The character of his services, and his advancement in the Confederate navy, will often have conspicuous and commendatory mention in this narrative. The *Fingal* was ready for sea about October 8th. Messrs. Foster and Moffat joined her at Greenock, and the captain was ordered to sail as soon as possible, and to call off Holyhead to take Colonel Anderson, Dr. Holland, and myself on board, it not being thought prudent to show ourselves at or about the ship until she was clear of the Custom House.

On the 11th we went to Holyhead, and learned by telegram that the *Fingal* was off from Greenock.

During the night it came on to blow a hard gale, which continued for two or three days, with thick weather and much rain. We could get no tidings of the ship, and although I felt reasonably satisfied that she had put into some harbour of shelter, yet the uncertainty and delay were perplexing. During the 14th the gale broke. Towards evening the weather was fine, and we had hopes of seeing or hearing from the missing ship on the next day. At about 4 a.m. on the 15th, I was aroused by a loud knock at my bedroom door, and a house-porter came in with a dark lantern, followed by Mr. Low. It had been raining, and Low had on a 'sou-wester,' and a long painted canvas coat, which were dripping with wet. I was only half awake. In the dim light of the lantern the figure before me loomed up like a huge octopus, or some other marine monster, and I was startled by a sepulchral voice which seemed to be mumbling under the breast of the peajacket like the last tremulous quivering of a thunderclap. But my ear caught the sound of a few articulate words, among which '*Fingal*,' 'brig,' 'collision,' 'sunk,' were fearfully jumbled together. It is astounding with what electric velocity the mind acts in the few seconds of awaking when one is suddenly aroused from sleep. Before I could leap out of bed a painful scene of wreck and disaster passed vividly through my brain, and I fancied the *Fingal* at the bottom of Holyhead harbour, with the fishes swimming among the shattered Enfields, sipping the mixture of sea-water and gunpowder through their gills, and wondering what it all meant. Low was, however, steady, cool, and unimpassioned, and put the facts into my mind without waste of words, and they may be briefly summarized thus: The *Fingal* was creeping cautiously round the breakwater when she suddenly came upon a brig at anchor, with no light up. The steamer had barely steerage way, and the engines were quickly reversed, but her sharp stem took the brig's starboard quarter. There was just a slight sound, like the quick snap of a gun-hammer upon the uncapped nipple, then a shout from the deck of the unhappy craft, and before a boat could be lowered she went down all standing. This is what usually happens when an iron steamer comes in contact with a wooden ship.

We roused up Colonel Anderson and Dr. Holland and got afloat as soon as possible.

Day was just breaking when we got alongside of the *Fingal*, and in the dim twilight we could see the upper spars of the brig standing straight up out of the water, with the bunt of the main top-gallant sail just a-wash. The vessel proved to be the Austrian brig *Siccardi*. She was loaded with coal, which accounts for her going down so quickly and standing upright afterwards.

It was manifestly out of the question to remain where we were. Customs officers would soon be on board; the *Fingal* would be detained to settle, or give security for a satisfactory settlement, with the consignees of the *Siccardi;* Colonel Anderson and I could hardly hope to escape notice; affidavits would be prepared by the United States Consul affirming the *Fingal* to be a suspicious vessel, and then there would surely be inquiry, further detention, and perhaps a final break up of the voyage. I thought of the rifles and sabres in the hold, and the ill-armed pickets on the Potomac, waiting and longing for them, and told the captain to weigh anchor at once.

There was no wish to defraud the owners of the *Siccardi* of any compensation they were entitled to. I wrote a hasty letter to Messrs. Fraser, Trenholm and Co., briefly reporting the circumstances and asking them to find out the consignees of the brig and make the best possible arrangement with them.* The letter was de-

* Messrs. Fraser, Trenholm and Co. communicated with the consignees very promptly. A friendly arbitration was agreed to, and the affair was satisfactorily settled.

spatched on shore by a boat we had engaged to bring our luggage off, and the *Fingal* was round the point of the breakwater, and steaming down Channel, before the accident at the mouth of the harbour was known to anyone who would have had authority to stop her.

For several days after leaving Holyhead we had fine weather, and were well satisfied in most respects with the ship. She was staunch, comfortable, and well-fitted in all particulars, but in the anxiety to get as much in her as possible, she had been loaded too deep, and I found that we could not get a higher speed than nine knots, which was rather disappointing, in view of a possible chase between Bermuda and the coast. About the 19th of October we caught a gale from the south-west veering to north and north-east. The sea was so heavy that we were compelled to ease the engines, and in a measure lay-to under fore and aft sails. While the gale was still blowing, the steward informed me that the fresh water seemed to be very low in the big iron tank which held the main supply. Upon examination it was found that we had only one or at most two days' supply left. It seems that after filling up the water-tank at Greenock, the ship continued to load for some days, and the crew, as well as a large number of stevedores employed in stowing the cargo, were permitted to use and to waste the water at will. When ready for sea, it did not occur to the captain to sound the tanks and fill them up. I do not wish to injure the captain by mentioning his name. He probably acted according to his lights, which were dull. He was very inefficient, and was of no use to us except as a medium of communication with Customs and other officials. The *Fingal* had no separate condensing apparatus, but fortunately the gale was moderating, and the wind was hauling to the north and east, and so we bore up for Praya, a bay and village on the north-east side of the island of Terceira, where we found good water, fruit, vegetables, fresh meat, etc.

This necessary deviation from our direct voyage, and the consequent delay, were not in the end without a compensating advantage. The bay afforded good anchorage, and the whole neighbourhood was so quiet and retired, so isolated from Europe, that I could not fail to note its fitness for a place of rendezvous at which to collect our cruisers with their tenders. Subsequently the *Alabama* was brought to this very spot and armed without hindrance. Perhaps if it had not been for the captain's forgetfulness in the matter of the *Fingal's* water supply, we might have gone to some less favourable place with the *Alabama* and failed in our purpose. The efforts of life in all undertakings are made up of alternate failure and success, and all that can be hoped for is a favourable balance-sheet at the end.

The *Fingal* proceeded on her voyage from Terceira, and arrived at Bermuda on the 2nd of November. Here we had the pleasure to find the Confederate States ship *Nashville*, Captain R. B. Pegram, from whom we learned much about the state of affairs in the beleaguered Confederacy. The *Nashville* was a paddle-steamer, built for the coasting trade between New York and Charleston. It has been already mentioned that she was bought by the Navy Department, and her appearance abroad was probably intended as a mere demonstration to prove the inefficiency of the blockade, and to make an exhibit of the Confederate flag upon the high seas and in Europe, because she was weakly armed and dependent upon her engines alone for motion. Nevertheless, she captured and burned the American ship *Harvey Birch* in the English Channel. There had been an original purpose to send the Confederate Commissioners, Messrs. Mason and Slidell, to Europe in the *Nashville*, but this intention was abandoned, and those gentlemen, with their suites, ran the blockade in a small steamer from Charleston, and proceeded to Havana. Captain Pegram handed me a despatch from the Hon. S. R. Mallory, Secretary of the Navy, acknowledging my reports sent *per* steamship *Bermuda* in August. He approved my contracts for the *Florida* and *Alabama*, and for naval ordnance stores, and also the proposition I had suggested of buying a steamer and returning in her to the Confederate States with supplies and for consultation. He furthermore informed me that he had sent out by the *Nashville* several pilots, and that Captain Pegram would let me have any one or more of them I might require. Mr. John Makin, a pilot for Savannah and the inlets to the southward, was transferred to the *Fingal*.

We were detained several days at Bermuda. The United States Consul suspected the ultimate object of the *Fingal's* voyage, and he did his best to put obstacles in the way of our getting coal and other supplies, and employed men to tamper with the crew and alarm them, and persuade them to leave the ship. However, the local merchants and the people generally were very friendly, and we got at last all that was wanted, and sailed for the coast on the afternoon of the 7th of November.

Up to the time of our departure from Bermuda, not a word had been said to a member of the crew, nor even to the captain, about the purpose to run the blockade, and the ship was cleared out from St. George's for Nassau. We had, however, several very active intelligent men forward, among them one named Freemantle, who followed me back to Europe and made the cruise in the *Alabama* as captain's coxswain. During the passage from England I had kept an eye to the men, and Low had been much with them as an officer of the ship, and we felt pretty sure that 'Jack' had his suspicions. That they should have resisted the persuasions and warnings of the United States Consul at St. George's was therefore a gratifying evidence of their willingness to take part in a little exciting adventure.

It was especially important to know whether the 'engineer department' could be relied upon, and I had often gone into the engine-room to have a talk with the chief. His name was McNair, a silent, steady, reliable Scot, immovable and impassive as the Grampian Hills when it was proper to stand fast, prompt, quick, and energetic when it was necessary to act. He was one of that thoughtful class of men who seem to be always thinking that something unexpected may happen, and to be preparing for the difficulty. From the very first I felt sure of McNair, and never parted from him until the *Alabama* was off on her cruise. In fitting out that ship he was of great service, and he had charge of her engines until she was joined at Terceira by Captain Semmes and his regular staff of officers.

The day after leaving Bermuda it was necessary to put the ship's head in the direction of the actual port of destination, and of course the men at the wheel, and in fact all on board, would soon perceive that we were not steering the course for Nassau. It would not have been fair to conceal the object of the voyage from the men until a critical moment, and it would also have been imprudent to go on to the coast without knowing their minds, because they had not agreed to undertake any such risk.

I determined, therefore, to settle the matter there and

then, and sent for all hands to come aft to the bridge. I told them very briefly 'that they had shipped in a British port, to make a voyage in a British ship to one or more British islands and back again to England; that I had no right to take them anywhere else without their consent, and I did not mean to use either force or undue pressure to make them do anything not set out in the shipping articles, but I thought they must have suspected that there was some other purpose in the voyage than a cruise to Bermuda and the Bahamas, and the time had arrived when it was both safe and proper for me to tell them the real port of destination, which was Savannah, and of course this meant a breach of blockade, with the risk of capture and some rough treatment as prisoners-of-war.' I added, 'If you are not willing to go on, say so now, and I will take the ship to Nassau and get other men who will go; but if you are ready and willing to risk the venture, remember that it is a fresh engagement and a final one, from which there must be no backing out.'

I had thought over what to say, and was prepared with a few exhilarating and persuasive phrases; but I caught Freemantle's eye and saw that several of the men were whispering together. It flashed across my mind at once that no further talk was necessary, and I put the question plainly, 'Will you go?' to which there was a prompt and unanimous consent. I thanked them, but said there was still something to explain, which I did to the following effect:

'The United States have been compelled to buy up steamers from the merchant service for blockaders. Many of them are neither so strong nor so efficient in any way as this ship, and they are not heavily armed. If we should fall in with any blockaders off Savannah at all, they are likely to be of that class, and Colonel Anderson and I, who represent the Confederate Government, and the gentlemen passengers, who are Southern men, do not feel disposed to give up this valuable and important cargo to a ship not strong enough to render resistance useless, or to open boats that may attempt to board us. So long as the *Fingal* is under the British flag, we have no right to fire a shot, but I have a bill of sale in my pocket, and can take delivery from the captain on behalf of the Confederate Navy Department at any moment. This I propose to do, if there should appear to be any likelihood of a collision with a blockader, and I want to know if you are willing under such circumstances to help in defending the ship?'

They answered 'Yes' to a man. These preliminaries being satisfactorily settled, all hands were set briskly to work to arm the ship. We mounted the two 4½-inch rifled guns in the forward gangway ports, and the two steel boat-guns on the quarterdeck. We got up a sufficient number of rifles and revolvers, with a good supply of ammunition, and converted the 'ladies' saloon' into an armoury, shell-room, and magazine.

The cases containing the made-up cartridges for the guns were stowed out of easy reach, so we hoisted out of the hold a few barrels of powder and a bale of flannel, and made ten or fifteen cartridges for each gun. Colonel Anderson had passed a good many years of his early life in the United States navy, and although he had been long out of the service, his 'right hand had not forgot its cunning.' He and I cut out the cylinders, the other passengers helped at the sewing, and the *Fingal* was on the next day ready to beat off a boat attack, or even to exchange shots with an impromptu blockader on a dark night, and thus perhaps prevent her closing. Freemantle and two or three others of the crew were old naval men, and took the leading positions at the guns. We had two or three drills, and found that we could handle the 'battery' satisfactorily.

I had a talk with McNair after settling everything with the men. Although he did not say so, I felt sure from his manner that he had been expecting the information, because he received it quite as a matter of course, and told me that he had been putting aside a few tons of the nicest and cleanest coal, and if I could give him time just before getting on the coast to haul fires in one boiler at a time, and run the scrapers through the flues, he thought he might drive the ship, deep as she was, at the rate of eleven knots for a spurt of a few hours. These preparations seemed to put all hands in good spirits; indeed, the men were quite jolly over the prospect.

On the 11th McNair got the chance to clean his flues. It was my purpose to make the land at the entrance to Warsaw Sound, through which Makin said he could take the ship by inland creeks into the Savannah river, and the course was shaped so that at noon on the 11th we should be on the parallel of Warsaw. From that position we steered in on a due-west course, and timed the speed to make the land about 3 a.m., or at any rate before daylight.

The moon set early, but the night was clear, and there was an unusually good horizon line. Several suitable stars passed the meridian between dark and 1 a.m., and Polaris was of course available, so we were able to get the latitude every half hour, and thus to check the course. At about 1 a.m. on the 12th we got alongshore soundings inside the Gulf Stream. Up to this time it had been uncomfortably clear, with a light south-east breeze, but it now fell calm, and we could see a dark line to the westward. Makin said it was the mist over the marshes, and the land-breeze would soon bring it off to us. In half an hour or so we felt a cool damp air in our faces, then a few big drops of moisture, and we ran straight into as nice a fog as any reasonable blockade-runner could have wanted. There was not a light anywhere about the ship except in the binnacle, and that was carefully covered, so that the man at the wheel could barely look at the compass with one eye, and the engine-room hatches were well-hooded. Not a word was spoken, and there was not a sound but the throb of the engines and the slight 'shir-r-r' made by the friction of the ship through the water, and these seemed muffled by the dank vaporous air.

When we got into six fathoms the engines were eased to dead slow, and we ran cautiously in by the lead, straight for the land, the object being to get in-shore of any blockaders that might be off the inlet. We supposed the ship to be drawing fifteen or sixteen feet, and we stood on into three and a quarter fathoms, when we turned her head off to the light easterly swell, and stopped the engines. The fog was as thick as, and about the colour of, mulligatawny soup, and the water alongside looked of a darkish brown. From the bridge it was just possible to make out the men standing on the forecastle and poop. We could not have been in a better position for a dash at daylight.

While we were thus lying-to and waiting, every faculty alert to catch the slightest sound, and every eye searching the fog for the first glimpse of land, or of an approaching ship, there burst upon our ears a shrill prolonged quavering shriek. The suddenness of the sound, coming upon our eagerly expectant senses, and probably much heightened in volume and force by contrast with the stillness, was startling. I am afraid to venture upon a superlative, but I may safely say it was unearthly. None of us could conceive what it was, but all thought that it was as loud and as piercing as a steam-whistle, and that it must have been heard by any blockader within five miles of us. In a moment the sound was repeated, but we were prepared, and it was this time accompanied by a flapping and rustling noise from a 'hencoop' in the gangway. 'It is the cock that came on board at Bermuda,' said some one. Several men ran to the spot. Freemantle thrust his arm into the coop, drew out an unhappy fowl, and wrung off its head with a vicious swing. But it was the wrong one, and chanticleer crowed again defiantly. 'Try again,' came up in an audible whisper from under the bridge; but Freemantle's second effort was more disastrous than the first. He not only failed to seize the obnoxious screamer, but he set the whole hennery in commotion, and the 'Mujan' cock, from a safe corner, crowed and croaked, and fairly chuckled over the fuss of feathers, the cackling, and the distracting strife he had aroused. At last the offending bird was caught. He died game, and made a fierce struggle for life; but Freemantle managed to catch him with a firm grip by the neck, and fetching a full arm-swing, as if heaving a twelve-pound lead, the body fell with a heavy thud upon the deck, and we were again favoured with a profound stillness.

By this time daylight began to break. Makin said the fog would settle and gather over the low marshes towards sunrise, and gradually roll off seaward before the light land-wind. I went aloft to look out for the first sight of the 'inlet.' Makin was right. In less than half an hour I could see the bushy tops of the tall pine-trees, then their straight slender trunks, then the brushwood, and finally the pale yellow streak of sand which formed the foreshore.

I reported this to Makin, who could not see it all from the deck, and he asked me to come down and consult. I assured him we were right abreast of Warsaw Inlet, and of this he was satisfied, but he said the buoys would all be up, and the low-lying fog would probably cover the distant leading marks, and we might go wrong in the intricate channels. He thought it would be some time before the fog would clear off to seaward, but as it was settling over the land and we would soon have a tolerably clear view in-shore, he proposed making a dash for Savannah, about 17 miles to the north and east, where he felt sure we could get in, buoys or no buoys.

In a few moments the engines were doing their best, and the ship's head was laid for the outer bar of the Savannah river. McNair fulfilled his promise, for the *Fingal* was making a good eleven knots. Meanwhile the fog continued to settle and roll off the land, and the low sandy beach, with the tall pines in the background, and a gentle surf just creaming its outer edge, was soon in full view from the deck. We skirted the shore in the least water the ship's draft permitted, and were much favoured. The land breeze dropped, and about half a mile off shore the fog hung heavily, a great grey mass, almost black at the water's edge. It served as a veil between us and any blockaders that might be enveloped in it.

We bowled along at a steady pace, and before long the beach and the line of pines trended abruptly away to the westward; we caught sight of the high brick walls of Fort Pulaski, and were off the estuary of the Savannah. In another quarter of an hour Makin had his marks on: 'Starboard,' 'Steady at north-west by north,' and the *Fingal* was over the bar and ploughing up channel, 'a big bone in her mouth,' the favouring fog still to the eastward, and the sheltering fort on the port bow. Before getting in range we fired a gun and hoisted the Confederate flag at the fore, which was answered from the fort. The parapet of the main works and the *glacis* of the outer were lined with men, and as we drew near we saw the caps waving, although we could not hear their cheers.

The entrance to the Savannah river is through a broad estuary, but though the expanse of water is wide, the ship channel is narrow and comparatively shoal. Nearly opposite Fort Pulaski two large wooden sailing ships had been sunk right in the fairway; but Makin thought with our draft we could probably squeeze by on either side, and he ported the helm to pass off shore of them, but just abreast of the outer ship we brought up in an oyster bank.

The tide was ebb, but the bottom was soft oozy mud, and as the ship could take no harm, we determined to let her lie as she was until we could find how it was possible to get round the obstructions. Colonel Anderson was a Savannah man, and he went on shore immediately to learn the news and to telegraph our arrival up to town.

Colonel Olmstead, the commandant of the fort, sent a boat off to the ship as soon as he perceived that we were aground, to inform us that a few days previously a large United States fleet, under Admiral Dupont, had attacked and driven the Confederate troops out of the batteries protecting Port Royal, and that place had been occupied by a strong land force. We were further informed that the Federal fleet was still at Port Royal, and that as there was interior water communication with the Savannah river, the enemy might send over small vessels or boats to cut us out; but the boarding officer was directed to say that a good look-out would be kept on the ship, and a sufficient number of men to defend her would be sent off if any such attempt should be made.

The distance from Port Royal, however, was much too far for us to be seen, and no danger was looked for from that quarter. The blockading vessels had probably been drawn off to assist in the operations at Port Royal. At any rate, we saw nothing of them, although later in the day several appeared off the outer bar. We had thus been able to effect a 'breach of blockade' with no graver incident than the scrimmage with the Bermudan cock, and the men appeared to be a little disappointed at the pacific and commonplace termination of the adventure.

At about 1 p.m. three river steamboats, being the main portion of Flag-officer Tattnall's so-called fleet, came down to look after us. Lieutenant-Commanding Johnston sent us a hawser from his ship, the *Savannah*, and dragged us out of the mud. After some pulling and hauling they got the *Fingal* above the obstructions, and escorted her up to the city, abreast of which we anchored at about 4 p.m., November 12th, 1861. The same afternoon I telegraphed my arrival to the Secretary of the Navy, and next day received orders by telegraph to go on to Richmond as soon as arrangements for the discharge of the arms, etc., could be made. On the 14th Flag-officer Tattnall detailed an officer to attend to the business of the ship, and I started in company with

Colonel Anderson, who was also going to Richmond to report to the War Department.

I knew from statistics and from personal knowledge of the country that the South was poor in military and naval resources, and that there had been no preparation for war, and no collection of material. But figures never carry to the senses full and clear impressions. When it is said that the drought in India has destroyed so many million tons of rice, the mind is at once impressed with the conviction that there will be a great deficit of food in Bengal; but it is only those who witness the sufferings of the famishing people who fully comprehend the melancholy import of the statement. On the route to Richmond I had ample and painful evidence of the strain which the sudden outburst of war had put upon the South, and the inadequate means to meet it.

The railways having only one line of metals, and the rolling stock barely able to satisfy the ordinary passenger and goods traffic, were already yielding to the increased wear and tear, and the heavy trains, filled with troops moving towards Virginia, and loaded with stores and supplies for the army, were dragged slowly along by the over-worked engines. The troops in the train with me were irregularly and indifferently armed, and were without uniformity of dress or equipment; but they were full of spirit, and laughed and sang songs around the impromptu fires which were quickly kindled wherever the train stopped, for we frequently waited for some purpose or other many miles from a station, often in the woods.

At a place called Goldsborough, in North Carolina, we remained for an hour or more, and while the passengers were getting dinner I heard loud singing in the street, mingled with the music of a band, and going out of the hotel I saw a long line of uncovered railway freight-trucks, with rough cross-benches uncomfortably close together, and each bench was filled with men. There was an engine at the end of the line, and I learned that the men were a regiment of North Carolinians from the Buncombe district, on the way to join the forces at Wilmington.

The troops were remarkably fine-looking men, mostly young and well-proportioned, but they were dressed in their ordinary clothing, and many had no great-coats, although it was November, and the air was keen and at night frosty. I walked along the whole line of trucks and spoke to some of the men, and asked about their arms. Some had old-fashioned flint-lock muskets, some had only double-barrel sporting guns, of course without bayonets, and a few had percussion lock muskets. I believe twenty or thirty had the old heavy small-bore weapon called the 'Mississippi rifle,' but I did not see a single modern military rifle in the whole battalion. In about half an hour the train moved on, the men singing 'Dixie,' and the people in the street cheering.

It would hardly be possible to exaggerate the discomforts and privations to which the Southern troops were exposed during the war. At first they were wholly destitute of camp equipage, and were compelled to bivouac in the open air without tent shelter or even the comfort of covered field hospitals, and these deficiencies were never more than partially supplied. The best manhood of the South, young men of spirit and good wiry constitutions, flocked into the army, and thousands were carried off by diseases always more or less prevalent in camps, but whose virulence and fatal effects are greatly lessened by good food and suitable protection from wet and cold.

No one will suppose that I depreciate the efforts or the services of those who held high commands, or occupied responsible positions, whether in the field or in the Cabinet, but I have always thought that the true heroes of the 'lost cause' were the rank and file—the men who, while in no sense responsible for the political events which produced the struggle, and the great majority of whom had not the least personal interest in that domestic institution which many assert to have been the underlying cause of the antagonism between the North and South, yet answered quickly and loyally the appeal of their States, and formed that splendid infantry which, though ill-armed and equipped, poorly clad, and often insufficiently fed, marched and countermarched, toiled in trenches, and fought in line of battle, with admirable patience and courage for four years, and who, in the depressing retreat to Appomatox Court House, when it was manifest that there was no longer a hope of final success, turned upon their pursuers with all the *élan* of Chancellorsville. No one can have witnessed what those men endured, or can know what they performed, without feeling impelled to speak a word of admiration; but the subject is one for the military historian of the war, and I have no space for more than a passing tribute.

After frequent delays *en route*, the train reached Richmond, and I lost no time in reporting at the Navy Department.

It would be both uninteresting and useless to record in detail the consultations with the Secretary of the Navy. I reported fully upon the state of affairs abroad, and the object of my return to the Confederate States was explained. The wants of the Department and the naval policy of the Government—how to supply the one and to carry out the other—were the chief considerations, and they were amply discussed. Finally it was decided as a first step that the *Fingal* should be filled up with cotton, on account of the Navy Department, and that I should return to Europe with her to carry out the further purposes of the Government; and while the ship was loading, my original instructions and powers would be revised, and the mode of furnishing funds would be arranged with the Treasury Department.

Messrs. John Fraser and Co., of Charleston, were instructed to buy in the interior and forward to Savannah the quantity of cotton necessary to fill up the *Fingal*, and the naval paymaster at that station was ordered to supply the coals required for the outward voyage. I got back to Savannah about November 23rd. The situation of affairs was interesting, and I think it will afford a better picture of passing events if I give the official correspondence which was carried on from that place, than if I continue the account in the narrative style.

'Savannah, *November* 25, 1861.

'Sir,—

'I have the honour to report that the steamship *Fingal* has been discharged, and now lies in the Savannah river ready to receive freight. Paymaster Kelly has written to Columbus to have the necessary quantity of coal sent down at once, and expects it to be here to-morrow or next day. I cannot refrain from urging the necessity of getting the ship off without delay. Yesterday five of the enemy's gunboats stood cautiously in, and after throwing a number of shell upon and over Tybee Island, a force was landed without opposition.

'This morning the Federal flag is flying from the

lighthouse, and they will doubtless soon have a battery upon the point of the island. The only egress left for the *Fingal* is through Warsaw Inlet, and it can scarcely be supposed that the enemy will permit it to remain open many days. . . . The small quantity of naval stores and cotton required for the *Fingal* could be got on board in a couple of days if they were brought here on the spot.

'I am, etc.,

'(Signed) James D. Bulloch.

'Hon. S. R. Mallory,
'Secretary of the Navy.'

The railways were so fully occupied with the transport of troops and material of war for Virginia, and other frontier points, that the local traffic was almost wholly stopped, and the cotton and coals for the *Fingal* were brought forward in the merest driblets. On the 4th of December I received the following letter of instructions :—

'Confederate States of America, Navy Department,
'Richmond, Virginia, *November* 30, 1861.

'Sir,—

'You will take command of the *Fingal*, receive on board so much cotton and rosin, to be delivered to you under the orders of the Secretary of the Treasury, as your judgment may approve, together with your coal, and proceed to such port in Great Britain as you may deem expedient, delivering your cargo as you may be requested by the Secretary of the Treasury. You will select two coast pilots to aid in bringing the *Fingal* safely back. On your arrival in Great Britain you will transfer the command of the *Fingal* to Lieutenant G. T. Sinclair, whom you will receive on board at Savannah.'

Then follows information in regard to funds, and instructions as to the articles most needed, which I was to buy, if not already included in the outstanding contracts, and ship back to a Confederate port in the *Fingal*.

'So soon as either of the vessels under contract in England shall be completed and delivered, you will adopt such measures as you may deem best to arm and equip her as a vessel of war, without infringing the laws of Great Britain, or giving to that Government just cause of offence; and having obtained a crew and all things necessary for an extended cruise, you will leave England in command, and proceed against the enemy in whatever quarter of the ocean circumstances may then indicate as affording the best chances of success. Lieutenant-Commanding Pegram (of the *Nashville*) is instructed to detail such officers from his vessel as you may require, and you are authorized to confer acting appointments upon such others as you may deem necessary. The Department, the speed and qualities of your vessel being unknown, is unwilling, so far in advance, to assign any particular locality for your operations, but desires to impress upon you the importance of rendering your vessel as formidable, and your cruise as destructive, as practicable, leaving to you entire freedom of action. Should your judgment at any time hesitate in seeking the solution of any doubt on this point, it may be aided by the reflection that you are to do the enemy's commerce the greatest injury in the shortest time. A speedy recognition of our Government by the Great European Powers is anticipated, and I have no reason to doubt that if you shall seek their ports, you will receive the consideration and treatment due from neutrals to an officer of a belligerent Power with which they desire to establish close commercial relations. The strictest regard for the rights of neutrals cannot be too sedulously observed ; nor should an opportunity be lost of cultivating friendly relations with their naval and merchant services, and of placing the true character of the contest in which we are engaged in its proper light. You will avail yourself of every opportunity of communicating with your Government, using, when you may deem it expedient, a cipher for this purpose. The Department relies with confidence upon the patriotism, ability, and conduct of yourself, officers, and men, and with my earnest wishes for the prosperity of your cruise, and your triumphant return to your country,

'I am, etc.,

'(Signed) S. R. MALLORY,

'Secretary of the Navy.

'Captain James D. Bulloch,
'Savannah, Georgia.'

In a subsequent letter the Secretary of the Navy directed me to arm the *Fingal* for the outward voyage, and I replied to the main points as follows :

'Savannah, *December* 5, 1861.

'SIR,—

'I have the honour to acknowledge, etc. . . . . The greatest obstacle will be met at the very outset in the difficulty of arming and equipping a cruiser in a neutral port; for even if Great Britain should have acknowledged the independence of the Confederate States, unless she has become a party to the war, her obligations under the International Code would force her to prohibit the equipment of an armed ship under a belligerent flag in her ports. You are better informed as to such contingencies than I can be, and I only allude to the subject to show that I am fully prepared to submit to the disappointment of not at once getting upon that element which is free to any flag when properly defended.

'Such portions of your instructions as are specific shall be carried out as strictly to the letter as possible, and in the exercise of the large discretion granted me, I will endeavour to act with as much caution and prudence as will be consistent with promptness and vigour. I particularly note your remarks in reference to neutrals, and will bear constantly in mind your suggestions upon this and other points. There has been much delay in getting the cotton forward, but I think the *Fingal* will be ready for sea on Saturday night. . . . I have not deemed it necessary to arm the *Fingal* for the return voyage, as it is important to preserve her original character as an English ship. This course will ensure her less trouble and annoyance in getting another cargo on board. If, on our arrival in England, the Confederate Government has been acknowledged, the flag can be changed. . . .

'I am, etc.,

'JAMES D. BULLOCH.

'Hon. S. R. Mallory,
'Secretary of the Navy.'

Owing to the continued difficulty of inland transportation and the delay in getting the cotton for the *Fingal* to the shipping port, she was not loaded until December 20th, and the following copies of the correspondence will best explain the attempts to get her to sea, as well as the condition of affairs at Savannah :

'Steamship *Fingal*, off Thunderbolt Battery,
'Near Savannah, *December* 24, 1861.

'SIR,—

'On Saturday morning the barometer and the general appearance of the sky indicating a favourable state of weather, I made preparations for sea, and on Sunday morning early dropped the ship down to a bight in Wilmington Island, where she can lie concealed from the enemy's ships at Warsaw as well as at Tybee. This bight is about one mile above a seven-gun battery on Skidaway Island, from which point there is a clear view of the opening to Warsaw Sound. Immediately after anchoring, the captain of this battery informed me that three blockading vessels were off the bar, and that one of them had chased his boat in on the afternoon before. Still, as all appearances indicated a dark and squally night, it was determined to get under weigh on the first quarter of the flood, so as to get down to the bar before the moon rose. At early dark a fog set in over the marshes, concealing the leading marks, and the pilots were unwilling to move the ship. This circumstance, sufficiently annoying at first, probably saved us from capture, as it appears that the enemy were keeping an especial look-out that night.

'No vessel could have seen to cross the bar before half-past seven o'clock, yet at 8 a.m. one of their small vessels appeared in full sight of the battery below us, and actually steamed up to within half a mile of its guns, turned, and steamed down channel again without receiving a shot. I am informed that the approach of this vessel was not reported to the commander of the battery until she was in the act of turning.

'Ignorant of the incident above mentioned, I sent an experienced pilot in an eight-oared boat with good sails, kindly furnished by Lieutenant-Commanding Kennard, of the Confederate States steamer *Samson*, to examine the bar and the coast north and south of the point of Warsaw Island, and to report as quickly as possible, so that if all was clear we might go to sea on the afternoon tide In the meantime two additional gun-vessels had joined the first, and the three coming rapidly up channel with the young flood, cut off our boat, compelling her, as it is now thought, to go into one of the creeks running through the Romerly Marsh, from which I trust she has been able by this time to reach Green Island. The enemy's three vessels took up an anchorage just opposite the main passage through Romerly Marsh, thus effectually closing all communication with Savannah from the sea, through any inlet. As the enemy could easily have discovered the position of this ship by landing upon Wilmington Island, and could have cut her out with boats at night, I took advantage of last night's flood to bring her up to this place, where there is another battery. For some time before last Saturday the enemy had not entered Warsaw Sound, their vessels simply cruising up and down the coast in very regular order. This movement, therefore, would seem especially intended to prevent the escape of this ship, and would indicate treachery somewhere. It may, however, only be the development of a general plan of attack upon Savannah, which place I consider far from being safe. The batteries are weak in guns and gunners, and whatever the gallantry of the men may be, which is undoubted, they could not withstand a vigorous attack from the ships which could be brought over Warsaw bar.

'I will remain in a position to take advantage of any

change in the enemy's plans, and will lose no opportunity of getting to sea.

'I am, etc.,

'(Signed) JAMES D. BULLOCH.

'Hon. S. R. Mallory,
'Secretary of the Navy.'

'Savannah, *December* 26, 1861.

'SIR,—

'On the 24th inst. I addressed you from the anchorage at Thunderbolt, reporting my failure to get the *Fingal* to sea, and informing you that the enemy had effectually sealed up all the approaches to Savannah from Warsaw Inlet and the other channels leading from the southward. The position of the *Fingal* below the battery at Thunderbolt was not safe, as the enemy might at any time cut her out with boats. I therefore, by the advice of Flag-officer Tattnall sent her back to the city on the afternoon of the 24th, and went down to Warsaw Island myself in search of the boat I informed you had been cut off by the sudden approach of the enemy's gunboats on the day before. I returned to Savannah last night, and have the satisfaction to report that the men (with Mr. Low and two midshipmen who were of the party) were found and brought safely to Skidaway, and are now here, with the exception of two of the crew of the *Samson*, who I regret to say deserted, and it is feared got on board the blockading vessels. Yesterday morning, while I was on Warsaw Island, a large paddle-wheel steamer joined the three vessels already anchored below Skidaway, and late in the afternoon a screw-steamer, barque rigged and pierced for eight guns, came in. There are thus five ships-of-war at the entrance to the Romerly Marsh, a force too powerful for the simple blockade of the *Fingal*, and this assembling of the enemy's fleet can only be regarded as preliminary to an attack in force upon the city. It is impossible to conjecture what chance may occur to open a passage for the *Fingal*. . . . If the *Fingal* is irretrievably locked up for the war, I presume you would desire me to get to England by some other means, etc.

'I am, etc.,
'(Signed) JAMES D. BULLOCH.

'Hon. S. R. Mallory.'

From the date of the foregoing letter I continued to report the condition of affairs at Savannah, and the position of the enemy's ships at the main entrance to the river, as well as in Warsaw Sound, and received various letters from the Department, increasing the orders for purchase of supplies in England, and enlarging the general scope of my duties there, and especially instructing me to 'examine into the subject of constructing iron and steel clad vessels in England and France.'

On the 3rd of January, 1862, I reported as follows:—

'Since my last letter there has been no change in the position of the blockading vessels off Tybee, but the enemy seems to have changed the design indicated by the first appearance of his squadron near Skidaway battery. On the 30th ultimo, three old sailing ships, probably part of the much-talked-of "Stone Fleet," were brought in and anchored at the entrance to the Romerly Marsh, and have since been stripped to their lower masts. If these vessels are sunk in their present position, the inland communication would of course be closed between Savannah and the more southern ports of Georgia; but should the enemy, content with this interruption of local trade, remove the men-of-war for other operations, or for outside cruising, the *Fingal* might yet be got to sea through the regular ship channel leading between Warsaw Island and little Tybee. Up to the present moment no opportunity has offered to pass the blockading ships. By way of Warsaw they occupy the entire channel with five ships, sometimes seven; and at the anchorage near Tybee there have never been less than four ships, frequently as many as eleven.'

January 13th I again reported:—

'I regret to say that this letter must be of the same tenor as the last. The enemy are fully informed of the *Fingal's* position and the intention to get her out if possible,' etc. 'Unless there be some changes in the political relations of the United States with the courts of Europe, I consider the port of Savannah as completely closed to commerce for an indefinite time; consequently my detention here with any hope of getting the *Fingal* to sea is not only unnecessary, but will occasion much delay and confusion in the settlement of the business for which I was originally sent to Europe. I therefore respectfully suggest that you order me to proceed at once to England for the purpose of completing that business, and of still further carrying out your instructions of November 30, 1861.'

In continuation I pointed out the effect of the delay, and the probable impossibility of completing or even fairly setting on foot the various duties with which I was charged, in time to go to sea in the first ship, which would probably be ready by the date of my arrival in England, and suggested that I should be transferred to the second ship, which would be finished three to four months later. In reply, my orders were modified in the above particular, and the Secretary of the Navy directed me to turn over the *Fingal* to Lieutenant G. T. Sinclair, and to proceed to England by any feasible route.

Mr. John Low, upon my recommendation, was appointed a master in the Confederate Navy, and was ordered to accompany me to Europe. Two midshipmen, E. C. Anderson, junior, and Eugene Maffitt, were ordered to join me, and also Mr. Clarence R. Yonge, an assistant in the paymaster's office at Savannah, the last named to act as clerk, and then to be appointed acting paymaster in one of the cruising ships.

Mr. Yonge afterwards left the *Alabama* when at Jamaica, somewhat unexpectedly, and as he took service on his return to England under the United States Consul at Liverpool, and afterwards took the prominent part of chief witness in the '*Alexandra* Case' (which will be dwelt upon in a subsequent chapter), his conduct was much criticised at the time.

The official correspondence quoted above has not been included in the body of this narrative merely to illustrate the movements of the *Fingal*, but chiefly to demonstrate the views of the Government in respect to the proposed naval operations abroad, and to make a fair representation of the enemy's operations and the condition of affairs at Savannah in December—January, 1861-62. My duties at that time compelled me to be much and often at both entrances to the Savannah river, and to examine carefully and critically the movements and force of the blockading fleet, and the strength and number of the Confederate defensive works.

The main approach to Savannah, *viâ* Tybee, was defended by two old brick forts, very inefficiently armed, chiefly with smooth-bore 32-pounders. The approach from Warsaw Sound, through Wilmington Creek, was protected by a battery of seven guns on Skidaway Island, and another battery of six or seven guns at Thunderbolt, further up the creek, and quite out of range of the first. Both of these fortifications were newly made earthworks, entirely open in rear, and the guns were mounted in barbette.

The United States ships at anchor off the entrance to Romerly Marsh were just out of gunshot from the Skidaway battery. They lay there for days, and so far as I could discover, never made a reconnaissance. There was no sleeping accommodation for the garrison inside the works at Skidaway, and the men lived in tents and huts some distance in the rear, a guard only being actually in the battery night and day. Among the blockading vessels was one fine steamship of the *Iroquois* class, and I often wondered why they did not come inside some dark night with boats, get round the flank of the battery, and spike the guns. The garrison were sturdy fellows, and would have been formidable in a stand-up fight, but the attacking party always have the advantage in a night surprise, and the ships could not only have chosen their time, but could have greatly outnumbered the guard.

The blockading squadron at Tybee was also very apathetic, and never, while I was there, came within range of Fort Pulaski. Among the vessels off Tybee, I recognised my old ship the *Bienville*, or it might have been the *De Soto*—they were sister ships. The gun-boats could have run past the batteries on Wilmington Creek at any time, and so have got into the rear of Fort

Jackson, driven the men out of it, and then gone on into the Savannah river, completely isolating Fort Pulaski. The men, working the guns in barbette, could not have stood a rapid fire from the ships ; grape and canister would have swept them off the parapet.

I do not know who commanded the United States blockading squadron at that time. Either Farragut or David Porter would have tried to get inside, if they had been there ; at least, they would have made some effort to discover the means of resistance. The Confederate naval forces at Savannah were commanded by Flag-officer Josiah Tattnall, as gallant a seaman as ever trod a plank. I suppose no officer of his rank and quality was ever doomed to the indignity of such an inefficient command. His flag-ship, the *Savannah*, was a paddle river-boat, with engines and boilers on deck, and her battery consisted of one smooth-bore 32-pounder gun, on a traversing carriage. A rocket exploding among the flimsy joiner-work of her deck cabins would have set her on fire, and a single shell from one of the gun-boats outside would have blown her up. When Tattnall would come down the river, as he often did, with his so-called 'Musquito fleet,' and flaunt his flag as a seeming challenge to the formidable ships of the enemy at Tybee, nothing saved the display from the appearance of bravado, or the manœuvre from ridicule, but the natural grace and dignity with which the fine old gentleman performed every act of his life.

Josiah Tattnall was a man out of the common, the *beau idéal* of a naval officer of what must now be called the old school, 'the sublime of Jack-tar.' He was punctilious on a point of honour, and rigid in the practice of official propriety ; but he was genial, modest and unassuming in his private intercourse with friends, and his manners were courtly, yet easy and unrestrained. He was charmingly fluent and entertaining in conversation, and had a very special gift for telling a story with liveliness and spirit, always illustrating the sense and point of his narrative with appropriate action and gesture. In positions of command fully testing his tact, judgment, courage, and professional skill, he almost invariably exhibited higher faculties than the occasions required, and no one can therefore fix the limit of his ability. He possessed all the traits which are found in heroic characters, and, with suitable opportunities, would have set his name among the great naval worthies who are historic. He was a high type of human nature—a 'perfect' man in the Scriptural sense—that is to say, complete in all his parts. He died in Savannah, his native place, and was buried near there in a grove of old live-oak trees planted to commemorate the wedding of the first of his ancestors who settled in the Colony of Georgia. A couplet from the touching requiem to 'Tom Bowling' would be a fitting epitaph to one who has been called the 'Bayard of the sea':—

> 'Though his body's under hatches
> His soul has gone aloft.'

The prediction that Savannah would be sealed up for the remainder of the war was fulfilled, and the *Fingal's* proposed voyage to Europe was definitely abandoned. She was not, however, lost to the Confederate States. The Navy Department took her into the service, and she was converted into an armour-clad, and christened *Atlanta*. To effect this conversion she was first cut down to her deck, which throughout about 150 or 160 feet amidships was widened (6 feet on each side, widest part, but tapering towards the ends) by a 'heavy solid overway of wood and armour,' sloping from a point several feet below the water-line to the edge of the deck. Upon this widened portion of the deck a casemate was built, the sides and ends inclining at an angle of about 30°. The top of the casemate was flat, and the house to cover the steersman and officer directing the fire rose above the roof about three feet. The sloping sides and ends of the casemate were covered with two layers of iron plates, each being two inches thick, screwed to a backing composed of three inches of oak upon fifteen inches of pine. The bolts were one and a quarter inch, countersunk on the outside of the plates, and drawn up by nuts and washers on the inside. She was provided with a beak or ram at the bow; and a pole and lever, which could be lowered at will, was also fitted at the bow, long enough to project beyond the ram. The pole was intended to carry a percussion torpedo. Her armament consisted of two 7-inch rifled guns on bow and stern pivots, and two 6-inch rifled guns in broadside. The 7-inch guns were so arranged that they could be worked in broadside, as well as for fore and aft fire, and the *Fingal* could therefore fight three guns (two 7-inch and one 6-inch) on either side. The guns were cast-iron with wrought iron bands, and were of the 'Brooke' pattern.

As soon as the *Atlanta* was finished, the Navy Department was desirous that she should be tried against the enemy's ironclads, eight or nine of which were known to be in the neighbourhood, off Charleston and the entrances to Savannah, or at Port Royal. The senior officers of the Confederate navy at Savannah did not think that she would be a match for the United States *Monitor* class at close quarters, and they did not think it prudent to take her out into Warsaw Sound, where two 'Monitors' were lying, except under favourable circumstances of spring-tide, because her draft had been increased by the weight of armour, ordnance, and necessary stores, and the channels were not only intricate, but the depth of water very scant at best, and besides this, the ship steered badly in consequence of the increased draft and the alteration of form caused by the projecting overway, which extended several feet below the water-line.

Flag-officer Tattnall's advice was to wait until the enemy collected his ironclads for a second attack upon Charleston, and then to send the *Atlanta* out on the first spring-tide, when she could be got to sea without the risk of being taken at a disadvantage in the narrow and shoal waters of the Romerly Marshes and Warsaw Sound. Once fairly afloat, and with ample sea-room, he thought she could strike a telling blow, either at Port Royal, where the enemy had a large collection of transports, or at some other point. This wise counsel was unhappily overborne by the weight of public clamour, and the Navy Department yielded to the outside pressure.

Commander Wm. A. Webb, a clever and spirited officer, was ordered to the *Atlanta*, and the condition of his appointment appeared to be that he should at once 'do something.' Before daylight on the morning of June 17, 1863, Webb got under weigh, and steaming past the old batteries on Skidaway Island, which had ere this been abandoned, entered Warsaw Sound. The United States 'Monitors' *Weehawken* and *Nahant* were at anchor in the sound. They made out the *Atlanta* at about 4 a.m., and the *Weehawken* immediately slipped her cable and steamed towards her, followed closely by the *Nahant*. At about 600 yards from the *Weehawken* the *Atlanta* grounded, but was backed off with some difficulty. Shortly after, the *Atlanta* took the bottom again, and stuck fast. The *Weehawken* approached to within about 300 yards, and choosing a position so that 'the *Atlanta* could bring her guns to bear with difficulty,' opened fire. The engagement, if it can be called one, lasted about fifteen minutes. The *Nahant* did not fire a shot, but the *Weehawken* hit the *Atlanta* four times, twice with 15-inch 'cored shot,' and twice with 11-inch solid shot. The *Atlanta's* pilot-house was knocked off, and one of the port-stoppers, or shutters, was driven in; the armour was crushed in at several points, although not pierced, and the backing was much damaged. One 15-inch shot struck fairly on the inclined side of the *Atlanta*, breaking the armour plate and driving a shower of splinters from the backing into the ship. Captain Webb has told me that the concussion knocked down about forty men, and sixteen were more or less wounded by the splinters.

Webb was in a sad plight. It can hardly be said that he was fighting his ship—he was simply enduring the fire of his adversary.

It was manifest that a few more concussions, and a 15-inch shot, perhaps a shell, would find its way into the casemate, and there would be great and useless slaughter among his men. When further resistance ceases to hold out any hope of final success, the dictates of humanity extort an acknowledgment of defeat, and the *Atlanta's* flag was hauled down.

The foregoing brief statement has been made up almost exclusively from the Confederate accounts. I have before me, while writing, a copy of the report of the commander of the *Weehawken*, and if it contained anything in conflict with the above, I would either mention the fact or give the report in full. Captain

John Rodgers, of the *Weehawken* (I hope I may still speak of him in the present tense), is an able officer. He accepted with promptness the *Atlanta's* invitation to battle, and handled his ship with skill and judgment. He took up a good position, awkward for his adversary and advantageous to himself, which he was bound to do, for it is clearly the duty of a commander so to dispose his force as to defeat the enemy with as little loss to himself as possible, and finally he reported the result of the engagement in a plain, manly, straightforward document, without the least brag or unbecoming elation. As a pleasing but somewhat unique feature in the report of Captain Rodgers, I may mention that he called the *Atlanta* the 'enemy,' and not the 'rebel,' an epithet chosen by the politicians at Washington for a purpose, and used by them as a reproach. It crept into the military and naval phraseology of the war, and was thrown broadcast over the correspondence of civil functionaries and United States Consuls ; but the old officers of the army and navy, for the most part, either avoided it, or at any rate seemed to use it as a technical phrase, without opprobrious meaning.

The encounter between the Federal 'Monitors' and the *Atlanta* illustrates no general principle applicable to engagements between iron-cased ships. The 15-inch guns of the *Weehawken* were superior in battering power at close quarters to the 6-inch and 7-inch guns of the *Atlanta*, and the only chance of success for the latter would have been to get into deep and broad waters, where she could manœuvre, and thus use her guns efficiently, and choose her distance as well as position. Lying helplessly aground, she was at the mercy of her opponent, who was able to come within the most effective range for her own guns, and to avoid almost entirely the return fire of her adversary. Captain Rodgers does not mention that his ship was hit, or that she received any injury whatever, except by collision with his own consort, the *Nahant*, after the surrender of the *Atlanta*.

When the Secretary of the Navy directed me to turn over the *Fingal* to Lieutenant G. T. Sinclair, and to proceed to England by any practicable route, I communicated at once with Messrs. John Fraser and Co., of Charleston, and they kindly offered me and my party passage in either of two steamers they were about to despatch, one from Charleston and one from Wilmington. The Charleston steamer would try the blockade first, but she was small, and would only go as far as Nassau, from which place I would have to find my way to Havana, and thence round by St. Thomas to Southampton, a circuitous route, and very uncertain as regards connection with packets, etc. The Wilmington steamer was larger, having been built for the coasting trade to Boston, and the purpose was to send her direct to Liverpool, only stopping at Fayal in the Azores to replenish her coals. I chose the latter ship and route, and went on to Wilmington, arriving there January 24, 1862. The steamer's name originally was *North Carolina*, but it had been changed to *Annie Childs*. She was coaling and taking in cotton, rosin, tobacco, and other cargo, until February 1st, when her commander, Captain Hammer, took her down to Orton Point, about twelve miles above the mouth of the river, from which position the ship was concealed from the blockaders.

General J. R. Anderson, commander of the Confederate forces at Wilmington, kindly put a small screw tug-boat at my disposal, and Captain Hammer and I went down to Fort Caswell, at the mouth of the river, every day to reconnoitre. The New Inlet bar was too shoal for the *Annie Childs*, and the only possible egress was by the main ship channel. Two gunboats were generally lying at anchor during the day about one mile west-south-west from the bar, and were sometimes joined by another from New Inlet. We learned from the coast-guard pickets that they did not get under weigh at night. The nights continued to be clear until February 5th, and there was no chance for a run. I find the following entry in my diary under February 5th, 1862:

'Early part of the day clear, but wind north-east, with passing clouds towards noon. In the afternoon got ready for a start. At 10 p.m. under weigh, moon shining, but light haze. Full tide at 12.7; moon set at same time. Timed the ship's speed so as to reach the bar just after the setting of the moon. Crossed 12.15; low fog, stars over head, smooth sea, calm, might have heard the dip of an oar or the swash of the screw a long way. Blockaders must have been fast asleep. Scarcely clear of the bar when the heating of a bearing made it necessary to stop the engine for at least half an hour. Fortunately it began to rain. The bearing being all right, we started again, and were soon safe in a thick drizzle, which lasted until we got to the eastward of the Gulf Stream.'

The *Annie Childs* had a single engine, one inverted cylinder, and was badly found for a voyage across the North Atlantic in the month of February, but she was a capital sea-boat and behaved admirably in a heavy north-west gale which we caught in the 'roaring forties.' At Fayal the American Consul gave a great deal of trouble, and if it had not been for Lloyds' agent we should not have got any coal at all. As it was, we had to be content with a scant supply. At 2.30 p.m. on the afternoon of March 8th, 1862, we made the Old Head of Kinsale, took a Cork pilot on board, and went into Queenstown that night, burning the sweepings of the bunkers mixed with rosin, and the spare spars cut into short lengths. The next day I took train for Liverpool *viâ* Dublin and Holyhead, and arrived there at 4 p.m. on the 10th.

CHAPTER IV.

The *Florida*.—Captain Duguid.—Correspondence concerning the *Florida*.—Her arrival at Nassau.—Commander Maffitt.—The United States blockade of the British Bahama Channel.—The equipping of the *Florida*.—Yellow fever.—The *Florida* runs the blockade at Mobile.—An unparalleled chase.—The *Florida's* cruise in the West Indies.—Vessels captured by the *Florida*.—Her stay at Brest.—Her second cruise.—Her assassination by the *Wachusett*.—Justification of the use of the term 'assassination.' —The Brazilian Government and the capture of the *Florida*.—United States treatment of prisoners-of-war.

Before leaving England with the *Fingal* in October, 1861, I drew up very particular and specific instructions with reference to the outfit of the *Oreto* (*Florida*), with the purpose of preventing any possible violation of the Foreign Enlistment Act, as it had been explained to me by counsel, and to ensure that the ship when delivered to me should be prepared to fulfil the conditions essential to a sea-going steamer of her class and nothing more.

On my arrival in Liverpool from the Confederate States (March 10th, 1862), the *Oreto* (*Florida*) was ready to take the sea. She had made a satisfactory trial trip, and was already provisioned for her outward voyage. I made a thorough investigation, and satisfied myself that not a single article contraband of war was on board the ship—not a weapon, not an appliance for mounting a gun. In this condition I was advised that according to the Municipal Law of Great Britain, she was a perfectly lawful article of traffic, that the builder could deliver her, and I could pay for and receive her, without infringing any statute, or transgressing any requirement of commercial propriety.

Captain James Alexander Duguid, a duly certificated master mariner, was appointed to command the ship, and the crew and engineer's staff were engaged in strict conformity with the conditions of the Merchant Shipping Act, signing articles for a voyage from Liverpool to Palermo, and thence, if required, to a port or ports in the Mediterranean Sea, or the West Indies, and back to a port of discharge in the United Kingdom, the voyage not to exceed six months. Not a single officer or man was enlisted for the service of the Confederate States, nor was a hint thrown out to the crew that the voyage would be other than the route specified in the shipping articles. Captain Duguid and the chief engineer were informed that the ship would go first of all to Nassau, but they knew perfectly well that a shipowner has the right to vary the order of visit to the ports specified in the shipping articles, and that it is not unusual to exercise that privilege when his interests or the special circumstances of the voyage suggest or require a variation within the general limits of the original engagement. Neither the captain nor the engineer were, however, employed, nor in any way pledged to depart from the general conditions set out in the articles, and they did not at any future time enter the service of the Confederate States, so far as I know.

In 'The Case of the United States,' laid before the Tribunal of Arbitration at Geneva, it is affirmed, on the authority of a despatch from the United States Consul at Liverpool, to Mr. Seward, that the *Oreto* 'took her gun-carriages on board at Liverpool,' and it is furthermore stated that she sailed with 'a crew of fifty-two men and *some* guns.'* In refutation of the foregoing, the evidence of the Customs officers at Liverpool was that they kept 'watch on the proceedings of the vessel *Oreto* from the time she left the Toxteth Dock, on the 4th of March last (1862), till the day she sailed, the 22nd of the same month. . . . we did not see at any time any arms, or warlike ammunition of any kind, taken on board, and we are perfectly satisfied that none such was taken on board during her stay in the river.'

One of the statements was very specific.

'I am one of the Surveyors of Customs at this port (Liverpool). Pursuant to instructions I received from the Collector on the 21st February in the present year (1862), and at subsequent dates, I visited the steamer *Oreto* at various times, when she was being fitted out in the dock, close to the yard of Messrs. Miller and Sons, the builders of the vessel. I continued this inspection from time to time until she left the dock, and I am certain that when she left the river she had no warlike stores of any kind whatever on board. After she went into the river she was constantly watched by the boarding officers, who were directed to report to me whenever any goods were taken on board; but, in reply to my frequent inquiries, they stated nothing was put in the ship but coals.

'(Signed) EDWARD MORGAN,
'Surveyor.'

The foregoing and other statements of like import will be found in the evidence laid before the Tribunal of

* 'United States Case,' p. 65.

Arbitration at Geneva.* They are confirmatory of my own declarations to the same effect, and the fact is therefore established beyond dispute that the *Oreto* left the Mersey wholly unarmed, and without any portion of her outfit which could render her liable to seizure or detention for violation of the Foreign Enlistment Act. As she lay in the river off the Egremont Ferry, she looked a comely craft, as much within her legal rights as a hundred cases of Birmingham rifles, or as many tons of gunpowder, about to start for New York in any other ship. This is not the rash assertion of an interested party, pronounced in a spirit of bravado, or by way of a retort; it is founded upon the decision of one of the highest Courts in the realm, as will be shown in due course.

It will be remembered that the orders of the Navy Department, dated November 30th, 1861, directed me to take personal command of the first ship completed in England, and to proceed to cruise against the enemy's commerce. But other duties assigned to me in Europe were largely increased before my departure from the Confederate States, and I was also instructed to examine into the subject of ironclads, and report whether vessels of that class could be built in England or France. When I called the attention of the Navy Department to the fact that the first ship would probably be ready for sea by the time I could reach England (I have already mentioned that the original orders were modified to suit the new conditions), I was directed to set in train the general business of the Navy Department in Europe, and to take command of the second ship (the *Alabama*).

It was not anticipated that this change would occasion any perplexity, because the *Nashville* (Captain R.

* See 'British Case,' p. 58, etc.

B. Pegram) was supposed to be in England at that time, and thus a commander, with a complete staff of officers, could be provided for the *Oreto* with little or no trouble. The two vessels could be cleared for an appointed rendezvous, and the transfer easily and safely effected. The Secretary of the Navy informed me that he had written Captain Pegram to order such officers to the *Oreto* as I might require, and that officer would have been only too happy to find that under the changed circumstances he would have the opportunity to command the *Oreto* himself. Unhappily, the instructions did not reach Captain Pegram, and when I arrived in Liverpool I learned with regret that he had sailed for a Confederate port, and was far beyond reach. The situation was perplexing. The ship was an object of suspicion and disquietude to the United States Minister, who was pressing her Majesty's Government to detain her, and his importunities might prevail. No inquiries could discover that she was thus far in default—of this I felt assured ; but still, the Confederate Government had no acknowledged advocate, and the Government might 'strain the law,' as the Attorney-General admitted they did at a later period.

It was imperative to send the ship away. Lieutenant (afterwards Commander) J. N. Maffitt, had been sent to Nassau on special duty, and I had reason to believe he was there at that time. I knew Maffitt well. He was a man of great natural resources — self-reliant, and fearless of responsibility. I determined to despatch the ship to him at once, and I ordered Low to go in her. The *Oreto* sailed from Liverpool on the 22nd of March, and Mr. Low's instructions were as follows :—

'Liverpool, 21*st March*, 1862.

'Sir,

'You will take passage in the steam vessel* *Florida*, now about to sail for the Bahamas. This vessel, for reasons already explained to you, is sent out under the British flag, and in command of an English captain, and it is of the utmost importance that nothing shall be done to compromise her character as a neutral vessel until she is safely delivered to an officer of the Confederate navy, or some agent especially appointed by the Confederate Navy Department. You are hereby charged with the care of all public property on board, a duplicate list of which is herewith furnished you, and the captain has been instructed after arrival at the first port of destination to be governed by your orders as to the movements and disposal of the ship. As soon as you arrive at the Bahamas, you will communicate with Captain J. N. Maffitt, Confederate States navy, whom you will hear of through Messrs. Adderley and Co., of Nassau, and you will forward the accompanying despatch to the Hon. Secretary of the Navy, reporting also your arrival to him in writing. If Captain Maffitt or any other commissioned officer of the Confederate States navy is at Nassau, give him all the information you have in reference to the ship, hand him the invoice of stores, with the enclosed letter addressed to Captain Maffitt, and make the best of your way back to this country as quickly as possible, as I have duties of great importance for you here. Should you not find Captain

* The *Florida's* dockyard name was *Oreto;* the name first assigned to her by the Navy Department was *Manasas*, by which she is mentioned in some of the correspondence, but to avoid confusion, or frequent explanation, she will hereafter be mentioned in this narrative as the *Florida.*

Maffitt in Nassau, put yourself in communication through Mr. Adderley with Major Charles J. Helm or Mr. Louis Heyleger, one of whom will doubtless be in Nassau. Consult with those gentlemen as to the propriety of keeping the ship in Nassau, and remain with her until you hear from the Navy Department. You must be careful to appear always as a private gentleman travelling on his own affairs, and let your intercourse with all persons known to be connected with the Confederate Government be very guarded and cautious. With the gentlemen mentioned above, you can of course speak freely, but let your interviews be private, so as to escape notice as much as possible.

'It is impossible to give you instructions to cover every emergency. I have had experience of your discretion and judgment, and must rely upon them now. You will be furnished with money to pay your personal expenses, and to meet any small demands against the ship. As the *Florida* has an extra quantity of coal on board, and the captain has been ordered to make the passage mostly under canvas, it is presumed no material outlay will be required for some time. Should there be absolute need of additional funds, you will apply to Messrs. Adderley and Co., or to either of the aforementioned gentlemen, pledging the Navy Department, through me, for the amount. You will, however, under all circumstances, practise the most rigid economy. You will keep a careful memorandum of the ship's performances, under steam and sail, noting her steering, working, stability, and all particulars of the speed under different circumstances, and the degree of pitching and rolling under various conditions of sea and weather. Furnish information on these points to the officer who may relieve you, and keep a copy for me.

'Among the papers are drawings to show how the sweeps and traverses for the pivot guns are to be put down. These, with the guns and all necessary equipments, are on board the steamship *Bahama*, now about to sail for Nassau. If the officer who will take charge on the part of the Navy Department needs your services for a short time, you are at liberty to remain with him, but unless otherwise directed by the Hon. Secretary of the Navy himself, after he has received the enclosed letter, you will return to England at latest by the first day of June, as your services will then be indispensable to me.

'Wishing you a safe and speedy passage, and a satisfactory consummation of the purposes of your voyage,

'I am, etc.,

'(Signed) JAMES D. BULLOCH.

'Master John Low,
'Confederate States Navy.'

The following letters were given to Mr. Low, along with his instructions, to be delivered to Captain Maffitt, and to be forwarded to the Secretary of the Navy from Nassau :—

'Liverpool, 21*st March*, 1862.

'SIR,—

'Day after to-morrow I despatch for Nassau a gun-vessel, built in England under contract with me for the Confederate navy. In all sailing and steaming equipment she is very complete, but I have been forced to dispense with all outfit suited to her true character. It has been with much difficulty, and only by the most cautious management, that she has escaped seizure or indefinite detention here, and I send her as she is, the first regularly built war-vessel for our navy, to your care. Mr. Low, Master, Confederate States navy, goes in her to take charge of the public property on board, and to place her in the hands of any Confederate officer who may be in the West Indies on her arrival. I hope it may fall to your lot to command her, for I know of no officer whose tact and management could so well overcome the difficulties of equipping her, or who could make better use of her when in cruising order.

'It has been impossible to get the regular battery intended for her on board, but I have sent out four 7-inch rifled guns, with all necessary equipments in the steamship *Bahama*, bound to Nassau, and Mr. Low will give you all particulars as to her probable time of arrival, and will also hand you a list of everything on board the gun-vessel, as well as an invoice of the shipment by the *Bahama*. Another ship will be ready in about two months, and I will take the sea in her myself by some means or other, although I perceive many difficulties looming in the future.

'The country seems to be hard pressed, but I hope no one at home despairs of the final result. Two small ships can do but little in the way of materially turning the tide of war, but we can do something to illustrate the spirit and energy of our people, and if we can arrange to meet, may yet repay upon the enemy some of the injuries his vastly superior force alone has enabled him to inflict upon the States of the Confederacy. Write me as soon as you receive this, and give me full information of the state of affairs on the other side of the Atlantic, and if you get to sea in the little cruiser I send out, appoint a rendezvous. I am too much pressed for time, and have too lately arrived, to write more fully now, but will communicate with you again soon.

'I am, etc.,

'(Signed) JAMES D. BULLOCH.

'Captain J. N. Maffitt,
'Confederate States Navy.'

'Liverpool, *March* 21, 1862.

'SIR,—

'On the 14th inst., in a necessarily short letter, I informed you of the safe arrival of myself and party in England, and will now report more in detail upon the matters which relate to my especial duties here. . . . . Although arrangements have been made by which correspondence with the Confederate States can be carried on with more freedom than formerly, yet as there is always a probability of letters going astray, such as treat of public affairs must obviously be worded with caution, and names of persons and places be suppressed. . . . .

'The *M.* (*Florida*) is ready for sea, with crew, provisions, and all boatswains', carpenters', and sailmakers' stores necessary for several months on board, and I will despatch her on the day after to-morrow to a West Indian port, the exact locality of which will be reported to you in a subsequent letter, as well as from the ship as soon after her arrival as possible. It is hoped that she will be able to communicate immediately upon arrival with the officer you have already detailed for duty between the southern coast and the Bahamas, and for this purpose I will send in her the very trusty and prudent officer you appointed especially to assist me in such affairs as require me to keep in the background.

'It has been found impossible to place any munitions of war on board the *M.* She has been twice inspected by the Custom House authorities, in compliance with specific orders from the Foreign Office, to see that nothing contraband of war has been placed in her, and notice has been given that any attempt to smuggle such articles on board would at once be followed by her seizure. The hammock-nettings, ports, and general appearance of the ship sufficiently indicate the ultimate object of her construction, but there is nothing to compromise the pacific character she must necessarily assume for this voyage. Registered as an English ship, in the name of an Englishman, commanded by an Englishman, with a regular official number, and her tonnage marked upon the combings of the main-hatch, under the direction of the Board of Trade, she seems to be perfectly secure against capture, or even interference, until an attempt is made to arm her, or to change the flag, and this, it appears to me now, can only be effected at sea. The late unseemly conduct of the captain of the Federal ship *Tuscarora* has caused the British Admiralty to issue very stringent orders in reference to the treatment of United States and Confederate vessels in English ports, whether home or colonial.'

Here follow specifications of the Admiralty Orders, which have been already mentioned in a previous chapter, and some details in reference to the shipment *per* steamship *Bahama*, sending out officers, pay of crews for the cruising ships, etc.

'I am, etc.,

'(Signed) JAMES D. BULLOCH.

'Hon. S. R. Mallory,
'Secretary of the Navy.'

The *Florida* arrived at Nassau on the 28th of April, and the subjoined letter is Mr. Low's report:

The *Florida* pursuing the *Star of Peace. (Century Magazine)*

Captain J. N. Maffitt, Commander of the *Florida*.
(Century Magazine)

'Nassau, 1*st May*, 1862.

'Sir,—

'I have the honour to report to you the safe arrival at this port of the Confederate States steamer *Florida*, on the morning of the 28th of April, after a passage of thirty-seven days, which, in compliance with your instructions, has been made principally under canvas. We wished to be as economical as possible in regard to the consumption of fuel, but were rather unfortunate in having light winds and frequent calms, more especially in the Trades. During the latter we thought it prudent to steam, thinking that if we made too long a passage the steamship *Bahama* would be here some time before us. The amount of coal, as you are aware, was one hundred and seventy-five tons, including Welsh and English. Our consumption of the former was eighteen tons per day, and of the latter twenty-four. We have now on board good two days' coal, so I trust you will find, after taking into consideration the weather, and our reasons for not making a long passage, that we have been as economical as possible, not only as regards fuel, but with everything on board.

'I took particular notice of the vessel as regards her speed under steam and canvas, and am happy to report most favourably of her in all respects. Our average steaming is nine knots and a half; her sailing averages, with the wind abeam or quarterly, so that the fore and aft canvas will draw, twelve knots. The above is the average; I now give you what I have seen her do during the passage. Under steam, with smooth water, ten and a half knots, and under canvas alone, with quartering wind, so that we could carry main top-gallant studding-sail, thirteen and a half good.

'As regards stability, I do not think there is a

stronger vessel of her class afloat; when pitching, you could not see her work in the least, not so much as to crack the pitch in the waterway planks, where I believe a vessel pitching is as likely to show weakness as anywhere else.

'I am, etc.,

'(Signed) JOHN LOW.

'Commander J. D. Bulloch.'

In the concluding portion of the above letter, Mr. Low reported that Captain Maffitt was not at Nassau when he arrived, but was expected shortly, and by the advice of Mr. Heyleger he determined to keep the ship there, but moved her to 'Cochrane's' or the 'New Anchorage,' about six miles from the town, where there was deeper water, and where the ship would be less conspicuous. I received several reports from Mr. Low while he was detained at Nassau, and the subjoined extract from one of them will be interesting as evidence of the rigorous 'blockade' which the United States cruisers had established over the British Bahama channels, even at that early date:—

'The steamer *Stettin* arrived here on the 30th of April from Falmouth. A short distance off the island she was chased and fired at several times by a United States gunboat, but the *Stettin* being a faster vessel, she ran away from her. The gunboat fired twelve shot and shell at the *Stettin*—several, as the passengers inform me, came very near. During the firing the *Stettin* had the English ensign flying, but it appears they have no respect for that.'

On the 13th of May Low had the happiness to advise me of Maffitt's arrival, and that he had taken charge of the *Florida;* he reported that although everything had been kept as quiet as possible, yet there had been many surmises in reference to the movements of the ship, and he feared there would be trouble if she was detained much longer at Nassau. Fearing this myself, I had advised that she should be run into a Confederate port at once, if there seemed likely to be any difficulty, and there equipped, and this was eventually done; but Maffitt, on the spot, was encouraged to hope that he might get her guns shipped to some neighbouring Cay or some point on the banks, and there complete the equipment without the delay and risk of running the blockade.

I never permit myself to criticize the action of an intelligent energetic officer when he is present on the scene and I am not. Throughout all the trying difficulties Maffitt showed great patience, astonishing endurance, and unflinching pluck. He wrote me a number of letters about the troubles and delays, but the details of the seizure of the ship and the proceedings against her in the Vice-Admiralty Court at Nassau are fully reported in the proceedings before the Tribunal of Arbitration at Geneva, and need not be repeated here. A short summary will suffice.

The United States Consul at Nassau had his suspicions aroused very shortly after the arrival of the *Florida*, and began at once to press the authorities to examine and then to detain her. She was several times inspected by officers of the Royal Navy, who reported, what was quite manifest, that she was in all respects suited for the purposes of a vessel-of-war, but that she was not armed, and had no warlike stores on board. On the 15th of June some of the crew of the *Florida* (she was still called *Oreto*) went on board of her Majesty's ship *Greyhound*, and stated to Commander

Hinckley that they had left the *Oreto* because they were not able to ascertain her destination, and that she was endeavouring to ship another crew. Thereupon Commander Hinckley seized the vessel, but on the morning of the 17th she was released, the Attorney-General being of the opinion that there was not evidence sufficient to justify a seizure. Notwithstanding this opinion, however, she was again seized on the same day (June 17th) by orders of the Governor, and proceedings were forthwith instituted against her in the Vice-Admiralty Court of the colony for violation of the Foreign Enlistment Act. Many witnesses were examined, and the trial was continued until August 2nd, when the judge pronounced judgment. After reviewing the evidence, he declared it to be insufficient, and made a decree for the restoration of the vessel 'to the master claiming on behalf of her alleged owner.'

Under date of August 1st, 1862, Maffitt wrote me from Nassau: 'The arguments (*in re Oreto*) were brought to a close last evening, and the judge reads in court to-morrow his decree. We have a clear case, but if the decision is favourable to us, I fear the Governor will order an appeal. Notwithstanding all I say, the *O.* may be released; in that event, six hours will not find her here.'

Having been released by the decree of the Vice-Admiralty Court, Maffitt, acting always through the consignees of the ship, cleared the *Florida* outward as a vessel in ballast for St. John's, New Brunswick, and went out of the harbour to a position near Hog Island, to try the machinery and to refit. The ship had been much neglected while under seizure, and many articles had been taken out of her which could not be recovered. At this time vessels were loading daily at Nassau for the purpose of running the blockade. The schooner *Prince Alfred* was engaged by the consignees of the steamship *Bahama*, and was loaded with the armament and other stores intended for the *Florida*, but unfortunately Maffitt was not able to personally supervise the transhipment, and many essential articles were overlooked.

This was one of the great difficulties the Confederates had to encounter during the whole war. Agents of the United States Government could ship war material of every description without disguise or the fear of interference. There were no Confederate Consuls to make up and forward affidavits affirming that the vessels thus loading were intended to be armed as cruisers, and the statement that many vessels were loaded in British ports with rifles, cannon, ammunition, and military equipments for the United States, expressly for use in the war against the Confederate States, requires no proof at this late date.

Maffitt's open personal interference with the *Florida* would have resulted in further detention, probably in another seizure. Every detail was necessarily left to agents, who in this case acted certainly with absolute good faith, but who did not comprehend the full extent of his necessities. About August 9th the *Prince Alfred* cleared out for St. John's, and proceeded to sea as if with the purpose to run the blockade. The *Oreto* (*Florida*) being already outside near Hog Island, soon followed her, and both vessels proceeded in company to Green Cay, a small desert island on the edge of the great Bahama Bank, about sixty miles from Nassau. The United States ships *Adirondack* and *Cuyler* were in the neighbourhood, and they were informed of the *Prince Alfred's* movements and her probable connection with the *Florida*, as appears from a despatch from the United States Consul at Nassau to Mr. Seward, dated August 12th,* but they either kept an indifferent look-out or Maffitt gave them the slip. At Green Cay the armament and other stores were transferred from the *Prince Alfred* to the *Oreto*, the Confederate flag was hoisted for the first time, but not until she was quite clear of the Bank. The ship was then regularly commissioned, and the name was finally changed to *Florida*.

Although Maffitt was now afloat in a Confederate ship-of-war, he was in no condition to begin a cruise. The necessarily quick departure from Nassau after escaping from the clutches of the Vice-Admiralty Court had made it impossible to engage a sufficient number of men to work the ship, far less to fight a battery. He had, moreover, only one officer of experience, Lieutenant J. M. Stribbling.

The work of transferring the armament was very laborious. The hot August sun, combined with night exposure and general want of physical comforts, told upon them all, and the much-dreaded yellow fever, that scourge of the West Indies, broke out among the men. There was no surgeon on board, and the care of the sick was added to Maffitt's other responsibilities. United States cruisers were following him ; he himself was ill ; it would have been folly to keep the sea—indeed, it was impossible. He succeeded in evading the United States ships which were blockading the Bahama channels, and finally found his way to the port of Cardenas, in the island of Cuba, where he was kindly received by the citizens, and the authorities made no objection to his obtaining such supplies as were needed.

* The letter is among the documents laid before the Tribunal of Arbitration at Geneva.

From Cardenas Maffitt wrote me the subjoined hasty note :—

'Cardenas, *August* 20, 1862.

'MY DEAR BULLOCH,

'I took on board at sea all my battery, but many things in the haste and confusion were forgotten, such as rammers, sponges, etc. Had but two firemen and eleven men; have run the gauntlet splendidly, my Coast Survey experience being of great service. Where I went the Federal ships dared not follow, and here I am, with prospects of filling up my crew and obtaining what is necessary. The "*prize-crew*" committed many acts of robbery, and left the vessel in a terrible plight. . . . I hope to give a good account of myself soon, if I get the men. I write in great haste. Have Lieutenant Stribbling—good officer; acting-master Bradford, acting-midshipmen Bryan, Floyd, Sinclair—young men of no nautical experience. No doctor, no paymaster. I have now three cases of yellow fever; have had seven. Am doing well in that line. You remember my fondness for doctoring the crew. I was fortunate enough to avoid any connection with the *Oreto* until the day before we gave the Yankees the slip. Semmes was looked upon as the person ordered to command her, and after he left, that Stribbling was to take her to him at a rendezvous. . . . This is written in extreme haste, to catch a chance to send it to Helm at Havana. Good luck, and a God's blessing.

'Yours affectionately,

'(Signed) J. N. MAFFITT.'

In the foregoing letter Maffitt complained bitterly of the heedless conduct of a Confederate officer to whose indiscreet and uncontrollable looseness in conversation he attributed the seizure of the *Oreto* and her subsequent troubles. It would be as painful to my own feelings as to those of Maffitt to mention any name in such a connection, because the loyalty and good intentions of the person to whom he alluded were beyond suspicion; indeed, it may be fairly said that he was probably unconscious of his failings, and a secret leaked through his mind and found expression from his lips just as the breath permeating through the lungs passes by its natural channels to the open air. There are some men who are wholly without the faculty of concealment, who cannot disguise or suppress their knowledge of important events which are in course of secret preparation, who have not the patience to await results and then to take their share in the credit of having contributed to success, but who are irresistibly impelled to manifest by their manner and speech that weighty concerns have been confided to them, and that the issues thereof are likely to be momentous. Many carefully laid schemes were frustrated during the late war by lack of prudence and for want of self-control on the part of men who were devoted to the South, and from whom nothing to its injury could have been wrung by violence.

From Cardenas Maffitt sent Lieutenant Stribbling to Havana, to communicate with Major Charles J. Helm, who was the Confederate agent at that place, and to see what could be done there in the way of engaging men. In three or four days Stribbling returned with twelve men, and on the 28th of August Major Helm telegraphed that the Captain-General desired that the *Florida* would come round to Havana. On the 30th Maffitt got under weigh and proceeded to Havana, where he arrived on the 31st, but finding the restrictions so severe that it was impossible for him either to increase his crew or to make good his other deficiencies, he resolved to run the ship into Mobile.

While the *Florida* was at Cardenas Maffitt himself was forced to succumb to the fever, which had already more than decimated his small crew. His strong constitution, and the hourly demand upon all his faculties, had kept him up until the ship was safe, but with the rest and relief from incessant care there came a reaction, and the fever took advantage of his relaxed energies and made a well-nigh fatal attack. Dr. Gilliard, a surgeon in the Spanish navy, kindly volunteered his services, and Maffitt probably owes his life, partly at least, to the skill and benevolent efforts of that philanthropic gentleman.

Dr. Barrett, of Georgia (I wish I knew his Christian name), was at that time in Cuba. He heard of the *Florida's* helpless condition, volunteered his services as surgeon of the ship, and joined her, thus facing all the perils of her hapless condition, with no visible motive, except the wish to be helpful to those in distress, and no expectation of reward except the 'answer of a good conscience.'

The object of the Captain-General in requesting Major Helm to get the *Florida* away from Cardenas, and to induce Maffitt to bring her to Havana, is not fully apparent. He may have thought that she could be better protected from violence on the part of the United States ships at the latter than at the former port ; or he may have wished to have her more completely under his own eye, and where he could with more certainty prevent her obtaining any supplies or reinforcement of her crew which would constitute a violation of Spanish neutrality.

The stringent orders Maffitt found in force on his

arrival at Havana suggest that the latter object was the reason; and finding that he could neither refit nor obtain men at Havana, he promptly determined to run into Mobile. On the afternoon of September 1st, the *Florida* was clear of the Moro Castle, and was steering boldly across the Gulf, which was then the highway for United States transports she had not the power to attack, and which was swarming with United States cruisers she was helpless to resist.

At 2 p.m. on the 4th the lighthouse on Sand Island, and then Fort Morgan, at the entrance to Mobile Bay, were made; but between the sheltering port and the devoted little craft lay three of the enemy's war ships. Maffitt had no purpose to retire and draw off the blockaders, and then endeavour to double and get in-shore of them. His determination from the first was to dash straight in whenever he made the land. But he hoped to get fairly among them, or even a little beyond, before they suspected his true character or purpose. With this object in view, he hoisted the British ensign and pennant, and stood on directly for the blockading squadron.

Commander Preble was the senior officer of the blockading force, and he placed his ship, the *Oneida*, directly in the *Florida's* course, the other ships taking up good supporting positions. When the *Florida* got close to the *Oneida*, Preble hailed and ordered her to stop. Maffitt perceived that he must either obey or draw upon the British flag an indignity, and he hauled it down and steered so direct for the *Oneida* that Preble was forced to reverse his engines to avoid a collision. There was no longer any disguise; the *Florida* was recognised, and Maffitt pushed on past the *Oneida*, taking her broadside at little more than pistol-shot. There is, so far as I know, no record of such a scramble as followed. The *Florida* stood steadily on for the bar, receiving broadside after broadside from the three United States ships.* She did not even cast loose a gun, because there were no men to fight them, and as there was nothing to distract the enemy's fire, it is marvellous they did not literally blow her to pieces. For nearly two hours the *Florida* stood this pelting *feu d'enfer*, drawing away little by little from her relentless pursuers, and at last the poor little crippled craft limped like a wounded stag into the friendly port, and anchored under the protection of Fort Morgan.

No shot or shell had got among the *Florida's* machinery, but she was much cut up. The fore-top-mast and fore-gaff were shot away, all the boats were cut to pieces, the hammock-nettings were nearly all swept off on one side, the main rigging was cut adrift, and she was hulled in many places. One 11-inch shell had passed clean through her just above the water-line, and another had entered the captain's cabin, fortunately without exploding.

During this unparalleled chase and escape, Maffitt sat most of the time on the quarter-rail, and steered straight for the bar; Stribbling was cool and self-possessed, and not one of the young officers or men flinched. Every man of true courage will say that this was a gallant deed, and will feel a generous regret that men of so much fortitude should have had no opportunity to show their metal except in the test of passive endurance.

It is not the purpose of this history to narrate in detail the cruises of the several vessels which were built

* Two of the blockaders, the *Winona* and the *Rachel, Seaman* did not get to very close quarters, but still they had a good chance for gun practice at the *Florida.*

or bought in Europe for the Confederate States. The late Admiral Semmes published before his death a full account of his adventures in the *Sumter* and *Alabama*, the journals of the *Florida* have been also published, and there have been accounts more or less complete of the performances of the other ships. I shall therefore give mere summaries of their movements, limiting my remarks upon their cruising careers to such incidents as suggest general reflections in respect to maritime warfare, or which have some special bearing upon the question of belligerent rights and practices.

The *Florida* needed extensive repairs and almost a new outfit, to make good her losses and injury at Nassau, and the terrible punishment she had received from the *Oneida* and her consorts; but at Mobile there was no dock, not even a slip upon which she could be placed, and almost everything required for outfit and armament had to be brought from a distance, the ordnance stores from far-away Richmond.

It was not until December that all necessary work was finished, and the *Florida* did not get to sea until some time in January, 1863. The blockading force had meanwhile been largely increased, with the special purpose to prevent the *Florida's* escape, and she had to wait some weeks before there was a favourable opportunity. The bold run into Mobile was justifiable only on the ground of its seeming necessity. An attempt to pass outward through the blockaders in the same daring manner would have been reckless and unworthy of Maffitt's reputation for prudence as well as courage. The opportunity came at last. One day, January 15th, 1863, there were signs of a 'norther' and everything was got ready for a run. At nightfall the gale began. There was no sheltering rain, but the wind was almost dead off-shore, the dark-blue surface of the Gulf was lashed into foam, and the spume of the sea was flying half-mast high. These northers in the Gulf of Mexico are spiteful, but no good well-found ship need fear leaving the weather-shore in one of them. The blockaders were no doubt doing their best to hold on to the land, for they must have thought the *Florida* would make the attempt to escape. She did, and got clear, although she was seen, and chased nearly across to Havana.

Maffitt did not remain long in the confined waters of the Gulf, but reappeared at Nassau, the scene of his first troubles, on the 25th of January, 1863,* where he remained only one day. From Nassau he cruised down to the southward through the West Indian Islands, touching at Barbadoes, February 24th, and Pernambuco, in Brazil, May 8th. At the last named place he stopped four days to get fresh provisions and make some repairs to his engines. Getting away from Pernambuco, May 12th, he cruised for a short time off the coast of Brazil, and worked his way up to St. George's, Bermuda, where he arrived July 16th, 1863.

During the *Florida's* run through the West Indies, Rear-Admiral Wilkes, of *Trent* notoriety, was commanding the United States naval forces in those latitudes, and he seems to have been looking especially after Maffitt, and to have had some inkling of his necessities, although not particularly well informed in regard to his whereabouts. On the 26th of February Admiral Wilkes wrote to his Government thus: 'The fact of the *Florida's* having but a few days' coal makes me anxious to have our vessels off the Martinique, which is the only island at which they can hope to get any coal or supplies, the English islands being cut off under the rules of her

* 'British Case,' p. 68.

Majesty's Government for some sixty days yet, which precludes the possibility, unless by chicanery or fraud, of the hope of any coal or comfort there.'* Two days before the date of Admiral Wilkes's letter, *i.e.*, February 24th, 1863, the *Florida* went into Barbadoes, and got what coal she required without practising either 'chicanery' or 'fraud,' but upon Captain Maffitt's simple statement that his fuel had been exhausted from stress of weather. In the 'British Case, Geneva Arbitration,' p. 68, it is stated on the authority of the Governor that both the United States ship *San Jacinto* and the Confederate ship *Florida* had been permitted to obtain coal at Barbadoes within a less period than three months after they had respectively coaled at another British colonial port, the commander of each vessel having alleged that his supply of fuel had been exhausted by stress of weather.

In the 'Case of the United States' it is demonstrated by official documents that the Governor of Barbadoes was mistaken in the supposition that the *San Jacinto* had received a supply of coal at a British port within three months; but it is not pretended that he had reason to doubt the fact at the time of the occurrence, because he mentioned it in a subsequent conversation with Admiral Wilkes, as the precedent which he had followed in extending a like privilege to the *Florida.* The Governor did not construe the regulations as applicable to cases of distress, and in his report he states that both vessels were 'dealt with as being in distress.'† The *Florida* was, however, only permitted to take on board about ninety tons of coal, which act of grace nevertheless offended Admiral Wilkes, and

* See 'United States Case, Tribunal of Arbitration,' p. 96.

† 'British Appendix,' vol. i., p. 92.

Destruction of the clipper ship *Jacob Bell* by the *Florida.* *(Harper's Weekly)*

The *Tacony*, commissioned at sea by the *Florida* to destroy shipping along the North Atlantic coast. *(Harper's Weekly)*

afforded the occasion for an indiscreet and intemperate protest. It is surprising to perceive how quickly a certain class of the United States naval officers adopted the phraseology of the politicians at Washington, and soiled their reports and marred the dignity of their official correspondence by the use of inelegant and opprobrious epithets in describing the conduct of their opponents, whose only offence was that they had conscientiously, and manifestly to their own injury, taken a different view of a great political question.

The *Florida's* short cruise in the West Indies and on the coast of Brazil caused much uneasiness in the commercial ports of the United States. The war premium advanced, and merchants hastened to register their ships in the names of British subjects, and to put them under the British flag. The *Alabama* was also by this time at sea and actively at work, as will afterwards appear, and her operations added to the panic.

The principal ships captured and destroyed by the *Florida* during the cruise above mentioned were the *Aldebaran*, *Commonwealth*, *General Berry*, *Crown Point*, *Lapwing*, *M. J. Colcord*, *Southern Cross*, *Oneida*, *Star of Peace*, *Rienzi*, *William B. Nash*, *Red Gauntlet* and *Henrietta*. I have before me, at the moment of writing, the ransom bonds of four other vessels which were taken by Maffitt from their respective captains, it appearing upon investigation that they were loaded on account of neutrals. Ship *Sunrise*, $60,000,* ship *Kate Dyer*, $40,000, ship *F. B. Cutting*, $40,000, schooner *V. H. Hill*, $10,000. The *Florida* left Bermuda July 25th, 1863, and arrived at Brest August 23rd. On the passage she captured the American ships *F. B. Cutting* and the *Avon*, but released the former.

* See p. 199 for copy of bond.

Besides the vessels above mentioned which Maffitt captured with the *Florida*, he captured the *Clarence* off the coast of Brazil, and fitted her out as a tender, and with her destroyed the *Kate Stuart*, the *Mary Alvina*, the *Mary Schindler*, and the *Whistling Wind*. On May 10th, 1863, he captured the *Tacony*, and finding her better suited to his purpose than the *Clarence*, he burnt the latter, and transferred her crew and armament to the *Tacony*. In conjunction with this vessel he captured the *Ada*, *Byzantian*, *Elizabeth Ann*, *Goodspeed*, *L. A. Macomber*, *Marengo*, *Ripple*, *Rufus Choate*, and *Umpire*.

On June 25th, 1863, he captured the *Archer*, transferred guns and crew from *Tacony* to *Archer*, and burned the former, and a few days after the boats of the *Archer* went into the harbour of Portland, Maine, and destroyed the United States revenue cutter *Caleb Cushing*.*

The *Florida's* arrival at a European port at that time was wholly unexpected by me, for I had received no communication from Captain Maffitt since his escape from Mobile, and had no advice of his intended movements. Maffitt, on his part, was ignorant where I was, although he knew that Liverpool was the most likely place to find me. Immediately upon the *Florida's* arrival at Brest, Maffitt reported to the Préfet Maritime, Vice-Admiral Count de Gueyton, the necessity which had compelled him to seek the shelter of a French port; and the first reply of the Admiral was that the ship might receive coals and other supplies, and effect necessary repairs on the same conditions as any 'merchant ship.' But the *Florida* needed a thorough refitting. On the 3rd of September Maffitt sent an officer to

* The officer who commanded the *Florida's* tenders and who executed the dashing affair at Portland was Lieutenant C. W. Read. The whole number of prizes taken during Maffitt's cruise was fifty-five.

Liverpool to see me personally, and to report defects and requirements, which were many and important. The officer brought me a letter from Maffitt, from which the following is an extract :

'We must dock, relieve our shaft, which has got out of line, and replace some of our copper. We want also a blower to get steam with the bad coal we are often obliged to put up with. While in Mobile we did all that could be done, and that was but precious little, for we lay in the middle of the bay, and the poverty of the city was painful in the extreme. Since leaving Mobile we have been under a constant pressure, without a friendly port in which to overhaul or give ordinary attention to the engines.'

I immediately sent a competent representative of the builders of the ship and engines to Brest to examine the *Florida*, and to report her condition. There was no commercial dock at Brest, but after some demur permission was given to use a Government dock. The *Florida* remained in dock five or six weeks, and the French authorities, when they became satisfied of her real wants, permitted them to be supplied in full. The rough handling to which the *Florida* had been subjected had told upon her armament as well as upon her general equipment. Permission was given to land the small arms to be overhauled by a local gunsmith, upon a guarantee through the Customs authorities that they would be re-shipped without any addition in quantity. Application was made to land some of the gun-carriages for the same purpose, but this was refused. However, two carriages and the necessary gear were made at Nantes for the pivot guns, and were delivered to the ship off the island of Belle Isle, together with some fusees and other articles contraband of war, without in any way violating the neutrality of France.

The repairs at Brest occupied several months, because applications had to be frequently made to the authorities for leave to do what was necessary as the need was discovered; and the requests had not only to be considered by the local authorities, but often referred to Paris. But there was difficulty, embarrassment, and delay from circumstances relating to the *personnel* of the *Florida*, as well as from the wear and tear of her hull, machinery, and armament. On the 3rd of September Captain Maffitt informed me officially by letter that he had been compelled to discharge a large number of his men at Brest, and had supplied each of them with money sufficient to carry him to Liverpool. He said that he had informed the men that they would not be entitled to be paid their wages in full unless they returned to the Confederate States, but they would be directed on the subject by me.

In writing an historical narrative it is necessary to record events which are often not of especial moment in themselves, but which in their consequences cause difficulties and create obstacles to the achievement of purposes with which they seem at first to have no connection, and they cannot therefore be omitted.

It will appear in a subsequent chapter that the *Florida's* arrival and delay in Brest, but especially the discharge of a portion of her crew there, caused infinite embarrassment, and contributed to the failure of an enterprise which would have been of incalculable advantage to the Confederate cause. Maffitt, of course, knew only of his own necessities, and his duty was therefore to do his best under the circumstances in which he was placed. His ship required overhauling, and he brought her to a port at which the defects could be made good, and from which he could communicate with the agent of the Confederate Navy Department, and he did not anticipate, neither could he have foreseen, that he would thus cause any trouble elsewhere.

The discharge of the men referred to above left the *Florida* so weak-handed that she would not have been fit to resume her cruise, and it was necessary to replace them. Application was made to the French authorities for leave to fill up the vacancies. There was at first some hesitation, and the application was referred to Paris. It appears from the proceedings before the Tribunal of Arbitration at Geneva that there was a good deal of correspondence on the subject between Mr. Dayton, the United States Minister, and M. Drouyn de l'Huys, the French Minister of Foreign Affairs, of which at the time we could know nothing. Mr. Slidell (the Confederate Commissioner), however, knew that the matter had been discussed by the Imperial Cabinet, and after due process of gestation the application was granted. M. Drouyn de l'Huys stated to Mr. Dayton that the Government had caused inquiries to be made, and had ascertained that seventy or seventy-five men had been discharged from the *Florida* at Brest, because the period for which they had been shipped had expired, and that the Government had concluded not to prohibit 'an accession to the crew, inasmuch as such accession was necessary to her navigation.'*

This, it must be admitted, was a strange and somewhat unusual proceeding, but we Confederates had no concern with the matter as a diplomatic controversy, or as a question of international law. The *Florida* wanted

* See 'British Case,' North America, No. 1 (1872), pp. 71, 72. Correspondence of Mr. Dayton.

a number of seamen, and the only question with Maffitt was, how to get them without violating the municipal laws of France, or imposing upon the credulity and friendly consideration which he had received from the local authorities at Brest. It would seem to be an easy matter to engage and get on board seventy seamen in a maritime port, but there was very great difficulty, and much time was consumed in accomplishing that apparently simple purpose. The permission to replace the discharged men did not carry with it the right to enlist them for the Confederate service even in France, and of course it gave not the semblance of a right to do so in England. The *Florida* wanted English-speaking seamen, and these had to be sought for chiefly across the channel. The men were engaged in small groups wherever they could be found, and were forwarded to Calais and other French channel ports, and then taken by rail to Brest. This was the only possible arrangement, and it required the employment of several agents, whose discretion was not always reliable. Manifestly the men could not be told what they were wanted for until they got on board the *Florida*. The mystery of the proceedings attracted notice, the suspicion of several of the United States Consuls was aroused, and they did their best to discover the true purpose of the unusual but systematic movement of nautical-looking men, with conductors in charge, and to defeat it.

With so much to accomplish, and by such indirect and tedious means, it is not surprising that the *Florida* was detained a long time in Brest; in fact, she was not ready for sea until February, 1864. All that the *Florida* required could have been completed satisfactorily in a few weeks, if she could have gone to any of the large English building-yards—say on the Clyde or Mersey—

and there have done the work openly and in the ordinary commercial way, and the expense would have been moderate. But the constant peril of being stopped for an alleged violation of neutrality, the necessary applications to official personages on every small matter of detail, the hesitations, references to Paris, and general circumlocution, caused great loss of time, and a large increase in the expenditure. The local authorities were most considerate and courteous, and for that very reason it was imperative to scrupulously respect their instructions and limitations, so as not to involve them in any trouble.

I have given the simplest possible synopsis of the cost and labour of refitting a Confederate ship. Full details would, I really think, astonish the reader, but the foregoing will suffice to suggest, if it does not abundantly demonstrate, the immense disadvantages under which the Confederate Government laboured in the effort to keep a small naval force at sea.

Very shortly after the arrival of the *Florida* at Brest, Maffitt's health completely gave way. The attack of yellow fever at Cardenas had left him in a weak state. Subsequent exposure brought on rheumatism of the heart. When at Bermuda in July, 1863, he had informed the Secretary of the Navy that he would feel bound to obtain a relief on the arrival of the ship in Europe, if he did not get much better, and as soon as the arrangements for the repairs were fairly in train, he resigned the command. Several Confederate naval officers were then in Paris, for purposes which will be subsequently explained. One of these, Commander J. N. Barney, relieved Maffitt, and he had much of the worry and labour of refitting the ship, but his health was not strong, and in January it became so feeble that he was compelled to retire, and he was relieved in the command by Lieutenant C. Manigault Morris, about January 4th.

The *Florida* was still short-handed, but there were men enough to handle the ship and work her pivot guns, and the Confederate cruisers were always able to recruit from prizes.

Morris got to sea from Brest on the 12th of February, 1864, took his new gun-carriages on board off Belle Isle, February 19th, and then proceeded to cruise through the West Indies, and up to the northward in the direction of the American coast. He touched at Martinique, April 26, for coal and supplies, called at Bermuda, May 12th, merely to communicate and land a sick officer, and went to that island again on June 18th, where he was permitted to make some necessary repairs and take in a small supply of fuel. July 27th he was off again, and made a bold dash straight in for the enemy's coast, which took him across the track of outward-bound ships. On the 10th of July, thirty miles off the Capes of the Delaware, he captured the United States mail steamer *Electric Spark*, bound from New York to New Orleans, with the mails and a number of passengers on board. Morris transferred the crew and passengers to a passing English schooner, which he chartered for the purpose, and then cut the steamer's pipes, opened her valves and ports, and thus permitted her to sink. During the run in shore from Bermuda the *Florida* captured and burned the following ships:—*Harriet Stevens*, *Golconda*, *Margaret Y. Davis*, and *Mondamin*. Manifestly the little Confederate cruiser could not remain in that neighbourhood long. The purpose was to alarm the enemy by a 'raid' on the line of his coasting trade, and having struck the blow, Morris ran across to Teneriffe, and then cruised leisurely across the line towards the north-eastern coast of Brazil, burning whatever prizes he made (in all about thirteen), including those captured during the run in and off the American coast.

On the 4th of October, at 9 p.m. the *Florida* anchored at Bahia, the purpose being to get supplies, make some slight repairs, and refresh the crew after a long and active cruise; for, in point of fact, there had been no chance to give the men a run on shore since the departure from Brest on the 12th of February. By this time the *Florida* was in good condition to fulfil the objects of those for whose service she was built. Officers and crew were in fine spirits, and hoped to accomplish a good deal of work still, although American ships were fast disappearing from the high seas, or at least they were rapidly sheltering from capture under the British mercantile flag. But there was another fate in waiting for the gallant little ship. She had braved and survived the lawful, though murdering, attack of the United States ships off Mobile; she surrendered to the treacherous and illegal assault of another United States ship at Bahia. The first encounter was a fair open 'stand and deliver,' the second was an assassination. This is a harsh word. It has been forced from me. The English language does not offer a milder phrase to fitly distinguish the occurrence, or I would gladly adopt it, but I feel, nevertheless, bound to justify the epithet.

It was dark when the *Florida* anchored, on the evening of October 4th. At an early hour on the morning of the 5th the customary visit of ceremony and inquiry was paid to her by the Brazilian naval authorities, and it was perceived that a United States ship-of-war was at anchor not far off, which proved to be the United States steam corvette *Wachusett*, Commander N. Collins. At about noon of the same day

Morris had an interview with the President of the Province, by special appointment, to explain his wants, and to get a reply to the request he had made to the Brazilian Admiral for permission to remain the necessary time to make some repairs to the engine, which request the Admiral had referred to his Excellency. The Admiral was present at the interview, and the result was very satisfactory to Morris. The President promptly consented to his remaining the customary forty-eight hours, to which time all belligerent vessels were limited, but added that if upon the report of a marine engineer, who would be sent on board to inspect, it should appear that the repairs could not be completed in that time, he would grant an extension sufficient to meet the requirements of the case.

The President, in the course of further conversation, remarked upon the presence of a United States ship-of-war in the bay, and impressed upon Morris that he would expect and rely upon him to do nothing that might occasion a hostile collision with her. He added that the United States Consul had given him a solemn assurance on behalf of Captain Collins that the *Wachusett* would do nothing while in the port which was contrary to the laws of nations, or in violation of the neutrality and sovereignty of Brazil, and expressed the desire that Morris would give him a corresponding promise, which he did. At this point the Admiral remarked that the *Florida* and *Wachusett* were lying in close proximity, and he suggested that Morris should move the *Florida* to a position between his (the Admiral's) ship and the shore. After the interview with the President, Morris went immediately on board and shifted his berth to the anchorage suggested by the Admiral. The marine engineer spoken of by the

President had preceded him, and soon reported that the repairs would require four days.

Morris now being quite easy in mind with regard to the privilege of remaining in port, and feeling no apprehension of an unpleasant, and certainly believing that there could be no hostile, collision with the *Wachusett*, or any of her belongings, determined to give his crew 'liberty.' The ship was put in usual harbour trim, the guns were unloaded, the running gear was flemished down, the awnings spread, and the port watch (one half the crew) were permitted to go on shore. The next day, October 6th, the 'liberty men' began to return on board at an early hour, and when most of them had returned, the starboard watch was sent on shore, Captain Morris and a party of the officers going at the same time.

When night set in on that 6th of October, 1864, the state of affairs was this: The *Florida* was lying in-shore of the Brazilian Admiral's ship (a small wooden sailing sloop-of-war), and the *Wachusett* was some distance off, and on the other or off-shore side of the Admiral. The first-lieutenant, J. K. Porter, with ten officers of all grades, and about seventy men, most of whom had just returned from 'liberty,' were on board the *Florida*, and Captain Morris, four officers, and the remainder of the crew were on shore. At about 3 a.m. on the morning of the 7th, Lieutenant Porter was aroused by the officer of the deck, Acting-master T. T. Hunter, who reported to him that the *Wachusett* was under weigh, and was standing towards the *Florida*. Lieutenant Porter had not turned in, but was asleep on a sofa in the commander's cabin, and being dressed, he got very quickly on deck, when he saw the *Wachusett* close aboard, and steering directly for them. Before he could give an order, or even hail the approaching ship, she ran violently into the *Florida*, striking her on the starboard quarter. The force of the collision crushed in the bulwarks, started several beams, broke the main-yard, and carried away the mizen-mast, which came down in three pieces. The *Wachusett* at or about the same time fired two shots from her battery, and opened a musketry fire upon the startled crew of the *Florida*, who, thus unexpectedly aroused, could have made no effective resistance, even if they had been armed, being embarrassed, and indeed prevented from even seeing the attacking ship, by reason of the awning, which, borne down by the wreck of the mizen-mast and its gear, covered and confined them as if in a net.

In the confusion of the collision, Lieutenant Stone managed to get clear of the awning, and standing upon a gun, he fired one shot from his revolver. About fifteen of the crew jumped overboard, but only six reached the shore. Those who succeeded in swimming safely to the shore reported to Captain Morris that they had been fired at while in the water by the men on the forecastle and in the boats of the *Wachusett*, and that the missing men had probably been killed or drowned. Immediately after the collision the *Wachusett* backed off a short distance and hailed the *Florida*, demanding an immediate surrender, on pain of being sunk there and then. After a moment's hesitation, and a hasty consultation with Lieutenant Stone, Lieutenant Porter replied that he would surrender. The *Florida* was then boarded, a hawser was made fast to her, and the *Wachusett* towed her to sea.

I have condensed the foregoing statement into the smallest possible space and into the briefest possible phrases, because I have thought it would be best and fairest to all parties to let them give their own version, and the official reports and statements with reference to the whole occurrence, together with the correspondence between the Brazilian Legation at Washington and the United States Secretary of State, will be found in full at the end of the chapter.

That portion of Captain Morris' report which refers to what took place on board the *Florida* during the attack was, as he himself says, gathered from the six men who succeeded in swimming ashore, and I am satisfied they were mistaken in saying that there was repeated firing on either side. From personal inquiry I feel assured that not more than two pistol-shots were fired from the *Florida*. I am inclined to think there was only one, by Lieutenant Stone, in the manner related above; on the other hand, I cannot learn that the *Wachusett* fired into the *Florida* after backing clear, although the men who escaped asserted that they were fired at in the water.

My object in giving a brief summary of the circumstances attending the capture of the *Florida* is to supply the text for the general remarks I feel called upon to make upon the whole occurrence, in order to justify the use of the word 'assassination' which I have applied to it, without being forced to refer frequently to the official documents, which the reader can consult at his convenience. There could hardly be a more flagrant and offensive violation ofnational sovereignty than that which Captain Collins committed upon the Empire of Brazil; but it is no part of my purpose to discuss the incident with reference to its diplomatic or legal bearings. I have no sentimental notions in regard to the precepts of public law, or the demands of international comity. I know full well that strong Powers have treated such considerations with indifference and contempt, whenever it suited their purpose to do so. Nelson sailed into Copenhagen and destroyed a great part of the Danish fleet without orders, even if not in violation of them, when England and Denmark were not at war, and he set up no pretence in justification, but simply affirmed that the safety and interests of his own country required him to act in that energetic way.* Captain Hillyar, with the British ships *Phœbe* and *Cherub*, followed the United States ship *Essex* into the harbour of Valparaiso, attacked, and after a desperate resistance captured her under the very guns of a Chilian battery, but both of those acts were done openly in the light of day, and in bold defiance of all consequences. When Buenos Ayres was fighting her war of independence with Spain, a ship-of-war of the 'so-called' insurgents, the *Federal*, boarded an American vessel on the high seas, and took out of her some goods alleged to be Spanish property. The *Federal* put into the Swedish island of St. Bartholomew soon after, and found there, or was followed in by, the United States ship *Erie*, Captain Daniel Turner. Captain Turner made a demand upon the Governor for the surrender of the *Federal* to him, she having done violence to the American flag. The Governor refused, on the ground that the ship in question was a commissioned vessel-of-war, belonging to a recognised belligerent Power, and Captain Turner sent in the *Erie's* boats, under command of his first-lieutenant, Josiah Tattnall, and cut her out from under the guns of the fort. The acts of

* 'Pictorial History of England,' vol. vi., book x., p. 162. When asked by the Crown Prince of Denmark why the British fleet had forced its way up the Baltic, Nelson replied, 'To crush and annihilate a confederacy formed against the dearest interests of England.'

the two Captains Hillyar and Turner were indefensible upon the principles of international law and comity as generally understood, but in neither case was the commander under a personal engagement, implied or otherwise, to respect the neutrality of the countries in whose waters the offences were committed. They simply acted in defiance of law, and were prepared to take the consequences.

There is no evidence that Captain Collins gave any personal assurance to the President of Bahia in reference to his conduct while in that port. He makes no allusion to the subject in his official report ; but that is not conclusive either one way or the other. I think those who read the various reports will not doubt that the Consul, Mr. Thomas F. Wilson, did give the assurance required by the President on behalf of the *Wachusett*, and it was his business, his imperative duty, to inform Captain Collins what he had done.

But apart from all technicalities and quibbles, it is perfectly well known that the regulations under which the Neutral Powers permitted the ships of the two belligerents in the American Civil War to enter and remain in their ports, were founded upon the assumption that in return for the hospitalities and shelter granted, there was an honourable and unqualified undertaking to respect the neutrality of the ports. Whenever a United States or a Confederate ship let go her anchor in a neutral port and asked leave to remain, her commander could only accept the privileges he asked under the above conditions, and when the alternative of compliance or departure was not directly and specifically proposed, it was from a feeling of delicacy on the part of the local authority, and of confidence in the good faith of the individual commander.

We come, then, to this final proposition. In stating it I hope to avoid the appearance of exaggeration. The United States ship *Wachusett* lay in the harbour of Bahia, in company with the Confederate ship *Florida* two days, both ships being under an obligation to keep the peace as the condition of their leave to remain. But when the *Wachusett*, by her quiet demeanour, had dispelled all doubt and apprehension, not only in the mind of Captain Morris, but in the minds of the Brazilian authorities as well, she crept stealthily, under cover of night, and struck her adversary a foul blow when there was no power to ward it off, and no possible ground for suspecting it. If Captain Collins had dashed into the harbour in the full light of day, and had made his attack upon the *Florida* without fear of the consequences, the proceeding would not have been more offensive to Brazil, nor would it have been a greater violation of her sovereign rights than the course he adopted, and he would have been equally sure of capturing, or at least destroying his enemy, because she would have been quite unprepared to make effective resistance, and the whole transaction demonstrates that the Brazilian Admiral's ship was too weak and inefficient to exercise any preventive force.* If the *Wachusett's* assault upon the *Florida* had been in the above manner, it could have been classed with that of the *Phœbe* and *Cherub* upon the *Essex*, or the boats of the *Erie* upon the *Federal*, and I should have been spared the pain of denouncing it as an assassination.

Captain Collins offers in justification, or at least in palliation of his offence against the sovereign rights of Brazil, the allegation that the *Alabama* had been permitted to burn some American ships near the island of

* See 'Admiral's Report,' p. 210.

The *Florida* captured by the U.S.S. *Wachusett*. *(Harper's Weekly)*

Captain C. M. Morris, Commander of the *Florida* when it was captured.
(Harper's Weekly)

Captain Napoleon Collins, Commander of the U.S.S. *Wachusett.*
(Harper's Weekly)

Fernando de Noronha, within the jurisdiction of the Empire without remonstrance, and he therefore thought it 'probable' that his attack upon the *Florida* would be treated with the same leniency. Captain Collins could have had no personal knowledge of the occurrence he mentions, and probably got the alleged fact from the United States Consul, who also put it in his letter to the President, requesting, or rather 'claiming,' that the *Florida* should in effect be treated as a pirate.* Admiral Semmes, in his history of the *Alabama's* cruise, writing from his diary, and without any knowledge of Captain Collins's counter allegation, gives the true version, which is that he burned the *Louisa Hatch* and the *Kate Cory*, 'taking the pains to send them both beyond the marine league, that I might pay due respect to the jurisdiction of Brazil.'†

The letter of Mr. Thomas F. Wilson to the President of Bahia is a fair example of the diplomatic literature with which the consular agents of the United States tried the patience and vexed the polite sensibilities of the local authorities to whom they were accredited during the Civil War. Brazil, in common with all the other Powers, great and small, had acknowledged the Confederate States as a belligerent, with a *de facto* Government, which conceded to them the same right to com mission ships-of-war as the United States had; and yet Mr. Thomas F. Wilson was apparently unconscious of the incivility and impolicy of asserting in an official communication to a high civil officer of the empire that the *Florida* was 'not commissioned by any recognised Government whatever,' that her officers and crew were

* See 'British Case,' p. 74.

† 'My Adventures Afloat,' by Admiral Raphael Semmes. London: Bentley, 1869.

'not subject to any international or civilized law,' and were consequently 'not entitled to the privileges and immunities conceded to vessels navigating under the flag of a civilized nation,' and then in conclusion setting up a 'claim' that the 'piratical cruiser' should be 'detained to answer,' etc.,* by which the writer probably meant that the officers and crew should be looked upon as Malay pirates, and treated accordingly.

The Brazilians are a very polite race. They are punctilious in the practice of official propriety and decorum. Their officials are easily conciliated by deferential treatment and outward forms of respect. They are very affable and obliging when approached with complaisance and frankness, but are reticent, suspicious, and unyielding at the slightest approach to rudeness or duplicity. I can well imagine the mingled feelings of surprise and repulsion with which his Excellency Antonio Joaquim da Silva Gomes, President of the Province of Bahia, read the letter of Thomas F. Wilson, Consul of the United States, and the effort it must have cost him to suppress his feelings within the limits of the mild and gentlemanly rebuke contained in the last paragraph of his reply.

When the *Wachusett* steamed out of the bay of Bahia with the *Florida* in tow, the Brazilian Admiral pursued her with the force at his disposal; but his three vessels were so small and so inefficiently armed, that he could have had no expectation of compelling the release of the *Florida*, and his demonstration was therefore only a spirited protest against the act of violence which had been committed under his eye. The *Wachusett*, towing the *Florida*, and with sail on both vessels, had no difficulty in getting away from her pursuers, and she finally

* Letter, p. 200.

arrived at Hampton Roads with her prize on the 12th of November.

On the arrival of the two ships at Hampton Roads the Secretary of State, Mr. William H. Seward, must have been promptly informed of the occurrence, and he must have known that the act of Captain Collins was wholly indefensible. His duty as a statesman, careful and jealous for the honour of his country as well as for its safety, would seem to have been quite clear. He admits, in his reply to the complaint of the Brazilian Minister at Washington, that 'the capture of the *Florida* was an unauthorized, unlawful, and indefensible exercise of the naval force of the United States within a foreign country, in defiance of its established and duly recognised government.' It is hardly possible to conceive that he should have hesitated one moment in deciding to release the *Florida*, and in offering an apology to Brazil, which would have been so much more gratifying to the recipient, and honourable to the giver, if promptly and spontaneously tendered. But Mr. Seward waited to see what the Brazilian Government would do. He knew that it would be some time, probably two or three months, before that Government could instruct their Minister at Washington, and he seems to have preferred yielding to a demand rather than to proffer a frank explanation.

At last the demand came, on the 12th December, through the Brazilian Legation at Washington, and Mr. Seward made the *amende*, in a despatch hardly ever paralleled in its tone of arrogant and offensive recrimination.

Brazil was too weak to protect the *Florida*. She was equally powerless to resent the injury this ungracious apology must have inflicted upon her pride. Diplomatically, her demands were complied with, but the *status quo* was never restored. Pending the arrival of the anticipated complaint from Rio de Janeiro, the *Florida* was permitted to founder in Hampton Roads, by a judiciously managed oversight in examining her valves, so Mr. Seward could not restore the ship. There were twelve or thirteen thousand dollars in gold in the paymaster's safe when the *Florida* was captured, a part of which belonged to the officers' mess. Mr. Seward did not mention that fact to the Brazilian Minister, nor was a single penny of it supplied to the officers when they were discharged from Fort Warren, after a rigorous confinement of about three months.*

The treatment of those officers is one of the most painful and discreditable incidents in this unhappy affair. When the *Wachusett* arrived in Hampton Roads the prisoners were sent *en masse* to the military prison at Point Look-out, where the officers and men were separated, and the officers were in a few days transferred to the 'Old Capitol Prison' at Washington. After three or four days' confinement in that gaol, they were sent back to the *Wachusett* at Hampton Roads, and were all conveyed by her to Fort Warren, a fortress on an island in the harbour of Boston, which had been converted into a 'lock-up' for prisoners-of-state as well as of war. In this cheerless place, and under the trying conditions specified in Lieutenant T. K. Porter's official report,† they were imprisoned until February 1st, 1865, which was nearly seven weeks after Mr. Seward had stated, in an official despatch to the Brazilian Minister at Washington,‡ that 'the capture of the *Florida* was an *un-*

* See Lieutenant Porter's official letter to Mr. Secretary Gideon Welles, p. 223.

† See Report, p. 219. ‡ Letter, p. 216.

authorized, *unlawful*, and *indefensible* exercise of the naval force of the United States,' and that the crew of the *Florida* were '*unlawfully* brought into the custody of this Government,' namely, the Government of the United States.

But this is not all. When the officers were set at liberty, they were forced to sign an undertaking that they would leave the United States within ten days from the date of their release. They were without any means to pay their expenses, and Lieutenant Porter wrote an application to Mr. Gideon Welles, the Secretary of the United States Navy, for a return to him of the money which had been captured in the *Florida*, and which, to the extent of the amount of pay due them, was as much the private property of the captured officers as Mr. Gideon Welles' watch was his, to say nothing of the obligation, under the conditions of the *amende* to Brazil, to restore the whole of it to Lieutenant Porter as the senior officer of the *Florida*.

To that application Mr. Gideon Welles did not see fit to reply; he did not even practise the commonplace courtesy of acknowledging its receipt, and the officers were turned into the streets of Boston, and among a population which was then hostile, with no means to pay their way out of the country, and yet under a forced engagement to depart within ten days. Lieutenant Porter was able to arrange for a passage for himself and party to England in the Cunard steamship *Canada*, by giving a draft on the Confederate financial agent, and they reached Liverpool about the middle of that month, and came to me very much in the condition of distressed seamen sent home under consular certificate.

I submit the foregoing without comment, as a plain unvarnished statement of the manner in which Mr.

Secretary Seward made the *amende* to Brazil for what he himself denounced as an '*unauthorized*, *unlawful*, and *indefensible* defiance' of her neutral rights, and of the spirit in which he affected to restore the *status quo*.

An historical narrative cannot be limited to a mere record of events in the form of a diary. The occurrences must be illustrated sometimes by explanatory comments, and by comparing or contrasting them with events or with actions upon which public judgment has already been pronounced. A military or naval officer in command of a national force loses, to a certain extent, his personal identity. He is merged in his office, and may thus be criticized without reference to his individuality or the personal qualities which make up his private character. Captain Collins was always looked upon as an honourable and truthful man in his intercourse with friends and acquaintances. If a proposition of doubtful propriety were suggested to him, I should feel sure that, if left to himself, he would come to a fair and just resolution, and that he would not leave it in the power of friend or foe to charge him with bad faith. With reference to his conduct in the adventure with the *Florida*, upon which it has been my painful office to comment, it seems to me that he made the mistake of placing himself in the hands of Mr. Consul Thomas F. Wilson, who appears to have imbibed the acrimonious temper of his departmental chief, and to have adopted the harsh epithets and the opprobrious phrases which that high officer of State did not think it unbecoming to introduce into his diplomatic correspondence when it was necessary to mention those who were opposed to him in the great Civil War.

Since Mr. Seward has thought it proper and dignified

to maintain in an official despatch* that 'that vessel (the *Florida*), like the *Alabama*, was a pirate,' and to further state in the same document that 'the crew,' among whom he contemptuously includes the officers, 'were enemies of the human race,' it seemed imperative upon me, as the historian of the little craft's origin and adventures, not only to relate the closing events of her brief career, but to comment upon the manner of bringing them about. I have no feeling of enmity against anyone. It would grieve me to know that I had wounded the feelings of one who was, in former years, a brother officer, or that I had cast an aspersion upon the service in which I once held a commission, by heedless statements or ill-digested comments. I confidently believe that in what I have felt it my duty to write there has been no warping of the facts, but that I have kept faithfully to the record. But the reader himself can judge, because I have annexed the official reports of all the persons involved in the affair.

DOCUMENTS ABOVE REFERRED TO.

FORM OF RANSOM BOND TAKEN FROM PRIZES WHEN RELEASED (SEE P. 177).

This bond, made and entered into this seventh of July, one thousand eight hundred and sixty-three (A.D. 1863), by and between Richard Luce, master and commander of the American ship *Sunrise* of the first part, and John N. Maffitt, lieutenant-commanding in the navy of the Confederate States of America of the second part, witnesseth:

That the said party of the first part is held and firmly bound (for himself, the ship and her owners) unto Jefferson Davis, President of the Confederate States of America, or his successors in office, in the full and penal sum of sixty thousand dollars ($60,000), to be well and truly paid, in gold or its equivalent, within six calendar months

* See p. 216.

after the ratification of a treaty of peace between the Confederate States and the United States.

The condition of this bond is such that the aforesaid party of the first part has this day been captured on the high seas, while in command of the ship aforesaid, by the Confederate States sloop-of-war *Florida*, whereof the party of the second part is commander, and has been allowed to proceed on his voyage without injury or detriment to the ship or cargo, and has been guaranteed against molestation during the present voyage from any and all armed vessels in the service of the Confederate States of America.

Done in duplicate on board the Confederate States sloop-of-war *Florida*, the day and date above written.

Witness: THOMAS BARRY, First Officer.
Witness: G. D. BRYAN, Mdn. C.S.N.

RICHARD LUCE (*seal*), Master-Comdg.
J. N. MAFFITT (*seal*), Lieut.-Comdg. C.S.N.

[*Copy.*]

THE UNITED STATES CONSUL TO THE PRESIDENT OF THE PROVINCE OF BAHIA.

To his Excellency Antonio Joaquim da Silva Gomes, President of the Province of Bahia.

Consulate of the United States of America,
Bahia, *October 5th*, 1864, 9 a.m.

SIR,—

This morning a steamer anchored in this port, bearing the flag adopted by those who are involved in the rebellion against the Government of the United States of America, and I am informed that the said vessel is the *Florida*, which is engaged in capturing vessels navigating under the flag of the United States of America, and in destroying them by making bonfires of them and their cargoes.

The vessel in question is not commissioned by any recognised Government whatever, and her officers and crew are composed of persons of various nationalities, who are not subject to any international or civilized law, and are consequently not entitled to the privileges and immunities conceded to vessels navigating under the flag of a civilized nation. I therefore protest, in the name of the United States of America, against the admission of this vessel to free practice, by which she might be enabled to supply herself with coal, provisions, tackle, or utensils of any kind whatever, or receive on board any persons whatever; finally, against any assistance, aid or protection which might be conceded to her in this port, or in any other belonging to this province.

I likewise claim that the piratical cruiser, which in combination with the pirate *Alabama* violated the sovereignty of the Imperial Government of Brazil, by capturing and destroying vessels belonging to citizens of the United States of America within the territorial waters of Brazil, near the island of Fernando de Noronha, in April, 1863, be detained, with all her officers and crew, in order to answer for so flagrant a violation of the sovereignty of the Government of Brazil, and of the rights of citizens of the United States within the jurisdiction of the Brazilian Government.

I avail, etc.,
(Signed) THOMAS F. WILSON,
Consul of the United States.

THE PRESIDENT OF THE PROVINCE TO MR. WILSON.

Palace of the Government of the Province of Bahia,
October 5th, 1864.

In a note dated this day, Mr. Thomas F. Wilson, Consul of the United States, claims that the steamer *Florida*, now anchored in this port, shall not be admitted to free *pratique*, nor obtain permission to provide herself with coal, provisions, supplies, and utensils of any kind whatever, nor receive on board any person whatever; he likewise requests that, as the cruiser, in combination with the *Alabama*, violated the sovereignty of the Imperial Government of Brazil by capturing and destroying vessels belonging to citizens of the United States of America within the territorial waters of the Empire, near the island of Fernando de Noronha, in April, 1863, she may be detained, with all her officers and crew, in order to answer for this flagrant violation of the sovereignty of the Government of Brazil, and of the rights of citizens of the United States, within the jurisdiction of the Brazilian Government.

In reply to the Consul, I have to inform him that, as the said vessel belongs to the Confederate States, in whom the Imperial Government recognised the character of belligerents, all the assistance required by humanity may be furnished her, which does in no wise constitute assistance for warlike purposes, as laid down by international law, and does not conflict with that neutrality which this

Government studiously seeks to preserve, and has always preserved, in the contest between the States of North America. The undersigned cannot, therefore, admit the first portion of the claim of the Consul, in the general manner in which it was presented, and particularly in relation to those articles considered as contraband of war, in conformity with instructions issued on that subject by the Imperial Government, and according to which the said vessel will only be permitted to remain in this port for the length of time absolutely indispensable.

In regard to the second part of his note, it is my duty to observe to the Consul that, even if it were fully established that the *Florida* had previously violated neutrality, such a proceeding would scarcely authorize us to refuse her permission to enter the ports of the Empire, and would never warrant us to commit the acts required by the Consul, which would be equivalent to a hostile rupture, without the intervention of the supreme Government of the State, which is alone competent to authorize such a rupture.

I renew, etc.,

(Signed) ANTONIO JOAQUIM DA SILVA GOMES.

To Mr. Thomas F. Wilson, Consul of the United States.*

[*Copy.* No. 38.]

To the Honourable Gideon Welles, Secretary of the Navy.

United States steamer *Wachusett*,
St. Thomas, W. I., *October* 31*st*, 1864.

SIR,—

The following is a detailed report of the capture of the rebel steamer *Florida* in the bay of San Salvador, Brazil, by the officers and crew of this vessel, without loss of life:—

At three o'clock on the morning of the seventh day of October instant, we slipped our cable and steered for the *Florida*, about five-eighths of a mile distant. An unforeseen circumstance prevented us from striking her as intended; we, however, struck her on the starboard quarter, cutting down her bulwarks, and carrying away her mizen-mast and mainyard. This ship was not injured.

* For the letter from the United States Consul to the President of Bahia and the reply of the President, see 'British Case,' pp. 74, 75.

Immediately upon striking we backed off, believing she would sink from the effects of the blow.

In backing clear we received a few pistol-shots from the *Florida*, which were returned with a volley, and contrary to my orders two of our broadside guns were fired, when she surrendered.

In the absence of Captain Morris, who was on shore, Lieutenant Thomas K. Porter, formerly of the United States Navy, came on board and surrendered the *Florida*, with fifty-eight men and twelve officers, making at the same time an oral protest against the capture.

Five of the *Florida's* officers, including her commander, and the remainder of her crew, were on shore.

We took a hawser to the *Florida* and towed her to sea.

In contemplating the attack on the *Florida* in the bay, I thought it probable the Brazilian authorities would forbear to interfere, as they had done at Fernando de Noronha, when the rebel steamer *Alabama* was permitted to take into the anchorage three American ships, and to take coal from the *Louisa Hatch* within musket-shot of the fort, and afterward, within easy range of their guns, to set on fire those unarmed vessels.

I regret, however, to state that they fired three shotted guns at us while we were towing the *Florida* out.

Fortunately we received no damage. After daylight a Brazilian sloop-of-war, in tow of a paddle gun-boat, was discovered following us. With the aid of sail on both vessels we gradually increased our distance from them.

We had three men slightly wounded ; one only of the three is now on the sick report.

I enclose a list of the prisoners. Those who have a star opposite their names were formerly in the United States navy.

This vessel is ready for service. The *Florida* will require repairs of machinery, a new mizen-mast, etc.

The officers and crew manifested the best spirit. They have my thanks for their hearty co-operation, in which I beg to include Thomas F. Wilson, Esq., United States Consul at Bahia, who volunteered for any duty.

I am, sir, very respectfully

Your obedient servant,

N. Collins, Commander.

[*Copy.* No. 39.]

To the Honourable Gideon Welles, Secretary of the Navy, Washington City.

United States Steamer, *Wachusett*,
Hampton Roads, Va., *November* 14*th*, 1864.

SIR,—

The following is a supplement to my report, No. 38, dated October 31st, 1864:—

1. On the morning of the 7th of October last, I directed to be cast adrift one of our whale-boats, just returned from reconnoitring the rebel steamer *Florida*, rather than attract attention of outside persons by the noise of hoisting her.

2. At the time of starting to run into the rebel steamer *Florida* on the 7th day of October last, I ordered thirty fathoms of our cable to be slipped without a buoy, as I feared the rope of the latter might possibly foul the propeller.

3. Our second cutter swamped alongside the prize steamer *Florida* while we were towing the ship to sea, and was cut adrift to avoid detention in range of the Brazilian guns. As the tide was flood, both the whale-boat and cutter will probably be recovered by the United States upon the payment of salvage.

Their probable value was, for the cutter, one hundred and fifty, and for the whale-boat, fifty dollars.

4. Thomas F. Wilson, United States Consul at Bahia, desired to remain on this ship during the nights of the 5th and 6th October last, in anticipation of a probable conflict at sea with the rebel steamer *Florida*, and was on board at the time of the capture of the latter vessel. As it was not convenient to land him, I brought him to this place.

5. At the island of St. Bartholomew, West Indies, where we called for supplies, every facility was granted us, although we had one case of varioloid on board. I trust the Department may make some official acknowledgment to the Governor of that island for his civility to us.

6. Walter Dulany, a citizen of Baltimore, a passenger on the American ship *Mondamin*, and captured by the rebel steamer *Florida* with the former vessel, was found on the *Florida* when we captured her, occupying such a position among the *Florida's* officers, some of whom were former friends and acquaintances, that I would suggest the policy of either holding him as a prisoner or of compelling him to take the oath of allegiance to the United States.

7. The authority to discharge such of our crew as have served out their period of enlistment is respectfully requested. Some have been on increased pay since June last, consequent upon having been detained beyond the time for which they shipped.

8. We touched at St. Bartholomew, West Indies, on the 29th October ult., and at St. Thomas on the 30th, where we remained till the 2nd inst., sailing on that day, and arrived here on the 12th.

I have the honour to be, very respectfully,

Your obedient servant,

N. Collins, Commander.

THE SEIZURE OF THE *FLORIDA.*

LIEUTENANT-COMMANDING MORRIS'S OFFICIAL STATEMENT.

Bahia, *October 13th*, 1864.

Sir,—

It is with great pain that I have to report the seizure of the Confederate States steamer *Florida*, lately under my command.

I arrived at this port on the 4th inst., at 9 p.m., to procure coal and provisions, and also to get some slight repairs after a cruise of sixty-one days. Just after anchoring, a boat passing around us asked the name of our vessel, and, upon receiving our reply, stated that the boat was from her Britannic Majesty's steamer *Curlew.* Next morning I found that the United States steamer *Wachusett* was at anchor near us, but no English steamer, so I at once concluded that the boat which had hailed us the evening before was from the *Wachusett.*

We were visited on the morning of the 5th by a Brazilian officer, to whom I stated my wants, and was informed by him that he would report the same to the President, and that until his answer was received we could hold no communication with the shore. At noon I received a communication—which was left on board the *Florida*—from the President, stating that he was ready to receive me. At our interview he informed me that forty-eight hours would be allowed me to fit and repair, but that, should his chief engineer, whom he would send on board to examine the machinery, deem the time too short, he would grant the necessary extension. He was most urgent in his request that I should strictly observe the laws of neutrality, at the same time stating to me that he had received the most solemn assurance from the United States Consul that the

United States steamer would do nothing in port contrary to the laws of nations and of Brazil; and that he desired the same from me, which I unhesitatingly gave.

The Brazilian admiral, who was present at the interview, suggested that I had better move my vessel in between his ship and the shore, as our proximity to the *Wachusett* might cause some difficulty. My assurance to the President seemed to set his mind at rest on the score of any collision between the two vessels, and upon leaving him I immediately repaired on board and moved the *Florida* close inshore to the position suggested by the Admiral. I found the Brazilian engineer on board and was informed by him that it would require four days to repair the pipe of the condenser. Feeling now no apprehension of any difficulty occurring while in port, and wishing to gratify the crew with a short liberty, not only on the score of good conduct, but also of health, I determined to permit one watch at a time to go ashore for twelve hours, and sent the port watch off that afternoon. About 7.30 p.m. a boat came alongside, stating that she was from the United States steamer *Wachusett*, with the United States Consul, who had an official communication for the commander of the *Florida.* The letter, with the card of the Consul, was handed to First-Lieutenant Porter, who, after examining it, and finding it directed to Captain Morris, "sloop *Florida*," returned it unopened to the Consul, stating that it was improperly addressed; that the vessel was the Confederate States steamer *Florida*, and that when the letter was so directed it would be received. The next day (6th) a Mr. de Vidiky came on board, having received a letter from the United States Consul, enclosing one for me. He requested me, before receiving my letter, to permit him to read to me the one sent to him.

It was a request of Mr. de Vidiky to carry a challenge to the commander of the *Florida*, and in case of its acceptance, to offer his (the Consul's) influence in having the repairs of the *Florida* speedily finished. I informed Mr. de Vidiky that I had heard quite enough, and, finding the letter to me improperly addressed, declined receiving it; but at the same time said to him that I had come to Bahia for a special purpose, which being accomplished, I should leave; but I would neither seek nor avoid a contest with the *Wachusett*, but should I encounter her outside the Brazilian waters, would use my utmost endeavours to destroy her. That afternoon, the port watch having returned, I sent the starboard watch, the other half of the crew, ashore on liberty, going also myself, in company with several of the officers. From our nearness to the *Wachusett*, persons on board that vessel could well see these men leave the ship. At 3.30 a.m. I was awakened by the proprietor of the hotel at which I was staying, and told that there was some trouble on board the *Florida*, as he had heard firing and cheering in the direction of the vessel, but on account of the darkness was unable to discern anything. I immediately hastened to the landing, and was informed by a Brazilian officer that the United States steamer *Wachusett* had run into and seized the *Florida*, and was then towing her out of the harbour. I hurried off to the Admiral's vessel, and was told by him that he was at once going in pursuit, which he did as soon as steam was raised on board a small steamer belonging to the fleet.

The Admiral's ship, being a sailing sloop-of-war, was taken in tow by the steamer and went out of the harbour. He returned in the afternoon with all his vessels, having been unable to overtake the *Wachusett*. Upon mustering the officers and crew left on shore, I found there four officers, viz., Lieutenant Barron, Paymaster Taylor, Midshipman Duke, and Master's-Mate King, and 71 men, of whom six escaped by swimming from the *Florida* after her seizure. Of the actual occurrences and loss of life on board the *Florida*, I have been able to find out very little. The substance of what I have gathered from the six men who escaped is as follows: That at 3.15 a.m. on October 7th, Master T. T. Hunter, Jr., being in charge of the deck, the *Wachusett* left her anchorage, and taking advantage of the darkness, steamed for the *Florida*, from which she was not seen until close aboard, when she was hailed by Mr. Hunter, who, receiving no answer, called 'all hands' to quarters. Before the officers and crew were all on deck the *Wachusett* struck the *Florida* on her starboard quarter, cutting her rail down to the deck and carrying away her mizen-mast, at the same time pouring a volley of musketry and a charge of canister from her forecastle pivot gun upon our decks. The *Wachusett* then backed off and demanded our surrender, to which demand Lieutenant Porter declined to accede. The enemy then fired again and again into us, which was returned by the officers and crew of the *Florida*.

Another demand was then made for our surrender, and Lieutenant Porter answered, 'I will surrender conditionally. The enemy then stopped firing, and the commander called for Captain Morris to come on board; Lieutenant Porter answered that Captain Morris was on shore, and that he, as commanding officer, would come on board as soon as he could get a boat ready. The enemy then sent a number of armed boats to take possession of the *Florida*. As soon as

Lieutenant Porter was heard to surrender, fifteen of our crew jumped overboard to escape capture, of whom only six succeeded, the remaining nine having been shot in the water by the men on the forecastle and in the boats of the *Wachusett*. Mr. Hunter was wounded and a number of men killed. The enemy made fast a hawser to the foremast of the *Florida*, and, after slipping her cable, towed her out to sea.

I called in person on the President as soon as possible, but could get no further information from him. On the 8th I sent a protest to the President, of which I send you a copy, marked 2. On the 10th our agent was informed by the interpreter that the President did not intend to answer my protest, as the Confederate Government had not been recognised by Brazil, and that I could find all the official correspondence in the newspapers.

I then wrote a letter marked 3, in which reference is made to a letter marked 4. Just before leaving Bahia, having received no answer, I sent our agent, Mr. James Dwyer, to the President. The result of his visit is contained in his letter, marked 5. The Bahia papers contain a number of reports as to the killed and wounded on board the *Florida*, all of which I have thoroughly sifted, and find no foundation for the same.

At the time of her seizure there was about twenty-five tons of coal on board, most of which was dust. The list of officers captured is contained in the report of Paymaster Taylor, marked 6.

The enclosed newspaper is an official extract containing all the Brazilian correspondence in reference to the *Florida*.

I am, very respectfully,

Your obedient servant,

(Signed) C. MANIGAULT MORRIS,

Lieutenant-Commanding, Confederate States Navy.

[*Copy.*]

LETTER OF THE PRESIDENT OF BAHIA TO THE AMERICAN CONSUL.

To Mr. Thomas Wilson.

Bahia, *October 7th,* 1864.
Palace.

SIR,—

Having reached this Presidency the grave attempt committed by the steamer *Wachusett*, of the United States of North America, and which, violating the neutrality of the Empire, treasonably and disrespectfully during the night set at defiance the respect due to the Empire, and in the harbour took prisoner the steamer *Florida*, setting aside the most sacred rights of people and civilized nations, that guards between nations belligerent any such acts, having this Presidency received the word of honour of the Consul, Mr. Wilson, to preserve the neutrality, that in explicit terms promised that the Commander of the steamer *Wachusett* should confine himself to his duties, and respect the neutrality due to the Empire, and not practise any hostile act in these territorial waters. The President cannot refrain from solemnly protesting against the act referred to, the more so that the Consul is therein implicated, seeing that, spite of his formal promise, he has not taken any measure to withdraw from the responsibility of this action. And as this fact and the silence preserved up to this date evidently prove that the President cannot confide in his endeavours to preserve the neutrality and sovereignty of the Empire, it is resolved to at once interrupt all official relations with him until further orders from the Government, where this unexpected and deplorable act will be related, and where, in its higher knowledge, final decision will be given. The Consul is in the meantime duly informed that orders are given to the respective authorities that in no 'harbour' of the Province the steamer *Wachusett* will be allowed entrance, resorting, if necessary, to force for this end. According to the terms of the instructions promulgated on the 23rd of June past by the Minister for Foreign Affairs, this, if the steamer obstinately and criminally persists in continuing in this manner, to infringe the rights imposed by the dignity of its own flag.

(Signed) ANTONIO JOACHIM DA SILVA GOMES.

LETTER FROM THE COMMANDER OF THE 2nd NAVAL DIVISION TO THE PRESIDENT OF BAHIA.

To the President.

Steamer *Paraense*, Bahia, *October 7th*, 1864.

ILLUS. E EX. SENHOR,—

It is my duty to state to your Excellency that to-day at daybreak the United States of America steamer *Wachusett*, without having previously given any symptom of moving, suddenly left the anchorage where she was, and approached the Confederate States steamer *Florida*. When she passed by the poop of the corvette *D. Januaria*, where I was, I intimated that she should anchor, and not doing so, sent an officer on board to give notice that all the ships of the division, as well as the forts, would fire if she attacked the *Florida*. To this intimation the commander replied that he should comply, and do nothing further, and that he would return to his anchorage, as your Excellency will see by the paper annexed signed by the officer who gave this notice.

Notwithstanding, the corvette, to ratify the intimation, fired a gun loaded with ball. Following, notwithstanding, her way outside, as it appeared to me to return to her anchorage, I observed as she passed by the bow that she was tugging the *Florida*. Immediately this steamer fired in the direction of the steamer *Wachusett* cannon loaded with ball; but escaping this attack, sailing in the direction of the bow, thus rendering useless the fire from the corvette, and I therefore ordered to cease firing. Having previously ordered that the *Paraense* should be made ready to move, I immediately that this was possible sailed, and went after her, seeing that the breeze was light, and made signal to the yacht *Rio de Contes* to follow us to the waters, which she did with all possible speed, sailing in our wake.

We chased the *Wachusett* outside the harbour as she tugged the *Florida*, both of which were little more than three miles off. I trust your Excellency will believe that when I left this port it was with the decided determination of sacrificing every consideration present and future to fight her, notwithstanding the small amount of force on which I could reckon, in order to vindicate the insult offered to the sovereignty of the country, thus taking by main force the steamer *Florida*; and this thought I expressed to the officers on leaving the harbour as they were united in the cabin, showing them the requirement in which we found ourselves to sacrifice every consideration without a thought to consequences, seeing that the proceeding of the commander of the *Wachusett* was of a nature to arouse the indignation of every Brazilian. A general and enthusiastic manifestation of complete adhesion to my opinion was the reply given by all the officers; and I am convinced that the other ships that accompanied me felt the same noble sentiments.

At seven o'clock in the morning the *Paraense*, tugging the yacht, gained considerably on the two American steamers, and I began to nourish the hope that we should satisfy our desires, when the wind calming, which the *Wachusett* soon perceived, always tugging the *Florida*, began steaming, increasing gradually the distance between our ships and their steamers flying before our bow, and being of considerably superior swiftness. Nevertheless, we chased them until eleven o'clock and forty-five minutes, when disappearing, I determined on returning to the port, returning to the *Paraense*, leaving outside the corvette and the yacht, with orders also to return to this harbour, where I dropped anchor at a quarter past three.

Before finishing this communication, I ought to give notice that a few moments before leaving this harbour I received offers from the Inspector of the Arsenal and Captain of the Port of assistance, or anything in their power, which I accepted, begging them to send me as many armed sailors as was possible. But it being necessary to use the greatest possible urgency in order to catch the flying steamers, I believed I ought not to wait, and immediately quitted without waiting for the offered help, also failing to wait on your Excellency for the same motive, according to the message I received.

God preserve your Excellency.

(Signed) GERVASIO MACEBO,

Commander of the Division.

NOTE.—The two foregoing letters are printed *verbatim* from the translations made by the public interpreter at Bahia, at the time of the occurrence. They were given in the above form to Captain Morris, and handed by him to me on his arrival in England. It has been thought best to reproduce them without putting the phraseology into better idiomatic English, for fear that the precise meaning of the writers might be inadvertently altered in the effort to express the sense in an easier and more graceful flow of language.

[*Copy.*]

LETTER FROM THE BRAZILIAN MINISTER AT WASHINGTON TO THE UNITED STATES' SECRETARY OF STATE.

(*Translation.*)

To his Excellency the Hon. William H. Seward.

Imperial Legation of Brazil,
Washington, *December* 12*th*, 1864.

The undersigned, Chargé d'Affaires *ad interim* of his Majesty the Emperor of Brazil, has just received orders from his Government to address himself without delay to that of the United States of North America about an act of the most transcendent gravity done on the morning of the 7th day of October last, in the port of the capital of the Province of Bahia, by the war steamer *Wachusett*, belonging to the navy of the Union, an act which involves a manifest violation of the territorial jurisdiction of the Empire, and an offence to its honour and sovereignty.

On the 4th day of the month referred to, there entered that port, where already had been lying for some days the *Wachusett*, the Confederate steamer *Florida*, for the purpose declared by her commander to the President of the province, to supply herself with alimentary provisions and coal, and to repair some tubes of her machinery.

The President, proceeding in accordance with the policy of neutrality which the Empire resolved to adopt on the question in which unfortunately these States are involved, and in conformity with the instructions in this respect issued by the Imperial Government on the 23rd of June of the year last past, assented to the application of the *Florida*, and fixed the term of forty-eight hours for taking in supplies, and fixing, in dependence on the final examination by the engineer of the Arsenal, the determination of the residue of the time which, peradventure, should be deemed indispensable for the completion of the repairs.

The same authority at once took, with the greatest impartiality, all the measures necessary to avoid any conflict between the two hostile steamers.

The *Florida* was placed under cover of the batteries of the Brazilian corvette *D. Januaria*, on the inshore side, at the request of her commander, who, reposing on the faith with which, without doubt, the chief authority of the province could not fail to inspire him, considered himself sheltered from any attack of his adversary, and in this confidence not only stayed a night on shore, but gave liberty to a great part of the crew of his vessel.

It behoves me to say that, as soon as the Confederate steamer entered the port of Bahia, the American Consul, Wilson, addressed to the President a despatch claiming that the *Florida* should not be admitted to free pratique, and that on the contrary she should be detained, alleging for this, that that vessel had, in concert with the *Alabama*, violated the neutrality of the Empire by making captures in 1863, near the island of Fernando de Noronha.

Such exaggerated pretensions, founded on facts not proven, which had already been the subject of discussion between the Imperial Government and the legation of the United States, could not be even listened to.

If the President should have refused the hospitality solicited by the commander of the *Florida*, he would have infringed not only the duties of neutrality of the Empire, but also those of humanity, considering that steamer, coming from Teneriffe, had been sixty-one days at sea, was unprovided with food. and with machinery in the worst condition.

Afterwards, the President having stated to the same Consul that he hoped, from his honour and loyalty toward a friendly nation, that he would settle with the commander of the *Wachusett* that he should respect the neutrality and sovereignty of the Empire, he was answered affirmatively, the Consul pledging his word of honour. Things were in this condition, the term of forty-eight hours being to expire at one o'clock of the afternoon of the 7th, when, about dawn of that day, the commander of the steamer *Wachusett*, suddenly leaving his anchorage, passed through the Brazilian vessels-of-war and approached the *Florida*.

On passing across the bows of the Brazilian corvette *D. Januaria*, he was hailed from on board that he must anchor; but, as he did not attend to this intimation, and continued to approach the *Florida*, at the same time firing a gun and some musketry, the Commander of the Naval Division of the Empire stationed in those waters sent an officer to board the *Wachusett* and inform her commander that the ships of the division and the forts would open fire upon her if she should attack the *Florida*. The Brazilian officer was not allowed to make fast to the *Wachusett*, but the officer of the deck hailed him, saying in reply that he accepted the intimation given, that he would do nothing more, and that he was going to return to his anchorage.

The commander of the Brazilian division then thought proper to ratify his intimation by firing a gun, upon which a complete silence followed between the two ships *Wachusett* and *Florida*. At the time this was passing the corvette *D. Januaria*, on board which the commander of the division had hoisted his flag, lay head to flood, the steamer *Florida* anchored B. B., side by side of her, and quite close to the shore, and between her and the corvette the *Wachusett* stopped her wheels.

The Commander of Division then observing—notwithstanding the darkness of the night—that the *Wachusett*, from the position in which she was, kept moving onward, and was passing ahead of the corvette, in a course E.B., became convinced that, in fact, she was steering for her anchorage, thus complying with the promise made.

But a few moments afterwards, perceiving that the *Florida* was in motion, the commander discovered that the *Wachusett* was taking her off in tow by means of a long cable.

Surprised at such an extraordinary attempt, the commander immediately set about stopping this, and redressing, at the same time, as behoved him, the offence thus done to the dignity and sovereignty of the Empire.

But availing himself of the darkness of the night and other circumstances, the commander of the *Wachusett* succeeded in carrying his prize over the bar, and escaping the just punishment he deserved.

The Consul, Wilson, preferred to abandon his post, withdrawing on board the *Wachusett*.

The Government of his Majesty, as soon as it had official information of the event, addressed to the legation of the United States at Rio Janeiro a note, in which, giving a succinct exposition of the fact, it declared that it had no hesitation in believing it would hasten to give to it all proper assurances that the Government of the Union would attend to the just reclamation of the Empire as promptly and fully as the gravity of the case demanded.

In correspondence with this expectative note, the worthy representative of the United States was prompt in sending his reply, in which he declares he is convinced that his Government will give to that of the Empire the reparation which is due to it.

Such are the facts to which the undersigned has received order to call the attention of the Honourable William H. Seward, Secretary of State of the United States.

The principles of international law which regulate this matter, and in respect of which there is not the least divergence among the most distinguished publicists, are common, and known to all. The undersigned would fail to recognise the high intelligence of the Honourable Mr. Seward, if, perchance, he should enter in this respect into fuller developments.

He limits himself then only to recall a memorable example, in which these principles, invariably sustained by the United States, had entire application. In 1793, the great Washington then being President of the United States, and the illustrious Jefferson Secretary of State, the French frigate *L'Embuscade* captured the English ship *Grange* in Delaware Bay, thus violating the neutrality and the territorial sovereignty of the United States. The American Government remonstrated energetically against this violation, and required from the Government of the French Republic, not only the immediate delivery of the captured vessel, but also the complete liberation of all the persons found on board. This reclamation was promptly satisfied. Much more grave, certainly, is the occurrence in the port of the province of Bahia which makes the subject of the present note. By the special circumstances which preceded and attended it, this act has no parallel in the annals of modern maritime war.

The commander of the *Wachusett* not only gravely offended the territorial immunities of the Empire, passing beyond the laws of war by attacking treacherously, during the night, a defenceless ship, whose crew, much reduced, because more than sixty men were on shore with the commander and several officers, reposed unwary beneath the shadow of the protection which the neutrality of the Empire guaranteed to them; and so open was the violation, so manifest the offence, that the enlightened American press was almost unanimous in condemnation of the inexcusable proceeding of Commander Collins.

On this occasion, remembering the United States, whose antecedents are well known and noted in history by the energetic defence and respect for neutral rights, of these unshaken principles, the undersigned cannot consider the event which occurred at Bahia otherwise than as the individual act of the commander of the *Wachusett* not authorized or approved by his Government, and that it will consequently give to the Government of his Majesty the Emperor the explanations and reparation which in conformity with international laws are due to a power which maintains friendly and pacific relations with the United States.

The just reclamation of the Imperial Government being thus presented, the undersigned awaits the reply of the Honourable Mr. Seward, and fully confiding in his exalted wisdom, and in the justice of the Government of the United States, he has not even for a moment doubted but that it will be as satisfactory as the incontestable right which aids the Empire, and the vast gravity of the offence which was done to it, may require.

The undersigned, etc.,

(Signed) IGNACIO DE AVELLAR BARBOZA DA SILVA.

MR. SEWARD TO MR. BARBOZA DA SILVA.

To Senhor Ignacio de Avellar Barboza da Silva, etc.

Department of State,
Washington, *December* 20*th*, 1864.

SIR,—

I have the honour to acknowledge the receipt of your note, which sets forth the sentiments of the Imperial Government of Brazil concerning the capture of the *Florida* by the United States war-steamer *Wachusett* in the port of Bahia.

You will, of course, explain to your Government that owing to an understanding between you and myself, your note, although it bears the date of the 12th December, was not submitted to me until the 21st inst.

Jealousy of foreign intervention in every form, and absolute non-intervention in the domestic affairs of foreign nations, are cardinal principles in the policy of the United States. You have, therefore, justly expected that the President would disavow and regret the proceedings at Bahia. He will suspend Captain Collins, and direct him to appear before a court-martial. The Consul at Bahia admits that he advised and incited the captain, and was active in the proceedings. He will therefore be dismissed. The flag of Brazil will receive from the United States navy the honour customary in the intercourse of friendly maritime powers.

It is, however, not to be understood that this Government admits or gives credit to the charges of falsehood, treachery, and deception which you have brought against the captain and the Consul. These charges are denied on the authority of the officers accused.

You will also be pleased to understand that the answer now given to your representation rests exclusively upon the ground that the capture of the *Florida* was an unauthorized, unlawful, and indefensible exercise of the naval force of the United States within a foreign country in defiance of its established and duly recognised Government.

This Government disallows your assumption that the insurgents of this country are a lawful naval belligerent; and, on the contrary, it maintains that the ascription of that character by the Government of Brazil to insurgent citizens of the United States, who have hitherto been, and who still are, destitute of naval forces, ports, and courts, is an act of intervention in derogation of the law of nations, and unfriendly and wrongful, as it is manifestly injurious, to the United States.

So, also, this Government disallows your assumption that the *Florida* belonged to the afore-mentioned insurgents, and maintains, on the contrary, that that vessel, like the *Alabama*, was a pirate, belonging to no nation or lawful belligerent, and therefore that the harbouring and supplying of these piratical ships and their crews in Brazilian ports were wrongs and injuries for which Brazil justly owes reparation to the United States, as ample as the reparation which she now receives from them. They hope, and confidently expect, this reciprocity in good time to restore the harmony and friendship which are so essential to the welfare and safety of the two countries.

In the position which I have assumed, the Imperial Government will recognise an adherence to rights which have been constantly asserted, and an enduring sense of injuries which have been the subject of earnest remonstrance by the United States during the last three years. The Government of Brazil is again informed that these positions of this Government are no longer deemed open to argument.

It does not, however, belong to the captains of ships-of-war of the United States, or to the commanders of their armies, or to their consuls residing in foreign ports, acting without the authority of Congress, and without even Executive direction, and choosing their own time, manner, and occasion, to assert the rights and redress the wrongs of the country. This power can be lawfully exercised only by the Government of the United States. As a member of the family of nations, the United States practise order, not anarchy, as they always prefer lawful proceedings to aggressive violence or retaliation. The United States are happy in being able to believe that Brazil entertains the same sentiments. The authorities at Bahia are understood to have unsuccessfully employed force to overcome the *Wachusett* and rescue the *Florida*, and to have continued the chase of the offender beyond the waters of Brazil, out upon the high seas. Thus, in the affair at Bahia, subordinate agents, without the knowledge of their respective Governments, mutually inaugurated an unauthorized, irregular, and unlawful war. In desisting from that war on her part, and in appealing to the Government for redress, Brazil rightly appreciated the character of the United States, and set an example worthy of emulation.

The disposition of the captured crew of the *Florida* is determined upon the principles which I have laid down. Although the crew are enemies of the United States, and, as they contend, enemies of the human race, yet the offenders were, nevertheless, unlawfully brought into the custody of this Government, and therefore they could not lawfully be subjected here to the punishment which they have deserved. Nor could they, being enemies, be allowed to enjoy the protection of the United States. They will, therefore, be set at liberty, to seek a refuge wheresoever they may find it, with the hazard of recapture when beyond the jurisdiction of this Government.

The *Florida* was brought into American waters, and was anchored under naval surveillance and protection at Hampton Roads. While awaiting the representation of the Brazilian Government, on the 28th November, she sank, owing to a leak which could not be seasonably stopped. The leak was at first represented to have been caused, or at least increased, by a collision with a war transport. Orders were immediately given to ascertain the manner and circumstances of the occurrence. It seemed to affect the army and the navy. A Naval Court of Inquiry and also a Military Court of Inquiry were charged with the investigation. The Naval Court has submitted its report, and a copy thereof is herewith communicated. The Military Court is yet engaged. So soon as its labours shall have ended, the result will be made known to your Government. In the meantime it is assumed that the loss of the *Florida* was a consequence of some unforeseen accident, which cast no responsibility upon the United States.

I avail, etc.,

(Signed) WILLIAM H. SEWARD.

NOTE.—The two foregoing letters, Senhor Barboza da Silva to Mr. Seward, and the reply of Mr. Seward, will be found in the 'British Case,' pp. 75-78.

COPY OF REPORT OF LIEUTENANT T. K. PORTER ON THE CAPTURE OF THE CONFEDERATE STATES STEAMER *FLORIDA* BY THE UNITED STATES STEAMER *WACHUSETT.*

To Lieutenant-Commander C. M. Morris, Confederate States Navy.

Liverpool, *February 20th,* 1865.

SIR,—

In obedience to orders I submit the following report of the capture of the Confederate States steamer *Florida* at Bahia, Brazil, on the 7th of October, 1864, by the United States steamer *Wachusett*, the treatment of the officers and crew while prisoners; and the manner of our release. But before commencing I beg to call your attention to the fact that before entering the harbour our shot were withdrawn from the guns; that after our being requested by the Brazilian naval commander to anchor in-shore of his squadron we let our steam go down and hauled fires.

At about 3 a.m. on the morning of the 7th October, the officer of the deck, Acting-Master T. T. Hunter, sent the quarter-master down to call me, and tell me that the *Wachusett* was underweigh and standing towards us. I immediately jumped on deck, when I saw the *Wachusett* about twenty yards off, standing for our starboard quarter. A moment after she struck us abreast the mizen-mast, broke it into three pieces, crushed in the bulwarks, knocked the quarter-boat in on deck, jammed the wheel, carried away the mainyard, and started the beams for about thirty feet forward. At the same time she fired about two hundred shots from her small arms, and two from her great guns. She then backed off about one hundred yards, and demanded our surrender. I replied to the demand that I would let them know in a few moments. The reply from the *Wachusett* was to surrender immediately, or they would blow us out of the water. As more than half our crew were ashore, and as those on board had just returned from liberty, I believed that she could run us down before we could get our guns loaded. But as I did not like to surrender the vessel without knowing what some of the other officers thought of it, I consulted Lieutenant Stone, the second officer in rank; and finding that he agreed with me that we could not contend against her with any hopes of success, I informed the commander of the *Wachusett* that under the circumstances I would surrender the vessel. I then went on board, and delivered to Commander Collins the ship's ensign and my sword. He immediately sent a prize-crew on board the *Florida*, and towed her out of the harbour. During the day he transferred about two-thirds of those captured to the *Wachusett*. He then paroled the officers, and put the men in double irons. As there were so few men compared to the *Wachusett's* crew, and those divided between the two ships, I tried to get Captain Collins to allow the irons to be taken off of all, or a part of them, during the day, but he refused to do so. Beyond keeping the men in double irons for nearly two months, there were but two cases of severity towards them that were reported to me. Henry Norman (cox.) was ironed to a stanchion with his hands behind him for having the key of a pair of the *Florida's* irons in his pocket. He, as well as all the other men on the *Wachusett*, was ironed with the irons belonging to her (the *Wachusett*). John Brogan (fireman) was kept in the sweat-box. Dr. Emory reported to me that he was sick and could not stand such treatment. I asked Captain Collins to tell me why he was so treated. His reply was that Brogan was seen talking, and that when his master-at-arms came up he stopped. He also said that Brogan had, the day the *Florida* was captured, cursed one of his engineers, who tried to get him to show him something about our engines. He said, though, that he had ordered his release two days before, and thought he had been taken out. This was about three weeks after our capture. Brogan informed me afterwards that he had been confined there for several days, and eighteen nights. A few days before going into St. Thomas, I went to Captain Collins, and told him that on a previous occasion he had informed me that he was going to put our men ashore at Pernambuco, and that as we would be in port a few days, I would like to know if he still intended to put them ashore, at the same time telling him that I thought the *Florida* would be given up by his Government, and that I thought any honourable man would try to return the ship and crew as nearly in the condition in which he found her as he could. His reply was, 'I have not thought of it—I have not thought of it to-day.' After further conversation I left him, believing that he would not try to break up the crew. But before leaving St. Thomas our men were informed that all of them who wished to go ashore could do so, and that Master George D. Bryan and one other officer would meet them to look out for them. They asked what was to become of their money, which had been taken for them, and were told that Mr. Bryan would take it ashore for them. A number of them thought this was a trick to get rid of them, and would not go, but eighteen were foolish enough to believe it, and had their irons taken off on the berth-deck, and were put in a boat from the bow port, and allowed to go ashore. The first Mr. Bryan heard of his part of the affair was when we left the *Wachusett* and had an opportunity of talking to the other men. After the men had time to get ashore, the commander of the *Wachusett* called away his boats, and sent an armed force after the boat in which our men had left. So anxious was he to get them ashore, that he sent them when the quarantine flag was flying at his fore in consequence of having the small-pox on board. The United States steamer *Keasarge* left St. Thomas while we were there, and Dr. Charlton and the eighteen men on the *Florida* were transferred to her. When we arrived at Fortress Monroe, we were sent up to Point Look-out Prison, and there the officers were separated from the men, and sent to the Old Capitol Prison in Washington. But in three or four days we were sent back to the *Wachusett* at Fortress Monroe to go to Fort Warren, Boston. On our return to Fortress Monroe, I heard that the *Florida's* money-chest had been opened, and I went to Captain Collins and reminded him that soon after we were captured, I informed him that there were three hundred and twenty dollars in it which belonged to the wardroom mess, which I had given to the paymaster the evening before we were captured, to keep till the caterer, Lieutenant Stone, should return from shore. He told me that he had mentioned it to Rear-Admiral Porter, but that the Admiral refused to give it to us. We saw the *Florida* before we left. She had lost her jibboom by a steam-tug running into her. A lieutenant-commander told me that if the United States Government determined to give her up, the officers of the navy would destroy her. Several other of our officers were told the same. Whilst in Fort Warren we heard these threats were carried out.

From Hampton Roads we were carried in the *Wachusett* to Boston, but before we were sent to Fort Warren, Lieutenant-Commander Beardsly went to the men and informed them that he was sent by Captain Collins to tell them that if they would take the oath of allegiance to the United States Government they would be released. He, meeting with no success, was succeeded by the master-at-arms of the vessel, and a sergeant from the fort, who told them that all the men but five of those who had come from St. Thomas on the *Keasarge* had taken the oath. I do not know by whose orders this was told them; but we found on arriving at the fort that it had no more truth in it than the report they gave the men at St. Thomas, that Mr. Bryan was to meet them on shore. I am happy to say that but one of the crew deserted his flag, and he did it the day we were captured. When we arrived at Fort Warren, the men were all put in one room, and the eleven officers were put into one with thirty-two other prisoners. These rooms were casemates, and were fifty feet long and about eighteen feet wide. At sunset we were locked up in these casemates, and released after sunrise, and allowed to promenade the extent of five such rooms. At 8 a.m. we were marched around to the cookhouse, and were all given one loaf of bread each, weighing fourteen ounces. After 12 we were marched around again, and were given our dinner, which consisted of about eight ounces of cooked meat, with half a pint of thin soup, three days, and two potatoes, some beans or hominy the other days. This was all we received each day. Many of the prisoners by economizing found this enough to appease their hunger, but a great many others were hungry all the time. If we had been allowed to buy sugar and coffee, and bread and cheese, a great many would have been able to do so, and divide with some of their friends who had no means, but we were allowed to buy nothing to eat without a certificate from the Post surgeon that we were sick. There is an arrangement between our Government and that of the United States, that prisoners-of-war may be allowed to receive boxes of provisions and clothing from their friends at home, but the United States Government now interprets this to mean that all boxes must come by a flag of truce. As half of the Confederate prisoners have their homes within what is now the United States military lines, this agreement works almost entirely for the Federals and against us. Half of the *Florida's* officers were in this situation, and they were compelled to decline the offers of their friends. On the 24th December all the *Florida's* officers except Dr. Charlton and fourteen other prisoners were locked up in a casemate, and kept in close confinement both day and night. We were not allowed to go out under any circumstances, except that for the first four days we were marched under a heavy guard to the cookhouse twice a day. After that our dinner was brought to us, and two of us were marched around to get the bread for all of those confined. This was for discussing a plan to capture the fort, which one of the prison spies, who pretends to be a lieutenant-colonel in our army, and a lieutenant in the English army, revealed to the authorities. We were kept in close confinement until the 19th of January, when Lieutenant Woodman, of the United States army, sent for me, and told me that he had an order from the Secretary of the Navy to release the officers and crew of the *Florida* from Fort

Warren, and that as such was the case he would release all of us from close confinement. He showed me the order from the Secretary of the Navy, which was that we would be released on condition that we signed a parole to leave the United States within ten days. I asked him if we would be given the money and our swords, and other articles captured on the *Florida*, which had not been sunk with her. He said that he knew nothing about them, but that if I wished to write to Mr. Welles, he would send the communication. I then gave him a copy of the following note, which he assured me was sent the same day:

'To the Hon. Gideon Welles, Secretary of the Navy.

'Fort Warren, *January* 19*th*, 1863.

'SIR,—

'I have just been informed by the commanding officer of this fort that the officers and crew of the Confederate States steamer *Florida* will be released on condition of leaving the United States within ten days. We will accept a parole to leave at any time when we are put on board any steamer going to Europe, but we would prefer to go to Richmond. We would call your attention to the fact that there were somewhere about thirteen thousand dollars in gold on the *Florida* when she was captured, which was taken out of her by order of Rear-Admiral Porter. And to leave the United States it will be necessary to have that to take us out, unless the United States Government send us away as they brought us in. If you will give us our money we would prefer remaining here till a steamer leaves here for Europe, or we would ask for a guard till we are put on one in New York, as so many of us being together might be the cause of an unnecessary disturbance, of which we would be the sufferers.

'Very respectfully,

'Your obedient servant,

'THOMAS K. PORTER,
'First-Lieutenant, Confederate States Navy.'

Mr. Welles made no reply to this. After waiting a week and finding that the United States Government neither intended to pay our passage away, nor to give us the money belonging to our Government, and not even our private money, I sent Lieutenant Stone to Boston with directions to procure a passage in the British and North American steamer *Canada*, or if he failed in that, to get us out of the

United States in any manner possible. He succeeded in getting passage for all of us on the *Canada*, by my giving a draft to be paid at Liverpool. And on the 1st of February we signed the following parole: 'We, the undersigned officers and crew of the steamer *Florida*, in consideration of being released from confinement in Fort Warren, do jointly and severally pledge our sacred word of honour that we will leave the United States within ten days from date of release, and that while in the United States we will commit no hostile act,' and I left the fort for the steamer *Canada*. It may be of importance to state that we were officially informed by Major Gibson, commanding the Post part of the time we were there, that we could hold no communication with the Brazilian authorities.

Very respectfully,

Your obedient servant,

THOMAS K. PORTER,

First-Lieutenant, Confederate States Navy.

CHAPTER V.

The building of the *Alabama*.—Suspicions of the United States Consul at Liverpool.—Captain Butcher.—The equipping of the *Alabama*.—Quitting Liverpool.—Bond, the Pilot.—Official Correspondence.—Captain Semmes.—The *Alabama* handed over to his charge.—Some matters connected with the clearance of the *Alabama* from Liverpool.—Mr. Price Edwards, the Collector of Customs at that Port.—The *Alabama's* first engagement.—The *Alabama* a legitimate vessel-of-war.—Action of the United States in regard to commissioning vessels at sea.—Influence of the cruisers on the United States carrying trade.—The *Alabama's* action with the *Keasarge*.—Mr. Seward and Earl Russell.

WRITING subjectively, and following the career of the *Florida* from her birth on the busy but peaceful shores of the Mersey to her violent seizure in Bahia, and thence to her final resting-place among the oyster-beds in the estuary of the River James, the narrative has been carried far beyond the regular course of events, and we must now return to March, 1862, and pick up that thread of the history which was woven into the general occurrences of the period by the *Alabama*.

At the time of the *Florida's* departure from Liverpool, her still more famous consort had not yet been dignified by any other name or title than the dockyard number '290.' Her comely frame had been covered in by the binding grip of the outside planking, which had developed the graceful curves of her counter and the delicate wave-lines of her bow ; but, nevertheless, I was disappointed to find that she was hardly up to specified time.

The builders were determined to turn out a first-class ship, and feeling perhaps that their obligation to do so was, if possible, increased by my absence, and the fact that there was no one to look after the interests of the owner, they were especially critical and hard to please in the selection of the timber for the most important parts, and had discarded two or three stern-posts * after they had been partly fitted and bored to take the screw shaft, because of some slight defect. This creditable, satisfactory, and punctilious care had caused some delay in completing the hull, but all the other work was in an advanced state, and the engines were ready to go into the ship as soon as she was off the ways.

The Birkenhead Ironworks lie some distance above the chief commercial parts of Liverpool, and being on the opposite side of the Mersey, they do not attract especial notice from persons engaged in business, or passing to and fro by the Woodside Ferry, and the boats plying to the lower landings on the river. But the large number of people passing up river to Tranmere, Rock Ferry, and Eastham, would often pass along the dock-walls of Messrs. Laird's establishment, and they could not fail to observe the gradual development of the graceful craft that stood out in bold relief at the extreme south end of the yard, and to contrast her with the large iron structures they were accustomed to see upon the adjoining building slips and ways.

The departure of the *Florida* without being called upon to give a particular account of herself and her

* The single piece of timber finally used for the stern-post cost £100.

intentions had grieved and vexed the United States Consul, and his suspicions having been once aroused, his mind was kept in a wakeful and agitated condition during the remainder of the war. The voluminous correspondence submitted to the Geneva Arbitrators, and which appeared from time to time in the Parliamentary Blue-books, gives proof of his nervous activity and the irritable and sometimes irritating persistency with which he pressed the local authorities to seize, or at least to detain, ships which he affirmed 'it was quite notorious were intended to be armed and equipped as privateers' for the 'so-called'—which latter appellation came to be a common designation of the Confederate States among those United States officials who were sometimes willing to drop the still more common epithets of 'rebel' and 'insurgent,' to which, however, the Liverpool Consul generally adhered.

The people who saw the '290' on the building-slip, and were attracted by her appearance, naturally talked about her, and no doubt remarks were often made in respect to her fitness for a cruiser, and it is not therefore surprising that she should have aroused the suspicions of those whose business it was to keep watch over the interests of the United States. I soon learned that spies were lurking about, and tampering with the workmen at Messrs. Laird's, and that a private detective named Maguire was taking a deep and abiding interest in my personal movements; but my solicitor assured me that there was nothing illegal in what I was doing, and there was nothing therefore to be done but to maintain a quiet reserve, to hasten the completion of the ship, and to get her away as soon as possible.

On the 15th of May '290' was launched, and as a matter of fact left that numerical title on the signboard at the top of the slip when she slid off into the Mersey, although it stuck to her some time, and continued to be the term used when mentioning her in the Consular affidavits, and in the diplomatic correspondence, until the frequent reports of her performances afloat gave greater notoriety and distinction to her now historical name of *Alabama.*

But this ship, like the *Florida*, bore more than one name in passing through the various phases of her life, from a mere entity in a dockyard to the position of a commissioned ship-of-war. It is one of the peculiar anomalies of our nautical English grammar that a man-of-war is feminine, and we should say of a frigate whose name was *Ajax*, or which bore the still more harsh and masculine appellation of *Polyphemus*, '*She* is a fine sea-boat.' The office of christening a ship is almost invariably performed by a lady, which is an aggravation of the anomaly about the sex, because if custom justifies a sailor in calling his ship 'she,' and if there is any propriety in his passionate affirmation, 'my barque is my bride,' the function of handing her into her natural element would be more fittingly, though not so gracefully done, by one of the 'opposite sex.' I could not take the liberty of introducing the name of the lady who christened '290,' into this narrative. She graciously consented to perform the office, and fulfilled it in a comely manner, little knowing that she was constructively taking part in a great Civil War, and wholly unconscious that she was helping to make work for five eminent statesmen at Geneva ten years after. I hope her conscience has never upbraided her since, and that she has not felt in any way responsible for the bill of £3,000,000, which her Most Gracious Majesty had to pay on account of the '*Alabama* Claims.'

When '290' was to be launched, it was necessary to provide an appellation for her. The Spanish language furnished a flexible and mellifluous equivalent for the Christian name of the lady who served the office, and when the ship got free of the blocks and glided down the ways, she had been christened *Enrica*. The Spanish name gave rise to another alleged mystery, and it was often asserted that there was a purpose to affect that the ship was intended for the Spanish Government, or at least for a Spanish firm in Spain; but I now state that there was no attempt to deceive anyone by any pretence whatever in the business of building and despatching the *Alabama* from Liverpool. I have already described the negotiations with Messrs. Laird for the building of the ship. There was no mystery or disguise about them, and it will be seen that all the further management of the transaction was conducted in the same ordinary commonplace way. A great effort was made by the United States Minister to induce her Majesty's Government to seize the ship, but no satisfactory evidence was produced that any violation of the Foreign Enlistment Act had been committed, and it appears from what is now known that the Government were not willing to 'strain the law' at that early date, or 'to seize a vessel which it would have been the duty of a court of law to restore.'

I have always attributed the success of getting the *Alabama* finished as a sea-going ship, and then despatched, to the fact that no mystery or disguise was attempted. I was well advised as to the law, and had the means of knowing with well nigh absolute certainty what was the state of the negotiations between the United States Minister and her Majesty's Government. For the rest, I merely practised such ordinary business prudence and reserve as a man would be likely to follow in the management of his private affairs. I never told any *employé* more than was necessary for him to know, and never gave any reason for an order having reference to the outfit or movements of the ship. Everything was done quietly, without any excitement or appearance of haste. At the last moment she was hurried off with some precipitancy, but this will be explained in due course.

The Messrs. Laird, conscious of being somewhat behind time with the hull, appeared desirous to make up the loss by quick work in setting up the engines and completing the outfit. The ship was no sooner in the water than two tugs took her to the entrance of the graving-dock, and she was warped into it, and placed over the blocks at once. The engineer department at the Messrs. Laird's is especially efficient. Before the *Enrica* was fully secured in her berth the great derrick was swinging over her decks, and the first heavy pieces of the machinery were going on board. The work was now rapidly pushed forward, and the progress was satisfactory. On about June 15th the ship was taken out for a trial trip, and was run over the usual course until all parties were satisfied.

As the ship approached completion, it was necessary to appoint a captain who held a Board of Trade certificate, to superintend the preparations for sea, to engage the crew, and transact all such business as by law and custom falls within the office of the commander of a vessel. The selection of the right man was a matter of grave consideration. The requirements were professional competency, prudence, control over the tongue, and absolute integrity. I consulted a friend, and he soon brought to me Captain Mathew J. Butcher, a gentleman who was then serving as first-officer in a Cunard steamship ; but he held a master's certificate, and was therefore eligible.

It turned out that I had met Captain Butcher two or three years before in Havana, he being then chief-officer of the Cunard steamship *Karnak*, and thus he was not wholly unknown to me. A conversation of a half to three-quarters of an hour brought us to a satisfactory understanding, and we went across to Messrs. Laird's yard, and I introduced Captain Butcher as the commander of the *Enrica*, through whom I desired them to receive all further instructions with reference to the outfit of the ship. To prevent repetition hereafter, I will take this occasion to say that Captain Butcher fulfilled all the requirements of the offices he engaged to perform, not only with tact, judgment and discretion, but with that nice and discriminating fidelity which marks the man of true honesty. He was engaged merely to take the ship to an appointed place without the United Kingdom; and he was especially warned that no men must be engaged under any pretence whatever, except to navigate the ship to a port or ports in the West Indies, with the privilege of stopping at any intermediate port.

It may be stated here, once for all, that no men were hired or engaged for any other purpose than that of navigating an unarmed ship, and no man was enlisted to enter the Confederate service, nor was a word said to any man to induce him to enter that service, by anyone having the slightest authority to make any such proposition, until after the ship had passed far beyond British jurisdiction. It would have been quite easy to prove that the affidavits obtained by the United States Consul at the time were either the fictitious conceits of the men who made them, or else that the men had been themselves deceived. But while Captain Butcher was only engaged to take out an unarmed ship, and he never did enter the Confederate Service, yet it was manifestly necessary to confide to him more than what appeared on the surface. He therefore knew enough before the arrival of the ship at Terceira to place the success of the whole enterprise in his power. An indiscreet remark, or a hint from him to a careless gossiping acquaintance, would have spoiled all of our well-laid plans. I shrink from seeming to suggest that there might have been a possibility of such a catastrophe; but there can be no doubt that the United States would have given a considerable sum to frustrate the departure of the ship, and a much larger sum still to have got possession of her. There was a time when the commander might have handed her over to an agent of the United States, or for that matter he might have taken her to New York, instead of to Terceira. I mention this to demonstrate the prodigious trust it was necessary to repose in Captain Butcher. But I never had the least uneasiness; men who have had much to do with their fellows, if observant, learn to understand them, and after our first interview I never hesitated to tell Captain Butcher all that was necessary for him to fully comprehend the actual state of affairs, although I never ceased to abide by the rule of burdening no one with more of a secret than it seemed good for him to know.

I was fortunate in having held on to my old friend McNair, the engineer of the *Fingal*, and he took charge of that department on board the *Enrica*, so that I was quite sure nothing would be neglected in the way of proper outfit.

About the 1st of July the *Enrica* was so nearly ready for sea, that I began to make preparations for my own departure in her. Lieutenant J. R. Hamilton had arrived in England from the Confederate States at the end of April, and reported to me for duty as first-lieutenant of the *Alabama* (still *Enrica*). When I was in Savannah with the *Fingal* in February, 1862, Lieutenant Hamilton had expressed an earnest desire to get afloat, and asked if I could bring it about that he should be detailed to serve with me. There appeared to be some difficulty at the time, but the Secretary of the Navy bore it in mind, and I was much gratified by Hamilton's unexpected arrival. He entered with much spirit into the arrangements for our cruise.

In the original instructions the Navy Department had left me a large discretion, and I had fully arranged and planned what, and in what direction, my operations should be. Maffitt and I had both served together on the United States Coast Survey. Both of us could find our way into about every harbour from Boston to the Mississippi. I had proposed a rendezvous with him, and a joint dash at a given point; but, failing the rendezvous, I had sketched out my own course separately. Just about this time, when in another week I should have been off, I received two despatches from the Navy Department of great length, the contents of which greatly disappointed my hopes and expectations in reference to getting afloat, but at the same time added largely to the sphere of my general duties.

The first despatch notified me that it had been thought advisable to order Captain Semmes to return to England from Nassau, and directing me to put him in command of the *Alabama*. That this change may be fully understood, I will just briefly mention that Captain Semmes, in the progress of his cruise in the *Sumter*, had found his way to Gibraltar, and finding it impossible to make at that place the repairs necessary to fit her for further cruising, and being also unable to obtain a sufficient supply of fuel to fetch the ship to a French or English port, he had laid her up and was *en route* with his staff of officers for the Confederate States when the fresh orders of the Secretary of the Navy met him at Nassau.*

The *Sumter* was for some time a *bête noire* to me. She was much in the way at Gibraltar, but having been turned over to me as Confederate property, there was both the necessity and the obligation to look after her. The United States kept two vessels in the neighbourhood to watch her, which was some offset to the inconvenience and expense, but when it became apparent that she could not be got away, and we began to have better and more efficient vessels for cruising, I sold her, and she was put under the British flag by her new owners, and was brought round to Liverpool and converted into a blockade-runner. She was never caught, but ended her days in the natural and ship-shape way by foundering somewhere in the North Sea.

The views of the Navy Department at this time will be best explained by quoting from the second of the afore-mentioned despatches: 'Captain Semmes returns to England to assume the command of the *Alabama*, and you will please afford him all possible assistance in getting her to sea and maintaining her as a cruiser.'

The Secretary then goes earnestly into the question of ironclads; directs me to build, if possible, two more vessels of the type of the *Alabama*, advises in what way

* A full account of all this will be found in 'My Adventures Afloat,' in which Admiral Semmes gives a history of his cruises in the *Sumter* and *Alabama*.

The *Sumter*, the first Confederate armed cruiser. *(Harper's Weekly)*

Raphael Semmes, Commander of the *Sumter* and the *Alabama.*
(Century Magazine)

he hopes to provide funds, adds orders for various supplies, and notifies me of some large contracts he has made with private parties, and instructs me to supervise them on behalf of the Government.

It may be interesting to the reader to know the opinion of a member of the Confederate Cabinet in *June—July*, 1862, in respect to the possible intervention of Great Britain and France, and I give it in the following extract:—

'We are all astonished here at the evident apprehension of the Government of Great Britain of a war with the United States. Mr. Seward's gasconades upon this subject excite but the contempt of his own people. . . . Should Great Britain and France acknowledge our independence, and send their products in their own ships to our ports, the war would not only cease, but their course would meet the approval of a vast majority of the people of the United States, for the war is carried on by a party in power, and not by the people.

'Enclosed you have a copy of my instructions to Commander Semmes. Your services in England are so important at this time, that I trust you will cheerfully support any disappointment you may experience in not getting to sea. The experience you have acquired renders your agency absolutely necessary. . . .

'I am, etc.,
'(Signed) S. R. MALLORY,
'Secretary of the Navy.'

Simultaneously with the notification of Captain Semmes's appointment to the *Alabama*, I received a letter from that officer himself, in which he advised me that he would join me in Liverpool by the first vessel leaving Nassau, and requesting me to make such arrangements to get the enterprise complete as I might deem best. This change, coming so late, when the ship was, in fact, ready for sea, and had been delivered to me by the builders, was very embarrassing. We knew that the American Minister was pressing the Government to seize the ship; and the frequent inquiries addressed to the builders by the Customs authorities at London, and the active watchfulness of the local officers of that department at Liverpool, warned me that the situation was critical.

Meanwhile the *Enrica* (*Alabama*) was taken into the Birkenhead Dock, where she was coaled and all her stores were put on board. Everything was kept in readiness for a start at short notice, but a full crew was not shipped, for fear that the men would be restive at the delay, and attract notice by their numbers and indiscreet talking.

In order to preserve due consistency in the order of events, it is now necessary to give an account of the arrangements for 'equipping' the *Alabama*—that is to say, the means adopted to supply that portion of her furniture which would complete her outfit as a vessel-of-war. It is not necessary to dwell long upon these arrangements. The battery was ordered very shortly after the contract for the ship was made, and all the ordnance supplies were put in train in good time; but such instructions were given as would ensure their being ready not much before the ship, although the parties contracted with were not informed for what purpose they were wanted, or even how they were to be shipped, until the time arrived for forwarding them. The necessary number of revolvers, short rifles with cutlass bayonets, ammunition, made-up clothing for 150 men, extra stores of all kinds, hammocks, and, in fact, everything required for the complete equipment of a man-of-war, were ordered, and instructions were given that the goods when ready should be packed, marked, and held for shipping orders.

About the end of May a suitable agent was instructed to look up a moderate-sized sailing-vessel in London, fit for a West Indian voyage, to carry heavy weights. She was to be staunch and in good condition ; but high finish not wanted, and a clipper not required. We got just the craft—a barque of about 400 to 450 tons. Her recommendation was that she had lately brought home ordnance stores—old guns, shot, etc.—from Gibraltar on Government account. She was bought, and in due time was entered out from London to Demerara. The agent was ordered to put 350 tons of coal in her, and the necessary shipping orders were given to the parties holding the *Alabama's* goods. Our barque was named *Agrippina*, and she attracted no especial notice and no suspicion while loading in the London Docks. It was easy to regulate the forwarding of the cargo and the lading, so as to fit in with the movements of the *Enrica* at Liverpool, without creating the suspicion that there was any connection between the two vessels.

I wished to know something definite as to the time of Captain Semmes's arrival, or at least that he had started from Nassau, before despatching the two ships, because it might be more dangerous to have them waiting at the rendezvous, where a passing United States cruiser might by chance fall upon them, than for the *Enrica* to remain in Liverpool, where no foreign enemy could touch her. But there was a domestic enemy—the Foreign Enlistment Act—upon whom it was necessary to keep a watchful eye.

On Saturday, July 26th, 1862, I received information from a private but most reliable source, that it would not be safe to leave the ship in Liverpool another forty-eight hours. I went immediately to Messrs. Laird's office, and told them that I wished to have a thorough all day trial of the ship outside. Although the testing trial trip had already been made, and the delivery of the ship to me in accordance with the terms of the contract was complete, yet it had been verbally agreed that there should be another trial, when coals and stores were all on board, if I desired it. Captain Butcher was ordered to ship a few more hands, and to have everything ready to come out of dock on Monday's tide. None of the crew were given an inkling of the contemplated movement ; but I informed Captain Butcher confidentially that the ship would not return, and directed him to get on board some extra tons of coal, and to complete his stores.

It was important to have as many trusty and intelligent men on board as possible, and I had already detailed Mr. John Low (now a master in the Confederate States Navy), who had rejoined me after going out to Nassau in the *Florida*, to be ready to accompany Captain Butcher.

On Monday the 28th the *Enrica* came out of dock and anchored off Seacombe, and every preparation was made for going out of harbour the next day. A small party of guests were invited to go out for the trial trip, and the next morning—Tuesday, the 29th—the ship was partially dressed with flags, and at about 9 a.m. we got under weigh and steamed down the river with a number of guests on board, and a party of riggers and additional engineers' men to assist if any help was needed. We had also in company the steam-tug *Hercules* as a tender.

The day was fine and the trials were very satisfactory. We ran several times between the Bell Buoy and the north-west lightship. The average speed was 12·8, the sea being quite smooth, and the wind light from north-west. About 3 p.m. I explained to the guests that it was my wish to keep the ship out all night to complete her trials, and that the sea being quite smooth we would run close to the bar, and every one could go up to town in the tug. Shortly after I asked Mr. George Bond, the Liverpool pilot, if he knew Moelfra Bay. He said 'yes.' I then directed Captain Butcher to take the ship down to that anchorage as soon as the rest of us left, and wait there until I came to him, which, if possible, would be the next afternoon. At 4 p.m. the guests, the extra men, and I, got on board the tug, and parting company from the *Enrica*, she proceeded to her place of anchorage on the Welsh coast, while we went up to town. On the way up the river I engaged the tug to be at the Woodside landing-stage at 6 a.m. on the next morning, telling the master that I wished him to take a few articles to the ship, which would probably remain outside at least for a day. A shipping-master had been previously engaged to have thirty or forty men on the landing-stage at the same time to join a ship at an outport, for a voyage to the Bahamas, and possibly to Havana.

I was on the Woodside landing-stage by 7 a.m. on the 30th. The *Hercules* was already there, and the articles wanted for the *Enrica* were on board. They were a spare anchor-stock, a large piece of scantling, intended for the frame to support the spare spars, and a few brass pieces belonging to the engines. There is reason for some particularity in these small details, as one of the Consular affidavits affirmed that gun-carriages were taken, which is quite untrue. The shipping-master was also on the stage. He had with him about thirty-five or forty men, and nearly as many women, of that class who generally affect a tender solicitude for Jack when he is outward-bound, and is likely to be provided with an advance-note. I told him to get the men on board, but of course the women could not go. He replied that he feared it was a case of all or none. The women, he said, stood in various degrees of tender relationship to the men, and would not part with them unless they could first get a month's pay in advance or its equivalent. There was no time for parley; the mixed group were hurried on board, and we proceeded down the river. As we approached New Brighton I told the master of the tug to take the Rock Channel, which would save distance, and go down to Moelfra Bay. At about 3 p.m. we sighted the *Enrica*, and at four got alongside of her. It had been raining, and the afternoon was dull and cloudy.

There had been nothing to eat on board the tug. Jack and his fair friends were therefore hungry, and not in suitable frame of mind for business. The steward was ordered to prepare a substantial supper as quickly as possible, and when it was ready all hands were refreshed with a fair but safe allowance of grog, to add zest and cheerfulness to the meal. When the men had well eaten, and had finished their pipes, they were called aft, and it was explained to them in few words that the ship had been 'cruising in the Channel to get her engines in good working order, and as everything was satisfactory it was proposed to proceed on the voyage without going back to Liverpool, which would be an unnecessary delay and expense. Would they ship for the run, say to Havana, touching at any intermediate port? If the ship did not return to England they would be sent back free of expense, or some other satisfactory settlement would be made with them. They should have one month's pay in advance, paid down on the capstan-head. The ship was a nice comfortable craft, and was well found, and well provisioned.' After a short consultation among themselves, all but two or three of the men agreed to go. Articles expressing the terms of the agreement had been prepared, and each man came down to the cabin in turn with his 'lady,' and signed, the latter receiving the stipulated advance in money, or a note for the equivalent from Captain Butcher.

It was near midnight before everything was arranged, and the tug was lying uneasily alongside; for the wind had shifted to south-west, and was blowing in spiteful squalls, with heavy rain. It seemed inhospitable to turn the ladies out on such a night, but there was no accommodation for them on board, and there were reasons why the *Enrica* should not be found in Moelfra Roads on the next morning. While the *Enrica* was still in Liverpool, it came to my knowledge that the United States ship *Tuscarora*, Captain T. A. Craven, had come up from Gibraltar to Southampton, some time in the early days of July, and that she continued to remain there, or in the near neighbourhood.

The nervous apprehension of the United States Consul in respect to the *Enrica* was well known, and it did not require much acumen to connect the presence of the *Tuscarora* in British waters with the supposed character and probable destination of the former vessel. Arrangements were made with a judicious friend at Southampton to keep me informed of the *Tuscarora's* movements, and I had received almost daily advices. Just before leaving the Woodside landing-stage in the tug with the men and women, a telegram was handed me, which contained the announcement that the *Tuscarora* had left Southampton, and it was believed that she had gone to Queenstown. Manifestly we were watched, and some one had put Captain Craven on our supposed track. It seemed so clear that he would touch at Queenstown for news, and then lie off Tuskar, or somewhere in the channel to intercept the *Enrica* on her way to sea, or follow her out by the usual route, that I determined to go 'north about.' I had already consulted with Captain Butcher and our excellent pilot, Mr. George Bond, on that point; both had agreed that it was the best course, and Bond knew that route as well as the other.

After the tug left us the weather grew worse. By 1 a.m. it was blowing hard from south-west, and raining heavily. It was not an opportunity such as a prudent seaman would choose to leave a safe roadstead and venture into the Irish Sea, but the circumstances appeared to justify the move; indeed, I thought them imperative. At 2.30 a.m. (31st), we got under weigh, and stood out of the bay under steam alone. At 8 a.m. the ship was off the Calf of Man, the sky clearing and wind dropping. We set all sail to a middling fresh breeze, and bowled along 13½ knots, good. By 1 p.m. the wind fell light, and we lost the effect of the sails; at noon passed South Rock, and steered along the coast of Ireland. At 8 p.m. entered between Rathlin Island and Fair Head. At 6 p.m. stopped the engines off the Giant's Causeway, hailed a fishing-boat, and Bond and I went ashore in a pelting rain, leaving Captain Butcher to proceed with the *Enrica* in accordance with his instructions.

During the evening it rained incessantly, and the wind skirled and snifted about the gables of the hotel in fitful squalls. Bond and I sat comfortably enough in the snug dining-room after dinner, and sipped our toddy, of the best Coleraine malt; but my heart was with the little ship buffeting her way around that rugged north coast of Ireland. I felt sure that Butcher would keep his weather-eye open, and once clear of Innistrahull, there would be plenty of sea-room; but I could not wholly shake off an occasional sense of uneasiness. Bond gave me the exact distances from point to point, from light to light, and having been taught at school to work up all sums to very close results, I made the average speed of the *Enrica* to have been 12·89 from Moelfra to the Giants' Causeway, and felt well satisfied with the performance. The next morning, August 1st, Bond and I took a boat and pulled along the coast to Port Rush. The weather was beautifully fine, and the effect of the bright sun and the gentle west wind was so exhilarating that I felt no further solicitude about the *Enrica*. From Port Rush we took rail to Belfast, and then steamer and rail *viâ* Fleetwood to Liverpool, where I learned that the *Tuscarora* had come off Point Lynas on the 1st, and then looked into Moelfra Bay, but found nothing there to engage her special attention.

I cannot dismiss Bond without a passing tribute; I came to know him well during the war, and for years afterwards. He was one of those men who perform every office of life with earnestness and zeal; who never complain of too much labour, or too little reward; whose conversation is without covetousness, and who always seem content with the things that are present. His position was not elevated. He began as a river and channel pilot, and ended his career as master of the Clarence Dock in Liverpool; but there was something in the heart and eye and manner of the man which gave an importance and dignity to his employment above its seeming consequence. We meet such men occasionally in what are called the humble walks of life, and they make labour honourable. After his short cruise in the *Enrica*, it would have been useless for me to attempt any special mystery in dealing with him; but he never asked an inquisitive question, and if it was necessary to give him any information, I never doubted that his lips would hold it as a sealed envelope.

When it became manifest that the *Enrica* must be sent away from Liverpool, I telegraphed the agents who were loading the *Agrippina* to despatch her forthwith, and sent up orders which the captain was not to open until all hands were on board and the ship was practically off. On my return to Liverpool, I learned with satisfaction that she was clear of the Channel, and that her cargo was complete. The two vessels were thus safely on their way to the rendezvous—that quiet little bay on the east side of Terceira, whose inviting shelter I would not have known but for the necessity of putting in there with the *Fingal* for water, which has been mentioned in a previous chapter.

I have thought that it will be best, in the further progress of this narrative, to give the actual official reports, explaining each important event, which were written at the time of the occurrence. This course will perhaps interfere with and interrupt the symmetry of the narrative, but I cannot doubt that it will add to its weight as a truthful uncoloured account of the various enterprises, and it will only be necessary to fill in the time between the dates of the reports with brief explanatory remarks. The instructions to the commanders of the two vessels should come first in order.

'London, *July 28th*, 1862.

'CAPTAIN,—

'You will proceed at once to sea with the barque *Agrippina*, now under your command, and make the best of your way to the bay of Praya, in the island of Terceira, one of the Azores. . . .

'Your experience as a seaman renders it unnecessary to give you special advice as to the care of your ship, and you will of course use all proper precautions in approaching the land; but it is advisable to give you some hints in respect to the anchorage at Praya and its approach. The bay of Praya is open to the east, and is easy and safe of access, there being no sunken rocks or danger of any kind not visible to the eye. With a leading wind, stand boldly in for the middle of the bight until a small islet off the north point is in range with the point of the mainland of the island itself; then haul up for the town, which lies in the northern curve of the bay, and anchor by the lead in eight to ten fathoms water. With the wind from the westward you can beat in by the lead, standing not quite so far on the southern as on the northern tack, and bring up in, say, eight to ten fathoms. You will be visited soon after anchoring by a health officer, to whom you will simply report that you are from London for Demerara, and have put in for supplies. It is hoped that the steamer will not be long behind you; indeed, you may find her there. The name of the commander of the steamer is Butcher. He will have a letter to you with authority to take whatever quantity of coal and other articles of your cargo he may require, and we particularly desire you to give him your best assistance, and afford him every aid in your power to transfer what he needs from the *Agrippina* to his own ship, and you will then proceed to any port he may direct, and land or deliver the remainder of your cargo. In fact, you are to consider all orders from the commander of the steamer as being authorized by us, with or without any other letter of advice.

'If any vessel is at anchor at Praya when you arrive, hoist your number, and should she be your consort she will show a white English ensign from the after shroud of the main rigging. If the steamer arrives after you, she will, after anchoring, make this same signal of the white ensign in the main rigging, which you will answer with your number, after which you can communicate freely. Relying with confidence upon your integrity and willingness to carry out our wishes in the prosecution of the voyage you have undertaken, we do not think it necessary to give you more minute directions in writing, but may find means to communicate with you again before your departure from Praya. Our interests are so deeply involved in the adventure entrusted to your management, that we will fully appreciate your exertions to bring it to a successful termination, and upon your safe return to England, we will be happy to make you a substantial acknowledgment for any extra exertions you may make for the satisfactory accomplishment of the voyage.

'We are, etc.

'Captain Alexander McQueen,
'Barque *Agrippina.*'

The above letter was 'signed by the registered owners.'

'Liverpool, *July* 30*th*, 1862.

'SIR,—

'You will proceed to sea in the steamship *Enrica*, now under your command, and taking the channel by the North of Ireland, will shape a course for the bay of

Praya, in the island of Terceira, one of the Azores. At that place you will be joined by the barque *Agrippina*, Captain McQueen, to whom you have a letter, and who will thenceforth be under your orders. As the *Agrippina* is a sailing vessel, and may not be at the place of rendezvous for a fortnight, it will not be necessary for you to arrive ahead of her, and you will therefore economise your fuel as much as possible, making the passage mostly under canvas. You have been informed of the manner of signalling the *Agrippina*, and when she joins you, if the weather permits, you will at once begin to transfer her cargo to your own ship. The paymaster has an invoice of her cargo, showing the contents of every case and bale, so that there can be no confusion or delay. All slops, clothing, and other articles in the purser's department you will please take on board first, and have them placed in the store-rooms, directing the paymaster to issue such of them as may be required by the men.

'Get the gun-carriages out of their cases and place them in their proper places, the carriage for 8-inch gun on the quarter-deck, and the one for the 7-inch rifled-gun immediately forward of the bridge. The carriages for the broadside-guns place opposite the side-ports. The cases containing the guns, being filled with small fixtures and equipments, had better be left as you find them until the Confederate States officer who is to command the ship arrives. The cases containing the shot can be opened, and the shot put in the racks, each rack being so fitted as to receive its proper shot. The shells you will place in the shell-rooms, each in its proper box, the spherical shells in the starboard, and the elongated shells in the port-room. The pistols are in four small cases, made so that two of them will fit into each of the arm-chests intended for the quarter-deck. Put them in the chests as soon as you get them on board. Fill the bunkers from the coals on board the *Agrippina*, and keep both vessels ready for a start at short notice. Captain R. Semmes, of the Confederate States Navy, is the officer who will, I hope, very soon relieve you. He will bring you a letter from me, and thereafter you will consider that all my control or authority over the ship is transferred to him. My private and official intercourse with you has been such as to give me a high estimate of your personal and professional ability, and as we have freely conversed as to the management of the adventure you have undertaken, I do not think it necessary to give you written instructions as to the simple care of the ship.

'You are to consider yourself my confidential agent, and I shall rely upon you as one gentleman may upon another. If you have an opportunity at any time, send me a line, and get out of the reach of the telegraphic stations as soon as possible. I do not anticipate that you will meet with any interruption in making the transfer of cargo, but an easterly gale may force you to get the *Agrippina* out of Praya Bay, in which case you can tow her under the lee of the island and lie by her until the weather permits you to return. In such a contingency leave a letter with her Majesty's Consul, directed to Captain J. W. Clendenin, saying where you have gone, and that you will soon be back.

'It is important that your movements should not be reported, and you will please avoid speaking or signalling any passing ship.

'Wishing you a successful cruise, and hoping to see you soon in good health,

'I am, etc.,

'(Signed) JAMES D. BULLOCH.

'Captain M. J. Butcher.'

'Liverpool, *July 28th*, 1862.

'SIR,—

'You will join the Confederate States steamship *Alabama* (*Enrica*) temporarily under the orders of Captain M. J. Butcher, and proceed in her to sea. The *Alabama* may have to cruise several days in the British Channel, and to touch at one or two ports. During this time you are strictly enjoined not to mention that you are in any way connected with the Confederate States Navy, but you will simply act as the purser of a private ship.

'In this capacity you will keep account of all money paid out, and you will assist Captain Butcher in any manner he may desire. You have been provided with an invoice of everything now on board the *Alabama*, as well as the cargo shipped on board the barque *Agrippina*, which vessel you will meet at the port to which the *Alabama* is bound. The invoice of the *Agrippina's* cargo gives the mark and number of every case and bale, the contents of each, and the part of the vessel in which it is stowed. You will endeavour to make yourself fully acquainted with the invoices, and examine the store-rooms, so that you will be able to give efficient aid in getting everything in its proper place when the transfer of stores is made.

'When the *Alabama* is fairly at sea you will mix freely with the "warrant and petty officers," show interest in their comfort and welfare, and endeavour to excite their interest in the approaching cruise of the ship. Talk to them of the Southern States, and how they are fighting against great odds for only what every Englishman enjoys—*liberty!* Tell them at the port of destination a distinguished officer of the Confederate States Navy will take command of the ship for a cruise, in which they will have the most active service, and be well taken care of. I do not mean that you are to make the men set speeches, or be constantly talking to them, but in your position you may frequently throw out to leading men hints of the above tenor, which will be commented upon on the berth-deck. Seamen are very impressionable, and can be easily influenced by a little tact and management.

'When Captain Semmes joins, you will at once report to him, and act thereafter under his instructions. He will be a stranger to the ship and crew, and will be in a position of great responsibility and embarrassment. You have it in your power to smooth away some of his difficulties in advance, especially in having all the stores and cargo of the ship in an orderly state, and the men settled and well-disposed, and I confidently rely upon your exertions to bring about such a state of things. You will consider yourself as temporarily under the orders of Captain Butcher, in whom I place great confidence, and by strict attention to your duties and the display of zeal and judgment in their execution, you will evince a just appreciation of the trust reposed in you, and will prove that your appointment to so important a post has been deserved.

'I am, etc.,

'(Signed) JAMES D. BULLOCH.

'Acting Assistant-Paymaster C. R. Yonge.'

The foregoing letters, together with the statement which immediately precedes, sufficiently describe the despatch of the *Alabama* and her tender. It will be perceived that the *Alabama* left the Mersey without any portion of her armament, and without any stores 'contraband of war.' The official report of the Surveyor of the Customs to the Collector at Liverpool, dated July 30th, 1862, contains the following paragraph:

'I have only to add that your directions to keep a strict watch on the said vessel have been carried out, and I write in the fullest confidence that she left this port without any part of her armament on board. She had not as much as a signal-gun or musket.

'(Signed) E. MORGAN,
'Surveyor.'

I got back to Liverpool from the Giants' Causeway on August 3rd, and immediately posted the following hasty despatch to the Secretary of the Confederate Navy by the Nassau closed mail:

'Liverpool, *September 3rd*, 1862.

'SIR,—

'For the last fortnight the United States officials in this country have used every possible means of inducing the British authorities to seize, or at least to forbid the sailing of the *Alabama*. Spies were employed to watch the ship while lying in a private dockyard, and affidavits were made that men had actually been enlisted by me to serve in the Confederate States Navy.

'This charge, although perfectly unfounded, for I had been very cautious not to violate any English law, gave me much uneasiness, and learning on Tuesday last from a very reliable source that the Government might not be able to resist much longer the importunities of the American Minister, I determined to get the ship out of British waters, and therefore went to sea in her myself, very unexpectedly, on Wednesday night. The United

States ship *Tuscarora* was known to be on the look-out, but favoured by thick weather, which enabled me to get quickly clear of stations from which our movements could be telegraphed, she was dodged, and I have just returned to this place, having left the *Alabama* well clear of the Irish coast, while the *Tuscarora* still remains on the look-out off Queenstown, as the telegraph reports. I have but a moment to mention this fact, as the Nassau closed mail leaves, or rather closes, in an hour. . . . I am in receipt of a letter from Captain Semmes, and from its contents hope to see him here in a day or two. The Nassau mail is safe, even though it passes through New York, and letters can be forwarded from Nassau by private hands through the agents of Messrs. John Fraser and Co.

'I am, etc.,

'(Signed) JAMES D. BULLOCH.

'Hon. S. R. Mallory,
'Secretary of the Navy.'

Not long after the above date the Confederate agencies at Nassau, Bermuda, and Havana were so well organized that there was no difficulty in sending reports by the British mails *viâ* Halifax and New York to either of those places, and the agents forwarded them to the Confederate ports by the best class of blockade-runners. It is quite astonishing how few letters from the regular official agents of the Confederate Government in Europe fell into the hands of the enemy. The agents at the islands practised great caution, and put their official mails in the hands of safe messengers, who destroyed them when capture seemed inevitable. There was often, of course, much delay, which caused embarrassment, but I never learned that any letter addressed by me to the

Secretary of the Confederate Navy at Richmond ever found its way to Washington instead, although lists of captured correspondence were frequently published in the New York papers.

I began now to look anxiously for the arrival of Captain Semmes, and knowing that he had left Nassau in the steamship *Bahama*, I arranged with the owners of that vessel to charter her for a voyage back to Nassau, and the purpose was that she should take Captain Semmes and his officers to the *Alabama* at Terceira. Some extra stores and two additional 32-pounder guns were got ready to be shipped by the *Bahama*, and Freemantle, who was with me in the *Fingal*, and a few good men were picked up to go also, ostensibly for Nassau. At the last moment about thirty men were induced to take passage in the *Bahama*, the plea being that they were to join a vessel at an outport.

The following extracts from my two next reports to the Secretary of the Navy will suffice to close the account of the outfit of the *Alabama*, and the beginning of her career as a Confederate cruiser.

'Liverpool, *August* 11*th*, 1862.

'SIR,—

'I have already informed you by letter, as well as by private messenger, that the *Alabama* is safely clear of British waters, and that another vessel, with her battery and ordnance stores, had previously sailed for a concerted rendezvous. I have now the satisfaction to report that Commander Semmes, with his officers, has arrived here, and will sail to-morrow in a steamer chartered for the purpose, to join the *Alabama*. It has been deemed advisable that I should go with Commander Semmes as far as the rendezvous, to smooth away as much as possible his embarrassments and difficulties in assuming the command of an entirely new ship with a strange and untried crew. My absence will not be prolonged beyond one month, and I have arranged all other business so that there will be no delay or interruption in the progress of other work. As soon as it would be safe to allude to the movements of the *Alabama* in detail, you shall have full accounts. . . . Suffice it for the present to say that the United States Consul . . . . has not been able to prove any violation of the Foreign Enlistment Act, or of her Majesty's Neutrality Proclamation. . . .

'It will give me the greatest satisfaction to know that Commander Semmes is fairly afloat in the *Alabama*, and confident of his ability to do good service in her, I will watch with pride her coming success, although I cannot overcome the feeling of disappointment I experienced when first informed that I was not to command her myself. The papers necessary to show all the plans, equipment, etc., of the ship are too bulky to send by the means now offering, but you shall have all these points as soon as possible. . . .

'I am, etc.,

'(Signed) JAMES D. BULLOCH.

'Hon. S. R. Mallory,
'Secretary of the Navy.'

'Liverpool, *September* 10*th*, 1862.

'SIR,—

'I have the honour to report my return to England after a short cruise to the Western Islands, where I had gone with Commander Semmes to see him fairly afloat in the *Alabama*. You have been already informed that I had taken the *Alabama* out of British waters, and leaving her off the north-west coast of Ireland, had returned to Liverpool to prepare a ship for the conveyance of Commander Semmes and his officers as soon as they arrived. The battery and ordnance stores, with a quantity of men's clothing and general supplies for a cruising ship, with 350 tons of coal, were despatched from another port of the kingdom in a sailing vessel bought for the purpose, and the two vessels were ordered to rendezvous at Praya, in the island of Terceira.

'Captain Semmes arrived from Nassau on the 8th of August, and on the 13th I sailed in the steamship *Bahama* with him and all his officers for the previously selected rendezvous.

'In seven days the *Bahama* reached Praya, and we had the satisfaction to find the *Alabama* and her consort at anchor in the bay. It was now Wednesday, August 20th, and no time was lost in commencing the transfer of stores from the tender to the *Alabama*. Favoured by Providence with mild calm weather, we met with no interruption, and the work progressed so briskly that at 10 a.m. on Friday, the 22nd, the last gun of the battery was mounted, the powder and shell all stowed, shot in their racks, and, in fine, the tender was discharged. The remainder of the day until 10 p.m. was occupied in coaling, at which time the "main-brace was spliced," and the hammocks piped down, the *Alabama*—so far, at least, as related to her equipment—being ready for action. On Sunday morning (the 24th), the *Alabama* and *Bahama* steamed slowly off the land, and when beyond the marine league which was covered by the jurisdiction of Portugal, our own national colours were hoisted for the first time at the *Alabama's* peak, welcomed by three cheers from the united crews of both vessels. Now came the business of shipping the men formally for the Confederate States service, making out their allotment tickets, arranging their accounts, etc. This could be done leisurely, for we were on the high seas, beyond the reach of Foreign Enlistment Acts and Neutrality Proclamations, the most annoying foes we have to contend with on this side of the Atlantic.

'By twelve o'clock at night all these matters were arranged ; the two steamers stopped their engines, and bidding Captain Semmes a cordial adieu, with heartfelt prayers for his success, I stepped over the *Alabama's* side. . . . Commander Semmes has written you enclosing crew-list, etc., and for further information I beg to refer you to his report. . . .

'I am, etc.,

'(Signed) JAMES D BULLOCH.

'Hon. S. R. Mallory,
'Secretary of the Navy.'

There were some minor adventures attending the equipment of the *Alabama* at Terceira which Captain Semmes has narrated in his very full and interesting history of his cruise. To repeat them here would be superfluous. My official reports were usually brief and concise, often written in great haste, and there was neither time to describe incidents of ordinary interest, nor would they have been suited to appear in official documents.

Captain Butcher returned with me in the *Bahama* to Liverpool. We parted company shortly afterwards and did not meet again for many years. I have already given my estimate of Captain Butcher's qualities, and as his name will now disappear from this narrative, I take pleasure in saying that his conduct up to the last moment was confirmatory of my first impressions. He carried out his instructions with zeal and intelligence, and when the *Bahama* arrived at the rendezvous, we had the satisfaction to find that he had already broken bulk on board the *Agrippina*, and had transferred a portion of the stores and some of the heavy weights to the *Alabama*, and had thus lessened the subsequent labour, and shortened the time of our detention at Terceira.

The whole story of the building and equipment of the *Alabama* has now been told, perhaps with unnecessary detail, but that offence may be pardoned, in consideration of the misapprehensions which have heretofore prevailed, the many misstatements which have been made with reference to her origin, and the obligation resting upon me to tell the whole truth, if I ventured to come forward as a witness at all.* Some of the statements respecting the departure of the *Alabama* from Liverpool require to be especially controverted and explained. It has been said that she 'escaped by a ruse,' and that an offence was committed by taking her away without registration, and without a clearance at the Custom House. The effect of registry in England is to entitle the ship to wear the British flag, and to assume the privileges of British nationality; but the law does not positively require an owner to register his ship.† Disabilities and disadvantages are, however, incurred by the failure to register, and thus the law may

* That the *Alabama* left Liverpool wholly unarmed is proved by the Report of the Surveyor of Customs. See note, Chapter II., p. 69.

† The law in respect to clearance and registration was altered in 1867, and the above remarks have reference to the law as it stood in 1861—1865.

be said to practically enforce registration in all cases of British ships employed in trade to and from the United Kingdom. When, however, a vessel is built in England, and is sent abroad for sale or for delivery to a previous purchaser, there is no violation of law, and no penalty is incurred, if she is sent away without a register.

The requirement to take out a clearance at a British port is purely for Customs purposes: (1) to obtain statistics of the quantity and description of merchandise entering and leaving the United Kingdom; and (2) to protect the revenue in the following particular. Ships taking on board, out of bond, such goods as are liable to import duty if consumed in the country, are allowed an exemption if the goods are intended for use during the outward voyage, or for final export, and before a clearance can be effected the Customs authorities require satisfactory proof that the goods of that class stated to be thus shipped are really kept on board and carried away. In the year 1862, and I believe until 1867, when the law was changed, no legal penalty was incurred by a vessel if she left a British for a foreign port without a clearance, provided she was in ballast, and had no stores on board except such as were exempt from duty, or had paid duty. I took legal advice on both the above points, and was fully instructed, besides which, I was furnished with specific examples of ships that had previously gone away direct from the hands of the builders, without registration or clearance. The *Alabama* was in ballast, and had no goods or stores on board that were not either free of import duty or had paid duty. She lay in a public dock for at least a fortnight. She was brought out of that dock in open daylight, and lay a night and part of two days in the river. She then got under weigh in a busy part of the day, when the whole neighbourhood was awake and active, and went to sea with colours flying.

There could hardly be a movement less like a clandestine 'escape,' and it has been shown that there was no violation of law. But it may be and has been said, that the party of guests, and the dressing with flags, were intended to convey the impression that the departure was not final, and that the ship would return. If the charge of 'escaping by a ruse' is founded upon those lawful and innocent proceedings, there is no occasion for much concern about it. I have never learned that the ethics of war forbid the practice of a ruse to deceive an enemy.

Not a single false statement was made with the purpose to mislead those having authority to make inquiries. No trust was betrayed, no confidence violated. The Foreign Enlistment Act, the Merchant Shipping Act, the Customs Regulations, were carefully examined, and in the opinion of experts none of them were transgressed, and no one has ever been indicted or made to answer in a court of law for his conduct in any matter concerning the building or despatch of the *Alabama*, although the parties implicated were at the time, and continued to be, resident in Great Britain.

Officers of her Majesty's Customs had been closely watching the ship. They were on board the very morning of her departure, and were satisfied that there were no arms or ammunition in the ship, and no goods except such as were free or had paid duty. The 'so-called' ruse was not intended to deceive them, but to mislead the United States consular spies, who I knew were ready to make any affidavit that might be considered necessary to effect a seizure of the ship for violation of the Foreign Enlistment Act.

It was furthermore said that the departure of the *Alabama* from the Mersey was 'hastened by the illicit receipt of intelligence of the decision of the British Government to stop her.' In the 'Counter Case' presented on the part of the Government of her Britannic Majesty to the Tribunal of Arbitration at Geneva, this statement is disposed of by pointing out that the report of the law officers was not made until the 29th of July, and therefore no decision had been come to when the *Alabama* left, early on the morning of that day; but the defence is set up that even if 'it had been so, the British Government could never be held responsible for the treachery of some unknown subordinate, who may have become informed of their decision or may have anticipated that it would be made.'

The statement referred to above is rather in the character of an insinuation than a charge, because it could not have been proved by any direct evidence, unless the alleged informer had been driven by a reproving conscience to confess his treachery. On the other hand, it cannot be proved to be false by any other evidence than a direct and categorical denial. It is not my office to defend, or explain, or to palliate the conduct of the British Government in any particular, but permanent officials, and especially the subordinates in the various departments, are in no way responsible for a policy, but only for the manner in which their specific duties are performed, and I feel it incumbent upon me to declare that no officer, high or low, in any department of the Government, did ever convey to me, or to anyone who afterwards repeated to me, a word or a hint which led me to anticipate what the action of the Government would be, or was likely to be, in any pending case. Although the Confederate Commissioners were not officially recognised, and therefore could have no diplomatic intercourse with the Government, it is well known that outside official circles they were received with very marked and gratifying cordiality, and it is probable that through private friends Mr. Mason could and did have very favourable opportunities of learning the general, and in some instances the specific, purposes of the Government. Whatever he learned that had any bearing upon our naval operations was always repeated to me without delay, and the information thus received often proved to be correct, although it was gathered merely from conversation with those who were accustomed to observe the conduct of Ministers and to draw their own conclusions, and not from the statements of any persons who were in a position to know the actual purposes of the Government.

But in the particular case of the *Alabama* the signs that something serious was about to happen were too visible to escape notice. The numerous statements and affidavits sent to the American Minister by the Consul at Liverpool were necessarily drawn up in legal form, and required the employment of solicitors. I cannot say whether there is, or is not, a species of magnetic sympathy between attorneys, or whether they have any special devices for finding out each other's ways, but I do know that my own solicitor managed to find out the particulars of some of the affidavits, and although they were inaccurate in the affirmations which were at all specific, yet some of them contained allegations which he thought would at least induce the Government to detain the ship for investigation.

Besides this, the Foreign Secretary, pressed by the United States Minister to take some action, referred the affidavits to the Commissioners of Customs, and directed them to inquire and report. For a fortnight before the departure of the *Alabama* inquiries came in showers from the collector, sometimes delivered in person by the surveyor or his subordinates, sometimes in the form of written memoranda. The inquiries were mostly addressed to the builders of the ship, and often referred to matters of which they knew nothing, and so could give no reply. My solicitor got possession of one of the lists of questions, and it lies before me now while I am writing. Almost every inquiry could have been answered by a direct and positive denial of the truth of the allegation; but at the same time it was possible, perhaps probable, that the Government would not be satisfied with denials, however categorical and explicit.

It must be manifest from the foregoing *resumé* that there was good reason for hastening the departure of the *Alabama*, and I trust it will be now admitted that the information which caused the somewhat precipitate movement came to those concerned in it, not by any treachery or breach of trust, but in a very simple, regular, and ordinary way.

The collector of the Port of Liverpool at that time was a Mr. S. Price Edwards. The official documents published in the proceedings before the Tribunal of Arbitration prove, it seems to me, that Mr. Edwards did his duty faithfully—in fact, zealously. On the 21st of July, 1862, eight days before the sailing of the *Alabama*, he appears to have written to his superiors in London informing them that the ship was quite ready for sea, and might sail at any moment, and he asked to be instructed by telegraph if the intention was to detain her.*

* Extract from a letter addressed by the Collector of Customs, Liverpool (Mr. Price Edwards), to the Commissioner of Customs,

When it was known that the *Alabama* was off, and all chance of seizing her had vanished, great annoyance and chagrin was felt at the United States Consulate and among the resident Americans who were in sympathy with the Federal Government. This feeling of disappointment was shown in many ways—among others, in harsh and ungenerous insinuations against the integrity of the local authorities, especially against Mr. Price Edwards himself, who was even accused of having been paid for shutting his eyes.

Many months afterwards I met a gentleman at the house of a friend, and we engaged in conversation for some time, neither knowing who the other was. Later in the evening we were joined by our host, who introduced us. There was a mutual expression of surprise, for the parties were Mr. Price Edwards and the writer. Mr. Edwards asked me if I was aware that he had been accused of taking a bribe from me for letting the *Alabama* go. I replied that I had heard some indefinite insinuations of the kind, but had not given them much heed. He affected to be equally indifferent, but I learned from other sources that he had been deeply pained, and that he never wholly recovered from the feeling of mortification produced by such an unfounded and gratuitous aspersion upon his official integrity.

Subsequently Mr. Edwards fell into some difficulties with the authorities at London in no way connected with Confederate affairs, and was removed from his office. I never knew the cause of his removal, but I met him some time afterwards. He appeared much broken in health and greatly depressed in spirits, and

London, dated July 21, 1862: 'I shall feel obliged by the Board being pleased to instruct me by telegraph how I am to act, as the ship appears to be ready for sea, and may leave at any hour she pleases.'

not long after I learned that he had passed beyond the reach of such 'ills as flesh is heir to.' I am glad to have it in my power to free his memory from the stain which may have clung to it in respect to the 'escape' of the *Alabama*, although it is hardly probable that any surviving relative will know that it has been done.

There is just one more disclaimer that I feel in some sort impelled to pronounce in this connection. I have said that no public official, either principal or subordinate, ever gave the faintest hint of the purposes of his superiors in respect to the seizure of Confederate ships. I can also affirm, without the least mental reservation, that no proposition, or suggestion, or promise of reward, was ever made to an *employé* of the Government which could have tempted him to swerve in his loyalty, or to turn one hair's-breadth from the straight line of his duty, and I never saw or heard of anyone who appeared likely to be accessible to such temptations, had they been put in his way.

When I parted from Captain Semmes off the island of Terceira, it was arranged that I should send out the *Agrippina* to him with a cargo of coals and certain other supplies, and the barque was ordered to Cardiff to load. This arrangement was carried out successfully. Semmes met his tender at St. Pierre, in the French island of Martinique, from which place he despatched her to Blanquilla, a small island off the coast of Venezuela, where he took from her a supply of coal, and then sent her to the uninhabited Arcas Cays, off Yucatan. Here he took the remainder of the coal and stores, and sent the barque to Liverpool, proceeding himself to look after General Banks's expedition against Galveston.

Semmes' hope was to catch the troop-ships and transports *en route*, and to make a dash in among them. He wrote me from Arcas Islands, January 4, 1863:—

'I have filled up with coal a second time from the barque, caulked the spar deck, overhauled and set up rigging, and shall sail again to-night on another foray against the enemy. My ship is getting in good order, and I have nearly a full crew, having added twenty-five men to the eighty-five that I brought with me from Terceira, and they are pretty well drilled at the guns. It is not unlikely that before I get out of the Gulf of Mexico I shall "put up" something, as this is a sort of "close sea" of the enemy, swarming with his cruisers. After leaving the Gulf I shall carry out the Secretary of the Navy's suggestion as to my cruising ground, and about which we (you and I) have consulted.'

In the same letter Semmes asked me to send the *Agrippina* to him again, first to the island of Fernando de Noronha, with instructions to wait there three days, and if he did not arrive to go on to Bahia. The expectation that he would 'put up something' before he got out of the Gulf was realized. He did not get among General Banks's transports, but he went off Galveston to look after them, and found there a powerful squadron under Acting Rear-Admiral H. H. Bell, who sent two or three of his ships to meet the approaching stranger and bring her to an account of herself.

Semmes ran slowly off shore, and drew one of his pursuers after him. When he found that the others did not follow, he waited until just at nightfall, when the enemy closed. There was a hail and a reply, then two quickly succeeding broadsides, and a sharp engagement of thirteen minutes, a cessation of the firing on one side, and a hail to report the vessel sinking. The hail was not from the *Alabama*, but it suspended her fire, and her boats were soon busy picking up the crew of the United States ship *Hatteras*.

It was a creditable performance for the first effort of a hastily improvised cruiser with a green crew, to sink an opposing ship in thirteen minutes in a night engagement, and then to pick up every man who had not been killed or mortally wounded in the action. On the other side, I take pleasure in saying that Lieutenant-Commanding H. H. Blake showed commendable spirit and courage in boldly running down upon a ship which he suspected to be the *Alabama*, and therefore knew was his superior in armament and general efficiency, when he had distanced his consorts and could expect no support from them.

The *Hatteras* was an iron paddle-steamer, bought out of the mercantile marine. Her engines were much exposed, and were of the 'top-lever,' or 'walking-beam' type. The armament of the *Hatteras* was four 32-pounders, two Parrot 30-pounder rifles, one 20-pounder rifle, and one 12-pounder howitzer—total, eight guns. The armament of the *Alabama* was six 32-pounders, one 8-inch smooth-bore gun (112 cwt.), and one 100-pounder Blakely rifled gun. The crew of the *Hatteras* was 108 men, that of the *Alabama* 110.

I do not describe the engagement in detail, because the reports of both commanders are on public record, and every incident has been minutely related in 'My Adventures Afloat,' by Admiral Semmes. There is no doubt that the *Alabama* was the superior ship, and barring an accident, or one of those unexpected chances which sometimes occur in contests between single vessels, and upset all calculations, she ought to have won, and the loss of his ship was no disgrace to the commander of the *Hatteras*.

The *Agrippina* was not a clipper. She made a long passage from the Arcas Islands to England, and sprang her foremast in a gale before getting into the Channel. She was refitted and despatched as quickly as possible, but this time the arrangements failed. Semmes touched at Fernando de Noronha, and then went on to Bahia, but not finding the tender at either place, he coaled from the shore, and proceeded on his cruise to the Cape of Good Hope, *en route* for the China Sea. The *Alabama* left Bahia on the 22nd of May, 1863, and the *Agrippina* arrived there on June 1st. Semmes was a little impatient to get away. He had done much damage to the enemy's commerce on the great ocean highway off the north-east coast of Brazil, and began to think that the neighbourhood could not remain safe much longer. He wrote me from Bahia, May 21st, 1862:

'I have coaled from the shore, and as the authorities are hurrying me off, I have appointed another rendezvous for the *Agrippina*. If you hear anything of my violating the neutrality of Fernando de Noronha, contradict it *in limine*, as being an invention of the enemy. We are having capital success. That "little bill" which the Yankees threaten to present to our Uncle John Bull, for the depredations of the *Alabama*, is growing apace, and already reaches $3,100,000.'

When the *Agrippina* arrived at Bahia, Captain McQueen found there two United States ships, the *Mohican* and the *Onward*. The United States Consul had suspected another British ship then in port of having stores on board for the *Alabama*, and had advised the commanders of the United States ships to capture her if she should leave the port. Captain

McQueen soon learned that his vessel had also attracted the notice and suspicions of the United States Consul, and he learned that the *Onward* was especially on the watch for him. In this dilemma he consulted her Majesty's Consul, who told him that he had not a shadow of doubt that if he went outside the *Onward* would capture him, and he would be sent before a United States prize-court.

Captain McQueen waited for some time in great perplexity, being most anxious to comply with Captain Semmes' instructions, but the *Onward* remained also on the look-out for him, and escape from her was impossible. Finally he applied again to her Majesty's Consul, who advised him to sell his cargo and take a freight for England, a proceeding which would protect him from capture, and would be the best possible arrangement for his owners. The Consul did not, of course, know of the *Agrippina's* connection with the *Alabama*, whatever the general belief at Bahia may have been, and his advice was given in the ordinary course of his duty as the guardian of British interests, the *Agrippina* being a duly registered British ship. Captain McQueen acted upon it, and to satisfy the owner that all was right, he brought home a consular certificate, which alleged that 'Bahia had been for some time virtually blockaded by the United States ships *Mohican* and *Onward*.'

The *Agrippina's* homeward freight amounted to £437 15s. 3d. She was too well known to be used for the Confederate service again, and was sold, after some delay, for a purchaser did not readily offer. Her original cost was £1,400, and she fetched at auction £860. The service she had rendered was more than compensation for the loss, but it was evident that the expense of providing a permanent tender for each cruising ship was more than the Confederate Treasury could bear, and besides this, I perceived that the probabilities of bringing the two together at distant and varying points, where they could communicate and make the transfer of stores safely, did not justify the labour and expenditure. The *Alabama* was therefore left to look out for herself, and I felt no great concern, because I was confident of her qualities and fitness for the work she had in hand. I knew that she could supply herself with provisions and various other wants from prizes, and the 'cruising fund' was sufficient to meet the requirements of fuel. Her commander writes of her thus :

'I was much gratified to find that my new ship proved to be a fine sailer under canvas. This quality was of inestimable advantage to me, as it enabled me to do most of my work under sail. She carried but an eighteen days' supply of fuel, and if I had been obliged, because of her dull sailing qualities, to chase everything under steam, the reader can see how I should have been hampered in my movements. I should have been half my time running into port for fuel. This would have disclosed my whereabouts so frequently to the enemy, that I should have been constantly in danger of capture, whereas I could now stretch into far-distant seas, and chase, capture, and destroy, perfectly independent of steam. I adopted the plan, therefore, of working under sail in the very beginning of the cruise, and practised it unto the end. With the exception of half-a-dozen prizes, all my captures were made with my screw hoisted and my ship under sail.'

The foregoing extract from 'My Adventures Afloat,' by Admiral Semmes, is confirmatory of what I have said in an early chapter respecting the suitable type for a Confederate cruiser; and the opinion I held at the beginning of the war was maintained to the end, and deterred me from buying any of the ordinary war-ships with non-lifting screws, or any of the wooden ships with insufficient sail power, which private parties desirous to make commissions were constantly pressing upon me.

The *Alabama*, it will be perceived, was commissioned on the high seas, and she never entered a Confederate port. This was always a sore point with Mr. Seward, the United States Secretary of State. He never ceased to call her a pirate, nor to press the British Government to seize her, even after she had been commissioned as a man-of-war under the Confederate flag. The tone of his despatches on the subject was not couched in such language as is commonly used by statesmen accustomed to diplomatic usage. His petulant complaints often gave offence, and brought upon him rebukes and retorts which must have been wounding to the national feeling in the United States if they were ever printed in the Congressional documents.

The European Powers having acknowledged the existence of a *de facto* Government at Richmond, that acknowledgment carried with it the concession of all belligerent rights. By the determination to acknowledge the Confederate States as belligerents, England, among other Powers, bound herself to extend the same privileges to Confederate cruisers as to those of the United States; and it was not only discourteous, but it was highly impolitic in Mr. Seward to taunt foreign Governments with precipitancy in the recognition, and then of harbouring 'piratical cruisers.'

I suppose there can be no principle of international law plainer than this, namely, when a ship is once commissioned by a recognised *de facto* Government, no other Power can inquire into her origin or antecedents.

The process of commissioning a ship is for the duly appointed captain, with his staff of officers, to take charge of her, read his commission, and hoist his pennant and the national colours. When these formalities have been complied with, no foreign Power can question the character of the ship, or enter upon any inquiry as to the place where she was commissioned. The British authorities could ask the commander of a Confederate cruiser for a sight of his commission, and if that was in order, no further inquiry was admissible.

No European or other neutral Power questioned the foregoing premises during the late Civil War, and it is not therefore necessary to mention any precedents from their history of vessels commissioned abroad or on the high seas.

Cooper, in his 'Naval History of the United States,' supplies many examples of vessels which were bought, armed, equipped, manned, and almost exclusively officered abroad and by foreigners, and which were then commissioned by the American Government and sent to cruise against English commerce, and to foray upon the British coasts, without previously entering an American port. As one case is sufficient to establish the precedent, I will just mention that of a fine fast English cutter bought at Dover by an agent of the American Commissioners in France. She was taken across the channel to Dunkirk, where her name was changed to the *Surprise*. She was fully equipped, officered, and manned. The Commissioners filled up a blank commission signed by John Hancock, President of Congress, and handed it to one Captain Gustavus Conyngham, who went to sea from Dunkirk on the 1st of May, 1777, and on the 4th captured the English packet *Prince of Orange.* Captain Conyngham took his prize into Dunkirk, the neutral port from which he had sailed only a few days before. The English Minister remonstrated, and the French Government seized the *Surprise*, imprisoned Captain Conyngham, and took away his commission ; but the American Commissioners at Paris found means to obtain his release. They bought and fitted out another cutter at Dunkirk, which was called the *Revenge*, and Captain Conyngham was recommissioned to her. The *Revenge* sailed from Dunkirk on July 18, 1777, and captured many British vessels. Some she destroyed ; the most valuable she sent into Spanish ports. Fenimore Cooper says that the *Surprise* and *Revenge* were spoken of in the accounts of the day as privateers, but that they were, as a matter of fact, bought and equipped by agents of the Diplomatic Commissioners of the United States.

Commodore Paul Jones fitted out his ship, the *Bon-homme Richard*, in a French port. His crew, picked up chiefly at Nantes, are thus described by Cooper: 'A few Americans were found to fill the stations of sea-officers on the quarter-deck and forward, but the remainder of the people were a mixture of Irish, Scotch, Portuguese, Norwegians, Germans, Spaniards, Swedes, Italians, and Malays,' etc. The Commissioners stationed in France at that time, and who conducted the naval operations of the American Congress abroad, were Benjamin Franklin, Silas Deane, and John Adams, eminent men, who would have indignantly repudiated the charge of piracy against their improvised cruisers, and yet no agent of the Confederate Government ever took such liberties with neutral rights, or with the laws of nations, as they did.

In regard to the right to commission a ship on the

high seas, I will refer to but one case, recorded also in Cooper's 'Naval History of the United States.' Commodore David Porter made a famous cruise among the English whaling fleet in the Pacific during the war of 1812-15, in command of the United States ship *Essex*. One of his prizes being armed and well suited for cruising, he manned her, partly from his own ship, put his first-lieutenant, John Downes, in command, and commissioned her as a United States ship-of-war, naming her the *Essex Junior*.

In view of these and other well-known examples recorded in the naval histories of England as well as the United States, Mr. Seward's continued harping upon the 'foreign origin' of the *Alabama* seemed puerile to the representatives of the various Powers to whom he addressed remonstrances on the subject. However, the *Florida*, although she went into a Confederate port, and was officered, manned, and recommissioned there, was also called by the generic name of 'pirate' in all the official correspondence of the United States during the war; and so it appears that, in Mr. Seward's opinion, deeds done by the *de facto* Government of the revolted colonies in 1777, or by the more formally recognised Government at Washington in 1812-15, were just and lawful acts of war, but that similar acts done by authority of the *de facto* Government of the Confederate States in 1862 were 'criminal' and 'nefarious.' The *Surprise*, fitted out, armed, and manned at Dunkirk, might with propriety capture a British vessel four days after she had left the neutral port; the *Essex Junior*, a captured prize, might be lawfully commissioned by a United States officer, at some savage island in the Pacific, and then sent to prey upon British whalers; but the *Alabama*, carrying the commission of a *de facto* Government, recognised as a belligerent Power by every civilized nation, was a 'piratical rover' unworthy of shelter or assistance, but fit only to be pursued and destroyed as a common enemy and a common pest.

Let us hope, if we can, that there will be no more wars, foreign or domestic; but Mr. Seward has done much by the pretensions he set up during the great contest of 1861-65 to embarrass the United States whenever they may be again placed in the position of a neutral or belligerent.

The *Alabama* left Liverpool on the 29th of July, 1862. She was commissioned off the island of Terceira on the 24th of August, and she kept the sea almost incessantly for two years. During that period she was rarely in harbour, and never long enough to effect a thorough and satisfactory overhaul of rigging, hull, or engines. She was kept while cruising chiefly under sail, with screw up; but she was purposely taken to the great thoroughfares of American marine traffic, to those well-known points towards which the trade of the world converges, and where it was reasonable to expect United States ships would be sent to keep guard. Hence she was in constant expectation of having to run or to fight. Any morning's light might find her close to an enemy's ship, and prudence required both a sharp look-out and constant readiness. Her engines got rest, but her boilers none. The fires were never allowed to go wholly out, but were banked; and the water was kept in such condition that steam might be quickly got. The chief engineer has told me that he rarely had an opportunity to cool the boilers and clean flues and pipes.

A great portion of her cruising was in the tropics, although she faced every vicissitude of climate. The

The *Alabama*, drawn from a description given by Captain Hagar of the *Brilliant*. *(Harper's Weekly)*

Winslow Homer depicts the consternation of passengers on an American ship when the *Alabama* approached. *(Harper's Weekly)*

icy fogs of the Newfoundland Bank, the steaming moisture of the equatorial belt, the burning sun of Malacca and the China Sea—all these in turn, and in quick succession, served to test her endurance. The wear and tear of such a cruise, such a lengthened period of restless activity, with no means to supply deficiencies or to repair injuries, except what might be found in captured vessels, told upon the little craft at last, and early in 1864 Semmes began to think of her requirements, and coming back round the Cape of Good Hope into the Atlantic, he worked leisurely up through the 'paths of commerce,' capturing a prize now and then, but finding few, for by that time the American mercantile flag had well nigh disappeared.

The effect produced upon the commerce and the shipping interests of the United States by two or three Confederate cruisers was a very striking peculiarity of the late war. While the *Alabama* was in the China Sea many American ships took shelter in the harbour of Singapore and other ports, and were partly dismantled and laid up at a time when trade was good, and there was an active demand for tonnage to all parts of the world. Semmes found on board a prize captured in the Straits of Malacca a copy of the Singapore *Times,* dated 9th December, 1863, containing a list of seventeen American ships, with an aggregate tonnage of about 12,000 tons, which were laid up at that port alone.

The Right Hon. Milner Gibson, President of the Board of Trade, made a speech at Ashton-under-Lyne, January 20th, 1864, in which he commented upon the transference of the carrying trade from American to British ships. He stated that during the year (1863-4) the number of British ships clearing had increased to something like 14,000,000 tons, as against 7,000,000 tons of all foreign tonnage inclusive, and he gave the actual decrease in the employment of American shipping in the trade between England and the United States as something like forty-six or forty-seven per cent.

Mr. Milner Gibson called particular attention to the foregoing results as an example of what could be done by two or three swift steamers, and commented upon the injury inflicted upon the commerce of the United States by the Confederate cruisers, as a warning to other Maritime Powers of what might happen to them. But I have always thought that the United States Navy Department showed either great apathy or was singularly blind to the real danger to the commerce of the United States, and strangely negligent in using the means to protect it. The points of attack were so apparent that it seems hardly credible that they were never occupied.

The whole traffic between the northern ports of the United States and the Pacific, as well as with Brazil and the states of the La Plata, passes through a belt of no great width, which intersects the equator at about the 30th meridian of west longitude. American outward-bound ships shape their course so as to leave the north-east Trades near the above-named meridian, then work their way through the equatorial 'doldrums,' and meeting the south-east Trade-winds, they are forced, after crossing the line, generally somewhat further west, thus passing in sight, or very nearly in sight, of the island of Fernando de Noronha. Homeward-bound American ships from the East Indies leave the south-east Trades at very nearly the same point, and those from round the Horn and the La Plata or Brazil pass sometimes rather more to the westward, between Fernando de Noronha and that portion of the South American coast which has its extreme eastern projection between Pernambuco and Cape St. Roque.

If the United States had stationed a few ships to cruise in couplets in the neighbourhood of the above-named 'forks of the road,' as they have been called by Maury, and a few more, say, in the Straits of Malacca, and on the principal and well-known cruising ground of their whaling-fleet, two or three Confederate cruisers could not have remained for weeks in the track of passing ships, capturing and destroying them without hindrance.

Neither the *Alabama*, *Florida*, nor *Sumter* was driven from her work in any particular latitude; they shifted their cruising grounds only when it seemed advisable to seek fresh victims elsewhere; and the *Shenandoah* went round the world, sought out the great American whaling-fleet in the North Pacific, and destroyed thirty-eight vessels without so much as seeing a United States ship-of-war.

It is not probable that any other Maritime Power will leave its commerce at the mercy of light cruisers of the *Alabama* type in a future war. In fact, a fair amount of British trade could be carried on in steamers capable of protecting themselves or of escaping by their great speed, because the majority of the modern steamers of the British mercantile marine could carry as heavy guns as the cruisers that would be sent after them, and they have very high speed.

On the 11th of June, 1864, the *Alabama* arrived at Cherbourg. The purpose was to give her a thorough refit, at least so far as the French authorities would permit. Captain Semmes soon learned that the United States ship *Kearsarge*, Captain John A. Winslow, was at Flushing. On the 14th she came round to Cherbourg, and Captain Winslow made a request of the local authorities that a number of prisoners landed from the *Alabama* should be permitted to join his ship. This request was refused, and the *Kearsarge*, without anchoring, went outside and took up a position off the breakwater. It was not probable that she would leave the near neighbourhood until the *Alabama* came out, and it was necessary therefore for Captain Semmes to consider whether he would complete his repairs, and then attempt to avoid an encounter by going out on a dark night, or whether he should go out openly and engage her.

The *Kearsarge* had some advantage in tonnage, and in weight and size of scantling, and she was probably in better condition generally. The effect of the *Alabama's* long and active cruise has been mentioned above. Captain Semmes, writing about two months before his arrival at Cherbourg, likens her to 'the weary foxhound, limping back after a long chase, footsore, and longing for quiet and repose.' The *Kearsarge*, on the contrary, was out in pursuit, and there is no reason to doubt that she was fit for any work suited to her class.

The *Alabama* carried six 32-pounder guns in broadside, one 8-inch smooth bore of 112 cwt., and one 7-inch 100-pounder rifled gun (Blakely pattern) on pivots. The *Kearsarge* mounted four 32-pounders in broadside, two 11-inch Dahlgren guns pivoted on deck, and one 28-pounder rifled gun, pivoted on the top-gallant forecastle. She had also a 12-pounder howitzer, which was used near the close of the action. The *Alabama* was pierced for eight 32-pounders, but was two short. However, by shifting one to the fighting side she could, and in fact did, use six guns in the engagement against the five which the *Kearsarge* fought.

In spite of the *Alabama's* extra 32-pounder in broadside, I think every professional man would say without

The U.S.S. *Kearsarge.* *(Official U.S. Navy Photograph)*

The officers of the *Kearsarge*. *(National Archives)*

The eleven-inch aft pivot-gun of the *Kearsarge*.
(Official U.S. Navy Photograph)

hesitation that the battery of the *Kearsarge* was the most effective. She not only threw more metal in broadside, but the larger calibre of her two chief pivot-guns gave her a great advantage against a wooden ship. I have not hesitated to point out, fairly as I think, the particulars in which I consider the *Kearsarge* to have been superior in condition and armament to the *Alabama.* The conditions under which the engagement was fought did not admit of any advantage being gained on either side by skilful handling, neither ship having sufficient superiority in speed to enable her to take a raking position. The result of the action was determined by the superior accuracy of the firing from the *Kearsarge.* The damage she inflicted upon the *Alabama* was more than sufficient to have destroyed her, and inasmuch as the *Kearsarge* received no mortal wound, and came out of the engagement with no material injury, it is only a fair admission to say that the result would probably not have been different under the existing circumstances, even if the *Alabama* had been a larger ship, and more powerfully armed.

The crew of the *Alabama* were in good discipline, and were well drilled in the manual of the guns, but the impossibility of replenishing the ordnance stores prevented target practice, and the battery had never been used with shot except in the short engagement with the *Hatteras*, which was fought at very close quarters, and a few rounds on one occasion fired at a prize, after the crew were removed. The men, therefore, had not been trained to judge of distances, and were wholly without the skill, precision and coolness which come only with practice and the habit of firing at a visible object and noting the effect.

Captain Semmes took a comprehensive view of the

relative force and condition of the two ships, and did not think the disparity so great as to render success hopeless. He thought of the cases in which a chance shot reaching a vital spot had disabled ships in previous engagements, or had at least balanced the initial disparity, and felt therefore justified in trying conclusions with his enemy, who it was quite apparent did not intend to grant him a free passage out to sea.

Captain Semmes notified Captain Winslow, through the United States Consul, that he would go out and fight him as soon as he had finished coaling, and it will not be doubted that both ships made the best possible preparations for the engagement. On the morning of the 19th of June, 1864, at about 9.30, the *Alabama* got under weigh, and steamed out of Cherbourg, passing to the westward of the breakwater. The *Kearsarge* took note of her movement, and knowing that there was no purpose to avoid an engagement, and desirous to prevent any encroachment upon the neutral rights of France, Captain Winslow turned his ship's head off shore, and steamed to a distance of about seven miles, followed by the *Alabama*. When it was quite certain that both vessels were well beyond the 'line of jurisdiction,' the *Kearsarge* turned her head in shore and steered towards the *Alabama*. The two ships approached rapidly, both were cleared for action, each with her battery pivoted to starboard.

When they were about one mile apart, the *Alabama* sheered to port, showed her starboard battery, and almost immediately opened fire, the shot mostly going high. The *Kearsarge* stood on until she had received three 'broadsides' from the *Alabama*,* the shot still going high, and doing no damage except to the rigging.

* Captain Winslow's official report.

At about a thousand yards' distance, Winslow began to be apprehensive of getting a raking shot, and he then sheered to port, bringing his own starboard broadside to bear, and opened fire.

The action now became active on both sides. Semmes, conscious of the inferiority of his crew in gunnery, had carefully considered the advantage he would gain by fighting at close quarters, and his purpose was to get within short range as soon as possible. Winslow, ignorant of this intention on the part of his adversary, pushed on at full speed to get in-shore of the *Alabama*, hoping thus to prevent any attempt to return into Cherbourg if he should succeed in disabling her. As soon as the two ships passed each other, the *Kearsarge* put her helm to port, with the object to pass under the stern of the *Alabama* and rake her. To counteract this movement and to keep her own broadside bearing, the *Alabama's* helm was ported also, and the two ships, keeping their helms to port, and steaming at full speed, fell into a circular course, and continued the action heading in opposite directions, in positions generally parallel to each other, while steaming round a common centre.

In about one hour and ten minutes after the *Alabama* fired her first gun, she was found to be in a sinking condition. The 11-inch shells of the *Kearsarge* had made several openings in her sides which it was impossible to stop, and at every roll in the very moderate swell large quantities of water rushed into her.

Semmes made an effort to reach the French coast by assisting the engines with the fore-and-aft sails, but the ship filled so rapidly that the fires were soon put out. Meanwhile the *Kearsarge* steamed ahead, and keeping her helm to port, she passed under the *Alabama's* stern, and ranging along her port-beam, finally got into a raking position across her bow; but by this time the *Alabama* was so manifestly sinking that the fire of both ships had ceased.

When Semmes discovered that his ship had got her death wound, and that she was hopelessly settling under him, he ordered the colours to be struck. There is some discrepancy in the reports of the two commanders as to the cessation of the firing. Captain Semmes says that the *Kearsarge* fired into him after his flag was down. On the other hand, Captain Winslow states that having ceased firing, he received two shots from the *Alabama's* port battery, which drew a return from him. Neither captain, however, charges the other with a wilful default. Semmes states the fact in his report, but in the comments upon the action in his narrative of the cruise, he acquits Captain Winslow of any intentional violation of the rules of humane warfare, and there can be no doubt that the alleged exchange of shots after the surrender arose from a mistake which is not without precedent in previous sea fights.

There was barely time to get the *Alabama's* wounded men into the boats and despatch them to the *Kearsarge*, when the ship went down, and the officers and crew were swimming for their lives. The *Kearsarge* did not immediately send assistance. It appears from Captain Winslow's report that the boats were disabled, but he managed, after some delay, to get two afloat, and they picked up a few men.

Captain Semmes and the greater portion of his officers and crew were rescued by two French fishing vessels and the English steam-yacht *Deerhound*, owned by Mr. John Lancaster. The French fishermen proceeded into Cherbourg, and the *Deerhound* to Southampton, and the rescued officers and men were landed at those two ports respectively.

The *Alabama* was so badly cut up in her hull that it is doubtful if she could have been again refitted for cruising, even if she could have been kept afloat long enough to reach Cherbourg. An officer told me the day after the engagement that he thought a barrel might have been passed through the hole made by an 11-inch shell at the gangway, and near the water-line. He said one of the men, while sponging his gun, saw the hole, and called his attention to it. He looked out of the port, and when he saw the aperture and the rush of water at every roll, he felt that the *Alabama's* last moments were close at hand. It is not possible to tell how many times the *Alabama* was hit, but it is quite certain that she received many shot in her hull, more than one of which contributed to her sinking.

The *Kearsarge* fired 173 shot and shell, apportioned as follows: From 11-inch guns, 55 shell; from 32-pounders, 18 shell and 42 solid shot; from 28-pounder rifled gun, 48 shell; from 12-pound howitzer, 9 shrapnel and 1 canister. She was struck twenty-eight times by shot and shell in various places. One shell exploded in her funnel, but except damage to some of her boats, she was but little injured, and strange to say, she had only three men wounded, none killed. The *Alabama* had twenty-one wounded and nine killed, and it is believed that ten were drowned.

I have read with care the reports of the two commanders. They are creditable to the writers, and give a fair, unpretentious account of the action, varying in no essential particular. I have not described the action with minute detail, because the official reports are on record, and Captain Semmes has published a full account of all the incidents appertaining to the engagement, and the events which preceded and followed it. I feel confident that I have given an impartial summary, and I think it may fairly be stated that the *Kearsarge* was in better condition and was more efficiently armed than the *Alabama;* but that she used her superior strength with commensurate skill and effectiveness, and gained the action by the excellence of her gunnery.

In mentioning the points it was proper for Semmes to consider before determining whether he would be justified in engaging the *Kearsarge*, I have said that he took into account the possible occurrence of one of those fortuitous chances which often produce very unexpected results. It appears from the details annexed to Captain Winslow's report that a shell from the *Alabama's* 7-inch rifled gun lodged in the stern-post of the *Kearsarge*, but did not explode. A ship's stern-post receives the 'wood-ends' of the planks which form the counter, and a vessel could scarcely receive a shell in a more vital point, if the shell exploded. I have been informed by an officer, who told me that he got the fact from the first-lieutenant of the *Kearsarge*, that this shell struck the stern-post about fifteen minutes after the beginning of the engagement. If, therefore, it had not failed to explode, the stern of the *Kearsarge* would have been shattered, the wood-ends opened, and she would have foundered instead of the *Alabama*. But without reference to time, if the shell had done its work, the result would have been to entirely change the issue of the action.

In all the remarks I have heretofore made with reference to the relative strength and condition of the two ships, I have compared them exclusively as two wooden screw-steamers, but it appears from Captain Winslow's report that, his ship being rather light, he had protected

The *Kearsarge* and the *Alabama* in mortal combat. *(Century Magazine)*

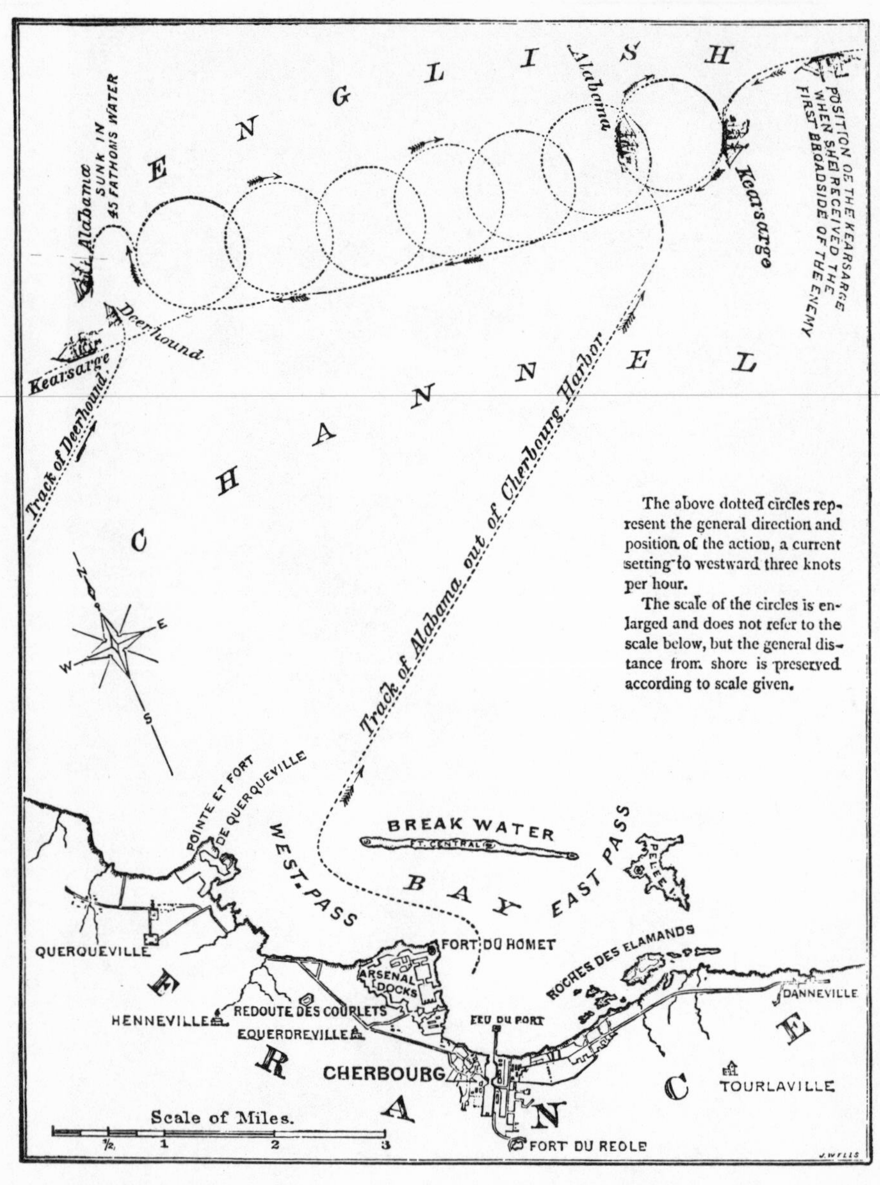

A chart showing how the *Kearsarge* and the *Alabama* circled around each other as they fought. *(Century Magazine)*

her midship section by stowing the sheet chain-cables outside. The chains were, it appears, arranged perpendicularly from the water's edge, so as to cover the engine space, and they were concealed by a thin plank covering. In fact, the *Kearsarge* over her most vital parts was armour-plated, and this is an important consideration in discussing the principles of naval warfare suggested by this spirited engagement between two single ships propelled by steam.

Captain Semmes, in his report, says that the officers whom he sent to the *Kearsarge* with the wounded, informed him that the covering boards had been ripped off in many directions, and in some places the chains had been broken and forced partly into the ship's side by the *Alabama's* shot and shells. It is manifest that if those projectiles had found their way into that protected section of the *Kearsarge*, the engagement might have had a different result.

Captain Semmes also states, in the history of his cruise, that the *Alabama's* powder was defective, which he attributed to the long time it had been on board, and the exposure to so many varying climates. It seems to me that there is some reason to accept the opinion that the powder was defective, because the details accompanying Captain Winslow's report mention that the *Kearsarge* was struck twenty-eight times in various places about the hull, but no damage is stated except the shattering of two boats. When the firing became active, the ships were about a thousand yards apart, and the distance was gradually reduced to four hundred yards. At this latter distance I think that the 100-pound elongated shot and shells from the *Alabama's* Blakely rifled gun would have carried the chain through the side of the *Kearsarge* if they had struck with the velocity due to the power of the weapon. The powder on board the *Alabama* was manufactured and put up into cartridges especially for her by Messrs Curtiss and Harvey. I do not mind mentioning their names, because they took the order as an ordinary business transaction, and without the slightest knowledge of the purpose for which the ammunition was wanted. The quality at the beginning of the cruise was perfect. Captain Semmes has told me that in the night engagement with the *Hatteras* her sides were all ablaze with the vivid light of the *Alabama's* exploding shells, and the sharp, quick, vigorous reports gave proof of the purity and strength of the charges.

In reference to the action with the *Kearsarge*, Captain Semmes says: 'Perceiving that our shells, though apparently exploding against the enemy's sides, were doing him but little damage, I returned to solid-shot firing;' and several naval experts who witnessed the engagement from the hills near Cherbourg have told me that they were struck with the difference in the appearance of the flame and smoke produced by the explosions of the shells from the two ships. Those from the *Kearsarge* emitted a quick bright flash, and the smoke went quickly away in a fine blue vapour, while those from the *Alabama* exhaled a dull flame and a mass of sluggish grey smoke. It is not unlikely that the effect of climate and the long stowage on board had helped to deteriorate the *Alabama's* powder, but I think the deterioration was hastened and increased by a local cause, and by a practice the ill effects of which were not suspected at the time.

The internal arrangements of the *Alabama* were designed to secure the largest possible space for essential stores; and as she had means of condensing, it was not thought necessary to provide tanks for more than two to three weeks' supply of water. The magazine was placed so that the top would be two feet and a half below the water-line, and the water-tanks, which were of iron, were fitted on each side and in front of it, and were carried up to the berth deck-beams, thus forming an additional protection. After the loss of the *Alabama*, I learned from the chief engineer that it was often the habit to condense in excess of the quantity which the cooling-tank held ; and that the boiling water, almost in the condition of steam, was often passed directly into the two iron tanks on each side of the magazine, and in contact with it. I think this practice contributed largely to the deterioration of the powder, and I have thought it worth mentioning as an element in the case.

Taking a comprehensive and impartial view of all the circumstances, I think it will be admitted that the probabilities of success were in favour of the *Kearsarge*. Captain Winslow was quite right in doing whatever he could to increase the defensive power of his ship, and he was not bound to inform his adversary that he had encased her most vulnerable parts with chain-cables. It has never been considered an unworthy ruse for a commander, whether afloat or ashore, to disguise his strength and to entice a weaker opponent within his reach. The *Kearsarge* was well fought. Captain Winslow reported the result in a clear, plain statement, neither concealing nor exaggerating any circumstance that would tend to enhance his own merit, or to depreciate his adversary, if it were differently told. Anyone who reads his report and the accompanying documents, and who is aware of the effect of her fire upon the *Alabama*, will admit that the *Kearsarge* was in a state of discipline and efficiency creditable to all on board, and to the United States naval service.

On the other hand, it seems to me that the *Alabama* could not have won, except by the occurrence of a fortuitous chance, such as the explosion of the shell which lodged in her enemy's stern-post. Captain Semmes says that every man and officer behaved well, and at the trying moment there was neither panic nor confusion. Captain Winslow says in his report that 'the firing of the *Alabama* was at the first rapid and wild; towards the close it became better,' which proves that her crew were steady and cool, and that they only lacked practice to make them effective gunners.

The fact that the *Kearsarge* was in some degree 'a protected ship,' and that the *Alabama* was somewhat inferior in force and general condition, besides having defective powder, are circumstances which sufficiently account for the result of the engagement. Nevertheless, the principle, admitted in theory, that good guns, well handled, are essential to success in naval warfare, found a confirmation in the damage inflicted by the *Kearsarge* upon her adversary, and the precision of her fire might have given her the victory even over a much larger ship, less efficient than herself in the above respects.

I hope there is nothing in the foregoing remarks which will appear like a purpose to lessen the credit due to Captain Winslow for the excellent performance of his ship, or to press into undue prominence the defects and inferiority of the *Alabama*.

I have not felt at all impelled to dwell upon Semmes' especial merits, or to take the occasion of this particular incident of his naval career to eulogise him. His defeat did not change the estimate I had formed of his capacity. If he had gained the victory it would not have added to my appreciation of his abilities. As a mere sea-officer under the ordinary requirements of the naval profession, he was not especially distinguished. He had neither the *physique* nor the dashing manner which combine to make a showy brilliant deck officer, and in the gift of handling a ship in fancy evolutions he had no special excellence. But in broad comprehensive knowledge of all the subjects embraced in a thorough naval education, in tact, judgment, acquaintance with diplomatic usage, and the requirements of international law and comity—in the capacity to generalize and to form plans, and in the latent nerve and mental vigour necessary to impress his views upon those under him, and thus to carry them out effectively, he had few if any equals in that service in which he passed the greater portion of his life, and which he left in obedience to a principle which was paramount with him, as it was in the minds of many others of unblemished character and unsullied honour, and who yet were classed together with him under the generic appellations of 'pirate,' 'rebel' and traitor,' in the political phraseology which grew up and was disseminated from the State Department at Washington.

Semmes managed the cruises of the *Sumter* and *Alabama* with admirable skill and judgment. He not only inflicted great injury upon the enemy, but he did much to enlighten the authorities at the neutral ports necessity forced him to visit upon the true nature of the war, and to remove the impression that Confederate cruisers were buccaneers, seeking only plunder, and willing to grasp it regardless of the rights of neutrals or the restraints of international courtesy. He was often compelled to correspond with officials of high position in civil service, as well as in military and naval rank. He had often to act, not only as the commander of a national ship, but as the diplomatic and consular agent of his country as well. In all of these trying positions he acquitted himself admirably. The local authorities perceived that he understood his belligerent rights, but also knew how to advance his claims with firmness and precision, without departing a hair's-breadth from the line of official courtesy and respect. He soon won the confidence of those with whom he came in contact, and his ships were generally received and treated in neutral ports with a kindly consideration which was gratifying to himself and beneficial to the cause he represented. In fact, he was capable of much more than sailing or fighting a single ship. He had the faculties and the acquirements which fit a man for high command, and if circumstances had ever placed him at the head of a fleet, I feel sure that he would have achieved important and notable results.

When the *Alabama* settled down to her final resting place at the bottom of the English Channel, and the *Kearsarge* steamed away with flying colours to announce her victory, it would seem that the pride of the victors might have been satisfied, and their anger appeased, after a little pardonable jubilation. But as the origin of the famous Confederate cruiser gave rise to much controversy, so likewise did the circumstances of her death furnish a topic for discussion, carried on with harsh and bitter petulance by Mr. Seward, and answered with singular forbearance, but with a touch of sarcasm and reproof, by Earl Russell. Captain Semmes and his officers, having landed from the *Deerhound* at Southampton, were free to go where they liked; but Mr. Adams, the United States Minister, soon sent in a complaint to her Majesty's Government and claimed them as prisoners-of-war.

The sinking of the *Alabama.* *(Harper's Weekly)*

The eleven-inch forward pivot-gun on the *Kearsarge* in action. *(Century Magazine)*

Lord Russell was evidently more surprised than vexed by this preposterous demand. In the official reply he says :—

'It appears to me that the owner of the *Deerhound*, of the Royal Yacht Squadron, performed only a common duty of humanity in saving from the waves the captain and several of the crew of the *Alabama*. They would otherwise, in all probability, have been drowned, and thus would never have been in the situation of prisoners-of-war. It does not appear to me to be any part of the duty of a neutral to assist in making prisoners-of-war for one of the belligerents.'

The answer to the above was written by Mr. Seward himself, in a despatch addressed to Mr. Adams—probably he thought Mr. Adams would be too mild. I shall only quote one paragraph, which sufficiently exhibits its general tone.*

'The Earl argues that if those persons had not been so taken from the sea, they would in all probability have been drowned, and they would never have been in the situation of prisoners-of-war. . . . I have to observe upon these remarks of Earl Russell that it was the right of the *Kearsarge* that the pirates should drown, unless saved by humane exertions of the officers and crew of that vessel, or by their own efforts, without the aid of the *Deerhound*.'

From Mr. Seward's point of view they were pirates—*hostes humani generis*. If, therefore, they had been saved by the 'humane exertions of the *Kearsarge*,' it would have been to meet the fate of hanging instead of drowning—an alternative that would not have tempted them to make much effort to get out of the water.

* See 'United States Appendix,' vol. iii., pp. 263, 273, and 'British Case,' p. 116.

The answer of the British Government to Mr. Seward's demand was 'that there is no obligation by international law which can bind the Government of a neutral State to deliver up to a belligerent prisoners-of-war who may have escaped from such belligerent, and may have taken refuge within the territory of such neutral.' He adds that they had been guilty of no offence against the laws of England, and had committed no act which would bring them within the provisions of a treaty between Great Britain and the United States for the mutual surrender of offenders, and states the following conclusion:—'Her Majesty's Government are, therefore, entirely without any legal means by which, even if they wished to do so, they could comply with your above-mentioned demand.'

The grounds of Lord Russell's refusal were unquestionable, and his reasoning was unanswerable. Mr. Seward must or should have known that the reply to his demand could not have been different from what it proved to be, and his motive in seeking the humiliation of a refusal is inexplicable. But Mr. Seward had fully impressed his views and his spirit upon many of his subordinates who represented the United States abroad at that time, and especially upon Mr. Thomas H. Dudley, the Consul at Liverpool, who manifested a bitterness of temper, and practised a sharpness and asperity in language and correspondence, and a recklessness in his statements, which would have been appalling, but for the conviction that public sentiment in Europe would revolt against such pretentious extravagance.

After the departure of the *Alabama* from Liverpool, many communications were addressed by Mr. Adams to the British Government dwelling upon her so-called escape, and the despatch of her armament from England.

In one communication he enclosed a letter from Mr. Thomas H. Dudley, dated January 11, 1864, in which that gentleman with the bitter temper and indiscreet pen enumerated the circumstances affecting the *Alabama*, which, he affirmed, proved her to be a 'British ship,' and her acts 'piratical.' The above letter was referred to the law officers of the Crown, who were asked to advise whether any proceedings could be taken with reference to the supposed breaches of neutrality alleged by Mr. Adams and Mr. Dudley. The law officers reported that 'no proceedings can at present be taken,' but they could not let Mr. Dudley's uncivil assertions pass without comment, and they closed their report with the following remarks:—'So far as relates to Mr. Dudley's argument (not now for the first time advanced) that the *Alabama* is an English piratical craft, it might have been enough to say that Mr. Dudley, while he enumerates everything which is immaterial, omits everything that is material, to constitute that character.' The law officers then demonstrate that the *Alabama* is a public ship-of-war of the Confederate States,* 'and has been ever since she hoisted the Confederate flag and received her armament at Terceira,' and they close their report, or rather their 'opinion,' in these words:—'It is to be regretted that, in any of the discussions on this subject, so manifest an abuse of language as the application of the term "English piratical craft" to the *Alabama* should still be permitted to continue.'

The law officers who gave the above 'opinion' were Sir Roundell Palmer, now Lord Selborne, who was generally supposed to be partial to the Federal cause, and Sir Robert Collier, who had been consulted by the

* For opinion of the law officers quoted above see 'British Case,' p. 117.

solicitors of the United States Consul in reference to the seizure of the *Alabama* before he received the appointment of Solicitor-General.

Northern men often complained of the sympathy exhibited in some parts of Europe, and especially in England, for the Confederate cause. I have reason to believe that at least five out of every seven in the middle and upper classes in England were favourable to the South, and I confidently believe that the majority were moved to favour that side by the haughty and offensive tone assumed by many of the representatives of the United States.

At the time of the rescue of the *Alabama's* drowning men by the *Deerhound*, many harsh things were said of her owner, Mr. John Lancaster, in the diplomatic correspondence of the United States, and high officials of that Government recklessly affirmed that the *Deerhound* was in collusion with the *Alabama*, and that Mr. Lancaster had taken his yacht out to watch the engagement under a covert understanding with Captain Semmes.

It is not probable that any American historian will give further currency to those statements. Mr. Lancaster proved to the satisfaction of her Majesty's Government, and to all who read his published letter, that there was not the slightest foundation in fact for the assertions of the United States officials in respect to his conduct, and he publicly offered to submit the whole of his proceedings to the yachtsmen of England for their opinion. I would have made no mention of the foregoing incident at all, except for the fact that it remains on record in the printed papers in reference to the Confederate naval operations, and it appeared necessary, therefore, to mention the satisfactory and conclusive proof that the accusations were not true.

CHAPTER VI.

The Confederate cruisers and the Foreign Enlistment Act.—The protest of the United States against the 'laxity' of the British Government.—The answer of the British Government.—The Confederate States admitted to be belligerents by the Supreme Court of the United States, and acknowledged as such by the European Powers.—Debate in the House of Commons.—European recruits for the United States Army in England.—Review of the situation of the belligerents in regard to neutral States.—The American and the English Foreign Enlistment Acts.—The *Alexandra* Case.—The Crown witnesses.—Conclusions to be drawn from this case.—After-history of the *Alexandra*.—Other vessels searched at the instigation of the United States Consul.—United States purchases in England. — The Board of Trade Returns. — Messrs. Baring Brothers and Co. and the United States.—Condition of the Confederates during the War.

A HISTORY of the efforts made by the Confederate Government to organize a naval force abroad would be very incomplete if the narrative was limited to a mere statement of the number and names of the vessels which were bought or built in Europe and a description of the arrangements which were made to effect their departure from the neutral ports and to equip them as fighting ships. It is well known that the few Confederate cruisers which may be said to have been of 'foreign origin' created much greater disturbance, and excited far more public interest, than their operations would have aroused if they had simply come out of the ports of one belligerent, in the ordinary way, and had inflicted a given amount of damage upon the other. They were the source of very serious complaints and much diplomatic correspondence between Great Britain and the United States, and pages of 'Hansard' are filled with the reports of debates in reference to them in both Houses of the British Parliament. They were the means of first drawing serious attention to the Foreign Enlistment Act, and caused the law officers of her Majesty's Government much trouble in expounding the meaning of that somewhat ambiguous statute. They gave occasion for a suit which resulted in a judicial exposition of the Act, and a judgment which has never been reversed, but which was so unsatisfactory to the United States, who were the real plaintiffs, and also to her Majesty's Government, who seemed desirous to satisfy them, that a Royal Commission, composed of learned judges and jurists and distinguished statesmen to the number of thirteen, was appointed to inquire into the character, working, and effect of the laws of Great Britain available for the enforcement of neutrality ; and finally, as everyone knows, they gave rise to so much controversy between her Britannic Majesty's Government and that of the United States, in reference to international rights and duties, that an agreement could only be effected by means of a special treaty and a great international arbitration. The diplomatic correspondence has been long since published, and is accessible to all who are interested in the subject.

The United States affirmed that the Confederate Government had established a bureau of their Navy Department in England. They charged the Confederate agents with wilfully and persistently violating the municipal laws of Great Britain, and denounced their acts as being 'criminal' and 'nefarious.' They complained that her Majesty's Government was both lax and slow in putting the law in operation, and that the subordinate officers of the Crown were wilfully passive in executing the orders of their superiors. The answers of the British Government to the complaints of the United States are fully set out in the correspondence and in the proceedings before the Tribunal of Arbitration at Geneva. The merest synopsis of them would require more space than would be admissible in this narrative.

The *gravamen* of the charges was that the British Government did not put the municipal law in operation with sufficient promptness and energy to prevent the acts complained of, and did not enforce the punitive clauses with the rigour which the nature of the alleged offences and friendly consideration for the United States justified the latter Government in expecting. The substance of the answer was that the Government of Great Britain was one of limited and legally defined powers, and that its authority could, therefore, be exercised only in subordination to law; that when there was interference by the Government with the rights of persons or property, redress might be immediately sought and recovered, provided the Government could not maintain its action, in a court of law. The Government could not, therefore, seize vessels alleged to belong to the Confederate States, or arrest persons accused of violating the law, unless there was sufficient *primâ facie* evidence to render a conviction probable; and neither the evidence obtained by the Government through their own officers, or tendered by the United States Minister and Consuls, was considered sufficient by the law officers of the Crown to justify either seizure or prosecution.

One ship was seized, and the United States officials exerted themselves to the utmost to provide evidence, but the prosecution failed, and her Majesty's Government had to pay damages. It was furthermore contended that acts prohibited by municipal law or by the orders and proclamations of the Executive Government were not necessarily prohibited by the law of nations, and there was no obligation to use executive power harshly, or in a manner at variance with the spirit of the national institutions, with no other purpose than to protect one belligerent against the other. In one of Earl Russell's despatches to Lord Lyons, the British Minister at Washington, he says that a phrase used by Mr. Seward in describing the conduct of Great Britain 'was rather a figure of rhetoric than a true description of facts;' 'that the Cabinet were of opinion that the law was sufficient, but that legal evidence could not always be procured.'* . . . 'That the British Government had done everything in its power to execute the law;' and that, in his belief, 'if all the assistance given to the Federals by British subjects and British munitions of war were weighed against similar aid given to the Confederates, the balance would be greatly in favour of the Federals.' † Lord Russell added, however, that Mr. Adams, the American Minister, totally denied the foregoing proposition. In this denial of Mr. Adams, we have the clue to the feeling which aroused the temper of the United States, and which caused Mr. Seward to put forward so many unreasonable complaints, and to use such strong and often abusive language in referring to the acts of the Confederate Government and their agents.

One of the most important lessons to be learned in

* Earl Russell to Lord Lyons, March 27, 1863.

† Parliamentary Document, 'North America,' No. 1, 1864, p. 2.

ordinary life in the management of every-day affairs, is that which teaches men to acknowledge and to submit with dignity and patience to the consequences of an 'accomplished fact,' even though the result may have disappointed their hopes and baulked their expectations. The statesman whose temper will not suffer him to admit that which is incontrovertible, whose faculties cannot discern the difference between his own will and the inevitable fulfilment of events, who persistently and with ever increasing warmth urges his own opinions and policy against the adverse convictions of those who have already scrutinized the question and pronounced their judgment, can hardly expect to control or direct public sentiment successfully, or to make the cause in which he is engaged acceptable to those not immediately connected with him by some common interest. The Cabinet of Mr. Abraham Lincoln during the period of the Civil War contained a number of able, energetic men, but they never could bring their minds to acknowledge that they were engaged in war with a *de facto* Government, and they never could treat with complaisance the representatives of those foreign Powers who ventured to act upon the principle that the contest between the States was a revolution and not an insurrection.

But the logic of facts proved too strong for them. One of the first acts of the Government at Washington for the suppression of the so-called rebellion was to proclaim a blockade of all the Southern ports. In the Proclamation, dated April 19, 1861, President Lincoln stated that the blockade would be 'set on foot' 'in pursuance of the laws of the United States, and of the law of nations in such cases provided.' The foreign Ministers resident at Washington immediately requested information as to the manner in which the blockade was to be enforced. To the British Envoy Mr. Seward gave the assurance that it would be conducted strictly according to the rules of public law, and with as much liberality towards neutrals as any belligerent could practise. In reply to the Minister of Spain he wrote thus: 'The blockade will be strictly enforced upon the principles recognised by the law of nations.'*

The proclamation of blockade was limited at first to seven specified States, but by the end of May it was extended to all the principal ports of the Gulf and Atlantic States, including Virginia. The Federal cruisers soon began to make prizes of neutral ships for alleged breach of blockade, and they were condemned with very short shrift by the United States prize-courts. Appeals were taken to the Supreme Court, and Mr. Justice Grier, giving the judgment of the court in a test case, said:

'To legitimatize the capture of a neutral vessel or property on the high seas, a war must exist *de facto*, and the neutral must have a knowledge or notice of the intention of one of the parties belligerent to use this mode of coercion against a port, city, or territory in possession of the other. . . . The proclamation of the blockade is itself official and conclusive evidence to the court that a state of war existed which demanded and authorized a recourse to such a measure under the circumstances peculiar to the case. The correspondence of Lord Lyons with the Secretary of State admits the fact and concludes the question.'

The Great Maritime Powers acted upon the foregoing statements of Mr. Seward and the judgment of the Supreme Court of the United States. They admitted the legality of the blockade, and as a necessary and

* See 'British Case,' part ii., p. 5.

legitimate consequence they acknowledged the Confederate States as belligerents, and threw open their ports to both parties on the same conditions and under precisely similar restrictions.

Here, then, was an accomplished fact—a *de facto* war. Europe refused to look upon the efforts of eleven great commonwealths, whose entire population, to the number of at least six millions of people, had united in asserting their right to retire from a voluntary union, as a mere insurrectionary opposition to an obnoxious Government. The common-sense, as well as the philanthropy of all nations, rejected the proposition to treat President Davis, Lee, and Stonewall Jackson as common brawlers or rebels, and the people of England especially could not be persuaded to denounce Josiah Tattnall, who towed the British boats into the Peiho, as a pirate, nor could they cast that stigma upon the naval service to which he belonged.

The acknowledgment of the Confederate Government as a belligerent met with such unanimous concurrence among foreign States, that it would have been only an act of common courtesy, and of judicious policy, to accept the judgment. But Mr. Seward could not bring himself to a dignified acquiescence in the common verdict. He indulged in repeated and petulant complaints, and urged with vehement earnestness that all the world should be subservient to his will, and should re-fashion the code of public law to suit his policy. It was a case of one sagacious juror against eleven stubborn men who took a different view of the criminal. What Mr. Seward wanted was that Europe should permit the United States to remain in the enjoyment of every privilege guaranteed by treaties of peace, free and unrestricted access to the ports, the right to buy arms and transport them unmolested across the sea, to engage men and forward them to the battlefields in Virginia without question, and, at the same time, that the whole world should tolerate a total suppression of trade with eleven great provinces, and suffer the United States to seize ships on the high seas and hale them before prize-courts, unless they were protected by the certificate of an American Consul.* He wished to practise all the rights which a state of war confers upon a belligerent, but begged to be excused from performing the duties which attach in equal degree to that condition.

The answer of the Great Maritime Powers was plain and to the point. Substantially it was this: 'You may be whatever you like—in a state of peace or in a state of war. If the political agitation which disturbs your country is a mere insurrection which you will suppress in "ninety days," the result will be quite agreeable to us; but meanwhile we must claim the right to go into the Southern ports, and get the staples our people want, and give in exchange the products of our industry, which their people want. If, on the other hand, you cannot maintain us in our privileges of trade with the South—if you cannot exercise jurisdiction there, and can only enter the country with great armies, which we perceive are often defeated; if to restore your authority it is necessary to resort to measures which are only admissible when exercised as a belligerent right, then by your own showing there is a state of war, to which there are of necessity two parties, each of whom must, by the common law of nations, have equal rights and duties, and we must protect our status as neutrals by seeing that neither party takes more than

* See Debate: Hansard, vol. clxx., 1863 (2), pp. 581, 582.

he is entitled to receive, or exacts more than he is justified in demanding.'

It will thus be seen that the outside world did not originate the event or create the fact. Eighteen or more great States, acknowledging a central Government at Washington, were engaged in war with eleven other great States adhering to a common authority at Richmond. This was the actual condition of affairs. All the special pleading of the politicians at Washington, all the *finesse* of diplomatic reasoning, could not alter the facts. Foreign Powers perceived the actual state of affairs, and the Proclamations of Neutrality, and the regulations specifying the conditions upon which their ports might be used, were framed in accordance with the fact that there was a state of war between two separate Powers, and although one could glory in the full-fledged title of 'a Government *de jure*,' and the other was shackled with the more restrictive appellation of 'a Government *de facto*,' yet in regard to belligerent rights and duties they were placed on precisely the same footing by the common consent and common action of the whole civilized world.

In discussing the acts of the Confederate Government, and the efforts made by them to obtain military supplies and a few cruising ships in Europe, it is only fair to call attention to the real position of the two belligerents in reference to the neutral Powers.

It has been often asserted in the diplomatic correspondence of the United States that the agents of the Confederate Government abused the hospitality and infringed the municipal laws of the neutral States, especially of Great Britain. 'Criminal evasion,' 'nefarious transactions,' and other cognate expressions, were among the milder forms in which their conduct was denounced by the United States Secretary of State and his consular representatives. Those charges and those epithets have been preserved in the pages of 'Blue Books,' and remain on record among the proceedings of the Tribunal of Arbitration at Geneva; and there are many people in England even now who think that there must have been some clever evasion of the law, some illicit 'tip' from a sub-official, which made the so-called 'escape' of the *Alabama* and her consorts possible.

If the charges and the epithets had merely been cast at an individual agent they would be of little importance, and it would hardly be worth while to intrude an explanation or a defence into a narrative of this kind, because an agent must be prepared to bear the consequences of the policy he undertakes to carry out, and if his principals have exacted from him the performance of any acts which may, when stripped of rhetorical flourish, be justly branded as 'criminal' or 'nefarious,' he must be content, if he has consented to retain his office, to assume the responsibility and to endure the ignominy. But I have shown in a previous chapter that it was the principle as well as the policy of the Confederate Government to practise a scrupulous and rigid deference to the rights of neutrals and the municipal laws of those countries from which they hoped to draw supplies. My own instructions were clear and explicit on this point, and I am in the position to know that all orders issued by the Confederate Government to agents and commanders of cruising ships were of the same tenor. If, therefore, the law of England was violated, or evaded in a criminal degree, the fault must be laid to the inadvertence or the negligence or the wilfulness of the agent, and not to the policy of those in whose behalf he was acting.

Seldom is a man competent to take up a complicated

Act of the British Parliament, or of any other Legislative Assembly, and define its scope and the limit of its sense and bearing upon his own conduct, especially when the Act contains many clauses combining prohibitory, preventive, and punitive enactments. What he is bound to do, however, is to take due precautions, by consulting experts whose office it is to examine and give opinions on points of law, who are familiar with legal phraseology, and are acquainted with the precedents and the previous judgments of the Courts in cases which may have arisen under the statute, so that he may escape danger of prosecution, and be free from the offence of misusing the hospitality of the country which has offered him shelter and protection. Those precautions were taken before a ship was bought or built in England for the Confederate Government, and the opinion of the learned barristers whose advice was asked has been already given in a previous chapter.* The only doubt that could be felt in regard to the advice was that it was founded solely upon the opinion of the eminent lawyers who gave it, and could not be confirmed by any precedent or previous judgment, because up to the year 1863 no ship had been seized and brought to the test of a trial under the Act.

The Governments at Washington and at Richmond stood at that time on a precise equality before the general laws of nations, and the municipal law of each neutral state. I mean, of course, with reference to their respective rights and duties as belligerents. Whatever was obligatory upon the one was equally binding upon the other. Whatever the agent of one could do without offence, the other could do also. The Foreign Enlistment Act defined the limits to which each could go. It laid down the precepts which each were alike bound to

* See chap. ii., pp. 66—69.

obey, and defined the consequences of disobedience to both without partiality or discrimination. If an agent of the United States could perform any service for his Government in England without infringing the law or laying himself open to the charge of 'criminal evasion,' an agent of the Confederate States might do the same or an equivalent act with corresponding innocence and propriety.

A member of Parliament—the late Mr. John Laird—stated in the House of Commons that the Navy Department of the United States opened negotiations with the firm from which he retired at the beginning of the Civil War for building a special class of ships. The correspondence, or at least sufficient to establish the fact, was read publicly before the whole House, and the member referred to stated that while he felt bound to suppress the names of the persons through whom the negotiations had been proposed, he would, if it was thought advisable, hand the whole correspondence, 'with the original letters,' confidentially to the Speaker of the House, or to the Prime Minister, in order that the public should have the assurance that he was not overstating the facts. One of the extracts read to the House was as follows :—'I have this morning a note from the Assistant Secretary of the Navy, in which he says, "I hope your friends will tender for the two iron-plated steamers."'

It is proper for me to mention that in a subsequent debate, about four months afterwards, Mr. Richard Cobden stated that he had received a letter from his friend, Mr. Charles Sumner, of the United States Senate, informing him that the Secretary of the United States Navy denied that any order had 'been sent from the American Navy Department to any shipbuilder in this country' (England). Mr. Laird did not assert that an order had been sent, but that proposals had been made and negotiations opened on the subject, and that the firm to which he belonged at the time were asked if they would undertake to build as desired, 'how soon, and for how much.' In reply to Mr. Cobden, he said that 'he was quite prepared, if necessary, to prove every word he had said in a former debate was perfectly true ; and as the question was one which affected her Majesty's Government, he was ready to put his proofs (namely, the original letters) in the hands of the noble lord at the head of the Government.'

The debates referred to may be found in Hansard, vol. clxx. Session 1863 (2), and vol. clxxii. Session 1863 (4). In the course of the latter debate the Prime Minister (Lord Palmerston) said :—'I cannot, in the abstract, concur with my honourable friend' (Mr. Cobden) 'in thinking that there is any distinction in principle between muskets, gunpowder, bullets, and cannon on the one side, and ships on the other.' . . . 'Therefore I hold, that on the mere ground of international law belligerents have no right to complain if merchants—I do not say the Government, for that would be interference—as a mercantile transaction supply one of the belligerents not only with arms and cannon, but also with ships destined for warlike purposes.'

The negotiations referred to by Mr. Laird were abandoned for reasons not necessary to mention in detail. The firm could not undertake the work on the conditions as to time of completion, etc., and I do not know whether the United States made overtures to other shipbuilders or not. The naval resources of the United States were so immeasurably superior to those of the Confederate States, both in the supply of materials and the mechanical means for utilizing them, that the Navy Department at Washington did not probably feel any anxiety on the score of ships. The chief supplies which the United States drew from Europe were arms, accoutrements, ammunition, and men. I say men, because it is well known that large numbers of emigrants were induced to go to the United States during the war under implied promises or allegations that they would find remunerative work, and the work supplied them after arrival was that of bearing arms in the United States Army and helping to subjugate the South.

It would be easy for me to name persons of unquestioned respectability in England, especially in Liverpool, who were well aware that bands of so-called emigrants were constantly passing through Liverpool and other English coast towns, *en route* for the United States, often in charge of men who were known to be agents of that Government. The diplomatic correspondence demonstrates incontestably that a system of 'evasive enlistment' for the United States army was practised in Europe during the Civil War, and Confederate officers would have no difficulty in proving, if there was any need, that whole battalions of Federal soldiers were captured during the campaigns in Virginia, composed of men who had not been six months in the country, and who could not speak a word of English.

There were two cases in which public inquiry was made as to the character of the passengers by American ships about to leave Liverpool for New York. In one of the cases the *prima facie* evidence of a clandestine enlistment was so strong, that the men were forced to land. I could name the solicitors who were the chief actors in the above mentioned cases. They are one of the leading firms in Liverpool. I am not repeating merely the current belief or suspicion that prevailed at the time, nor am I affirming the existence of a practice the proof of which rests upon such vague evidence as is often tendered in the phrase 'it is quite notorious.' Perhaps the subject is of sufficient importance to justify, if not to require me to give a particular example.

One day in the very height of the war, a gentleman called at my office and told me that he had reason to feel satisfied that a large number of men would arrive in Liverpool that afternoon, who were really recruits for the United States army ; that they were in charge of a person who he thought was a commissioned officer in the United States Service ; that they were to embark on board the American ship *Great Western*, then lying in the river, and he thought I ought to take some steps to bring the matter before the proper authorities. I replied that my duties could only be satisfactorily and successfully performed by a prudent reserve, and by maintaining a retiring and unobtrusive attitude. If I ventured into the arena of legal strife with the American Consul, or with persons supposed to be engaged in unlawful proceedings, I should necessarily be forced out of my retirement, which I thought would be more injurious to the interests of the Confederacy than the addition of a few hundred men to the armies of the United States.

My informant, although an Englishman, was a warm partizan of the south. He admitted the soundness of my reasons for not interfering, but was not satisfied to leave the affair to take its course without some opposition. He went to a few others who were known to be 'Southern sympathizers,' and they placed the evidence in the hands of a local solicitor, who communicated it to the Customs authorities. The alleged facts were forwarded to London, and a junior solicitor of the Customs was sent to investigate the case. I believe the ship was detained one or two days, or at least her clearance was held back. The solicitor of the Customs who made the investigation reported that the evidence of a violation of the Foreign Enlistment Act was not sufficient to justify the arrest of any of the parties, and the ship and her passengers were allowed to proceed. The gentleman who gave me the information went on board with the solicitor he had consulted, and he told me that the men, many of whom were Irishmen, seemed to know that he and those with him were trying to stop them; but feeling safe from interference, they chaffed and indulged in a good deal of rough humour, and he furthermore told me that he saw a person on board who was a cabin passenger, and appeared to have charge of the men, and that he wore a military dress, which some of the men told him was the uniform of a lieutenant in the United States army.

Now, the foregoing incident would prove nothing if there were no sequel to it, but in the winter of 1871 I went to New York on a visit. I was stopping at the house of a gentleman—a New Yorker, of high social position. He had neither a military education nor what may be called the military instincts, and being a man of great practical sense, with a sound perception of the fitness of things, he did not seek a commission in the army, and he was far too valuable a man to be wasted in the office of carrying a rifle in the ranks. But his temperament was too ardent, and his convictions too strong, to admit of his remaining inactive in the struggle, which he perceived was likely to be long and arduous. There could not have been a man more loyal to the United States, more willing to make greater personal sacrifices for the success of the Federal cause. I believe he did as much as any one to keep up the spirit of the men in the field, and to animate the hopes of the desponding who were not in the field; and his services were as important and as conducive to the final success of the Federal Government as those of any man at the North who was not in high command, or in some equally important civil executive office. I could say much of his personal qualities, which made him lovable by those who knew him well, but this is no place for a tribute of that kind.

The gentleman to whom I refer was firmly impressed with the feeling that the neutrality of England was more favourable to the South than to the North, but one of his characteristics was to take fair and reasonable views of other men's motives, and to express his own opinions with moderation and courtesy. One day we were discussing the action of Great Britain, the effect of the Proclamation of Neutrality, and the manner in which the municipal law was applied in restraining the operations of the Confederate agents. He took the ground that they were allowed too great latitude, and that the British Government showed an unfriendly feeling towards the United States in permitting the *Alabama* and other ships to leave England. I, of course, took an opposite position, and we argued the point in a temperate and friendly spirit. I contended that her Majesty's Government could not have stopped the *Alabama* without acting arbitrarily, and going beyond the limits of a fair, impartial neutrality, and to demonstrate that the preventive clauses of the Foreign Enlistment Act were not applied very strictly against the

United States, I cited the incident of the ship *Great Western*, which I have mentioned above.

My friend smiled. He could be as reticent as anyone when there was necessity for reserve, but he was too honest to shrink from admitting a fact, or to hedge himself behind a prevarication in a friendly argument. He left me, and went into another room. In a few moments he returned, bringing a small package of papers, filed and backed in voucher form, and then told me that he had been, during a portion of the war, a member of a committee whose office it was to look after men who had been brought over from Europe without any definite purpose on their own part, and who might therefore be available as recruits for the army; that he had nothing whatever to do with engaging the men abroad, and never inquired what inducements were held out to them to come over, but when they were safe across and were of willing minds, the committee paid the expenses, etc. 'These papers,' he said, 'are the documents and vouchers relating to that voyage of the *Great Western* you have just mentioned. And the information upon which your Liverpool friend acted was probably correct.'

We were both amused by this accidental discovery of our common connection with a transaction eight years after the event, and I was well satisfied to have such a complete demonstration of the facility with which the United States could and did recruit their armies, without infringing the British Foreign Enlistment Act, because it confirmed me in the opinion I had previously maintained, that the Act was not intended to protect one belligerent from another, but to prevent prejudice to Great Britain herself by acts done within the kingdom which would endanger its peace and welfare. Her Majesty's Government brought the subject of the alleged enlistments to the notice of the American Minister, and appeared to be satisfied with the declaration that there had been none. The Confederate Government had no recognised diplomatic agent to whom inquiries could be addressed, and who could make explanation, and after the departure of two or three ships the complaints and remonstrances of the United States Minister induced her Majesty's Foreign Secretary on more than one occasion to seize and detain vessels in which the Confederate Government had no interest whatever, or, as the Attorney-General expressed it, to 'strain the law.'

I assert nothing more than the fact that the United States, by means of authorized agents, did induce many men to go from Europe to America during the war, the intent being to enlist them into the army after their arrival. I do not affirm that there was an actual enlistment in any part of Europe, and the disclaimer of the United States Minister was no doubt justified. The process was carried out thus: Able-bodied men were persuaded or stimulated by judicious representations to emigrate to the United States, and they were kindly looked after and cared for on the journey to the ports and on the voyage across the Atlantic by friendly intermediaries. There was nothing illegal in this. Rifles, accoutrements, and ammunition were bought at Birmingham and elsewhere, and were shipped through the great houses of Baring, and Brown, Shipley and Co., to the United States, in the ordinary way of business. There was nothing illegal in that. When the men and the arms arrived in New York, or Boston, or Philadelphia, they were brought together by a happy accident; the emigrants were persuaded that it was a very fine thing to be soldiers, they were dressed in the traditional 'blue,' the equipment was completed, and they were marched off to Virginia, to be shot down at Seven Pines and Chancellorsville, or to perish by fever in the swamps of the Chickahominy.

The Confederate Government did not require men so much as arms. They were never able to equip the fighting population of the country. They wanted, however, besides arms, ships suitable to cruise and to destroy the enemy's mercantile marine; and the manner of accomplishing their purpose may be briefly described as follows:

A ship suited in structure and general arrangements to carry the weight of a battery on deck, to berth a sufficient crew, and to keep the sea for a long time, was bought or built in England. She was then despatched to an outport without a weapon or an ounce of powder on board, and with a crew just sufficient to navigate her in safety. According to the best advice available, there was nothing illegal in that transaction. Guns, cutlasses, revolvers, ammunition, and stores of all necessary kinds, were bought in London, Birmingham, Sheffield and elsewhere, and were shipped in due form, by a vessel loading in the ordinary way, for the West Indies, or other suitable market for such supplies. There can be no doubt that this part of the transaction was perfectly legal. The two vessels—one fit to bear arms, but having none; the other full of arms, but unable to use them—shaped their respective courses so as to gradually converge until, at some point far removed from British jurisdiction, they found themselves in a fortunate conjunction. The equipment of the ship fit to bear arms was then completed; passengers or seamen from the two vessels, and perhaps from a third, were persuaded that they might have a jolly cruise, and they donned the familiar and jaunty serge frock of the man-of-war's-man, and went to 'battle the watch' and to take their chances under the Confederate flag.

I think the foregoing sketches clearly and fairly demonstrate the attitude of the two belligerents in the late Civil War in respect to the British Foreign Enlistment Act, and I should be much surprised to hear anyone not biased by prejudice, or pledged in advance to a particular assertion, say that there is a shade or a shadow of difference between them, whether viewed as a matter of principle or as a question of evading the law.

Now that seventeen years have passed since the end of the war, it is to be hoped that the passions which were then aroused have sufficiently subsided on both sides to make it possible for each to take a fair and equitable retrospect of what the other did. I have met many Northern men who were loyal to their Government, who sacrificed their business and risked their lives in its support, and who never did fall into the frenzied state of bitterness which many of the political party leaders manifested, and who never had any sympathy with the violent and abusive language used by Mr. Seward and some of his consular agents.

In the British counter-case presented to the Tribunal of Arbitration at Geneva (p. 57), I find the following paragraph, which serves as an illustration of the extreme pretensions set up by the United States, and the effect produced by the ill-advised complaints and demands of their representatives. 'Pressed by the difficulty of distinguishing between their own operations in Europe and those of the Confederate States in such a manner as to make it appear that the British Government was bound to give free scope to the former and repress the latter, the United States appear to imagine that they found such a distinction in two circumstances.

One of these is, that the needs of the Confederacy were, as they allege, more urgent than those of the Union: the former could only obtain their military supplies from abroad; the latter could manufacture some of theirs at home.* The other is, that the United States, having the command of the sea, could transport the goods purchased by them freely and openly, or (as it is expressed) "in the ordinary course of commerce;" whilst the Confederates were obliged to "originate a commerce for the purpose"—that is, to get their goods transported by way of Nassau and Bermuda, which are commonly places of no great trade—and further, to make use of those concealments by which the traffic in contraband of war, when not protected by a powerful navy, usually tries to elude the vigilance of the enemy's cruisers. Are we, then, to understand that, according to the views put forward in the case of the United States, the "strict and impartial neutrality towards both belligerents," which it is the duty of a neutral Government to maintain, obliges it to find out which of the two stands in the greater need of supplies, and consists in lending aid, by measures of repression, to the belligerent whose force is the greater and his wants the less pressing of the two, and thus assisting him to crush more speedily the resistance of his weaker enemy? Her Majesty's Government is unable to assent to this novel opinion, advantageous as it would doubtless prove to States which, like Great Britain, possess a powerful navy.'

The last sentence in the foregoing quotation is pertinent to a comment I have previously made upon the pretensions set up and exacted by the United States during the war. They advanced and were permitted to enforce belligerent rights which were strongly resisted

* 'Case of the United States,' pp. 310—312.

when applied to themselves in former years, and thus established precedents which will occasion much trouble and perplexity to some future Government at Washington, if the United States should be neutral in a war between two countries having powerful navies. It is well known that the great autocratic and monarchical Powers of Europe had shown a willingness for years before the American Civil War to relax the extreme application of the belligerent rights heretofore claimed by them, and relentlessly enforced whenever their interests required. England, once so persistent and arrogant in practising the 'right of search,' has, during many past years, taken a leading part in the effort to modify the harsh restraints upon neutral commerce, which she herself was formerly so ready to inflict, and to abolish or prohibit the destruction of private property on the high seas. The Great Powers who joined in the Declaration of Paris in the year 1856, agreed to several very important rules which greatly relaxed the oppressive restraints on neutral commerce in times of war. The most beneficent provisions of that famous Declaration were those which practically affirmed the doctrine that 'free ships made free goods,' and which furthermore exempted neutral goods from condemnation as prize, if found in an enemy's ship. It is remarkable that the United States, professing the freest and most liberal institutions, and up to 1861 vehemently urging and insisting upon the fullest immunity for their flag, should have so suddenly made a retrograde movement in the liberal policy of their past history, while even the autocratic States of Europe were discarding their dictatorial traditions, and were advancing in the path of greater freedom to commerce, and less interference with the rights and privileges of neutrals.

In the year 1863 Messrs. Pile, Spence and Co., of the City of London, advertised a line of steamers to run regularly between England and Matamoras, in Mexico. The first vessel despatched on the line was the screw steamer *Gipsy Queen*, which performed her voyage and returned in safety. The second vessel was the *Peterhoff*, also a screw steamer. The *Peterhoff* left London with proper clearances from the Custom House, but for greater precaution took a certificate of clearance from the Mexican Consul. In the due progress of her voyage she arrived in the neighbourhood of the island of St. Thomas, where she was stopped by a United States ship-of-war and boarded. Her papers were examined and endorsed with a statement that they were in order, and she was then permitted to proceed on her voyage. In accordance with the original intention of her owners, she went into St. Thomas, replenished her coal, and sailed again for Matamoras. Just as she was leaving the harbour of St. Thomas the United States ship *Vanderbilt* was coming in, and Admiral Wilkes, the senior American naval officer present, ordered the commander of the *Vanderbilt* to pursue her. He did so; he captured her and brought her back to St. Thomas, whence she was afterwards taken to Key West to be adjudicated upon by a prize-court.

The above facts are condensed from a debate on the subject in the British House of Commons, March 27, 1863 (Hansard, vol. clxx., Session 1863 (2), p. 71, etc.). In the same volume (p. 575, etc.), will be found another long and spirited debate on the 'Conduct of Admiral Wilkes' and 'American Cruisers and British Merchantmen.' Those debates go further than anything I have written to demonstrate not only the harsh and rigorous manner in which the United States enforced their belligerent rights during the Civil War, but the surprise which was aroused in England by the sudden and complete abandonment and reversal of their previous principles in respect to the 'right of search.' The purpose of the United States was to hermetically seal up the Southern ports, to deprive the South of every possible means of obtaining supplies from abroad, whether by direct trade or through ports contiguous to it either by sea or by land; and to accomplish that purpose appeared to be of greater importance to the Government at Washington than to maintain a character for consistency in the interpretation of International Law.

At the present day the American shipping trade has fallen to a very low point, but all who are acquainted with the resources of the country, the activity and commercial intelligence of the people, and the mechanical skill they have exhibited in the past, will expect to see their trade revive and American ships again taking their due part in the marine traffic of the world whenever the country can persuade its rulers to remodel the navigation laws. But when the United States resume their due place among the Maritime Powers, they will require a powerful and ubiquitous navy to protect their commerce against the encroachments of some future belligerents, who may, and probably will be, inclined to follow the precedents of 1861—65.

The statements in the foregoing pages having reference to the operations of the United States in England, and the comparison of their conduct with that of the Confederate States in respect to alleged violations or evasions of the municipal law, and of neutral rights, are not made as a reproach to the former, nor are they set forth as grounds upon which to found an argument, or to build up a defence. Whatever was done by a

Confederate agent in Europe, can be made to appear neither better nor worse, by proving that some one else has committed or avoided the same errors, and I heartily renounce all faith in, and all tolerance for, the weak and puerile plea of '*Et tu quoque.*' But the facts which I have mentioned are parts of the current history of those troublous times when the American Union was suffering its great national convulsion, and the general historian of the future will require information on all such points, in order that he may have the data for a fair impartial judgment.

I have stated that before a keel was laid, or a ship was bought in England for the Confederate Government, advice was taken as to the legality of the proceedings, and that everything was done thereafter in strict conformity with the advice obtained. I can affirm, without the least mental reservation, that no deception whatever was practised upon the Customs authorities in respect to the registry or clearance of the *Alabama*, for as the law then stood, neither registry nor clearance was required, and with reference to the other ships built or bought by me, I can state with equal confidence that every requirement of the law was complied with, whether affecting the registration, clearance, or shipping of the crews.

But to determine whether the agents of the Confederate Government infringed or evaded the municipal law of England, something more will be required by those who are interested in the questions than the mere opinion of lawyers, however eminent, or the assurance of an implicated party, however conscientiously he may affirm his innocence of an evil intent. The course of events has furnished the only authoritative rule which can be applied to the elucidation of any doubtful or ambiguous point of law—that is, a trial before a duly constituted court, and a judicial exposition and decision.

In the well known case, 'The Attorney General *v.* Sillem and others,' commonly called 'The *Alexandra* Case,' the Foreign Enlistment Act was discussed at great length by several of the most distinguished lawyers of the English bar, by Sir William Atherton, her Majesty's Attorney-General, Sir Roundell Palmer, her Majesty's Solicitor-General, and Sir Robert Phillimore, the Queen's Advocate, on one side, and Sir Hugh Cairns, J. B. Karslake, Esq., Q.C., George Mellish, Esq., Q.C., and James Kemplay, Esq., on the other. The judgment rendered in the above case has never been reversed, and the interpretation of the Act as laid down by the learned judge on that occasion fixes its meaning and settles the question of the culpability of the Confederate agents. The '*Alexandra* Case,' was what lawyers call a prosecution *in rem*, and the Crown contended for a forfeiture of the ship for or upon an alleged violation of the Foreign Enlistment Act, chiefly with reference to the seventh section. It will probably help the reader to understand the case, and to duly estimate the effect of the judgment, if I give a brief history of the circumstances under which the Act was passed, and a short explanation of the principles of neutrality involved in it.

The United States have an Act very similar to that of Great Britain, both as regards the object of the statutes, and the causes which appeared to render them necessary. In the year 1778, the American Colonies, then engaged in their War of Independence with Great Britain, made a treaty (in fact, there were two) with the Government of Louis XVI., by which very large, important and exclusive privileges were granted to the respective parties with reference to the use of each other's ports for the condemnation and sale of prizes, and for the visit, shelter, and equipment of their ships-of-war. Very shortly after the execution of Louis XVI., the French National Convention plunged into a war with England and Holland.

Whatever may be said of the cruelty and arrogance of the men who assumed the control of the French Government in those days of terror, it must be admitted that they did not lack audacity and vigour. They appeared at once to look to the United States as a convenient *point d'appui* for their naval operations, and jumped to the conclusion that under the aforementioned treaties of 1778 they would be permitted to arm and commission privateers in the American ports, to bring into them their prizes, and to have the prizes condemned by the French Consuls. The French Republic declared war against England on February 1st, 1793, and one of the first acts of the Government was to send a Minister to the United States, to inflame the people against Great Britain, and to claim and use the rights and privileges conceded by the treaties of 1778. M. Genet, the person selected for the mission, was certainly not wanting in the qualities of self-assurance, energy and presumption. He arrived at Charleston on the 8th of April, 1793, and began forthwith to organize a system of privateering. He also issued instructions authorizing the French Consuls to hold courts of Vice-Admiralty for condemning the prizes which the cruisers of France might capture and bring into the ports of the United States. Having thus put these naval operations in train, he set out for Philadelphia, and during his journey he resorted to every possible means of inciting the people of the country to acts of enmity against England.

Washington, who was then President, and whose wise judicial mind would have revolted against this presumptuous conduct, even if good faith to England had not influenced him, did not wait for a remonstrance from the British Minister, but issued a proclamation of neutrality on the 22nd of April, 1793. There was some opposition to Washington's prompt and decisive action, for in his Cabinet were several members who were favourable to the French cause, but his strength of character and firmness of will enabled him to put his own views in practice, and to maintain an attitude of strict neutrality. M. Genet appears to have carried matters on with a very high hand, and he tried the temper and the forbearance of the President greatly. He not only persisted in violating the neutral territory, but he entered into various offensive political intrigues, and made himself so obnoxious that his recall was demanded, and the United States Minister in Paris was instructed to say to the French Government that if M. Genet persevered in his proceedings the United States Government would be forced to suspend his functions before a successor could arrive. The result of those troublesome proceedings was to bring the majority of the Cabinet into complete agreement with the President, and they gave rise to the first Act for the Preservation of Neutrality, or what may be called the first American Foreign Enlistment Act, which was passed by Congress early in 1794, re-enacted March 2, 1797, and made final April 24, 1800.

The Act thus made perpetual in 1800 did not, however, prove strong enough for the purpose. The revolt of the Spanish Colonies in South America gave much trouble to the Government of the United States. Agents from those colonies came to New York, Baltimore, and other ports, and bought and equipped vessels to cruise against Spanish commerce, and American citizens fitted out vessels which were officered and manned exclusively by Americans, and after being thus fully equipped for immediate hostilities they were commissioned by the several revolted colonies. Those proceedings involved the United States in constant complaints from Spain, and in diplomatic remonstrance and correspondence with her representatives, and finally, to meet the fresh necessities, a further Foreign Enlistment Act was passed, April, 1818, which was the American Act in force during the late Civil War.

The contests between Spain and her American colonies beginning in 1810, attracted much notice in England, and were from the first regarded with warm interest by the people of Great Britain. The old spirit of maritime adventure, and the passion for enterprises to the Spanish Main and the 'El Dorados' on the west coast, which aroused the temper and inspired the actions of Drake, Cavendish, Hawkins, and their contemporaries—those splendid buccaneers, whose deeds have added piquancy and glory to the reign of the Virgin Queen—had not yet been completely superseded by the more peaceful instincts of the nineteenth century, nor wholly and effectively shackled by the growing stringency of a recognised International Code.

It appears that in 1814 Spain was able to persuade England that she ought to do something to check, if not to prevent, the participation of British subjects in the war she was then waging with her recalcitrant subjects in the 'Golden South America,' and in August, 1814, a supplementary treaty was made between the two Powers, which declared in Article III. that 'His Britannic Majesty being anxious that the troubles and disturbances which unfortunately prevail in the dominions of his Catholic Majesty in America should cease, and the subjects of those provinces should return to their obedience to their lawful sovereign, engages to take the most effectual measures for preventing his subjects from furnishing arms, ammunition, or any other article, to the revolted in America.'

The treaty did not, however, meet the purposes which inspired it, because we find that in 1818 the interest in the strife had again been greatly aroused throughout Great Britain, partly in consequence of the instinctive attachment of the people to the cause of freedom, and partly in consequence of the extravagant expectations which interested parties had excited by highly coloured statements of the wealth of the Spanish American colonies, and the vast field that their independence would open up to British commerce and enterprise. But in addition to the foregoing causes, much irritation had been produced throughout Great Britain by the reactionary policy of Ferdinand VII., the prohibitory duties he had imposed upon British commerce, and the resentful feelings which were provoked by the alleged ingratitude he had shown to many British officers who had served him in Spain.

There was at the time a strong party even in Parliament who were in favour of supporting the claims of the colonies and giving them help to win their independence. There was an old statute of James I., which specified the conditions upon which British subjects might enter into the service of a foreign prince; and there were further Acts, in the reign of George II., forbidding enlistment or the procuring others to enlist in a foreign service 'without licence under the King's sign-manual.' By Statute 29 George II. c. 17, it was enacted 'that to serve under the French King as a military officer shall be felony without benefit of clergy; and to enter the Scotch Brigade in the Dutch service without first taking the oaths of allegiance and abjuration, shall be a forfeiture of £500.'*

The foregoing may be taken as the substance of 'British neutrality law' in 1818, when Spain was striving to suppress the revolt of her American colonies.† But neither the treaty of 1814 nor the prohibitory Acts of Parliament were sufficient to prevent aid being sent to the insurgents, both in men and materials of war. There does not appear to have been any attempt at disguise. Great numbers of Peninsular veterans, officers and men, went to the revolted provinces, and gave them the benefit of their experience and the prestige of their military fame. An adventurer of some note, who assumed the title of general, and was known as Sir Gregor McGregor, collected an expedition in the ports of Great Britain, with which he sailed in British vessels and under the British flag. He attacked and took Porto Bello, in South America, then in the undisturbed possession of a Spanish force. This violent act of aggression led to strong remonstrances on the part of the Spanish Government, and the British Ministry, on the 10th of June, 1819, introduced a Bill for the Amendment of the Neutrality Laws, which was passed on the 21st by a majority of sixty-one. The Act was strongly opposed, the Opposition being led by Sir James Macintosh, who denounced it as a 'left-

* Phillimore's 'International Law,' vol. iii., ed. 1857, p. 212.

† For the dates and facts in respect to the origin of the British Foreign Enlistment Act, see Appendix to Report of the Neutrality Laws Commissioners, issued for the information of the House of Commons, 1868, from which the account herein is abridged in the leading points.

handed neutrality, aimed at the struggling independence of South America.' In the year 1823, Lord Althorp moved for the repeal of the Act, but the motion was defeated, and the statute, as passed on the 21st June, 1819, remained the 'Neutrality Law' of Great Britain up to and during the American Civil War. It is known, and was generally alluded to, as the 'Foreign Enlistment Act,' and it is the Act which is applicable to all cases of alleged violation of the neutrality of Great Britain by either belligerent in the American Civil War.

The passing of the Act of 1819 seems to have put an end to the despatch of expeditions from Great Britain against Spain, for a time, at least; but it was necessary to put it in force on several occasions to prevent or to arrest expeditions fitted out to operate against other countries with which England was at peace. In 1835 an Order in Council was passed exempting British subjects who might engage in the service of Queen Isabella of Spain from the penalties of the Foreign Enlistment Act. Under the terms of this exemption, a British legion was formed, which went to Spain under the command of Sir De Lacy Evans, and served there during the war against the Carlists. In 1862 an Order in Council was again issued suspending the Foreign Enlistment Act so as to allow Captain Sherard Osborne, R.N., to fit out ships and engage British subjects to enter the service of the Emperor of China.

In the Appendix to the Report of the Neutrality Law Commissioners in the year 1867, it is said that 'in all, or nearly all, the cases up to the time of the American Civil War, the Foreign Enlistment Act had been invoked to prevent the enlistment and despatch of recruits and soldiers rather than the equipment of vessels.' There are only three cases mentioned of interference with, or seizure of vessels, and in each of them the ships were so completely equipped and manned that they might have engaged in hostilities as soon as they were clear of the British port, or else they had emigrants or volunteers on board which it was proved were intended for the service of a belligerent, and no case is mentioned of any vessel being brought to trial.

In order to comprehend the application of the Foreign Enlistment Act to the cases of Confederate ships built or bought in England, it is necessary to bear in mind the circumstances which produced the amendment of the Neutrality Laws in 1819, and the evil it was intended to guard against, and to remedy, by the Act of Parliament.

Mr. Canning, in his speech in support of the Bill, gave a graphic description of an expedition prepared in a British port for hostile attack upon some foreign Power, and he said that if a foreigner visiting England at the time should see the ships with their armament and crews on board, and the transports with the troops, he would naturally ask with what country England was at war. When he was told that the country was not at war, but was in peace and amity with the whole world, he would doubtless be greatly surprised.

The Attorney-General of that day, in introducing the Bill into Parliament, said: 'It was extremely important for the preservation of neutrality that the subjects of this country should be prevented from fitting out any equipments, not only in the ports of Great Britain and Ireland, but also in other parts of the British dominions, to be employed in foreign service.' He explained that by fitting out 'armed vessels, or by supplying the vessels of other countries with warlike stores, as effectual assistance might be rendered to a foreign Power as by enlistment in their own service,' and he added 'that in the second provision of the Bill, two objects were intended to be embued—to prevent the fitting out of *armed* vessels, and also to prevent the fitting out or supplying other ships with warlike stores in any of his Majesty's ports, not that such vessels might not receive in any port in the British dominions, but the object of the enactment was to prevent them from shipping warlike stores, such as guns and other things—other things obviously and manifestly intended for no other purpose than war.'

It is usual for Legislative Acts to be headed or preceded by an explanatory clause, or preamble, as it is called, which states the object of the Act and the evil to be remedied by it. The preamble to the English Foreign Enlistment Act is as follows: 'Whereas the enlistment or engagement of his Majesty's subjects to serve in war in foreign service without his Majesty's license, and the fitting-out, equipping, and arming of vessels by his Majesty's subjects for warlike operations in or against the dominions or territories of any foreign Prince, State, Potentate, or persons exercising or assuming to exercise the powers of Government in or over any foreign country, etc., may be prejudicial to and tend to endanger the peace and welfare of this kingdom, etc.' It would appear from the foregoing explanations, and the preamble of the Act, that the object was to provide against the fitting out of warlike expeditions in the ports of Great Britain which might be in condition to engage in acts of hostility as soon as they left the neutral port, and to prohibit British subjects from practically engaging in war on their own account, by taking part in the preparation of warlike expeditions in Great Britain, or the arming of ships for war within the United Kingdom. This was the view taken by the learned barristers whose opinions were asked before the contracts for the *Florida* and *Alabama* were made. They advised that it was not illegal for a builder to build, or a purchaser to buy, a ship of any description whatever, provided she was not armed for war and no men were enlisted or engaged to go in her for the service of a foreign State.

The ground is now clear for the report of the test case which has been mentioned above—a case which resulted in a judicial exposition of the law, and an authoritative verdict upon the acts of the Confederate Government in respect to the building or purchase of ships in England.

About the 7th of March, 1863, a small wooden screw-steamer was launched from the building-yard of Messrs. W. C. Miller and Son, at Liverpool. The material of which the ship was built, her general arrangements, and the fact that she was launched from the same yard in which the *Florida* was built, soon attracted the notice of Mr. Dudley's spies, and they began to manufacture affidavits for the information of the American Minister. On the 28th of March, Mr. Dudley made a formal 'affirmation' (being, as he stated, averse to taking an oath) that he had reason to believe that the above mentioned vessel, which had been named *Alexandra*, was intended for the Confederate States. The 'affirmation' began with the preamble or introductory prelude which was commonly adopted by the American Consuls of the period, namely, that the Government and people of the United States were engaged in a war with 'certain persons who have rebelled against such Government, and pretended to set up and assume to exercise the powers of Government, styling themselves the Confederate States of America;' then was added a synopsis of the grounds of Mr. Dudley's faith in that to which he affirmed, and a declaration of his belief in the truth of the affidavits of certain other persons, whose statements were duly sworn to at the same time.

The foregoing 'affirmation' and 'affidavits' were forwarded to the United States Minister in London, and on the 30th Mr. Adams addressed a letter to Lord Russell on the subject, and an active correspondence appears to have been carried on between that gentleman, the British Foreign Office, the Customs authorities, the Mayor and Head-Constable of Liverpool, the Treasury, and the Home Office. The correspondence fills twenty-four pages of the appendix to the 'British Case.' A synopsis of it would hardly interest the reader. It is sufficient to say that the upshot of it all was the seizure of the *Alexandra*, and a suit in her Majesty's Court of Exchequer for her forfeiture to the Crown.

The little vessel which had occasioned all this commotion had been launched on the day the Princess of Wales entered London, previous to her marriage, and had been christened *Alexandra*, in commemoration of that interesting event. She was taken into the Toxteth Dock to complete her outfit, and to have her engines placed, and there the work went peacefully on, her builders and owners having some consciousness that the United States Minister was uneasy about her, but not dreaming that they were doing anything illegal, and therefore attempting no concealment or disguise.

On the 5th of April, 1863, the Surveyor of Customs at Liverpool seized her, and all work upon her was suspended. The trial was not begun until the 22nd of June, and as the decision was important, besides furnishing the first and the last judicial exposition of the Foreign Enlistment Act, I feel that a synopsis of the proceedings would not be inappropriate, and I will now give an abridgment of the report which my solicitor got for me at the time.

The 'information' in the case was dated May 25th, 1863, and stated that a certain officer of her Majesty's Customs had seized and arrested, to the use of her Majesty, as forfeited, a certain ship or vessel called the *Alexandra*, together with the furniture, tackle, and apparel belonging to and on board the said ship or vessel. Then followed counts to the number of ninety-eight, charging the offences by reason of which the ship had become forfeited to the Crown. The 97th and 98th counts were abandoned by the Crown. The remaining ninety-six counts consisted of the first eight counts repeated twelve times, merely varying the offence charged. Thus, the first eight counts charge that the defendants did *equip* the vessel, the next eight counts that they did *furnish* the vessel, the next eight that they did *fit out*, then they did *attempt or endeavour to equip*, and so on, exhausting the various offences enumerated in the seventh section of the statute, with the exception of *arming* the vessel, which was not charged at all. The first eight counts therefore represented the rest, and were in substance as follows. The first count charged that 'certain' persons within the United Kingdom, without having any leave or license of her Majesty for that purpose first had and obtained, *did equip* the said ship or vessel, with intent and in order that such ship or vessel should be employed in the service of certain foreign States, styling themselves the Confederate States of America, with intent to cruise and commit hostilities against a certain foreign State, with which her Majesty was not then at war, to wit, the Republic of the United States of America, contrary to the form of the statute in that case made and provided,

The *Alexandra* lying alongside a dock at Liverpool after being seized by the British. *(Harper's Weekly)*

Charles Francis Adams. *(Library of Congress)*

whereby and by force of the statute in that case made and provided, the said ship or vessel, together with the said tackle, apparel, and furniture, became and was forfeited. The second count differed from the first only in charging that hostilities were to be committed against the *citizens* of the foreign State. The third count omitted the words 'that such ship or vessel should be employed in the service,' etc., and merely charged that the defendants *did equip* the vessel with intent to cruise and commit hostilities against a certain foreign State, etc. The fourth count resembled the third, merely varying the description of the belligerent party against whom hostilities were to be committed. The fifth, sixth, seventh and eighth counts resembled the first and second counts, and merely varied the description of the belligerent parties who were affected by the conduct of the defendants. The *intent*, therefore, was stated in two different ways, to meet the ambiguous language of the seventh section, wherein the clause 'with the intent or in order that such ship,' and the clause 'with the intent to cruise,' may be regarded either as alternative or cumulative propositions. The defendants pleaded that the vessel was not forfeited for the supposed causes in the information mentioned.

At the trial, which took place on the 22nd June, 1863, and following days, before the Lord Chief Baron of the Exchequer (Sir Frederick Pollock, Kt.), the evidence for the Crown was directed to prove, first, that the vessel was built for the purpose of a warlike equipment; second, that she was intended at some stage or other of her construction for the service of the Confederate States. It may be assumed that the Crown succeeded in proving that the vessel was built for the purpose of a warlike equipment, or at any rate that she was suited to receive a warlike equipment, but on the second point the witnesses were so discredited on cross-examination, that neither judge nor jury appeared to give much, if any, credence to their evidence, and the counsel for the defendants did not call any witnesses. The judge, in charging the jury, after explaining the information, and citing Kent and Storey, proceeded thus :

'These are authorities' (Kent and Storey) 'which show that where two belligerents are carrying on war, the subjects of a neutral Power may supply to either, without any breach of international law, and certainly without any breach of the Foreign Enlistment Act, all the munitions of war, gunpowder, every description of firearms, cannon, every kind of weapon—in short, whatever can be used in war for the destruction of human beings. Why should ships be an exception ? In my opinion, in point of law they are not.' His lordship then, having adverted to the statute and read the seventh section, said : 'The question that I shall propose to you' (the jury) 'is this—whether you think that this vessel was merely in the course of building for the purpose of being delivered in pursuance of a contract, which I own I think was perfectly lawful, or whether there was any intention that in the port of Liverpool, or any other English port (and there is certainly no evidence of any other), the vessel should be equipped, fitted out, and furnished or armed for the purpose of aggression. Why should ships alone be themselves contraband ? . . . . What the statute meant to provide for was, I think, by no means the protection of the belligerent Powers, otherwise they would have said, "You shall not sell gunpowder, you shall not sell guns." The object of the statute was this—we will not have our ports in this country subject to possibly hostile movements. You shall not be fitting up at one dock a vessel equipped and ready, not being completely armed, but ready to go to sea, and at another dock close by be fitting up another vessel, and equipping her in the same way, which might come into hostile communication immediately, possibly before they left the port. Now and then this has happened, and that has been the occasion of this statute. The offence against which this information is directed is the "equipping, furnishing, fitting out, or arming." From Webster's dictionary it appears that to "equip" is to "furnish with arms." In the case of a ship especially, it is to "furnish and complete with arms"—that is what is meant by "equipping." "Furnish" is given in every dictionary as the same thing as "equip." To "fit out" is to "furnish and supply," as to fit out a privateer, and I own that my opinion is that "equip," "furnish," "fit out," or "arm," all mean precisely the same thing. . . . The question is—Was there any intention that in the port of Liverpool, or in any other port, the vessel should be, in the language of the Act of Parliament, either "equipped, furnished, fitted out, or armed," with the intention of taking part in any contest? If you think that the object was to equip, furnish, fit out, or arm that vessel at Liverpool, then that is a sufficient matter. But if you think the object really was to build a ship in obedience to an order, and in compliance with a contract, leaving it to those who bought it to make what use they thought fit of it, then it appears to me that the Foreign Enlistment Act has not been in any degree broken.'

The jury found a verdict for the defendants. The counsel for the Crown tendered a Bill of Exceptions to the direction of the judge, in order that all the points of law involved might be argued and decided in the Exchequer Chamber (the Court of Appeal). The Bill of

Exceptions was subsequently abandoned, and in November, 1863, the Attorney-General moved a 'rule' in the Court of Exchequer to set aside the verdict found, and for a new trial. In the same month cause was shown against and for this 'rule' before the Lord Chief Baron and the Barons Bramwell, Channel, and Pigott. The question was very fully argued, and the four judges read very long opinions, two, namely, the Lord Chief Baron and Baron Bramwell, giving judgment for the claimants of the ship, and two, namely, Barons Channel and Pigott, for the Crown. Inasmuch as the four judges were divided, Baron Pigott, according to practice, withdrew his judgment in order that the Crown might appeal. The Crown subsequently appealed to the Court of Exchequer Chamber, but the appeal was dismissed on a preliminary objection of a technical nature. The appeal was then carried to the House of Lords, but was also dismissed on the same grounds. The judgment for the claimants of the ship therefore remained undisturbed, and the questions raised as to the interpretation of the seventh section of the Foreign Enlistment Act have never received any other solution than that which is set out in the charge of the Lord Chief Baron to the jury, which it will be perceived exactly agrees with the opinions given by the learned barristers who were consulted before any effort to build ships in England was made at all.

The United States authorities appear to have been satisfied with the action taken by her Majesty's Government in the matter of the *Alexandra*. On the 6th of April, the day after the seizure, Mr. Adams wrote to Earl Russell: 'It is a source of great satisfaction to me to recognise the readiness which her Majesty's Government has thus manifested to make the investigations desired, as well as to receive the assurances of its determination to maintain a close observation of future movements of an unusual character that justifies suspicions of an evil intent.'* Mr. Seward, writing to Mr. Adams after the verdict, says: 'You are authorised and expected to assure Earl Russell that this Government is entirely satisfied that her Majesty's Government have conducted the proceedings in the case with perfect good faith and honour, and that they are well disposed to prevent the fitting-out of armed vessels in British ports to depredate upon American commerce, and to make war upon the United States. This Government is satisfied that the law officers of the Crown have performed their duties in regard to the case of the *Alexandra* with a sincere conviction of the adequacy of the law of Great Britain, and a sincere desire to give it effect.'†

It must have been refreshing to Earl Russell to receive a commendatory notice from Mr. Seward, for the general tone of the communications from Washington could not have been agreeable reading at the British Foreign Office. The satisfaction of Mr. Seward and of Mr. Adams was confined to the approval of Lord Russell's readiness to seize the ship, and the zeal displayed by the law officers of the Crown in the prosecution of the suit, but they could not have been gratified by the result of the suit, although it was her Majesty's Treasury which had to bear the consequences of the failure to effect a forfeiture. The builders of the *Alexandra*, Messrs. Fawcett, Preston and Co., made a claim for damages, and after much delay and negotiation their

* 'British Appendix,' vol. ii., p. 171, and see also 'British Case,' p. 40.

† 'United States Documents,' vol. ii., p. 291, quoted in 'British Case,' pp. 40, 41.

solicitors agreed to receive £3,700, 'on the understanding that the amount shall be paid without delay,' and that amount was paid to them by order of the Treasury.

It is necessary to say something in reference to the witnesses brought forward by Mr. Thomas H. Dudley, the United States Consul, in support of the 'information' in the '*Alexandra* Case,' in order that the evidence which her Majesty's Government was urged to act upon in this and other cases may be fully understood, and a correct judgment may be formed in respect to the action of that Government in applying the Foreign Enlistment Act to the operations of the Confederate agents during the war.

I have said in a previous chapter that the affidavits upon which the United States Minister based his complaints and accusations were for the most part either wholly false or they contained gross exaggerations. A man may be deeply impressed with the expectation that a certain event is about to happen ; the expectation may be fully realized, and yet the information upon which his convictions were formed may have been false in all specific particulars. The *Florida* and *Alabama*, as is now well known, became Confederate cruisers, and Mr. Dudley's predictions in regard to their ultimate purpose have been fulfilled ; but the statements made in the affidavits of Da Costa, Passmore, and others, which appear in the proceedings before the Geneva arbitrators, are false ; and if either of the ships named had been seized by the Government, their falsehood would have been proved, not only by rebutting testimony, but by cross-examination of the witnesses themselves. This is precisely what happened in the '*Alexandra* Case.' The Crown proved by its own witnesses, who were experts, that the ship was so constructed as to be well suited to the purposes of a cruiser, but not for purposes of commerce. When, however, the prosecution attempted to prove specific facts in regard to the intent to equip, etc., the evidence failed, and failed because it was untrue, and therefore entirely broke down in cross-examination. Counsel for the defence were so satisfied that the witnesses had discredited themselves to the jury, that they called no witnesses to deny their statements. Men who are employed as spies, or who are paid to give evidence in regard to matters upon which they can have no personal knowledge except what they may have acquired by dishonest and unworthy means, are easily exposed by skilful cross-examination in the witness-box ; and anyone who was present at the trial of the *Alexandra*, or cares to read the report of the proceedings, will feel a contemptuous pity for Mr. Dudley's three witnesses—John Da Costa, George Temple Chapman, and Clarence Randolph Yonge. Sir Hugh Cairns (now Earl Cairns), in his address to the jury, summed up and commented upon the evidence of the above-named 'worthies' as follows :

'I cannot help pausing to remind you of the kind of evidence that Da Costa gave. He came forward, and what did he tell us he was ? He said he was a shipping-agent and a steamboat-owner ; that is his own account, in the first instance, of his character. I am sorry to destroy that illusion ; but it turns out, on cross-examination, that he is a crimp and a partner in a tug. He says he is a shipping-agent and a steamboat-owner. How easily great titles may descend to something smaller ! He is a crimp and a partner in a tug. He is brought forward by the Crown—I beg pardon, not by the Crown ; he is one of the witnesses of Mr. Dudley, the Liverpool Consul. . . . My learned friend for the Crown could not moderate him. He had one thing to say, and he was always saying it, and whatever he was asked it always came out. "There is a gunboat"—that is what he came to tell, and he would say nothing else—the "*Phantom*" and "gunboat;" all I know is "that was a gunboat." He would give no answer without mixing up with it that which he thought he came here to prove.'

After pointing out the irrelevancy as well as improbability of Da Costa's statements, Sir Hugh Cairns proceeded:—

'I have still to deal with the two illustrious witnesses who remain—the two spies. I will take first Mr. George Temple Chapman. . . . George Temple Chapman's story is this: He went to the counting-house of Messrs. Fraser, Trenholm and Co., and has an interview with Mr. Prioleau; he represents himself to be a Secessionist, and a warm supporter of the Southern States. He goes with that lie on his lips to have a conversation with Mr. Prioleau. Now, what was the object of telling that lie on the 1st of April (while the seizure is being prepared for)? Mr. George Temple Chapman was sent to the office of Messrs. Fraser, Trenholm and Co., to have an interview with Mr. Prioleau, and to beguile him by a false statement into making admissions to him. I suppose you will see that Mr. George Temple Chapman was sent by the American Consul as a spy, in order to obtain some admission about the *Alexandra*. Well, what came of it? . . . Does he say that he was able to extract one single sentence from that firm, or to obtain from Mr. Prioleau, who was confiding in him, believing in him as a compatriot,—does he say that he obtained one single piece of information with respect to the *Alexandra?* . . . Nothing of the kind. The whole thing is a failure which recoils on the Crown. . . . The witness who comes forward and tells this story, cannot put his finger upon a single fact that could bear upon the case of the *Alexandra*.'

I was at the office of Messrs. Fraser, Trenholm and Co. when Mr. Chapman called, and after his interview with Mr. Prioleau, he asked to see me. He introduced himself as an ex-officer of the United States Navy, and told me that although a Northern man, his sympathies were, and had been, wholly with the South, and for that reason he had been obliged to leave Boston. I instinctively distrusted him, but he had the external appearance of a gentleman, and I received his visit with as much courtesy as I could command for the occasion. He showed me a letter which he said he had got from the 'mulatto wife of Clarence R. Yonge,' mentioned elsewhere, and he thought I might like to have it. The letter purported to be a copy of an official letter written by me many months before, and he said Mr. Yonge had kept this copy, and might make improper use of it. The contents of the letter were of no importance, and I handed it back to him, merely saying that it did not concern me. On the trial it came out that his object was to obtain some admission from me, but he failed, and his evidence in respect to our interview was false.

After fully exposing the character of Chapman, and the worthlessness of his evidence, Sir Hugh Cairns proceeded to deal with the third of the trio, thus:—

'Well, but, gentlemen of the jury, I come to the greatest witness of all in this case, the witness who was reserved by the Crown to the last, and was brought forward certainly with some pomp and ceremony. I mean Mr. Clarence Randolph Yonge. How am I to describe this specimen of humanity?—the man who began his career by abandoning his wife and child in his native country . . . who became Captain Bulloch's private secretary, had access to his papers, was the companion of those who were engaged in the Confederate cause, persuaded them that he shared in the feeling of patriotism which actuated them ; who came over to England, who still assumed the same character—who, received by Messrs. Fraser, Trenholm and Co., became possessed of every secret with regard to the proceedings of those who were engaged in war on the part of the Southern States ; who accepted a commission from his native country in her service, became an officer enrolled in her navy, owning allegiance to her, received her pay, distributed her money; who then became a deserter, slipping overboard on leaving the ship of which he was an officer, in order that he might by a lying pretence of a marriage effect the ruin and plunder the property of a widow, who had the misfortune to entertain him in her country and to be possessed of some property of her own ; who succeeded in possessing himself of that property ; who brought her over to Liverpool, and who then turned her adrift, penniless, on the streets ; who then hurried up to London in order to pour into the ear of Mr. Adams, the American Minister, his tale of treachery, betraying every one of his familiar friends, and every one of his brother officers, and the cause of the country to which he had promised allegiance ; who stood there in the witness-box before you, who denied no crime and blushed at no villainy, until, indeed, it was suggested that the victim of his villainy had been a mulatto woman, and not his wife, and then all his feeling of self-respect recoiled, and he indignantly denied the charge. This, gentlemen, is the man who is brought forward at the end as the climax of the case on the part of the Crown ; but I beg pardon, he is not the witness of the Crown—he is the witness of Mr. Adams, the United States Minister. It is Mr. Adams who forwarded him to the Crown to be put into the witness-box before a jury of English gentlemen, to repeat the tale which that unmitigated villain told in our ears. Gentlemen, I know the honourable and straightforward character of my honourable and learned friend, the Attorney-General, and I felt how he must have loathed and recoiled from his task when, reading from the brief of the American Minister, he put questions to this witness, question after question, which elicited the tale which we heard from Mr. Clarence Randolph Yonge. . . . But what was it that Mr. Randolph Yonge told us, after all? He gave us a great deal of information about the *Alabama*, he told us how the money was procured to pay the officers on board the *Alabama*, he told us where the *Alabama* went to, etc.' Counsel then pointed out the folly as well as the fatality of bringing forward such a witness, and added, 'I do not merely mean to say that this evidence would cover with shame any case that was ever brought before a jury, though that is perfectly true. . . . But consider this. . . . We have now got laid before us, by one of the agents, as it was said, of the Confederate Government, everything they contemplated last April at the time when they were engaged in the fitting out and sending away the *Alabama*. . . . He has disclosed the secrets of the Cabinet Councils in Liverpool, and not one single secret of those Cabinet Councils has reference to the ship you are now trying.'*

* When I went to Savannah in the *Fingal*, in November, 1862, Mr. Clarence R. Yonge was an assistant, or clerk, in the paymaster's office at that naval station. He had served as acting-paymaster on board of one or two of the vessels of Flag-officer Josiah Tatnall's squadron, and was reported to be fully competent to perform the

The trial of the *Alexandra* afforded the opportunity to discover and expose the character of the witnesses which the United States Consul offered to produce in support of his allegations, and looking over the affidavits published among the documents laid before the Tribunal of Arbitration at Geneva, and in the diplomatic correspondence, I find they are nearly all of the same stamp as those of Mr. John Da Costa, namely, utterly inaccurate as regards the specific statements. But although the witnesses in the '*Alexandra* Case' were so thoroughly discredited that the jury could not have believed their testimony, yet the verdict of the jury was really given for the defendants in consequence of the directions of the Lord Chief Baron on the points of law, which may be summed up in the following sentence: 'But if you think the object really was to build a ship in obedience to an order and in compliance with a contract, leaving it to those who bought it to make what use they thought fit of it, then it appears to me that the Foreign Enlistment Act has not been in any degree broken.'

If it had not been for the trial of the *Alexandra*, the

duties of a naval paymaster. Just before leaving the Confederate States to return to Europe in January, 1862, the Secretary of the Navy directed me to take Mr. Yonge out as my private secretary, and to give him an appointment as acting-assistant-paymaster for the *Alabama* when she was ready for sea. When Captain Semmes joined the *Alabama*, I told him that Yonge was an unsteady and unreliable young man, whose judgment and discretion were not to be trusted, but I had no suspicion in regard to his integrity in money matters, and, of course, could not have dreamed that he was capable of treachery and treason. He was dismissed from the *Alabama* in disgrace, but Captain Semmes did not report the fact to me at the time. He came to Liverpool, but never came near me; he went instead to Mr. Dudley, the United States Consul, to whom he sold himself, with the results specified in the speech of Sir Hugh Cairns, the facts having been drawn from him in the course of his evidence.

judicial exposition of the law, and the verdict of a jury, there would have been no sufficient and unanswerable reply to the reiterated assertions of the United States Consul and of Mr. Seward, that the acts of the Confederate Government in attempting to procure ships in England were 'criminal' and 'nefarious.' But we have cumulative evidence in almost every form in which independent and authoritative opinion can be pronounced, in regard both to the spirit and the letter of the Foreign Enlistment Act, and I will now give a synopsis of that evidence, in order that the reader may have the data upon which to found his own judgment.

First,—there is the legal opinion of the two learned barristers who were consulted before the contract for the *Alabama* was made, and which has already been mentioned.*

Second,—Lord Palmerston, the Prime Minister of England, during the Civil War, when all these '*Alabama* questions' were occupying the public mind, in a speech in the House of Commons, July 23rd, 1863,† said: 'I cannot, in the abstract, concur with my honourable friend' (Mr. Richard Cobden) 'in thinking that there is any distinction in principle between muskets, gunpowder, bullets and cannon on the one side, and ships on the other. These are things by which war is carried on, and you are equally assisting belligerents by supplying them with muskets, cannon, and ammunition, as you are by supplying them with ships that are to operate in war.' After citing cases from United States history, he further said: 'Therefore I hold, that on the mere ground of international law belligerents have no right to complain if merchants—I do not say

* See chap. ii. pp. 66, 67.

† See Hansard, vol. clxxii., Session 1863 (4), pp. 1269, 1270.

the Government, for that would be interference—as a mercantile transaction, supply one of the belligerents, not only with arms and cannon, but also with ships destined for warlike purposes.'

Third,—Earl Russell, the Secretary of State for Foreign Affairs, in a letter to Mr. Adams, argues the question upon the Foreign Enlistment Act, and cites to the American Minister two cases—the *Independencia* and the *Alfred*, which were decided in the United States Supreme Court, and then, appealing to the American Minister upon the authorities of his own country, he says: 'It seems clear on the principles enumerated in these authorities that, except on the ground of any proved violation of the Foreign Enlistment Act, which those cases decided had not been violated, in those cases her Majesty's Government cannot interfere with commercial dealings between British subjects and the so-styled Confederate States, whether the object of those dealings be money, or contraband goods, or *even ships* adapted for warlike purposes.'*

Fourth,—her Majesty's Solicitor-General, Sir Roundell Palmer—now Lord Selborne and Lord Chancellor of England—in a speech made in the House of Commons, during a debate on the Foreign Enlistment Act, March 27th, 1863, said: 'It would be a great mistake to suppose that the Foreign Enlistment Act was meant to prohibit all commercial dealings in ships-of-war with belligerent countries. It is not intended to do so. Two things must be proved in every case to render the transaction illegal: that there has been what the law regards as the fitting-out, arming, or equipment of a ship-of-war; and with the intent that the ship should

* Quoted or read to the court by Sir Hugh Cairns in the *Alexandra* trial, p. 173.

be employed in the service of a foreign belligerent.'* The Solicitor-General then recites two cases in which decisions have been rendered by the United States Supreme Court upon the corresponding American statute, to demonstrate to the House 'what may lawfully be done on the showing of the Americans themselves;' and he then adds: 'The circumstances of the case tried before Justice Story were so far exactly the same as those which occurred in the case of the *Alabama*, and, in the absence of any further evidence, the seizure of that ship would have been altogether unwarrantable by law. She might have been legitimately built by a foreign Government, and though a ship-of-war, she might have formed a legitimate article of merchandise, even if meant for the Confederate States.'

I might cite many familiar cases from the history of the United States, and from the judgments of the Supreme Court of that country, in opposition to the views put forward by Mr. Seward in respect to the Confederate ships; but the charge was that *English* municipal law was violated and 'criminally evaded,' and that *British* hospitality was abused in a manner which was 'nefarious,' and therefore it is not necessary to appeal to any other tribunals than those of the country in which the alleged offences were committed. That appeal has been made, and the verdict rendered is that the Confederates have done no violence either to British law or to British hospitality. We have the judgment of the Prime Minister of England that there is no distinction in *principle* between supplying belligerents with arms and ammunition, or 'with ships that are to operate in war,' and that a British merchant may sell either guns or ships to a belligerent without infringing either

* Hansard, vol. clxx., Session, 1863 (2), pp. 47—52.

local or international duties. We have the declaration of Earl Russell, the Minister especially charged with the diplomatic relations of the kingdom, that the Confederate States had the right to procure 'money or contraband goods, or *even ships* adapted for warlike purposes' in England, provided only they did not violate the express conditions of the Foreign Enlistment Act. We have the Solicitor-General, one of the highest legal advisers of the Crown, stating with all the authority of his office, and with all the prestige of his position as a Member of Parliament, that it would be a great mistake to suppose that the Foreign Enlistment Act was meant to prohibit commercial dealings in ships-of-war with belligerent countries, and assuming that the *Alabama* was not 'equipped' in England, she was a legitimate article of merchandise, even if meant for the Confederate States. Finally, we have had the trial of a test-case, and the verdict of a special jury, under the direction of one of the highest judges in the kingdom, and the decision was that an English shipbuilder may build any kind of ship, to a commercial order, or merely in compliance with a contract, and the purchaser may take her away and do what he likes with her afterwards, without any violation of English law.

It is manifest, therefore, that in the opinion of the highest personages in England, of those who during the whole period of the Civil War were responsible for the Government of the country, who had the exclusive authority to interpret the law and to administer it, who from their exalted position, their experience, and their knowledge of public affairs, were eminently fitted to pronounce judgment upon what was due to her Majesty's Government, both in reference to acts of obedience and acts of courtesy—in the opinion of such men, expressing their views under circumstances of the gravest official responsibility—the Confederate Government, by buying or building ships in England, did nothing contrary to commercial usage, international comity, or municipal law. If the charges of 'criminality' and 'nefarious evasions of law' had been merely cast at me as an individual, or against any other agent of the Confederate Government, I would not have made the foregoing elaborate explanation, but I have learned the application of the legal phrase, '*qui facit per alium facit per se.*' I have always felt that the object was to discredit the Government of the Confederate States, as well as to defeat their purposes, and every feeling of loyalty has impelled me to give all who care to form an impartial judgment the facts and circumstances which should be taken into account. The epithets have already passed into history. They can never be erased from the public documents which they deface. Some future American Secretary of State—perhaps now that the country is reunited it may be an ex-Confederate or his descendant—may look over the files of his Department and wonder at the heat and passion of his predecessor; but I will venture to say that no member of the late Confederate Government, and not one of their representatives abroad, ever has felt a pang of conscience on the subject, or has ever had his peace of mind disquieted by the thought that he was doing, or had done, in respect to the matters at issue, anything of which a loyal man should be ashamed—loyal, I mean, in the broad sense of duty to others as well as to himself.

At some future day, when the actors have passed away, a true and impartial history of the great Civil War and its causes will be written, for it was too notable an event to remain as a mere item in the course of God's providence. Then the truth, and the whole truth, will appear, and the world will be surprised to learn how much the South has been misrepresented, the motives and doctrines of her public men distorted, and even the private life and social habits of her people caricatured for political purposes. Those who were inimical to the South, or were, at least, instigated by motives of political necessity to misstate facts or to suppress a part of the truth, have had the opportunity to publish their statements and to impress them upon the public mind of the present generation, with hardly an effort of retort or correction on behalf of the Southern people.

But the history of the past cannot be wholly forgotten. It must be and is known that in the pure days of the Republic, before the tyrannous 'caucus' and the iniquitous 'machine' had usurped the control and direction of the public will—when men were judged upon their merits, and political parties were separated by honest diversity of opinion, and not by sectional lines—the South, though greatly inferior in voting power, furnished four out of five consecutive Presidents. She has given such men as Clay, Calhoun, Crittenden, Crawford, and Forsyth to the civil service since the great struggle for independence, and the greatest of the Chief-Justices of the Supreme Court was a Southerner. She has contributed many gallant and able men to the army and navy. The 'Father of his Country' was a Virginian planter, and even Farragut, who made his reputation in helping to defeat the South, and has been called the 'Nelson of the American Navy,' was by birth, by early training, by marriage, by all the domestic and social associations of his life, a Southern man, possessing in a marked degree the peculiarities, and even what may be called the provincialisms, of that part of the United States.

I have mentioned but a small number of the Southerners who helped to elevate the national fame before dissension and distrust had alienated the two sections, and I feel sure that the day will come when justice will be done to the Southern leaders of 1861-65, and that an impartial posterity will by its verdict free their names from the calumnies which have been spoken against them, and will pronounce a retributive censure upon their traducers. After the trial of the *Alexandra*, and the clear, emphatic opinion expressed by the highest authorities of the kingdom in regard to the sale and purchase of ships in England on behalf of a belligerent, it might have been supposed that the Confederate Government would have been permitted to supply its necessities, at least, under restrictions no greater than those imposed upon the United States. But such was not the case. Whether Mr. Seward's warm commendation of the 'good faith and honour' of her Majesty's Government, and the zeal of the law officers of the Crown in the prosecution of the *Alexandra*, won Earl Russell to the Federal cause, or whether he yielded to the importunities of Mr. Adams in the spirit of the judge 'in a certain city' of whom we read in Scripture, that unfortunate ship was pursued with relentless persecution until the end of the war. She was held under seizure by the Government until April, 1864.* When released, her name was changed to *Mary*, her fittings on deck and below were altered and made suitable to a vessel of commerce, and in July she sailed from Liverpool for Bermuda, and thence to Halifax. Mr. Seward at once addressed a communication to the British Chargé

* See 'British Case,' p. 41.

d'Affaires at Washington, and the letter was forwarded to the Lieutenant-Governor of Nova Scotia. That functionary replied that he could not 'interfere with any vessel, British owned, in a British harbour, on mere suspicion;' nevertheless, he promised to institute inquiry and to have a strict watch kept on her. The *Mary*, finding no rest for the sole of her foot, or rather for her keel, at Halifax, returned in December to Bermuda, and thence proceeded to Nassau, where, on the 13th of December, 1864, she was seized by order of the Governor, and proceedings were instituted against her in the Vice-Admiralty Court of the colony. The cause was heard on the 22nd and 23rd of May, 1865; and on the 30th of May the Court decided that there was no 'reasonably sufficient' evidence of illegal intent to support a sentence of forfeiture, and the vessel was accordingly released. The war had by that time ceased, and the little craft was freed from further persecution.

Before turning to another subject, I will just mention that, in spite of Da Costa's sworn statements to the contrary, I never saw the *Alexandra* until after she was seized, I never had the slightest control over her, and never gave an instruction in reference to her. She was built under a contract with Mr. Charles K. Prioleau, of Liverpool, at his own private cost and risk exclusively. He told me, while she was building, that his purpose was to send her as an unarmed ship to run the blockade into Charleston, if possible, and after her arrival there he meant to present her to the Confederate Government. This transaction would have been perfectly regular and unobjectionable, according to the decision in the trial before the Lord Chief Baron of the Exchequer, and the views of the eminent statesmen whose opinions I have given above; but it was violently interfered with and prevented by authorities deriving their power from those Ministers who had declared that there was no difference in principle between selling a gun or a ship to a belligerent, and no violation of neutrality in permitting it to be done; and I assume that if a British merchant may sell a ship, there can be no iniquity in his giving one away. It must be borne in mind, too, that there was no evidence that the *Alexandra*, or *Mary*, was intended to be given to the Confederate States. After her release she was loaded and cleared for Halifax as any other British ship.

Under date of September 1st, 1863, I wrote to the Secretary of the Navy at Richmond on this subject, as follows:—

'The favourable decision in the "*Alexandra* Case" has not made our operations in Europe less difficult. Federal spies have rather increased than otherwise, and I am convinced that nothing more should be attempted in England. While the shipment of arms and every description of warlike implement for the North is freely allowed, while armour plates are being rolled in this country for United States ships, and recruiting is notoriously going on in Ireland for the Federal army, a vessel cannot clear for an island, even though it be a British island, contiguous to the Confederate States, without inquiry, interruption, and delay; and a ship building anywhere in private yards with the external appearance of a man-of-war, is not only watched by Yankee spies, but by British officials, and is made the subject of newspaper discussions, letters and protests from lawyers, and even petitions from the "Emancipation Society." The South derives some advantage from her recognised status as a belligerent, but the neutrality of Great Britain discriminates too palpably in favour of the North to deceive anyone as to the fears, if not the sympathies, of the present Ministry.'

In the Appendix to the British Case, Geneva Arbitration, vol. ii., there is a list of twelve vessels which were made the subject of correspondence between the United States Minister and her Majesty's Government, and all of them, upon the simple allegations of the United States Consuls at Liverpool and elsewhere, were interrupted in their loading, and interfered with, more or less, by the Customs authorities. Some of them were loading in part with contraband of war, and a portion of the shipments were on behalf of the Confederate Government. In none of those ships did the Confederate States have any interest whatever, except as shippers by them to Bermuda, the Bahamas, and Havana. One of them, the *Phantom*, became a blockade-runner, but she sailed from Liverpool in a perfectly legitimate way.

Some of the cases demonstrate very strongly the recklessness of the United States Consuls in their allegations, and the readiness with which Earl Russell acted upon them. On March 24th, 1863, Thomas H. Dudley, the United States Consul at Liverpool, wrote Mr. Adams that 'this vessel' (the *Southerner*) 'came here yesterday either to load or to fit out as a privateer. There is no doubt about this vessel. I suppose it will be impossible for me to obtain legal evidence against these two vessels,* and nothing short of this will satisfy the Government.'† Mr. Dudley never permitted himself to doubt, and generally indulged in a sneer at the British Government; but, notwithstanding his positive assertion, Mr. Adams, in forwarding the statement to Earl Russell on the 26th, was obliged to inform his lordship that

* *Phantom* and *Southerner*.

† 'British Case,' Appendix, vol. ii., p. 167.

Mr. Dudley was mistaken, and that the ship referred to had not yet reached Liverpool.* The *Southerner* was a large screw-steamer, built at Stockton-on-Tees for a passenger and freight trade. She was provided with all fittings necessary to handle her cargoes, and her saloons were arranged in every respect as a first-class passenger ship. No one fairly inspecting her could have supposed that she would have been fitted up in that style if the intention was to convert her into a 'privateer,' and her size and draft of water manifestly unsuited her for even blockade-running. Yet the British Foreign Office acted upon Mr. Dudley's allegations, and twenty-four pages of the 'Appendix' (pp. 185—209) are occupied with a correspondence in respect to her between Mr. Adams, Earl Russell, the Treasury and Customs officials, the Town Clerk, the Mayor, and Head-Constable of Liverpool. Finally she was surveyed by Mr. T. Hobbs, Admiralty overseer, assisted by Mr. W. Byrne, Assistant Surveyor of Customs at Liverpool, and Mr. Hobbs reported to the Controller of the Navy on June 23rd, 1863, as follows :†

'She is fitted with top-gallant forecastle and poop-deck, with deck-houses continuous fore and aft with the same, in the same manner as the Inman line of screw-boats, now sailing between this port and New York. She is fitted aft under the poop-deck with accommodation for about sixty-six saloon passengers, etc. . . . I find that her topsides are of iron-plates, three-eighths of an inch thick, and in no way fitted or secured, as I consider, necessary for the working of guns. . . . I cannot find anything with regard to construction or

* She arrived a few days after.

† 'British Case,' Appendix, vol. ii., p. 206.

fittings that would lead me to suppose that she was intended for belligerent purposes.'

In consequence of the above report, the Head-Constable of Liverpool advised the Mayor that the officer especially appointed to watch the ship should be relieved, and on the 3rd of July Earl Russell reported the facts to Mr. Adams, and the ship was permitted to go about her business. It appears that she went on a voyage up the Mediterranean, in the course of which she touched at Algiers, from which port another American Consul, by the name of Edward L. Kingsbury, wrote to Mr. Dayton, the United States Minister at Paris, on October 2nd, 1863 :

'I have the honour to inform you that, while absent from my post by special permission, I received information that "the suspected pirate steam-ship *Southerner*" was at Malta, *en route* from Alexandria to Algiers.'*

Mr. Kingsbury then gives a full description of the ship, her cargo, passengers, etc., which particulars he got from 'a perfectly competent and reliable gentleman of my acquaintance at this place,' and adds : 'I am also informed that the British and United States flags are painted upon the partitions of the companion way, etc., the ship having been built, it is said, to run between Liverpool and Charleston.'

The *Phantom* was detained and watched and written about in the same way. I have said that she became a blockade-runner, but she was wholly private property. The Confederate States never had any interest in her whatever. Mr. Thomas H. Dudley got a man by the name of Robert Thomas to swear that he knew me, and had seen me frequently giving directions about the *Phantom*, and especially on one occasion inspecting and

* 'British Case,' Appendix, vol. ii., p. 209.

giving orders about the screw, during a trial which occupied twenty minutes.* As a fact, I never was on board the *Phantom*, nor even alongside of her, in my life, and never heard of Mr. Robert Thomas until I saw his name at the bottom of the above affidavit, and I solemnly declare his statements to be false in every particular, so far as they relate to me. Mr. Dudley's affidavits always had a wonderful particularity in the details. He seemed to have been determined, as he had to pay for them, to get his money's worth.

Another one of the suspected craft was an old ricketty fifty-gun ship called the *Amphion*, which had been sold out of one of her Majesty's dockyards 'as old material,' and yet the United States Consul at London succeeded in putting her purchasers to considerable trouble and expense with the Admiralty about her. One vessel—the *Hector*—turned out to be building for the British Admiralty ; nevertheless, when she was launched Mr. Adams contrived to get up a correspondence with the Foreign Office and the Admiralty on the subject.†

It would be easy for me to give many more cases of interference with the loading and despatch of vessels from British ports during the war in deference to the suspicions of the United States Minister. Whenever an American Consul thought the Confederate Government had an interest in the cargo, or he felt the desire to show his animosity to a supposed friend or sympathizer with the South, he could always find some one to make the stereotyped affidavit, and the inquiry, interference and delay would almost invariably follow. There is no exaggeration in saying that there was much difficulty and trouble in making shipments by vessels of

* 'British Case,' Appendix, vol. ii., pp. 171, 172.

† 'British Case,' Appendix, vol. ii., p. 143, etc.

any description to Halifax, Bermuda, the Bahamas, Havana or Matamoras during the war, and the restrictions and necessary concealments added much to the labour and expense of forwarding supplies to the Confederate States. And yet it must be remembered that the trade, by the repeated declaration of her Majesty's Ministers, was perfectly legitimate, and they professed to enforce their neutrality with impartial fairness, or, rather, indifference to the interests of either belligerent.

I have stated, in the letter to the Secretary of the Confederate Navy quoted above, that the neutrality of England was practised in a way to give great advantages to the United States. While the restrictions placed upon all shipments which were made in vessels not loading for one of the northern ports amounted almost to a prohibition, I never heard of a single interruption to the trade in contraband with the United States, nor do I know of a single instance in which a vessel bound to that country was delayed a moment, or asked what was the destination of her cargo, or made to show whether the purpose was to arm her as a national cruiser, or privateer, after her departure.

The United States Minister at London gave certificates to British vessels loaded with arms and other contraband articles for Mexico during the French invasion of that country, when he had satisfactory proof that the arms were intended for the Mexican Government, but he refused certificates to others who applied to him without such proof. The former were protected from capture by United States ships, but the latter were in several cases captured on the high seas, and carried before the American prize-courts (*vide* the case of the *Peterhoff*, mentioned above).

In Hansard, vol. clxx., Session 1863 (2), p. 576, etc., there is a report of a debate in the House of Commons on the above subject (there were several debates). Mr. Roebuck, commenting upon one of the permits given by Mr. Adams says: 'That permit is granted. Why? Because that ship carried out arms to the Mexicans, to be used against our ally, France.' In another case he says: 'The permit was refused; and now I must say that Mr. Adams, the American Minister, is the Minister for Commerce in England.'

In the same debate another member, Mr. Peacocke, gave a very graphic and circumstantial account of the manner in which the giving of the permits came about. He said: 'The Mexican Government ordered supplies of arms in the United States. The Government of the United States, however, arrested the vessel which was to carry these arms. The Mexican Government, as well it might, remonstrated; whereupon Mr. Seward informed the Mexican Minister that he did not wish to deprive him of a supply of arms to carry on the war against France, but the United States wanted those arms themselves. "If, however," added Mr. Seward, "you will send over to England and get arms, we will give you every facility in our power." Mr. Peacocke then explained that the Mexican officer charged with the purchase of the arms came over to England, provided with a letter to Mr. Adams, requesting that Minister to give him every assistance in his power, in order to obtain arms to help the Mexicans in their war with France. 'It was under these circumstances,' adds Mr. Peacocke, 'and not from any individual action taken on his own responsibility, that Mr. Adams furnished the pass.' This, it must be admitted, was permitting a very unusual power to the

United States Minister, and the exercise of a very comprehensive belligerent right.

But in demonstration of the favour and privileges granted to the United States, as compared with the watchful restrictions imposed upon the Confederate agents, it is not necessary for me to go beyond the unlimited freedom to get and to ship whatever they wanted for their own use which the United States enjoyed during the whole war. I will confine my statement to the official returns, as printed in the British Counter-case, p. 54, etc. It appears that in May, 1862, Mr. Adams, in compliance with instructions from Mr. Seward, pressed on Lord Russell, in conversation, the expediency of revoking the recognition of the belligerent status of the Confederate Government, and mentioned, in connection with this subject, the irritation produced in the United States by the reports of supplies furnished by private persons in England to the Confederates. Lord Russell, in his reply, said 'that large supplies of similar materials had been obtained in England on the part of the United States, which had been freely transported and used against the "insurgents."'* Mr. Adams admitted that at one time a quantity of arms and military stores had been purchased in England 'as a purely commercial transaction,' for the use of the Federal army; but said that he had early objected to the practice, for the reason that it prevented him from pressing his remonstrances against a very different class of operations carried on by friends and sympathizers with the 'rebels' in England, and it had been discontinued. Mr. Adams added that 'we' (the United States) 'had, indeed, purchased largely

* Mr. Adams to Mr. Seward, reporting the conversation with Lord Russell; the word 'insurgents' is Mr. Adams's, not Lord Russell's, who never speaks of the Confederates in that character.

in Austria, but that Government had never given any countenance to the insurgents.' Mr. Adams, courteous as he generally was, could not, it appears, refrain from having his fling at Lord Russell on this occasion. He would have no more arms bought in England 'as a purely commercial transaction,' because so many people sympathized with the 'rebels' in that free country; he would go to autocratic Austria, where there was no sympathy with 'insurgents.'

But Mr. Adams was mistaken in the statement that purchases in England for the United States army had been discontinued. Messrs. Naylor, Vickers and Co., of New York, Liverpool, and London, bought and shipped large quantities of small arms to the United States. They were supplied from Birmingham alone with 156,000 rifles between June, 1862, and July, 1863. They acted very extensively as agents for the United States Government. The Assistant Secretary of War at Washington, in a letter addressed to them on the 20th of October, 1862, sanctioned an arrangement for the supply of 100,000 rifles, and the acceptance of this order was duly notified to the Secretary of War by a letter from Birmingham, dated November 4th, 1862. The arms were sent to Liverpool for shipment. In December, 1863, *fifty 68-pounder guns were proved at the Royal Arsenal at Woolwich*, at the request of Messrs. T. and C. Hood, and after proof they were taken away by Messrs. Naylor, Vickers and Co. and shipped to New York. There were other large purchases on behalf of the United States.

The general results of these operations may be traced in the official returns of exports from Great Britain to the northern ports of the United States, published by the Board of Trade. These show that, whereas the average yearly export of small arms to those ports for the years 1858, 1859, 1860, were 18,329; it rose in 1861 to 44,904, in 1862 to 343,304, and amounted in 1863 to 124,928. These are the recorded shipments of small arms; but there is reason to believe that other shipments, to a considerable extent, were made under the denomination of hardware. Of percussion caps, the average export in the years 1858, 1859, and 1860 was 55,620,000; in 1863 it rose to 171,427,000, and in 1864 was 102,587,000. Of cannon and other ordnance the exports in the year 1862 alone were valued at £82,920, while the aggregate value of the exports for the other nine years, from 1858 to 1861, and from 1863 to 1867, was but £3,336. The exports of saltpetre for the years 1858 to 1861 had averaged 248 tons yearly. The purchases for the United States Government raised the amount to 3,189 tons for the year 1862 alone. The amount of lead shipped, which had averaged 2,810 tons yearly, rose in 1862 and 1864 to 13,148 and 11,786 tons respectively. I might give further statistics in reference to military clothing and other supplies, but the foregoing is sufficient to show the enormous quantity of articles contraband of war which were bought by the United States in England during the war, and then shipped, chiefly from Liverpool, without let or hindrance, interference, vexatious inquiry, or delay, on the part of any local authority, and I wish particularly to call attention to the fifty 68-pounders proved at the Royal Arsenal at Woolwich and then shipped to New York.

The State Department at Washington, and the Consuls who received their inspiration from its chief, indulged often in what Lord Russell called 'figures of rhetoric' when addressing her Majesty's Government on subjects appertaining to the war. The compilers of the 'Case' presented to the Tribunal of Arbitration at Geneva on behalf of the United States, appear to have drunk deeply from the same fountain. It is stated by them, as a complaint, that England was 'the arsenal, the navy-yard, and the treasury of the insurgents.' There is no doubt that the Confederate Government bought supplies of all kinds in England, and that money was provided to pay for them, and persons were employed to purchase, forward, and ship them ; but the quantity of articles bought and money expended must have been, I was almost going to say insignificant—at any rate it was small—in comparison with the operations of the United States.

I have read nearly the whole 'Case of the United States,' and do not find it asserted that the rifles, cannon, saltpetre, etc., mentioned above, found their way to New York without any purchasing or financial agents to transact the business. It is probable that many agents were employed in such large transactions, and therefore branches of the War, Navy, and Treasury Departments of the United States were to be found in England, in the same sense that those departments of the Confederate Government were represented there. However, we are not left in doubt on this point. From the documents laid before the Tribunal of Arbitration, we learn that the United States engaged large warehouses at Birmingham for the reception of arms when completed, after which they were shipped through the agency of Messrs. Barings and Messrs. Brown, Shipley and Co.,* and we have already seen that they had guns proved at Woolwich. There also appears in the British Appendix, vol. vi., p. 154, a letter from

* 'British Counter-Case,' p. 53.

the Secretary of War at Washington to one of his agents—a Mr. Schuyler—in which he says: 'You will please express my acknowledgments to Messrs. Baring Brothers and Co. for their prompt and patriotic action in facilitating your operations. The terms offered by Messrs. Baring Brothers and Co., namely one per cent. commission, and five per cent. interest per annum, as agreed upon by them with the Navy Department, are approved.'

Messrs. Baring Brothers and Co. are a very eminent banking firm, as all the world knows. Their financial arrangements with the War and Navy Departments of the United States were no doubt in strict conformity with neutral duties—at least, that may be inferred from the statements of Earl Russell, for in a letter to Mr. Adams already quoted above, he said: 'Her Majesty's Government cannot interfere with commercial dealings between British subjects and the so-styled Confederate States, whether the object of those dealings be money, or contraband goods, or even ships adapted for warlike purposes.' The Confederate agents have advanced this declaration of her Majesty's Secretary of State for Foreign Affairs as a complete justification for all their dealings with British subjects, and they do not deny that it can and should be applied to the agencies of the United States with equal pertinence and comprehensiveness. But there is a special difference between the financial operations of the two belligerents in England in this particular, that while the Confederate Government dealt with private merchants and tradesmen exclusively, who were not bound by any specific undertaking to investigate the spirit and letter of the neutrality laws, but might fairly and conscientiously deal in money, contraband goods, or ships 'as purely mercantile transactions,' the United States had their Treasury Department in England at the office of bankers whose leading partner was a member of Parliament, who was bound by his oath, as well as by the ordinary precepts of loyalty, to follow with scrupulous nicety the spirit as well as the letter of the law, and to set an example of strict and impartial compliance with her Majesty's Proclamation of Neutrality.

Mr. T. Baring's name appears in Hansard* as a warm advocate of the North in the debates on the *Alabama* question, and he urged the Government to give the United States some assurance that they would prevent the Confederates obtaining ships in England, which he said might be the cause of a war between Great Britain and the aggrieved Republic across the water. Now, the Government of the United States invariably denounced the shipbuilders, the tradesmen, the financiers, who in the ordinary and legitimate course of their business had commercial dealings with the Confederate Government. They charged them with disloyalty, with violating the neutrality of their country, and endangering its peace, and often added epithets and insinuations which were personal and offensive. Did Mr. Seward and his Secretary of War really think that the house of Baring Brothers, with its Parliamentary member, could lend them money to buy guns, and rifles, and saltpetre—could forward the goods for them and perform such other services in 'facilitating the operations' of their agents as to earn the highest commendation they could bestow, and yet be wholly free from a like criminality with those who were only doing the same things in kind, but hardly in degree, for the Confederates? I suppose the use of the word '*patriotic*' in the commendatory

* See especially vol. clxx., 1863 (2), p. 59.

letter of the United States Secretary of War in reference to Messrs. Baring must have been a slip of the pen. It is one of those infelicitous and inappropriate expressions which sometimes creep into hastily written documents, or escape from an over-fluent orator. A member of the British House of Commons is quite free to advocate any cause which appeals to his sympathies, and whose principles coincide with his convictions ; but when the great commercial firm to which he belongs embarks in a large financial operation with a foreign belligerent, however ably, faithfully, and energetically he may serve the interests of his clients, we must look for some other word to describe his conduct than that expression which can only be fitly used in reference to services rendered from *amor patriæ.*

I most earnestly and emphatically disclaim the slightest wish or purpose to reflect in any way upon the house of Messrs. Baring Brothers, or to intimate that the member of the firm who sat in the House of Commons committed any fault. I have mentioned their name, and commented upon their transactions with the United States, historically. The facts are recorded in the diplomatic correspondence, and in the proceedings in the Geneva Arbitration, and I have used them, together with other statements mentioned above, to illustrate the relative attitudes of the two belligerents in respect to the neutrality of Great Britain, and to demonstrate that if England was the 'arsenal and treasury' of the Confederate Government, as has been alleged, the same may be said in a stricter as well as in a still more comprehensive sense with reference to the United States, whose War Offices were so completely and definitely established that they had warehouses for the storing of arms and the use of public arsenals for proving guns, and whose

Treasury may be said to have been represented in the British House of Commons.

In a debate on the Foreign Enlistment Act, March 27th, 1863, Lord Palmerston,* commenting upon the allegation that the Government had failed to detain vessels supposed to be intended for the Confederate States upon reasonable suspicion, said, 'Is it not fair for us to say that so far as suspicions go, we have been informed—perhaps erroneously—that not only have arms been despatched to the Northern ports of the United States, but that efforts have been made, in Ireland especially, to enlist persons to serve in the Federal army and navy? Unquestionably a great many cases have occurred in North America in which British subjects have been seized and attempts made to compel them to serve against their will in the Civil War.'

I have already mentioned two cases in which the suspicions caused interference with two vessels alleged to be taking recruits from Liverpool for the United States army, but I have not been able to discover a single instance of interference with a vessel loading with arms and other war supplies for the United States, and I can find no record of a single ship being detained an hour to give account of her cargo, or her destination, if she was clearing out for a Northern port, and was duly certified by the local United States Consul. It was very different with ships of any description loading for a British colony, for Cuba or for Mexico. The mere allegation of an American Consul that he had reason to believe that she was intended for a Confederate cruiser was sufficient to cause immediate investigation, often complete stoppage of the work during the inquiry, and in many instances a complete prevention of the voyage. Sometimes the com-

* Hansard, vol. clxx., 1863 (2), p. 93.

plaints of the United States were couched in such exaggerated terms,* and they put forward such astounding claims against Great Britain for the depredations of Confederate cruisers, that Lord Russell ventured upon a retort, as, for example, October 26th, 1863,† he tells Mr. Adams that if her Majesty's Government were to apply the principle of interfering with the trade of shipbuilding as broadly as the United States wished, a source of honest livelihood to great numbers of British subjects would be seriously embarrassed and impeded; and he then remarks: 'I may add that it appears strange that, notwithstanding the large and powerful naval force possessed by the Government of the United States, no efficient measures have been taken by that Government to capture the *Alabama*.'

I do not propose to discuss the conduct of her Majesty's Government towards the Confederate States during the Civil War with reference either to international law or comity. The result of the war has been to obliterate the political status of those States as a separate and *de facto* Power, and no one is now competent to argue such questions on their behalf with any practical purpose. Nevertheless, it will always remain a subject of interest to the five or six million people of the Southern States and their posterity, and it will always be an embarrassing problem for them to determine the reasons why the British Ministry of 1861—65 acted towards the Confederate States in a manner so inconsistent with their own interpretation of the Foreign Enlistment Act, confirmed as that interpretation was by the unreversed

* See letter of Mr. Adams to Earl Russell, dated October 23rd, 1863, 'North America,' No. 1, 1864, Parliamentary Blue Book, p. 26.

† Reply to Mr. Adams's letter above, p. 42, No. 19.

judgment of a court of law. 'There is no difference in principle between supplying a belligerent with muskets, cannon, and ammunition, or with ships that are to operate in war.' 'Her Majesty's Government cannot interfere with commercial dealings between British subjects and the so-styled Confederate States, whether the object of those dealings be money, or contraband goods, or even ships adapted for warlike purposes.' 'The *Alabama* might have been legitimately built by a foreign Government, and though a ship-of-war, she might have formed a legitimate article of merchandise, even if meant for the Confederate States.' 'An English shipbuilder may build any kind of ship to a commercial order, or merely in compliance with a contract; and the purchaser may make what use of her afterwards he sees fit.' These are the official declarations of the two principal members of the Ministry which governed England during the American Civil War, of the Solicitor-General under the same Government, and the unreversed judgment of the Lord Chief Baron of the Exchequer.

I think anyone who fairly and impartially examines the facts connected with the seizure of ships alleged to have been bought or built for the Confederate Government, and the repeated detention of vessels, and interference with their loading, when it was supposed that their cargoes were ultimately intended for a Southern port, will admit that the Foreign Enlistment Act was not administered in accordance with the above declarations and judgment, so far as the Confederate States were concerned; and that the neutrality of Great Britain was practised in such a manner as greatly to embarrass and hinder the efforts of that belligerent who most needed what she could supply, and which the said belligerent was desirous to buy in a fair way of trade.

When the American colonies rebelled against the British Crown, they obtained substantial aid from France, before the Government of Louis XVI. became a party to the war. When the Spanish American provinces revolted from Spain, England and the United States did not preserve a very rigorous neutrality, but permitted the struggling colonists to get much help in men and ships. When Greece was labouring for her freedom, almost the whole Christian world sent her succour of some sort. When Queen Isabella was battling for her crown against Don Carlos, the English Foreign Enlistment Act was suspended to permit a British general, with a British legion, to fight in her behalf. When the conflicting claims of Doña Maria and Don Miguel had kindled the fires of Civil War in Portugal, a British admiral was permitted to command the naval forces of one of the parties and to retain his commission in the British navy. When Pope Pio Nono was fighting for his temporalities, he had his Irish battalion and his foreign legion, recruited without much difficulty among the Catholic States. When the Italian people were expelling King Bomba and the reigning dukes, the chief combatants on the popular side were Garibaldi's volunteers, including many foreigners and 'Garibaldi's Englishman' among them. When Servia was striving to free herself from the suzerainty of Turkey, a Russian general commanded her active army in the field, and volunteers from neutral Russia filled her ranks. Even in the Franco-Prussian War of 1870, Garibaldi, the restless Revolutionist, broke up his hermitage at Caprera, and brought a band of men in the traditional red shirt to fight for France.

The list is not exhausted. Memory furnishes me with no record of a struggle for freedom, or between two great contending factions of the same people, or of a weaker state striving to maintain itself against the aggression of a stronger, in which the merits of the contest, the gallantry of the weaker side, or the common human instincts which have impelled men in all past time to help those who appeared to need help, did not bring the required succour in some practical form. The South alone, so far as I know, was left to fight her arduous and prolonged battle with no foreign aid, and with but a grudging allowance of the necessities she was able to pay for. A few gallant, sympathetic men like Prince Polignac and Heros von Borke brought their stout hearts to her aid; but the men who followed Lee and Beauregard, Stonewall Jackson, Longstreet, and other Confederate chiefs, were the sons of the soil, and a few English and Irish, and still fewer Germans, who from long residence had come to love the country and its people and were practically Southerners.

I cannot call to mind—I believe there never has been—a great war, fought against such odds, not in men alone, but in every element of military power, in which the weaker side has persevered so long and endured so patiently, and then after defeat has murmured so little and set so manfully to work to retrieve its losses.

I wish to draw no comparisons between the combatants, and I know too much of both North and South to doubt that there are thousands of brave, earnest, true, and loyal men in each and every section of the Union. Many thousands of gallant men went from every Northern State to the battlefields of the South, and sacrificed their lives, honestly believing that the national life was bound up in the Union of the States, and that they must fight to maintain that Union. There were hundreds of men in the armies of the United States, subalterns and field-officers of regiments, brigade and division commanders, who filled their offices not only with admirable courage, but with all the dash, judgment, and tactical skill that their positions required ; but taking a comprehensive view of the war at this distance of time, with temper cool and judgment free from bias, I am of the opinion that the United States did not find the man—he might have been there—I only say that they did not find the man for a chief-commander, who displayed more than average ability as a military strategist.

Sadowa was won, and the Austro-Prussian War was ended in a campaign of about seven weeks, by the superior skill of the Prussian Chief-of-Staff. France was crushed, two of her great armies capitulated, one in the field, one from the shelter of a strongly fortified position. The whole of her eastern and northern provinces were overrun, and her capital was occupied by a German *corps d'armée*, after little more than a year's fighting. No one believes that the Austrians are wanting in courage, or in high military qualities ; and French troops have marched as victors over nearly the whole of Continental Europe. Facts now known have proved that Prussia in 1866 was better prepared for active war than Austria, and the German armies were doubtless more efficiently organized in 1870 than those of France. But looking at the relative military strength of these three Powers, their population, wealth, war material in possession, and ability to keep up the supply, it must be admitted that the difference, if any, was not sufficient to account in any way for the quickness and thoroughness of the results, and we must look to the genius of Von Moltke for the explanation.

The South was almost wholly destitute of war material, and could supply herself only by driblets, and at very great cost. Almost from the start she was isolated by blockade from communication with the countries from which she might have drawn supplies. She had no natural lines of defence, but was open to invasion along a frontier of many hundreds of miles. Rivers, sounds, and inlets, which she had no naval force to defend, afforded access to her very heart. Her means of inland communication were hardly more than equal to the requirements of ordinary passenger and goods traffic, and proved wholly insufficient for war transport. The difficulty of arming the troops in the field was so great that they never were supplied with a uniform weapon, and powder was so scarce and difficult to obtain, that it was found necessary to form artificial nitre beds for its manufacture, and some of them were not 'ripe' for use at the end of the war. The difficulty of transportation was so great that it was impossible to get supplies to the front, and the troops in the field were often on poor and insufficient rations. The medical staff was so deficient in all kinds of necessaries for the comfort and treatment of the sick and wounded, that many men died from sheer want of them, and thousands were unshod and without greatcoats, even in winter. When all these drawbacks and deficiencies are considered, there still remains the important item of numbers, and I think it is only a fair estimate to say that the actual fighting population of the South, that is to say, the number of males capable of bearing arms, was not more than one-fifth of those of the same class in the States which adhered to the Union. Thus over-matched, the South resisted for four years, and some of the most desperate combats of the war were fought during the advance upon Richmond, and along the lines between the James River and Petersburg, during the last months of the struggle, when she was well-nigh exhausted—when, as General Grant is reported to have said, she had 'robbed the cradle and the grave' to supply her armies in the field.

It appears to me that the South could not have held out so long if the opposing power had been wielded with a superior military skill. But I have no wish to pursue this topic further. The military historian of the future will duly consider all these facts, and the generals who figured in the great Civil War will be placed in their relative positions, without reference to the adulations which partial friendship, or partizan bias, may have heaped upon them in the years just passed.

The Southern people know that many persons in England sympathized with them, and that their cause was not without able and eloquent advocates in both Houses of the British Parliament. It was very generally thought that at least two members of the Cabinet were also very favourably inclined towards the South, but that prudential and other reasons, and the belief that the rupture was final, induced the Cabinet, as a whole, to decline committing the Government to an open recognition of the Confederate States.

The action of the Ministers, I think, demonstrated clearly that they were agitated by unsettled views ; they vacillated and did not act up to their own declarations ; they did and said things which deceived both sides—which excited hopes at the South, and caused irritation at the North ; and this wavering policy ended at last in the payment of £3,000,000 to the United States, for alleged offences which Lord Russell had often repudiated, and for not restraining the Confederates from doing in

England what he more than once declared he neither could nor would prevent. Perhaps now that the war is over, the States reunited, and the people of the two sections are drawing near to each other in sympathy, and in the bonds of common interests, it is well that the South has no debt of gratitude to pay, and that the North is finding out that she has no real grudge to nurse against England. These great political convulsions follow the inscrutable laws of Providence, and when the main issues and the grand results are controlled by a Power we cannot resist, and dare not question, it is hardly worth while to perplex our minds, and to vex our souls by snarling at each other over the paltry details.

It is necessary, perhaps, to state that the Foreign Enlistment Act referred to in this narrative is the Act of 1818, and all the remarks upon the neutrality laws of Great Britain, and the registry and clearance of vessels, have reference to the condition of the law during the years 1861-65, when the alleged offences of the Confederates were committed. Since then (1867) the law in respect to the clearance of vessels has been changed, and in consequence of the report of the Neutrality Commission, a new and very stringent 'Foreign Enlistment Act' was passed in 1870. The statute as it now stands will prove very vexatious to the ship-building trade whenever England is again a neutral during a great war. It seems to me that the ship-building trade will then be at the mercy of the Consuls of the contending parties.

CHAPTER VII.

Review of the Situation in November, 1861.—Changed purposes of the Confederate Government in regard to their naval operations.—Armour-clad vessels required.—Two contracted for with Messrs. Laird Brothers.—Correspondence concerning them.—Their transfer to Messrs. Bravay, and their ultimate purchase by Government and enrolment in her Majesty's navy as the *Scorpion* and the *Wivern*.—Action of her Majesty's Government and that of the United States in reference to these vessels.—Inconsistency of the declarations and actions of the British Government.

An explanation of the Foreign Enlistment Act, and the manner in which it was made applicable to the operations of the Confederate agents in England appeared to be a necessary part of the history of those operations; and the account of the '*Alexandra* Case,' which furnished a practical exposition of the statute, has again carried the narrative far in advance of the due course of events.

The chief purpose of the Confederate Government in sending me to Europe was at first to get ships afloat capable of keeping the sea as long as possible, and otherwise fitted to cruise and destroy the enemy's commerce; and my original instructions were to put six suitable vessels in commission with all reasonable despatch. Insufficiency of money, and the pressing wants of the Navy Department in other respects, compelled me to limit the number to the two whose despatch from

England has already been described; and it soon became manifest that they were enough to drive the American commercial flag away from the principal routes of trade. But the designs of the Government assumed a broader range after my departure from Montgomery, and the reality and magnitude of the war in which the country was involved had become apparent.

By the time of my return to the Confederacy in the *Fingal* (November, 1861), the battles of Bull Run and Leesburgh had been fought; there had been some active campaigning in Western Virginia; Port Royal and the chief inlets of the great North Carolina Sounds had been occupied by the United States forces; and a blockade of the southern coast from the Chesapeake to the Mississippi, and even beyond as far west on the gulf-shore as Sabine Pass, had been proclaimed. The coast was too long for the number of ships then on the United States navy-list to guard effectively; but Europe, and indeed all the neutral states, were satisfied with the assurance that a sufficient force would soon be placed off the ports and chief inlets to justify the distinction between a genuine and a paper blockade, and they had acknowledged the state of war and the legitimate consequences appertaining to that condition.

The Confederate Government had also removed to Richmond, the several Executive Departments had been more completely organized, and there was a general conviction among the higher and more experienced officials that the contest would be fierce, and probably long. Winter weather had set in. Active campaigning had ceased along the northern frontier of Virginia. The two combatants were warily watching each other, and each was preparing to renew hostilities on a large scale. The United States were organizing a great army on the Potomac, for an effective, and they hoped a crushing, advance upon Richmond in the early spring of 1862. The Confederate Government was straining every nerve to equip the forces necessary to repel the threatened invasion, and to occupy the many weak points along the extended line of land frontier and sea coast.

Although the enemy's naval strength had enabled him to occupy with but little resistance a number of important points, such as Port Royal, Roanoke Inlet, etc., and to place there, under cover of his ships, military forces which proved to be a constant and embarrassing menace, yet on the whole the balance of success up to that time was in favour of the Confederates. The advance upon Richmond by way of Bull Run had certainly been the largest and most important operation of the war at the close of 1861, and the invading army had been so thoroughly beaten at that now historic creek, that the remnant fled into Washington without organization or cohesiveness, a mere flying rabble. General McDowell's army at Bull Run was a larger and more efficient force in every respect than the hastily gathered and ill-armed volunteers under Beauregard and Johnston, and I believe it is generally admitted that his dispositions were judicious, and that his plan of advance and attack was skilfully and energetically executed, so far as his own efforts and those of his staff were concerned. According to all sound rules of calculation, he ought to have won the battle in spite of the unquestioned gallantry and stubborn hardihood of the Southern troops. The sudden panic which seized the Federal army, and which drove whole brigades into confusion, and then precipitated them into a headlong rout of unparalleled confusion and dismay, is simply a fact in the history of the war which I shall not attempt to explain. I saw the effect in the feeling of hopeful confidence which the event had inspired among the Southern people, and yet it was manifest that the higher authorities at Richmond were not possessed by any vain expectation that another Federal army would run away, or that the Confederate States would win their independence, except by hard fighting and patient endurance.

The War Department was steadily and systematically collecting material, and massing troops. The Navy Department was striving to build and equip vessels at several coast places, and on some inland waters, for harbour and river defence, and had begun to entertain hopes of doing something more abroad than to commission ships to cruise against the enemy's commerce. The Treasury Department was hard at work upon the finances, devising means of converting the great staples which remained in the country into money, or discussing how they might be used as the basis of credit in Europe to meet the wants of the two fighting departments of the Government.

I have already (Chapter III.) given some account of the views and purposes of the Navy Department at the time above referred to, and of the especial duties assigned me. In the subsequent course of the narrative the change in respect to my own services and employment has been necessarily mentioned, and now I must further relate a still more important advance in the purposes of the Confederate Government with respect to naval operations against the enemy.

It will be remembered that on my arrival at Savannah with the *Fingal* in November, 1861, I was immediately ordered to Richmond for consultation with the Navy

Department. Among the many matters discussed was the subject of ironclad vessels, and the Secretary of the Navy (Hon. S. R. Mallory) was much impressed with the importance of getting vessels of that description to match the enemy's 'Monitors,' and to open and protect the blockaded ports. He told me that he had sent Lieutenant James H. North to England to inquire into the construction of such vessels, but had not yet heard from him.

Mr. Mallory's earnest desire was to find the money to build, and to decide upon the best type of armoured vessels for operations on the coast. It was impossible to build them in the Confederate States—neither the materials nor the mechanics were there; and besides, even if iron and skilled artizans had been within reach, there was not a mill in the country to roll the plates, nor furnaces and machinery to forge them, nor shops to make the engines.

I gave all the information I then had on the subject, and Mr. Mallory directed me to make further and more especial inquiries as soon as I got back to England, but nothing definite was decided when I left Richmond. Just before leaving Savannah *en route* for Wilmington, to run the blockade of that port, I received specific instructions on the subject in a letter from the Navy Department, of which the following is a copy:—

'Navy Department,
'Richmond, *January* 14*th*, 1862.

'Sir,—

'I desire more particularly to direct your attention to the subject of constructing iron or steel clad ships in France or England than was done in my letter of the 11th inst. Lieutenant North has had this matter in charge, but has not yet been able to do anything with it. I earnestly desire to have an armoured steam-sloop of moderate size, say of about 2,000 tons, and to carry eight or ten heavy guns, built in England upon the most approved plan and in the shortest time, and the evident change of feeling and opinion in England in relation to our country induces me to believe that we may now contract for the construction and delivery of such a vessel.'

Then follow some general comments upon the *Gloire*, *Warrior*, and *Black Prince*:

'Many plans of such a vessel have been submitted, and herewith I send you the drawings, without specifications of the one devised by Naval-Constructor Porter and Chief-Engineer Williamson. . . . . I submit this plan for your information only; but so anxious am I to have an ironclad ship built, that should you and Lieutenant North, with whom I associate you in this matter, be able to contract, or to make the preparatory arrangements to contract, for an armoured, either steel or iron clad, ship, you will proceed with despatch to prescribe the character of the vessel, and I will place the funds in England at once. . . . .

'I am, etc.,

'S. R. Mallory.

'Secretary of the Navy.

'Captain James D. Bulloch,
'Savannah, Georgia.'

Anyone who cares to refer to the leading newspaper articles, and who remembers the general tone of public sentiment in England at about the date of the above letter, will, I think, admit that there was a very apparent tendency of opinion towards a feeling of sympathy with the Confederate cause, and that the Government at Richmond had reason at that time to expect, if not formal recognition, at least that degree of passive encouragement which would enable their agents to obtain all necessary supplies without further restraint than was sufficient to maintain a fair impartial neutrality.

I arrived in Liverpool on the 10th of March, and began at once to examine into the question of ironclads, which the Secretary of the Navy had so much at heart. On the 21st of March I advised him that I was in full treaty with competent builders, and hoped to be able to send a detailed report, with plans, etc., in a very short time. I soon perceived, however, by the strict watch upon the *Florida*, which I was then trying to despatch from Liverpool, and from the espionage upon the *Alabama*, and other signs, that the Foreign Enlistment Act would be most rigorously enforced in respect to all undertakings on behalf of the Confederate Government, and in a despatch dated April 11th, 1862, I reported my fears on the subject, and ventured to ask whether it would not be well to concentrate all the resources of the Navy Department for the defence of the home ports, and I then added :—

'I find that several parties would contract for any description of ship, but, as I have before remarked, an ironclad sea-going ship must be large, and would require at least a year to complete after the order was received on this side. I would therefore respectfully suggest that wooden vessels be laid down at once at the various ports in the Confederacy, where timber is abundant, then, by sending over scale drawings, or working plans, of their decks and sides, the iron plates, rivets, bolts, etc., could be made here, marked, and shipped to arrive as soon as the vessels would be ready to receive them.'

Later in the war, vessels were built in the Confederate States—at least they were begun—and engines were sent from England for them ; but my suggestion did not promptly reach the Navy Department, and at the beginning the Government was impressed with the feeling that the arrogant tone of Mr. Seward's despatches to the United States Ministers abroad, and the excessive harshness with which the right of search and of capture was practised by the United States cruisers upon neutral vessels, would either create active opposition, and perhaps interference with the blockade, or would so irritate the Maritime Powers that they would not be over-strict in pressing their neutrality laws. Hence it was thought advisable to begin a few ironclad vessels at once.

At any rate, it was my duty to carry out the views of the Executive Government, and I pushed on with all possible arrangements, so as to be ready to act promptly as soon as definite instructions were received. Communication by letter with the Confederate States was generally slow, as our mails had to go to Bermuda and Nassau, and thence wait the departure of a blockade-runner which the Government agent would be willing to trust. Sometimes, however, we sent cypher despatches through Baltimore, and got very quick replies ; but this could only be done under great reserve, and for very special purposes. On the 10th of June, 1862, I received a long despatch from the Navy Department, treating of general matters. It was dated April 30th, and so had been forty-one days coming. That letter contained specific instructions to begin at least two iron-clad vessels, and I replied by the first returning mail for Bermuda, *viâ* Halifax.

The following extract from my despatch relates to the above-mentioned instructions :

'Finding, on my arrival in England in March, 1862, that Lieutenant North had, as he informed me, specific orders to buy or build a frigate, and that he had already made arrangements to contract for such a vessel as soon as the necessary funds arrived, I devoted myself primarily to the especial duties assigned me; but as vessels (iron-clad) capable of acting efficiently either in the attack or defence of our coast must necessarily be of light draught, I put myself in communication with eminent iron-shipbuilders, whose position enabled them to obtain the official reports of all experiments, with the view of determining the minimum draft compatible with sea-worthiness. It resulted, from a close calculation of weights and form of model, that by using turrets instead of broadside batteries, whereby the sides would be relieved from much strain and the heavy weights be thrown over the centre, a vessel might be built of about the following dimensions: length, 230 feet; beam, extreme, 42 feet; draft, with crew and stores for three months, 15 feet; engines, 350-horse-power nominal; speed, $10\frac{1}{2}$ knots; tonnage, 1,850.

'I immediately directed the plans and scale-drawings of such a ship to be made, and reported to you by letter that I would forward them as soon as they were ready and an opportunity offered. While this was going on—I think about the middle of May—Lieutenant North received a remittance of $150,000, unaccompanied by any letter of advice, as I was informed; and supposing it to be for the uses mentioned in his original instructions, he prepared at once to close up a contract for an armoured frigate, and notified me of the fact.

'I advised him that a ship of less size, cost, and draft could be built; but he deemed his orders specific and peremptory as to class of ship, and contracted for a

Lieutenant North's ironclad steam ram. *(Harper's Weekly)*

OLD MARM BRITANNIA, as she will catch it, one of these fine days, from her own Rams.

A contemporary cartoon from *Harper's Weekly*.

frigate of 3,200 tons accordingly. About the 10th of June I received your letter of April 30th, in which you say: "I write to Commander Semmes to take command of the largest of the two vessels built by you, and I write also to Lieutenant North to take command of the other vessel;" and you direct me to furnish those officers with funds for cruising expenses. As to myself you say: "I hasten to urge upon you the necessity of having at least two armoured vessels built and equipped at the earliest possible moment." "Act upon your own judgment, to save time. British inquiry and experiments, and your own knowledge of the bars and waters of our country, will enable you to act advisedly."

'To render these instructions possible of fulfilment, you inform me that one million of dollars has already been placed to my credit with Messrs. Fraser, Trenholm and Co., and that you hope to increase the amount to two millions very soon.

'Fortunately, I was in a position to act promptly upon those instructions. The drawings and plans ordered were nearly finished, and on the day after the receipt of your letter I requested the parties who had been assisting me all along to make a tender for the contract, having previously provided myself with estimates from other builders who competed for Admiralty contracts. In a few days the price was agreed upon, and I gave a verbal order for two vessels, so that no time should be lost in contracting for the large quantity of armour plates required. By giving the order for both vessels to the same builders I got a reduction of £1,250 on the cost of each, and by adopting the same size and model of ship, and a like form of engines, they can both be completed in very nearly the same time. Besides this, experience has taught me that it is far safer to keep our business as little extended as possible, as otherwise the chance of our transactions being ferreted out by the Federal spies, who abound even in this country, is greatly increased.

'For full description of these vessels, I beg to refer you to the drawings. . . . A clause in the contract gives me the right to modify or alter them in certain particulars, as experience, during the progress of the work, may suggest.'

Here follows a minute description of the peculiar construction and rig of the ships.

'The first of these ships will be ready for sea in March, 1863, and the second in May. Cost of each, fully equipped, except magazines and battery, £93,750.'

I added that the contracting parties had shown great confidence in me by taking this large contract upon my assurance that the money would be forthcoming, and I hoped that the remittances would be forwarded so as to ensure prompt payment of the several instalments as they fell due. The builders with whom I contracted for the above ships were Messrs. Laird Brothers, of Birkenhead, and the whole of the arrangements were made in the same way as those for the building of the *Alabama.* They treated with me as a private individual, and the contract was a purely 'commercial transaction,' the agreement being that they should build and deliver the two vessels to me in the port of Liverpool, finished according to the stipulated specifications, but furnished only with such fittings and outfit as were required for an ordinary sea-voyage. In order to avoid every possible appearance of an intent to arm them within British jurisdiction, it was arranged that no magazines were to be placed in either ship, nor any special places for stowing shells and ordnance stores.

I have stated very confidently that at the time of contracting for the *Alabama* the Messrs. Laird knew nothing of my connection with the Confederate Government, but at the date when the contracts for the two armoured vessels were concluded, the *Florida* had already left Liverpool and the *Alabama* was nearly ready to start. My name had been often mentioned in the United States Consul's affidavits as an agent of the Confederate Navy Department, and they (the Messrs. Laird) had no doubt been informed of those affidavits, and knew therefore as much, but no more, than anyone else whose attention had been attracted to the two handsome-looking and handy vessels which were alleged to be the property of one of the belligerents across the sea.

I wish to make no mystery of these proceedings, nor to set up a pretence that the Messrs. Laird did not believe that the two formidable vessels they were about to build would ultimately find their way to a Confederate port; all that I affirm is that they never heard from me that I was not building the vessels for my own personal account, and throughout the whole of the transactions nothing was said by them as to the intent. They undertook 'to build the two ships in obedience to an order, and in compliance with a contract, leaving it to those who bought them to make what use they thought fit of them,' a transaction which, it must be remembered, was subsequently pronounced by the Lord Chief Baron of the Exchequer to be perfectly legitimate.

Before closing the contracts with the Messrs. Laird, I had of course considered and discussed with my solicitor whether armour-plating a ship could be considered 'equipment' within the meaning of the Foreign

Enlistment Act. He went carefully over the opinions given by counsel with reference to the *Alabama*, and said that the statute did not forbid the building of any description of ship, that the prohibitory clauses referred to the arming or furnishing a vessel with ammunition and ordnance stores for warlike purposes. I afterwards learned that Messrs. Laird took counsel's opinion also before undertaking to build the ships, and they were informed that there was nothing illegal in the proposed transaction. It will be perceived that every possible effort was made to get at the meaning and application of the Foreign Enlistment Act, so that there might be no intentional or heedless violation of the municipal law, and no reckless indifference to the Queen's neutrality.

The judgment of the court in the case of the *Alexandra* was not rendered until April, 1863, and the explicit declarations of Lord Palmerston, Earl Russell, and the Solicitor-General (Sir Roundell Palmer) were not made until March, 1863; but it was shown in the preceding chapter that those declarations and that judgment confirmed the opinion previously given by counsel, namely, that it was perfectly legal for a British subject to build a ship of any description as a purely mercantile transaction, and deliver her unarmed to a purchaser, even though the ship was 'destined for warlike purposes;' or 'even if meant for the Confederate States' as the Solicitor-General expressed it.

By the middle of July, 1862, the work on both ships had fairly begun, and there were reasonable grounds for hope that they would be permitted to leave Liverpool, when completed, in an unarmed state. They were known in the yard while building as '294' and '295,' but those numbers did not attract the notice, nor suggest the mystery attributed to the figures '290,' by which the *Alabama* was at first known. The circumstances connected with the building of these two vessels, and the very peculiar arrangement by which they were taken into the Royal Navy as her Majesty's ships *Scorpion* and *Wivern*, are important and interesting as historical reminiscences, and to avoid the possibility of overdrawing them or of giving a fresh colouring to a single incident, I shall, at the cost of sacrificing some regularity and smoothness in the narrative, merely give extracts from my official reports to the Confederate Navy Department on the subject, in the precise order of date, with such other correspondence as may appear necessary to a full and clear illustration of the whole matter.

In a despatch dated 'Liverpool, August 11th, 1862,' I reported as follows :—

'The armour-clad ships are getting on finely, and I have great hopes that I shall be allowed to use the revolving turrets. . . . If the war continues until spring, these vessels may yet have important and conclusive work in the question of the blockade. The difficulty of getting them fairly to sea will be very great, however, and I confess that thus far I do not see the means to be adopted.'

September 10*th*, 1862, I wrote to the Secretary of the Navy thus :—

'I trust you have learned by this time what I am doing in iron, and have received my plans, etc. The work is going on to my entire satisfaction, and if funds do not fail, you shall have two formidable ships ready in the early spring. . . . At the proper time I will suggest the means of getting officers out for these ships. For the present I think they had better not be sent here. The presence of a number of naval officers in England could not fail to excite comment, and their movements would be closely watched. I do not hesitate to say that embarrassment has already been occasioned by the number of persons from the South who represent themselves to be agents of the Confederate States Government. There are men so constituted as not to be able to conceal their connection with any affairs which may by chance add to their importance, and such persons are soon found out and drawn into confessions and statements by gossiping acquaintances, to the serious detriment of the service upon which they are engaged.

'The proper armament for the turret-ships is engaging my serious thoughts. Experiments are in progress at Shoeburyness to determine this very point, and I will watch the results until the time requisite for the construction of the guns compels me to make a choice. . . . I have resolved to construct the turrets to revolve, and run the risk of being interfered with, and there will be two guns of the heaviest calibre practicable for actual service in each turret, mounted parallel to each other, and four and a half feet from centre to centre. The ports will be oval, large enough vertically to give twelve degrees of elevation and five degrees of depression, with just width enough to clear the chase ot the guns, so that an object can be seen over the side sights.

'I have the working drawings of Captain Cowper Coles' turret, and will send them by first safe opportunity. You are aware of the difficulty of sending letters, and the consequent necessity of being as brief as possible. I cannot, therefore, reason upon points of interest, but must request you to be satisfied with simple statements. I am making a collection of all the official reports of expriments upon matters connected with ships and their armaments, and have the evidence given before the "Defence Committee" and the "Plate Committee" of the House of Commons. These are in pamphlets, are too valuable to be lost, and could not be replaced, so I must await a safe opportunity to send them.'

'*Liverpool, September* 24*th.*— . . . I have nothing to add except that the ships are progressing as rapidly as could be expected, and that I am more pleased with them every day. The ships being of entirely new design, I see reasons to modify the plans from time to time, but only in immaterial points not involving important alterations. . . . I confidently expect to afford you great satisfaction in the character of these ships. I think they will be as near an approach to cruising ships as can be devised, when the powers of defence and offence are considered in conjunction with their light draft of water, fifteen feet extreme.'

'*Liverpool, November* 7*th*, 1862.— . . . *Armour-clad Ships.*—An unusual amount of bad weather has somewhat interfered with a certain portion of the work upon the ships of this description; but the builders are as anxious as I am to have them ready in the stipulated time, and have covered them with comfortable sheds, and have even introduced gas, so as to insure additional hours for work during the short foggy days of this climate. I have decided upon the means of getting the first of these ships clear of British jurisdiction in a manner not to infringe her Majesty's proclamation; but the attempt will be attended with difficulty, and will require to be conducted with such caution and secrecy that I fear to mention the plan even in this way. . . . In each attempt to get a ship out a different plan must be pursued. As the first of these ships will be ready in April, it is time to arrange for getting the officers detailed and in a position to join her.

'I am still firmly of the opinion that to send a staff of officers to this country would excite comment and suspicion, and would probably end in failure to accomplish the end in view. I have reason to be sure that if I had not sent the *Alabama* and her armament away before the arrival of Captain Semmes and his officers, she would have been stopped. I beg leave, therefore, to throw out the following suggestion for your consideration. Select the officers for each ship, also a few leading men and marines—non-commissioned officers who are natives of the South, or *bonâ-fide* citizens of the Confederacy—to give nationality to the crew and to ensure the actual possession of the ship until the men shipped at large are got into a good state of discipline.

'Send the first detachment out in a steamer especially provided for the purpose, so as to be under the control of the senior officer, and direct them to proceed at once to the island of Madeira. Upon arrival at Madeira, the senior officer should be instructed to notify me by the English, as well as by the Portuguese, mail, to coal his ship, have everything ready to sail at short notice, and if he finds his presence excites comment, to go out on a short cruise, leaving a letter with her Majesty's Consul, addressed to Captain W. Arkwright, British ship *Carnatic*. . . . . The steamer employed for this service should be sailed under the British flag, or, better still, the French flag, if a French owner can be found for her, and she should be managed in every way as a merchant vessel, the officers and their staff being simply passengers. The *Julia Usher*, a small steamer belonging to Messrs.

Fraser, Trenholm and Co., will very shortly sail for a Southern port. If she gets in you might employ her for the service—or the *Giraffe*, if she can be supplied with coal, would be a still better ship, from her great speed. It would be well to combine movements, so that the officers should not arrive much ahead of the ship they are to join, and with the state of the blockade under your own eye, you can arrange their departure from the Confederate port, so as to reach Madeira about the 10th of April. . . . As Captain Semmes will soon have a thoroughly organized crew, I respectfully suggest that one of these ships be put at his disposal. The officers sent out could be transferred to the *Alabama*. I am sure Captain Semmes would be pleased with such an arrangement, and I have written him that it was my intention to bring the matter to your consideration. There may be difficulty in communicating with Captain Semmes, but I shall soon know, as he will probably be at the first rendezvous agreed upon in a fortnight. I have already sent out a cargo of coal to meet him at Port Royal, Martinique. . . .

'I will not add anything on the subject of my being detailed for the command of one of the ships, but beg to refer to a previous letter in which I have set forth my feelings and hopes. My ambition is to get afloat, but after what you say in your letter of July 12th, I feel bound to submit with becoming grace to any assignment of duty for myself you may think the interests of the public service may require. You will pardon, I trust, the personal character of these remarks. They are induced by that professional pride you are well aware an officer should always possess.'

'*Liverpool, November* 21st, 1862.— . . . . The work upon the armoured ships progresses favourably.'

'*Liverpool, December* 18th, 1862.—I am gratified to learn that you approve of the designs for the two armour-clad ships. . . . As their life must necessarily begin with a sea-voyage of over three thousand miles, it was absolutely necessary to secure good sea-going qualities and fair speed, which I think could not have been accomplished on less draft and dimensions. I designed these ships for something more than harbour or even coast defence, and I confidently believe, if ready for sea now, they could sweep away the entire blockading fleet of the enemy.'

'*Liverpool, January 23rd,* 1863.— . . . . I was prepared for all ordinary opposition, and no mere physical obstruction could have prevented our ships getting out, partially equipped at least. There has arisen a political question which is very embarrassing. The Ministry have ordered the Collectors of Customs to examine and report frequently upon all vessels building in their districts, and armoured ships cannot escape notice. Our transactions have become well known—Southern papers received lately publish them, and a letter in the *Times* from the South clearly indicates that armoured ships are expected from this side to break the blockade. I have been aware that indiscreet persons who should have known better have written to private persons at the South on such matters, and I am not surprised at the result. Lord Russell says in effect that the "290" evaded the law, and rather intimates that it shall not be done again. I am convinced that the present British Ministry will do almost anything the United States Government asks, and you are well aware that an "Order in Council" will override the ordinary rules of law. Parliament meets February 5th, and I am reliably informed that the question of furnishing supplies to the belligerents will come up. I am consulting the best legal authority, but confess that the hope of getting the ships out seems more than doubtful—indeed, hopeless, unless there should be a change in the political character of the Ministry. I will of course go on as if no obstacle existed, so as to be ready to avail myself of chance circumstances.'

'*February 3rd*, 1863 (cypher despatch, *viâ* Baltimore).— . . . . I have been delayed in giving orders for ordnance stores, etc., for iron ships, by want of money; but financial agent authorizes me to order them, and says in any event he can and will manage to supply the necessary funds when the payments are required. Unforeseen causes have kept back work on iron ships. Have tried very hard to hasten the completion, but insurmountable difficulties have occurred. No armoured ships for Admiralty have ever been completed in time specified; whole character of work new, and builders cannot make close calculations; great labour and unexpected time required to bend armour-plates; and the most important part of the work, the riveting, is far more tedious than anticipated. . . . Think British Government will prevent iron ships leaving, and am much perplexed; object of armoured ships too evident for disguise.'

On the 9th of March, 1863, I received a despatch from the Secretary of the Navy, dated 'Richmond, January, 1863.' In reference to sending out officers for the armoured vessels, the Secretary wrote thus:—

'I concur with the views you express upon the inexpediency of sending naval officers to England. The plan suggested in your despatch of November 7th, 1862' (see p. 392) 'is so difficult of accomplishment that I will at once submit to your judgment another, and request you to give me your views as promptly as practicable. It would be difficult, if not impossible, for us to obtain the services of a suitable steamer; and failing in this, we should be compelled to charter an English sailing vessel at Nassau for the purpose. I suggest to you, therefore, that you at once put yourself confidentially in communication with Mr. Slidell, and learn from him whether you cannot fit out the vessels at a French port, in which event the officers could go to France, *incog.*, *viâ* England, in the ordinary way, and escape observation. I do not suppose that the French Government would give any formal assent to this proposition, but I do suppose that not only no obstacle would be offered, but that facilities would be extended. . . . I am not at liberty to state the reasons of this opinion, but they are sufficiently strong to induce me to press the subject upon your attention. If you could run over to Paris and see Mr. Slidell it would be the best, perhaps the only course to pursue. I do not desire, by any suggestion here made, to change any plan that you may deem best for getting the ships to sea. I do not know your entire plan, and offer my suggestions for your consideration, content to leave the matter to your uncontrolled discretion. I trust you will be able to advise me of your determination in time to avoid any delay in my co-operation.'

On the very day of the receipt of the above despatch I was able to send, *viâ* Baltimore, a reply in cypher, dated 'Liverpool, March 9.'—'Completion of armoured ships having been delayed, change of plan can be made. You can send officers to France as soon as possible. Will go to consult with our commissioner in France (Mr. Slidell) in a few days,' etc.

I must call particular attention to the cautious intimation of the Secretary of the Navy that the Government at Richmond had good reasons to suppose that facilities would be extended to us in France. The grounds upon which such expectations were based will appear very clearly in the subsequent arrangements with reference to the two English ironclads, and in the account of the efforts to build and fit out ships in France. On the 11th of May, 1863, I received two despatches from the Secretary of the Navy in cypher. The first, dated 'Richmond, March 19th, 1863,' contained the following:—

'Your despatch of February 3rd, 1863' (see p. 395), 'reached me yesterday. I share your apprehensions as to our ships. The importance to our cause of getting them to sea at an early day renders the subject one of great anxiety. I am in possession of information which prompts me to suggest to you the following proposition, should you find that the [British] Government designs to prevent their departure. Do not risk correspondence, but proceed to Paris and consult Mr. Slidell, after conferring fully with Mr. Mason, and arrange, in the manner which your judgment shall approve after such consultation, for the transfer of the vessels to French owner, and their equipment in a French port. M. ——*, a Member of the Corps Législatif, and who is said to have the confidence of the Emperor, is indicated as a party willing to receive the transfer and complete the outfit,' etc.

The second despatch was dated 'Richmond, March 27th, 1863,' and merely enclosed copy of a letter from the Secretary of the Navy in cypher to Mr. Slidell, our commissioner to France. The letter to Mr. Slidell was

* The name is suppressed because the person was not the one with whom the arrangement was subsequently made.

in the Navy Department cypher, and I was directed to translate its contents and then to act upon them in conjunction with Mr. Slidell. The following is a copy of the letter, which I transcribe in full, as it bears upon other operations in France which will be narrated in a subsequent chapter:—

'Richmond, *March 27th*, 1863.

'The Secretary of State having laid before me certain portions of your despatch of January 11th, No. 23, I am induced to invoke your aid in such manner as you may deem most advisable in the attainment of two objects of the first importance to the interest of our country. You have doubtless noticed certain indications in England of a disposition to prevent the departure of the ships built there for our service. The officer in England in charge of this duty, a close observer of public sentiment there, expresses much anxiety upon this subject, in which I fully share. Under these circumstances, Commander Bulloch is instructed to confer fully with Mr. Mason and yourself as to the practicability of transferring those ships to M. ——, or other French citizen, with the view of removing them from England as early as possible, and fitting them out in France. If this can be accomplished, they might be probably loaded with supplies for the French army in Mexico, cleared for Vera Cruz, and sold to us at Terceira or elsewhere. Our early possession of those ships in a condition for service is an object of such paramount importance to our country, that no effort, no sacrifice, must be spared to accomplish it. Whatever may be the terms which M. —— may prescribe as the conditions of thus placing them at our command will be promptly met, and apart from all pecuniary consideration involved in the enterprise, its success would entitle him to the gratitude of the country.

'To the good judgment of Commander Bulloch I must necessarily leave all details, earnestly asking your assistance to open and conduct this measure to a favourable conclusion.

'The second subject referred to is the construction of new ships for our country in France. The size and general character of the ships would be best determined by Commander Bulloch, after consultation with the builders, and due consideration of the means of construction, the time involved, etc. The character of our rivers and harbours, however, necessarily demands light draught. Payment for contracts would be made in interest-bearing bonds, or in cotton delivered here upon demand at prices controlled by its current value in this market.

'I am, etc.,

'(Signed) S. R. MALLORY.'

'Hon. John Slidell,
'Paris.'

Before the receipt of the foregoing despatch, Mr. Slidell had communicated to me his belief that we should be allowed much more latitude in our naval operations in France than in England, and I had already been in conference with him on the subject. My next despatch to the Navy Department of importance in reference to the ironclads was under date of 'Liverpool, June 30th, 1863':—

'First in importance as well as interest are the ironclads already under construction. These should have been ready for sea between March and June, according to the original terms of contract. I have already reported that mechanical difficulties of construction, not within the reach of foresight, had delayed the progress of these vessels, but the action of the British Government in reference to our operations in Great Britain, culminating in the seizure of the *Alexandra* and her trial in the Court of Exchequer, has still further delayed their completion. As long ago as the latter part of March, I went to Paris to consult with Hon. John Slidell with reference to a possible sale of these ships to a French subject. Through M. Arman, a distinguished naval architect of Bordeaux, Mr. Slidell and I were introduced to the Messrs. Bravay and Co., of Paris, with whom a satisfactory arrangement has been made. Messrs. Bravay and Co. have bought the ships from me for a nominal sum,* and the contract with the builders has been transferred to them, or rather, the builders have made a new contract agreeing to complete the ships for the Messrs. Bravay and Co. precisely as they were to have been finished for me.

'This exchange of property required to be managed with great caution, because it was well known that the true ownership of the vessels was suspected, and that any attempt to equip them for sea, or even to launch them, would result in their seizure and indefinite detention by means of the interminable proceedings of the Court of Exchequer. In order that the transaction might bear the scrutiny of an English court, I thought it advisable to take the advice of counsel on the points of English law. His opinion was that the mere building of a ship in England, for whatever purpose, was not contrary to the Foreign Enlistment Act; that the

* The precise facts are, that Messrs. Bravay bought the ships for a specified amount, and they engaged to re-sell them beyond British jurisdiction for an amount which should include a commission to them.

seizure of the *Alexandra* and the stoppage of several other ships for inquiry in consequence of affidavits lodged by the United States Consuls were illegal and arbitrary acts, but that the ironclads were liable to the same proceedings, and if they should be seized we could not expect to release them from the Court of Exchequer during the war, if at all.

'It was known that . . . . Clarence R. Yonge had already stated to the United States Minister in London his belief that the ironclads referred to were intended for the Confederate Government; that the United States Consular spies were already watching their daily progress, and that the British Foreign Office would act promptly whenever it suited Mr. Adams' purpose to demand their seizure. It was therefore necessary to disconnect myself with the ships as quickly as possible. I was advised by counsel that under any circumstances there would doubtless be a legal inquiry into the title to the property, and that all the papers and letters relating to the sale must be such as would bear judicial scrutiny and tend to prove the *bonâ fide* character of the transfer. As the builders would naturally be the principal witnesses, it was absolutely necessary to prevent them from suspecting that there was any collusion between the nominal purchasers and myself. With this view I first wrote a formal letter to the Messrs. Laird, stating that the interference of the British Government in all attempts to build ships suspected of being for the Confederate States was such as to make it certain that they would not be allowed to complete the ironclads for me; that I was not willing to run the risk of their seizure, which would either result in entire confiscation or my being kept out of the use of the large sum of money already expended for an indefinite time, and requesting them to sell the ships for such sum as would ensure me a reasonable profit, and to release me from all further obligations under the contract.

'Fortunately, just at this time the Russian Government made an offer for the ships, and I hastened to Paris to regulate the correspondence on the part of the French purchasers, to suit the advice of my English solicitor. As you will readily perceive, the affair required a good deal of management, and occupied far more time than if the transaction had been a real one. It is not necessary to go into further details. Suffice it to say that our two ironclads are now the property of Messrs. Bravay and Co., of Paris, agents for the Pasha of Egypt. The papers are all in proper legal form, the Messrs. Laird are convinced that the sale is *bonâ fide*, and I have expressed the most cordial regrets that there should have been a necessity for such a proceeding.

'To keep up this illusion I can no longer appear on board the ships, or even in the yard of Messrs. Laird, but can only direct their further completion from behind the desk of the Messrs. Bravay and Co. These necessary proceedings have created additional delay in finishing the ships, but the work shall now be pushed on as rapidly as possible.'

Then follows a specific report of the condition of the ships.

'The engines of both ships have been ready for several months. One ship is entirely plated, and could have been in the water six weeks ago if it had not been for the political necessity of keeping her back. . . . I cannot hope that these two ships will be ready to take the sea before October. I can only assure you that every effort will be made to hasten their completion. I will keep the Messrs. Bravay under a constant pressure.'

In an historical narrative of this kind it is the duty of the writer to take care that no persons who were connected with the transactions, and whose names and credit as men of business are in any way implicated, shall be left in a doubtful position, by reason of a looseness in the general statements, or a want of particularity in the details. I have stated in the letter to the Secretary of the Navy, quoted above (June 30th, 1863), that it was necessary to manage the arrangements with Messrs. Bravay so that the Messrs. Laird should not suspect that the sale of the ships was not *bonâ fide* and final. Every step in the business was taken, in conjunction with my solicitor, in the ordinary somewhat circumlocutory way, which appears to be unavoidable in the legal transfer of property, and I believe that if the Messrs. Laird ever read this book, they will receive the first intimation of the true character of the transaction from the disclosures on the subject here made. The Messrs. Laird acted as agents for the sale of the ships, and I simply arranged with Messrs. Bravay that they should apply for tenders for two ships in the ordinary way of business. The Lairds would naturally have preferred building new ships in response to this proposition, but they acted with their accustomed good faith, and promptly reported to me the offer they had received as a probable opportunity to sell the two ironclads.

When in the course of the arrangements they applied to me for definite and specific authority to sell the ships which they could produce to Messrs. Bravay, they wrote thus: 'It will be necessary that we should have clear instructions, either direct to Birkenhead or through your solicitor, of the price at which we are to negotiate the sale.' After giving their own views of the price which might be fairly asked, they add: 'As the inquiry came to us in the ordinary course of our business for building vessels, and not with any special reference to vessels we might have in course of construction, we hope that you will agree with us that these prices should include a commission of two and a half per cent. on the transaction to us, as we not only lose the opportunity of tendering to our correspondent for new vessels, but shall have considerable trouble in making the transfer and arranging money matters and other details.'

In reply to the foregoing I wrote to the Messrs. Laird that, having made inquiry through my bankers, I was satisfied in regard to the financial position of Messrs. Bravay, and had learned that they had executed large commissions for the Egyptian Government, and had at the time an open order for two ironclad vessels from the Pasha. I therefore felt assured that they were able to carry out the proposed transaction, and it might therefore be closed on the terms proposed; and I added:

'Your claim for a commission upon the amount of the sale is, under the circumstances, quite usual and justifiable, and if two and a half per cent. is the established commission in such cases, I readily agree to it. . . . . Hoping that in better times we may be able to renew our business associations, which have been as satisfactory to me as our social intercourse has been agreeable, and assuring you of my personal esteem and regard,

'I am, etc.,

'(Signed) JAMES D. BULLOCH.'

During the negotiations an offer was made for the purchase of the ships on behalf of the Russian Government, and Messrs. Laird, looking to the official and therefore reliable source from which the inquiry came, and the financial security of such a transaction, were inclined to entertain it. To refuse the offer upon grounds which would seem reasonable to them was at first a little embarrassing, but I wrote my solicitor, who of course knew of the arrangement with Messrs. Bravay, that the excessively friendly relations which appeared to exist between Russia and the United States made me suspicious of any proposition coming from St. Petersburg. It was possible, I said, that the Russian Admiral might be acting on behalf of the United States Navy Department, and the ships might get under the wrong flag, and I suggested that this was a sufficient reason for declining the proposition.

It is useless to give further details. The sale to Messrs. Bravay, and the transfer of the property, was effected by my solicitor and the Messrs. Laird in conformity with strict commercial and legal usage and requirement. The chief object was to keep the Messrs. Laird free from any knowledge of the secret understanding with Messrs. Bravay, so that they might be able to answer all inquiries, either from the Foreign Office or the Customs authorities, without embarrassment or hesitation. This purpose was effected, as will appear to anyone who cares to read the official correspondence on the subject, which fills one hundred and forty-five pages of the Appendix to the 'British Case,' Vol. II.

The arrangement with Messrs. Bravay, regarded as a mere business transaction, was based upon a letter from M. François Bravay, the senior partner, dated 'Alexandria, Egypt, 28th December, 1862,' to his brother, M. Adrien Bravay, who was the resident managing partner of the firm in Paris, and the reply to that letter, dated 'Paris, 15th January, 1863.' In the above-mentioned letter from M. François Bravay, he writes generally about his business relations with the Viceroy, but the first paragraph of the letter is the only one which need be quoted here.

'I write you a few lines' (he says) 'to inform you that the Viceroy positively wishes me to complete some commissions for him, in spite of the resolve I have manifested to him not to execute them. He has ordered me to have built for him in France two armoured frigates, after the best and most perfect designs. He stipulates above everything that it shall not be made known that they are for the Egyptian Government, for he has political reasons for that. Make arrangements to get designs and the contracts in the best form.'

The reply acknowledges the receipt of the above letter, and in reference to the particular subject says:—'Your letter transmits to us the commission which his Highness the Viceroy has given, to have built in France two armoured frigates, after the latest models. We will at once take the necessary steps for the execution of that order, in obtaining from the French Government the same facilities for its execution that have been already granted us in reference to the guns that we have had constructed for his Highness,' etc.

These and other letters, which were shown to Mr. Slidell and to me, sufficiently demonstrated that the Messrs. Bravay had extensive business relations with the Viceroy of Egypt, and that they were therefore in a position to justify the purchase of such vessels as the two at Birkenhead. It was necessary to have the *status* of the Messrs. Bravay fully established in the above respects, for manifest reasons of a purely business character, because the Messrs. Laird would not have paid attention to an offer coming from irresponsible parties. But Mr. Slidell had received private and confidential information that the Imperial Government would not interfere with any subsequent arrangement Messrs. Bravay might make for the delivery of the ships to the Confederate Government, after they had been despatched from England, and, moreover, it was intimated to him that if her Majesty's Government objected to a private firm taking the ships away without a guarantee that they were not intended for a belligerent, the Imperial Government would state on behalf of Messrs. Bravay that they were satisfied with the explanations of that firm, and would request permission for the departure of the ships as the property of French subjects. This hint, conveyed to Mr. Slidell through a very direct and satisfactory source, was the foundation of the whole agreement with the Messrs. Bravay.

The order of the Viceroy for the two armoured vessels was dated before we had met either of the Messrs. Bravay, or had thought of an arrangement of the kind for getting the ships out of British jurisdiction. It was made use of only as a plausible reason why a private firm should want vessels of such formidable structure and armament, and was not manufactured for the occasion. Subsequently it will appear that the Grand Vizier of Egypt denied that an order for ironclad vessels had been given to Messrs. Bravay. Perhaps there were political reasons for the denial, just as there were for keeping the order secret. Or perhaps the order, being rather in the character of a request, or what may be called a 'permissive commission,' the Grand Vizier might have found it convenient, at the particular time when the inquiries were made, to deny any knowledge of it.

The arrangement by which it was hoped that the departure of the two ships from Liverpool would be assured having now been fully explained, it only remains to describe the progress and result of the undertaking, which can best be done by a transcript of such portions of my official despatches to the Secretary of the Navy as relate to the subject.

'*Paris, July 8th*, 1863.—I have the honour to send you with this letter a complete set of drawings of our two ironclad vessels, which in future reports I will allude to as Nos. 294 and 295. I also send the detailed specifications upon which the ships are being completed.' After a full and most specific explanation of the drawings, the despatch continues: 'I reserve my remarks upon the special service upon which it would be advisable to employ these ships for a separate despatch.'

The Secretary of the Navy had previously alluded to the desirability of using the ironclads for re-opening the Mississippi and regaining possession of New Orleans, and had invited me to comment upon that proposition. The work on the vessels had up to this time progressed without interference, although we had been well aware that they were closely watched. After the arrangement with the Messrs. Bravay, which was completed on the 17th of June, 1863, it was of course my duty to proceed with all contingent plans as if expecting that the ships would be permitted to sail, and I reported on the subject of their employment as follows:—

'Paris, July 9th, 1863.

'Sir,—

'The several despatches I will now have the honour to send you are of such a nature, and treat upon subjects a knowledge of which by the enemy would be so ruinous to our interests, that I have thought it advisable to send them by a special messenger, and have selected Lieutenant W. C. Whittle, Confederate States Navy, for this important service. It is possible that Lieutenant Whittle may be forced to destroy the despatches, and yet may be able to reach you in person; I have therefore fully instructed him as to their contents, and have given him full verbal explanations of the drawings of the ships and turrets. . . .

'No very great difficulty was experienced in getting crews for the *Florida* and *Alabama*, and I think any vessels fitted out to cruise against commerce, thereby holding out to the men not only the captivating excitement of adventure, but the possible expectation of prize-money, might almost at any time pick up a goodly number of passable seamen. But the ironclads are too manifestly for other purposes to deceive any mere adventurer. Their grim aspect and formidable equipment clearly show that they are intended for the real danger and shock of battle, and I do not think reliable crews could be obtained from among the floating population of European seaports. The ships are so rigged as to require but few able seamen. The actual force of the crews need be only artillerists, but these must be men willing to fight for the sake of their country alone, and must be actuated by the same spirit which has converted our farmers and backwoodsmen into the veterans who are now sweeping irresistibly through Maryland and Southern Pennsylvania under the leadership of our great General Lee. Engineers and firemen can be got here, and men enough to work the ships and perhaps one gun on each. They would thus be able to overcome any wooden ship, or fleet of them. I respectfully propose, then, that the ships, when ready for sea, should be ordered to proceed as quickly as possible to Wilmington, North Carolina. One could fall in with the land at New Inlet, and the other at the main "ship bar" at the mouth of Cape Fear river.

'By steaming quietly in at early daylight, they might entirely destroy the blockading vessels—not one should be left to steal away and make known the fact that the ironclads were on the coast. Crews might be ready at Smithville or Fort Caswell, to be put on board the ships as soon as they had destroyed or dispersed the blockaders, and in a very few hours afterwards the two vessels would be ready to strike a decisive blow in any direction, north or south. I am earnest and anxious on the subject of crews, because the ships are too formidable and too valuable to be trusted in the hands of a mere set of adventurers, who, actuated by no feeling of patriotism, and controlled only by force, might fail at a critical moment, either from indifference or disaffection, thus disconcerting the best devised plans, or perhaps even occasioning fatal disaster. When the departure of the ironclads from Europe can be definitely determined, say within two weeks, a special messenger can be sent to report specifically to you, so that all necessary steps may be taken and arrangements made to carry out the further views of the Department.

'In view of the intimate knowledge I necessarily possess of the construction and capabilities of the ironclads 294 and 295, I feel called upon to throw out a few suggestions as to the service for which they would be most available, and I trust you will not think me presumptuous for doing so. I feel confident that they will be as good sea-boats and as easily handled as armoured vessels can be, but as you will perceive from the drawings and descriptions, they are large ships, both in length and breadth, and in the rapid current and short turnings of the Mississippi, they would be at great disadvantage, and their full force and power as rams could not be made use of. If they could be accompanied by smaller and shorter vessels to assist them in turning, or to occupy the enemy's ironclads while they were thus engaged, the difficulty might be somewhat removed, but in such narrow waters they would be very much in the condition of a boxer with one arm tied behind his back. I am supposing now that they would have to fight their way up the river in face of the enemy's fleet of ironclads. If these latter can be held above Vicksburg or Port Hudson, and "294" and "295" were simply expected to force their way past the forts and steam up to the city, that object could easily be accomplished. Of course, in such an event, there would be a movement of troops by land, and also of the Mobile flotilla, through Lake Pontchartrain; otherwise, on the approach of the ships by the river, the garrison of New Orleans would burn the city, retire upon the lake, and escape by means of their transports through Ship Island Pass.

'The Atlantic coast offers enticing and decisive work in more than one direction. Without a moment's delay, after getting their crews on board off Wilmington, our vessels might sail southward, sweep the blockading fleet from the sea-front of every harbour from the Capes of Virginia to Sabine Pass, and cruising up and down the coast, could prevent anything like permanent systematic interruption of our foreign trade for the future. Again, should Washington still be held by the enemy, our ironclads could ascend the Potomac, and after destroying all transports and gun-boats falling within their reach, could render Washington itself untenable, and could thus create a powerful diversion in favour of any operations General Lee might have on foot. Third, Portsmouth, New Hampshire, . . . is a wealthy city in itself, and opposite the town is an important national dock and building-yard. The whole lies invitingly open to attack and destruction. Suppose our two iron-clads should steam, unannounced, into that harbour on some fine October morning, and while one proceeded to demolish the navy-yard and all it contained, the other should send a flag of truce to the mayor, to say that if $1,000,000 in gold or $5,000,000 in greenbacks were not sent on board in four hours the city would be destroyed after the manner of Jacksonville and Blufton.* Portsmouth could afford to pay for its existence. Philadelphia is another point open to such an attack. The river is navigable, the banks comparatively low, so that no plunging fire could be brought to bear upon the ships, and once in front of the city they could dictate their own terms. Such operations as are thus hastily sketched would inflict great damage upon the enemy, besides creating a striking effect in Europe, and the ships would thus be employed in a manner which would bring into use their full power, so that no strength would be wasted. . . .

'I am, etc.,

'(Signed) JAMES D. BULLOCH.

'Hon. S. R. Mallory,

'Secretary of the Navy, Richmond.'

To the Secretary of the Navy I wrote :—

'Liverpool, *July* 20*th*, 1863.

'You will remember that Lieutenant R. R. Carter was ordered to report to me for duty in the ironclad you

* Two Southern towns which had been just then reported to have been burned by the United States forces.

originally intended me to command. Although you have changed the sphere of my duties, I continue to employ him as an assistant in the inspection of work actually in progress, as well as to advise with on all matters of importance. I propose in a few days to put him in communication (through the purchasers of "294" and "295") with Captain Blakely, to arrange for the arming of those ships, as it is important that I should keep entirely out of sight in the matter. I take pleasure in saying that Lieutenant Carter yields me the most cheerful and intelligent assistance, and I esteem myself fortunate in having him with me at this time. . . .

'The opportunity to send this has unexpectedly occurred, and I am forced to be brief and hurried, only adding that matters still progress favourably with "294" and "295." . . . Application will very shortly be made for permission to arm them in England, and the French owners anticipate no difficulty. If, however, their application is refused, we will have to transport the armament to a Continental port, which will involve some delay. . . .

'As I can only shape plans to suit possible changes of circumstances, it is quite impossible to go further into detail on this subject.'

Not long after the date of the above despatch we began to feel the effects of Mr. Adams' representations to Earl Russell, especially on the subject of the ironclads. Under date 'Liverpool, October 1st, 1863,' I reported to the Secretary of the Navy thus:—

'The newspapers, which seem to pass very regularly through the lines of the armies, will doubtless have prepared you for disappointment in all our English undertakings. Of course, I shall continue to act as if certain of success, but am forced to acknowledge that I have but little hope. . . .

'The articles alluded to in my despatch of June 30th, 1863,* would have been ready for departure now if it had not been for interference, such as you can readily imagine. They cannot, however, be wholly lost, for reasons you will understand by referring to the letter alluded to above.'

The difficulty and delay in communicating with Richmond was always a cause of great embarrassment in arranging for co-operative movements and in exchanging views. Opportunities were often lost, from the miscarriage of despatches, and suggestions which were approved in purpose were only known when it was too late to act upon them. About October 15th, 1863, I received a despatch from the Secretary of the Navy, advising me of the safe arrival of Lieutenant Whittle with a large batch of despatches from me, including that of July 9th, 1863, on the subject of the proper service for the ironclads. Lieutenant Whittle left Paris on July 10th, and reached Richmond on August 20th. The despatch of the Secretary of the Navy just above mentioned was dated 'Richmond, August 29th, 1863.' He said:

'I have very carefully examined the drawings (of "294" and "295"), and so far as I can form an opinion of structures so novel in all their details, I think they will be very efficient ships; and that they will probably excel all other ironclads of which I have any knowledge in sea-going qualities. . . . My regret and disappointment at their delay in England is very great, but I understand the difficulties in your path, and cannot well see how you could have done better than you have.

* Nos. 294 and 295.

Their presence at this time upon our coast would be of incalculable value, relieving, as they would be able to do, the blockade of Charleston and Wilmington, and nothing must be suffered to interfere with their completion at the earliest practicable moment. . . . It is deemed expedient to send an officer of rank out to bring over "294" and "295," and Captain Barron has been selected. To him I have communicated your views as to appropriate employment for them, and I will thank you to confer with him freely about them. He will receive them from you, as did Captain Semmes the *Alabama*, for I deem it important that you shall carry out the plans you have devised for placing them in our possession. . . . The arrangements made by you for the completion of "294" and "295" and their final transfer, seem the very best that could have been effected, and I doubt not your judgment and discretion will conduct the negotiation to a successful conclusion. Your suggestions as to the enterprises to be undertaken by them command much consideration, and Captain Barron will receive upon this subject especial instructions.'

In respect to manning the vessels, the Secretary of the Navy said: 'The method suggested by you would meet the case if Wilmington should at the time be in its present condition with reference to the enemy. . . . You will regard this plan, however, namely, manning the vessels from Wilmington as suggested by you, as the one to be carried out unless otherwise changed.' A great portion of the above despatch was devoted to the subject of supplying funds, which was always weighing upon the minds of the heads of Departments at Richmond.

Captain Barron arrived in due course, and there came with or followed him a sufficient number of other officers to supply the staff for the two ironclads. By the time of his arrival it was already manifest that our expectations with reference to those vessels could not be realized, and he retired to Paris and there waited, hoping against hope that some fortunate turn of events, or some change of policy in the two chief Maritime Powers, would enable him to get afloat. Captain Samuel Barron was well known in the United States service before the war as a gallant dashing officer, and he had some fine young officers with him. Sometimes a sense of companionship in misfortune serves as a consolation, but it was rather an aggravation than a relief to my own disappointment, to contemplate those ardent men yearning for employment and chafing at their compulsory inactivity. It was a hard case to be so near to a great opportunity and yet to miss it. The final annihilation of all hope of getting our ironclads and so ending the blockade and securing supplies to the famishing armies in the field, was reported in the following despatches to the Navy Department:—

'Liverpool, *October* 20*th*, 1863.

'Sir,—

'In my despatch of October 1st, 1863, I called your attention to the newspaper accounts of the seizure of the ironclads "294" and "295," which had doubtless reached Richmond, but feared to trust particulars to the ordinary mails. Now, by the hands of Lieutenant R. R. Carter, I will report in detail all that has transpired in reference to those ships. When the proceedings in the case of the *Alexandra* had exposed the extent and unscrupulous character of the system of espionage the United States officials had established in this country, and had developed to the full the great treason of Mr.

Clarence R. Yonge, it became evident that no ships partaking of the character of war-vessels would be safe from seizure unless they were known to be the property of some foreign Government not a belligerent. It was of pressing importance to destroy any trace of Confederate ownership in "294" and "295" at once, and the arrangements with Messrs. Bravay, of Paris, previously discussed as a probable and very plausible means of security, were speedily consummated in the manner already reported to you in my despatch of June 30th, 1863. The transfer papers, and indeed all the correspondence involved in the negotiation, were so carefully drawn in accordance with British law, that the solicitor employed to conduct the sale remarked on its completion, "The ships are now irretrievably the property of Messrs. Bravay and Co., and could not be recovered by any process they might think proper to resist." It certainly seemed that the British Government, when informed of the ownership, could and would reply to the further demands of the United States Minister that, the ships being the property of French citizens, their completion and final departure, at least to a French port, could not be forbidden. Under these circumstances I was naturally hopeful of success in getting them both to sea, and once more in our own possession; for even though the British Government might refuse Messrs. Bravay permission to arm them in England, it was difficult to see how that Government could be compromised as towards the United States by permitting a French subject to take his property, even though in the shape of ships, to his own country.

'Under any circumstances, it would have been prudent for me to absent myself from this neighbourhood; but at the time of the Bravay operation I was just beginning some new contracts on account of the Navy Department in France, and thus my absence from England involved neither loss of time nor waste of opportunity. During the month of July everything seemed to progress favourably; the ships steadily advanced towards completion, and there did not appear any reason to doubt that they would be ready to take the sea during the month of October.

'In August it became evident that the United States officials were getting uneasy, a fact made manifest by increased activity and boldness on the part of their spies, and undisguised efforts to tamper with the *employés* of the Messrs. Laird. Towards the end of that month these causes began to operate in such a manner as to seriously interfere with and retard the progress of the work. At the same time the Custom House officials began to make visits of inspection to the ships, and to press inquiries as to their destination and ownership, indicating that the Government was listening to the affidavits and persistent protests of the American Minister. Finally, the Messrs. Laird, hoping that if the Government were furnished with proof that the ships did not belong to the Confederate States, they would be relieved from further annoyance and inconvenience, asked and obtained the permission of the Messrs. Bravay to avow their ownership of the vessels. The result of this was a call upon M. A. Bravay at his house in Paris, by Captain Hore, R.N., who, on the part of his Government, made minute inquiries as to the intent of the purchase by Messrs. Bravay of such formidable ships.* Receiving apparently satisfactory answers to all of his questions, Captain Hore then made a direct offer to purchase them for the British

* See 'British Appendix,' vol. ii., p. 372.

Admiralty, which proposition M. Bravay declined to entertain, at least until the vessels were fully completed according to their designs, and had been delivered to him in a French port. This ended the interview with Captain Hore, and the circumstances were minutely detailed to me by M. A. Bravay on the day of their occurrence.*

'In the meantime, matters continued to grow worse at Liverpool. The nature of some of the affidavits sent up to the Foreign Office by the United States Consul leaked out, and although most of them were glaringly false, still they seemed to be whispered into willing ears, and had such effect that the Lairds were directed not to attempt a trial trip with either ship without giving notice to the Customs officials, and were finally forbidden to do so at all, except with a guard of marines, or other force from one of her Majesty's ships, on board.

'During most of this time I was in France, coming to Liverpool only for a day or two at a time to receive and write letters by the Bermuda mail, yet the United States Consul, through his spies, was swearing to my constant presence here, and superintendence of the ships. The local authorities are well aware that this latter statement is untrue. It has also been discovered that most, if not all, the affidavits upon which the Government is acting have been furnished by Chapman, Yonge and others, whose utter want of character was so clearly proved in the proceedings against the *Alexandra*. The course pursued by the Foreign Office can only be accounted for upon the supposition that the head of that Department is a partizan of the North, and is acting for its interest, instead of simply and consistently following the strictly neutral course he professes to have adopted.

* The statement of M. Bravay is confirmed in all essential points by Captain Hore's letter, 'British Case,' Appendix, vol. ii., p. 372.

No one would expect this Government to permit the equipment of a ship-of-war for one belligerent, any more than it would be expected to permit the open enlisting of troops for the other belligerent. Yet interference with either of these should, it would seem, be conducted according to the law of the land, and not in accordance with the whim or partiality of a Minister of State.

'The fact that men are constantly enlisted in Ireland for the Federal army, and have been shipped by hundreds from this port, is so notorious as to be generally discussed, yet I have not heard up to this date, that the rights of a single British shipowner have been violated, nor his ship detained for a single hour in order that the destination or character of the passengers might be inquired into, while in the case of a ship building in a private yard, this Government furnishes detectives to watch her progress, listens to and acts upon the statements of perjurers and avowed traitors, and finally interferes and prevents her completion in a most unusual and illegal manner, as I am informed, for fear that she may at some future time fall into the hands of the Confederate States.

'The inference is so clear that I shall not suggest it, but will simply particularize by repeating that the two rams building by Messrs. Laird have been virtually seized by orders from the Foreign Office, and are now in the possession of the Customs officers of this port, assisted by one of her Majesty's gunboats, and a guard of marines from her Majesty's ship *Majestic*. The actual seizure took place only about a fortnight ago (October 9th), although the public has been prepared for such an event by intimations in the so-called Government organs, and discussions upon the matter in all the newspapers of the kingdom.

'I have inquired into the causes of this act, and learn, from the best possible sources, as follows:—It has been made known to the authorities that a large number of Confederate naval officers have during the past three months arrived in England. The *Florida* came off the Irish coast some six weeks since, and proceeding to Brest, there discharged the greater portion of her crew, who were sent to Liverpool. These circumstances were eagerly seized upon by the United States representatives here, and they have so worked upon Lord Russell as to make him believe that the presence of those officers and men has direct reference to the destination of the rams. At any rate, the declaration of the United States Consular spies to that effect has been the cause of their seizure at this time, because the reason assigned is that the ships may be captured on their trial trips, or even forcibly carried out of Liverpool, without the consent of the Messrs. Laird, by these very officers and men.

'The precautions taken to prevent such an attempt are, under the circumstances, ludicrous. One of the rams is in the Great Birkenhead Float. To be got out she must pass through a kind of lock; a large *caisson* must be lifted, which can only be done at a certain stage of the tide; and finally, a gate requiring machinery to move it must be opened to give her egress. I learn upon inquiry that if it were desired to remove her from the dock, the keeper would require five hours' notice. Yet this Government have thought it necessary to place a gunboat with extra marines alongside of her, the fasts of the gunboat being actually placed over those of the ram, and until within the last few days have kept a sixty-gun frigate at anchor opposite the dock-gate, for fear that this formidable ship might jump over all the obstructions and proceed to sea in charge of the aforementioned officers and discharged seamen, without bending a sail or lighting a fire.

'Now, sir, the final issue of this affair is no longer a practical question. No amount of discretion or management on my part can effect the release of the ships. Mr. Slidell has always given me to understand that the Emperor of the French was aware of the nature of the transaction with the Messrs. Bravay, and that at the proper time the French Government would come forward in support of the claims or assumed rights of its subjects. I have already intimated to Mr. Slidell, in a cautiously worded letter, what has happened here, and asked what steps the French Government will take. . . . It is my opinion that the British Government will not let the ships be removed from their present position unless the French Government comes forward and relieves it from all responsibility or presumed obligation to the United States, by requesting that the ships may be allowed to leave Liverpool as the property of a French subject. Whether the Emperor is prepared to change places with her Majesty's Government or not can only be determined when M. Bravay asks the protection or countenance of his own Government; and I will do all in my power to press a decision in the matter, and will report to you the result at the earliest possible moment.

'I have always been under the impression that it would have been better for the Messrs. Bravay to have avowed their ownership of the ships at the time of the assumed sale, and to have asked permission to complete them. Thus would our minds have been at least set at ease. If the answer had been "No," we should have saved the money since expended, and could have sold the ships in reality, as they were, and have put the proceeds to other pressing uses. I waived those views in deference to those of Mr. Mason and Mr. Slidell, who thought that I should not interfere with or dictate too much to Messrs. Bravay in the management of details, and who thought that we should await some direct act of interference on the part of the British Government before calling upon the French owners to act. My hands are now tied until those French subjects succeed in effecting the release of the ships, which can only be done through the medium of their own Government. Under all the circumstances, you will perceive how impossible it is for me to predict the future of these ships. I can only say that if they are released from seizure, no time will be lost in getting them clear of such a casualty again. I feel bound to say that the presence of the *Florida* in these waters, and the discharge of her crew, have very materially added to our complications here ; but I need not go into detail upon matters which have already taken place, and can only be felt in their effects without the possibility of prevention.

'I have conversed freely with Lieutenant Carter (bearer of this) upon all our affairs in Europe, with the view of his mentioning the substance to you, and I respectfully request that you will give him an opportunity to explain some things to you which would unnecessarily swell the dimensions of this despatch, and which I do not wish to put formally upon paper.

'I have the honour, etc.,

'(Signed) JAMES D. BULLOCH.

'Hon. S. R. Mallory,
'Richmond.'

I reported in the above despatch that the 'actual seizure' of the rams was effected about one fortnight before the date upon which it was written, namely, about October 9th, 1863. This was sufficiently correct for the information of the Navy Department at that time; but for a clear and complete exposition of the case in all its bearings, a more precise statement of dates is necessary. It appears from the official correspondence that Mr. Layard, the Under-Secretary of State for Foreign Affairs, wrote to her Majesty's Minister at Washington on the 5th of September thus :—'We have given orders to-day to the Commissioner of Customs at Liverpool to prevent the two ironclads leaving the Mersey. . . . Mr. Adams is not yet aware that orders have been given to stop the vessels. You may inform Mr. Seward confidentially of the fact.'

In pursuance of the above intimation, the Messrs. Laird were notified on the 9th or 10th of September that the ships would not be permitted to sail or even to make a trial trip, without special notice and permission ; but the actual or formal seizure was not effected until October 9th, 1863. On the 27th of October a body of marines was put in charge of the ships, and two gunboats stationed to watch them, the workmen being sent on shore.

The facts, then, are briefly as follows. The ships were 'detained' September 9th, and 'seized' October 9th, after which they were closely watched and guarded, and the work of completing them virtually stopped, to the great inconvenience and injury of the Messrs. Laird, who were simply executing an ordinary commercial order. Finally, after much correspondence and remonstrance, they were permitted to go on with work, but always under vexatious inspection and restraint.

This state of affairs continued for four months, during which long period no steps were taken to test the

H.M.S. *Majestic* keeping watch over the Laird rams in the Mersey after they were seized by the British. At left is *El Tousson;* anchored to the right of the *Majestic* is *El Mounassir. (Harper's Weekly)*

JOHN BULL. "Well, Friend BONEY, that looks like a Good Blockade. I don't think there's any use trying to break it."

A contemporary cartoon from *Harper's Weekly*.

legality of the seizure, or to bring any of the parties alleged to have been implicated in the equipment of the ships to an account. The particulars of the proceedings against the ships were reported by me to the Confederate Navy Department in the following despatch :

'Liverpool, *February* 17*th*, 1864.

'You have doubtless learned by means of newspapers, which seem to pass very regularly through the lines of the opposing armies in Virginia, as well as from the published correspondence between Mr. Seward and the United States Minister at the Court of St. James, that every attempt to build a ship for the service of the Confederate States is opposed not only by the active exertions of the American Minister and his numerous subordinates, the Consuls of that nation, but that through Lord Russell the entire machinery of the British Government which can in any way be used for such a purpose has been set in motion and put at Mr. Adams' disposal, not to be worked in accordance with English custom and English law, but in such a manner as may be dictated by the Cabinet at Washington.

'The spies of the United States are numerous, active, and unscrupulous. They invade the privacy of families, tamper with the confidential clerks of merchants, and have succeeded in converting a portion of the police of this country into secret agents of the United States, who have practised a prying watchfulness over the movements and business of individuals intolerably vexatious, which has excited the disgust and openly expressed indignation of many prominent Englishmen, and the frequent criticism of that portion of the British press which is really neutral. These practices, though wholly inconsistent with the spirit of justice and the fundamental principles of constitutional government, are not only permitted, but to all appearance are directly countenanced and encouraged by the present Ministry, and the rights of British subjects are violated, and their pecuniary interests damaged, by the seizure of property in their hands upon the affidavits of persons who have already perjured themselves before her Majesty's Courts.* A nation is undoubtedly justified in the enforcement of its neutrality by all legal processes, but where the customary forms of law are departed from, where a large latitude is permitted to one belligerent and the other is watched with a jealous and even vindictive scrutiny, the obligations of neutrality are violated. That these obligations are violated in the action of Great Britain to the Confederate States must be apparent to the world at large. The point is conceded by many Englishmen, at any rate.

'The conjoint efforts of Lord Russell and Mr. Adams have proved irresistible, and it is now settled beyond a doubt that no vessel constructed with a view to offensive warfare can be built and got out of England for the service of the Confederate States. The arrangement by which I hoped to get the two ironclads, "294" and "295" beyond the jurisdiction of England, depended, as you have already been informed, mainly, if not exclusively, upon the intervention of the Emperor of the French. It was hoped, and there was good reason for the hope, that such intervention would come to our aid at the proper time.

'It was confidently believed that if the British Government, fearing that the Messrs. Bravay would resell the rams to the Confederate States, should cause them to be seized, and should demand of those gentle-

* *Vide* Yonge and Chapman *in re Alexandra.*

men any guarantee that the vessels should actually be delivered to the Pasha of Egypt, the Emperor of the French would express to her Majesty's Government his knowledge of the connection, in a business way, of Messrs. Bravay with the Egyptian Government, and would request the release of the ships as the property of French subjects. In this expectation, based upon intimations purporting to have come directly from the Emperor, we have been grievously disappointed. It has been intimated to Mr. Slidell, through no less a personage than the Duke de Morny, that the Emperor cannot make such a request at this time, although his desire is that somehow or other the release of the rams should be effected, and their possession by the Confederate States be again secured.

'Thus reduced to a struggle with the British Government, who, in case of a decision favourable to us in the Court of Exchequer, will exhaust us by continual delays and appeals even up to the House of Lords, it has been determined to make a *bonâ fide* sale of the ships, if possible, and I have given Messrs. Bravay instructions to that effect, in a letter, a copy of which I enclose, marked *A*. It is possible that the Government may not allow the sale of the ships, and we may be forced to defend the suit, but the lawyers are so confident that the title of the Messrs. Bravay will be sustained, that I hope with some degree of confidence that Lord Russell may abandon the case and permit Messrs. Bravay to sell the ships, although I am satisfied he would never suffer them to leave England, except as the property of some responsible Government other than that of the Confederate States.

'Under date of October 20th, 1863, I had the honour to report very fully to you on the subject of the seizure of the rams, and I will now briefly trace their fortunes to the present time.

'It was naturally supposed that as British subjects of position and wealth were interested pecuniarily in the case, and as it was one of great public interest, the Government would take steps to bring it at the earliest possible time before the Exchequer Court. My solicitor was of opinion that it would be brought up during the January term; and I patiently awaited the turn of the year. There seems to be something peculiar in the construction of the Court of Exchequer and in the mode of procedure therein. The defendants in a suit have no power to hasten proceedings, but must await the action of the prosecution. The solicitors for the Messrs. Laird and for the Messrs. Bravay were at first of the opinion that the Government was only desirous of affording the United States Minister a hearing in support of his suspicions, and that in justice to their clients a hearing would be granted at the earliest possible time. Weeks passed, however, and no 'information' was lodged in the Exchequer Court, nor could the solicitors for the defendants obtain from the Government any assurance as to when the case would be tried, or what would be the precise nature of the indictment, or 'information,' as it is technically called, in the Court of Exchequer.

'About the end of December (1863) I took legal advice on the following points: (1) Is there any way of forcing the Government to take action? (2) Can any damages be recovered from the Government if the verdict is favourable to the defendants? (3) Will the Government permit the ships to be sold to a foreign Power? On the two first points counsel gave technical opinions not necessary to insert here. In reference to the third, the opinion was 'The Government would not probably allow the ships to be sold to a foreign State, but might be willing to settle the whole matter in full by making the purchase themselves, provided Messrs. Bravay would sign a quit claim.' My own solicitor, who from his professional as well as political associations was favourably situated for coming to a correct conclusion, expressed to me very decidedly his opinion that Lord Russell would not act in accordance with law; that he was in feeling a thorough partizan of the United States, and, acting in that spirit, he would create all the delay possible in bringing the case to trial, and would further embarrass the defendants by successive appeals from each consecutive verdict. He also felt convinced that Lord Russell would never permit the rams to leave England, unless the Emperor of the French would claim them as French property, and thus relieve her Majesty's Government of all responsibility to the United States.

'My own observation of the progress of the case had brought me to like conclusions, and on the 27th of January I went to France to bring the matter to a close without further delay, and by direct appeal to the Emperor, through Messrs. Bravay. Although in the beginning there was good reason to hope that the Emperor would intervene at this stage of our proceedings, I had for some time begun to doubt it, and on my arrival in Paris the doubt was confirmed. The Emperor caused the Messrs. Bravay, as well as the Hon. John Slidell, to be informed that he could not make the request to the British Government to release the rams. There was a good deal said about the personal sympathy of the Emperor for the South, and his earnest desire that by some means or other we might get our ships out, but he could not help us, so the sympathy and the hope were sheer mockery, when we had been buoyed up with the expectation of something more.

'I now laid the whole case before Hon. John Slidell, Hon. James M. Mason, and Captain Barron, all of whom were in Paris. . . . They expressed the unanimous opinion that there was no hope of getting the ships out, and that there was nothing left for me to do but to recover, if possible, the money expended. I lost no time in settling preliminaries with Messrs. Bravay, and to put the transaction in a formal business shape handed them the enclosed letter, marked *A*, already alluded to above—an act which, I assure you, sir, gave me greater pain and regret than I ever thought it possible to feel. The British Government have within the last two or three weeks filed the 'information,' which includes 130 counts. The case is set for trial, I believe, in April or May. Messrs. Bravay will not receive an answer to their application to sell in time for me to report the result by Commander Wm. L. Maury, who will take this despatch, but you will probably see the result in the newspapers before I shall have an opportunity of writing again.'

On the 3rd of April, 1864, I received a short cypher despatch from the Secretary of the Navy, dated 'Richmond, February 24th, 1864,' expressing the greatest reluctance to part with the rams, and saying that nothing short of the impending loss of them would justify their sale. He had not then received the above explanatory report upon the whole case, and I replied, under date of 'Liverpool, April 14th':—

'You may rest assured that nothing has been done in the matter alluded to by you except from necessity. I have freely consulted with Mr. Mason and Mr. Slidell, and their opinions were identical with my own. Commander Wm. L. Maury is, I trust, ere this in Richmond, with despatches fully explaining the causes which compelled the course adopted. I send you by to-morrow's mail, *viâ* Halifax, a number of Parliamentary papers relating to the rams. The affidavit of Chapman, with reference to a pretended conversation with me, is wholly untrue. Not one single sentence which he has sworn to ever passed between us. As this man perjured himself in the case of the *Alexandra*, his testimony would not probably be received if the case of the rams is ever brought to trial; yet it is upon such testimony as this that Lord Russell orders the forcible seizure of the ships. The letter from Commander Maffitt to me, which you will perceive was used by Mr. Adams to induce the seizure of the rams, did not reach me through the men of the *Florida*, by whom it was sent. When those men arrived in Liverpool I was absent on the Continent. They got into the hands of a solicitor, and gave him the letter, which he seems to have sent to the United States Consul, and the immediate cause of the seizure of the ships was due to this circumstance.'

On the 2nd of May, 1864, I received another despatch from the Navy Department on the engrossing subject of the rams. It was dated 'Richmond, March 21st, 1864.' The Secretary of the Navy was still ignorant of the critical state of affairs, not having received my despatches forwarded by Commander Maury, and he directed me not to sell the rams 'until that measure shall have been submitted to the President, with the reasons for it.'

I got an opportunity to reply on the 13th of May, as follows:—

'I should never think of departing from your instructions nor the implied wishes of the President, except in a case wherein such a course alone would prevent positive disaster, the danger of which you could not have foreseen, nor even then without the advice and support of my natural and proper counsellors, the Commissioners of the Confederate States. I may say, however, that in this particular instance I am no longer a free agent, but am in the condition of a disabled ship taken possession of by a current she has no power to stem. The rams are in the possession of the law officers of the British Crown, and they are acting under the instructions of a Minister who has on every occasion shown in practice personal animosity to the Southern cause, and who seems regardless of the forms of law in his efforts to prevent our getting any material aid from Great Britain. Hoping to regain possession of these much-needed ships, or, failing in this hope, at least desiring to recover the large sum of money expended upon them, I have placed the case in the hands of able solicitors, who are acting in accord with eminent counsel.

'Now, sir, unless it is desired to establish a great grievance against the British Government, and it is thought that the money already expended upon the ships may be advantageously sacrificed to gain that end, I respectfully submit that my duty is to manage the case in a practical business way, and to be governed by the advice of the counsel employed. The only chance of gaining the pending suit rests upon the ability of Messrs. Bravay to prove their contract with the Pasha of Egypt, and upon the consistency of their own testimony. If the case goes to trial and the Bravays fail in the above points, the verdict will undoubtedly be in favour of the Crown, and our ships and money will both be lost.

'This is the opinion of counsel, and I am advised to let Messrs. Bravay sell the vessels to the British Government if they do not feel quite prepared to go into court with a clear case. On the very day of the receipt of your despatch of March 21st, I notified Messrs. Bravay to suspend all pending negotiations for the sale of the rams. The elder M. Bravay is now in Egypt. If on his return he expresses confidence in himself and in his case, we will stand to the issue of the trial. If, on the contrary, he professes doubt, or unwillingness to submit to a personal examination, it is Mr. Slidell's opinion that I should permit the actual sale of the ships, he being satisfied, as well as myself, that such would be the decision of the President, and of yourself also, if you were aware of the actual state of affairs. The solicitors and counsel employed are of opinion that if the first verdict is for the defendants the Crown will appeal to the Exchequer Chamber, and from thence to the House of Lords, and that the case will not reach this latter Court of Appeal during this entire year.

'I trust you have not thought that I have been needlessly fearful of the result, and have yielded too readily to the advice of my solicitors. . . I held out as long as was justifiable, and clung to hope as long as there was a ray of it. No one could have had stronger inducements to get the rams to sea than I had. Suppressing all allusion to patriotic impulses, and setting aside the loyal duty and allegiance I owe to the country, there are personal reasons which could not fail to have spurred me to great exertions. Although I was not to have had the honour of commanding either of the ironclads, I felt satisfied that their qualities and performances would redound to my professional credit, and if they fail to do service for the country in this great war for its independence, I frankly confess that with a feeling of deep regret for the public loss will be mingled one of purely selfish personal disappointment.'

On the 30th of May, 1864, I again received a despatch from the Navy Department, written this time with a full knowledge of the state of affairs affecting the rams. The above mentioned despatch was dated 'Richmond, April 7th, 1864,' and began thus :—

'Commander Maury reached Richmond on the 3rd inst., and delivered your several despatches. The hopes in which I have long and confidently indulged of certain important results to our country from your efforts abroad, and which hopes were shared by thousands around me, are prostrated by the intelligence he brings. One reflection alone can alleviate the bitterness of this disappointment, and this is the reflection that it results not from any cause within our control, and that your whole course, as the immediate and principal agent in the enterprise, has been marked by equal energy, sagacity, and tact. Knowing from my own what must be your depression under this great national misfortune, I deem it proper to say this in reference to your action.'

The Secretary of the Navy confirmed the decision to sell the rams, and the remainder of the despatch was devoted to other matters of business. During the whole of the time, from the first 'detention' of the rams, on September 9th, 1863, until the 'information' was filed in the Exchequer, namely, February 8th, 1864, a period of five months, not a single step was taken by her Majesty's Government to justify the seizure, or to show cause for the detention. It now appears, from the official correspondence published in the 'Appendix to the British Case,'* that those five months were diligently occupied in looking up evidence and in digesting the numerous affidavits of the United States Consul at Liverpool.

* '*Alabama* Claims, British Case,' vol. ii.

That gentleman manifested his usual fecundity of resource in supplying 'statements.' Those in this case were of the stereotyped form, the persons swearing to them being generally of the well-known type of 'affidavit monger.' They 'believed this,' and had 'heard that,' but were always wide of the mark when they came to deal with specific facts.

After the formal seizure on the 9th of October, the ships were kept literally in a state of siege—Captain Inglefield, of her Majesty's ship *Majestic*, was the officer charged with their special custody. The Government had been persuaded by Mr. Adams that the discharged crew of the *Florida* had been sent to Liverpool for the purpose of forcibly seizing the rams and taking them to sea, and if there had been a hostile fleet off the harbour, Captain Inglefield could not have been more perplexed and anxious, more nervously active and watchful in his precautions and preparations to discover and defeat a cutting-out expedition, than he appears to have been with respect to the alleged hostile seamen from the *Florida*, who were probably smoking their pipes at the 'Sailors' Home,' or were already dispersed in other ships, in happy or careless unconsciousness of the agitation they were creating.

On the 6th of October, 1863, Captain Inglefield wrote, in reply to 'confidential instructions' from the Admiralty: 'I conceive the possibility that an attempt might be made to carry the vessel in question out of British waters by force.' . . . 'The Custom-house authorities having placed their means entirely at my disposal, I have organized a system of espionage which cannot fail to give me the earliest possible information of any movement on the part of the ironclad vessel in question.'* On the 8th of October he received orders by telegraph 'to give every assistance to officers of the Customs in effecting and maintaining the seizure of both iron ships,' etc.; and on the 9th he wrote in reply:† '. . . . In obedience to the above, I consider it most expedient that the *Liverpool*‡ should be moved down the river to a berth immediately abreast of the entrance to the Great Float, so that she may perfectly command the basin, and be nearer her guard-boat. The gunboat will remain within the entrance to the Great Float, and during the night an armed pinnace will row guard.' On the 11th of October he reports further: 'The gunboat will take up a position beside the ironclad vessel, and during the daytime the marines will remain on board of her. After the workmen have left, a sentry will be placed on the forecastle, and another on the poop of the ram; Messrs. Laird's shipkeepers remaining in charge of stores. . . . I shall then direct a lieutenant of marines to remain on board the iron ship during the night, only withdrawing his party when the workpeople return in the morning.'§ On the 25th of October he wrote again: 'If an effort is made to carry off the rams, I think it will either be at night, or in such thick weather as we constantly experience at this time of year. Unless the gunboat arrives to-day, I must employ the ferry-boat to-morrow morning; for though the *El Mounassir* is not masted, nor are her turrets on board, she is, nevertheless, an available ironcased ram, which would be of considerable service (even in her present condition) for breaking a blockade.'‖ . . . 'The arrival of the *Heron* and *Britomart*, which I am looking for anxiously, will

* 'Appendix to British Case,' p. 384. † Ibid. p. 393.

‡ The *Liverpool* was a large screw frigate of sixty guns.

§ 'Appendix to British Case,' p. 400. ‖ Ibid. p. 418.

obviate the necessity of seeking the assistance of the ferry-boat, etc.'

In consequence of the above letter, the Secretary to the Admiralty wrote to the Under-Secretary for Foreign Affairs on October 26th :—' My lords are quite prepared, if Earl Russell thinks it desirable, to send the *Prince Consort** to anchor at the mouth of the Mersey.'†

There are more documents of similar purport in the official correspondence, but the above quotations will sufficiently demonstrate the great naval force that was employed in guarding these mastless and turretless rams from being carried off, the items being: her Majesty's ship *Majestic*, say sixty guns; her Majesty's ship *Liverpool*, sixty guns; three gunboats—say one pivot-gun each—and the proffered reinforcement of her Majesty's armour-cased ship *Prince Consort*.

Captain Inglefield is a gallant officer, I have no doubt on that point, and he would probably make skilful and suitable arrangements to repel a sea attack upon the Mersey, if he should be appointed to the naval command at Liverpool in a time of war; but I cannot help thinking that, as he sipped his wine at dinner in the *Majestic's* cabin, after writing one of the above reports to the Admiralty, there must have floated athwart his mind a suspicion that there was a comical side to the whole transaction. I cannot bring myself to believe that an experienced naval officer would give credence to such a preposterous allegation as that an attempt would be made to carry off the rams by force, or that any effort would be made to move them from their positions, which could not have been prevented by the remonstrance of a single

* The *Prince Consort* is an ironclad.

† 'Appendix to British Case,' p. 417.

Custom House officer, with a pen behind his ear and a memorandum-book in his hand.

The Confederate Government was impelled by every motive of policy, if not of principle, to conciliate foreign Powers, and especially Great Britain, and it is inconceivable that any Minister of State, nay, I may say that any reasoning being, could have supposed that the President of the Confederate States would have countenanced, or that any responsible agent of that Government would have made, such an attempt.

It was said, I believe, that as the *Alabama* was taken out of the Mersey without permission, the same thing might be done with the ironclads, but the cases are not comparable with each other. There is a great difference between taking up your hat and quietly walking out of a man's house without asking his leave when he has not forbidden your departure, and the act of knocking him down and stepping over his prostrate body to get out when he has prohibited your going. It has been shown, and I think it will be admitted by all fair-minded people, that the taking away of the *Alabama* infringed no law, and it has never been alleged that she was restrained in any way, or that a single false statement was made in reference to her movements. I mean that her Majesty's Government have never alleged it. But in the case of the rams, they were restrained by the orders of the duly authorized civil authorities from making even a trial-trip without especial permission, and the Messrs. Laird would not have connived at their being removed from their works; and no one acting on behalf of the Confederate Government would have dreamed of attempting a forcible removal. Besides, as a mere practical question, the condition of the vessels was such that they could not have been carried off without so much open preparation, and so much assistance from local people, that there could have been no disguise and no *coup-de-main.* The 'scare' originated at the United States Consulate. The arrival of the *Florida's* men was seized upon as a fortuitous circumstance. Mr. Adams appears to have convinced Earl Russell of 'the desperate character of the chief persons engaged in the insurrection in the United States,' of whom he says, in one of the letters to his lordship:—'I shall be little surprised at learning of their resort to any expedient, however audacious or dishonest, which may have for its object the possession of these formidable ships.'*

It is well known among business men that a ship remains exclusively in the custody of the builder, and is in fact his property, until the last instalment of her price is paid and the builder's certificate is handed over to the contractor or purchaser. The latter has, of course, a contingent interest in her, equivalent to the portion of the stipulated price he has paid, but he cannot take possession or remove her until she is completed and paid for. If there is delay in the completion beyond the time specified for delivery, or injury to the ship in course of building, the loss falls upon the builder, and not upon the purchaser.

The inconvenience and injury to the Messrs. Laird by the seizure of the rams, and the lashing of gun-boats alongside, and the mounting of guards on board, must have been serious. They protested, and pointed out the improbability—in fact, the impossibility—of any party of men being found who would attempt to take the ships away from them by force. On the 17th of October, 1863, they wrote to the Under-Secretary of the

* Published in Liverpool *Daily Mercury*, with other official correspondence, March 10th, 1864.

Treasury:—'Both vessels are incomplete, and unfit for sea-going. The second vessel has not even got her masts or funnel in, and both are in the sole charge of our own people. We believe, further, that if any such project as the forcible abduction of these vessels had ever been thought of, it could not successfully have been carried out in the port of Liverpool.'

At one time it was proposed to stop the work upon the ships entirely, but this would have compelled Messrs. Laird to discharge a large number of men, which Captain Inglefield thought would increase the ill-feeling already exhibited by the operatives in Messrs. Laird's yard towards the naval officers and men employed in maintaining the seizure, and the builders were permitted to go on with their work, although under such restrictions and 'espionage' the progress was necessarily slow and unsatisfactory.

Meanwhile, the Government was diligently employed looking up evidence. They even went to the expense of sending a commission to Egypt to examine the Viceroy and his Grand Vizier as to their business relations with Messrs. Bravay. Finally, after coquetting for some time about the purchase of the ships, they sent down experts from the Admiralty, who carefully examined and valued them, and then, with the law-suit in one hand and the valuation in the other, they made a direct offer to Messrs. Bravay, which was accepted, and the preliminary terms upon which the two rams should pass into the Royal Navy were settled on about the 20th of May, 1864.

Formal notice of suit for the forfeiture of the rams had been given on the 8th of February, and in the 'information,' both the Messrs. Laird and Messrs. Bravay were made parties to the suit. It is ordinarily supposed, when a defendant in a case of this kind abandons his defence and accepts the terms offered by the Government, that he admits the weakness of his position, and the legality of the proceedings which have been taken against him. But after the withdrawal of the case by the Crown it was thought advisable to prevent any such conclusion with reference to Messrs. Laird and Messrs. Bravay. On the day after the formal notice of withdrawal of the suit, namely, May 27th, 1864, the Attorney-General, with Sir Hugh Cairns, appeared in the Court of Exchequer at Westminster, and the former said:—

'The Crown had asserted that there was a valid seizure for a valid cause of forfeiture. The claimants had to the last asserted that there was no such valid cause of forfeiture, but the matter had been by arrangement withdrawn from the cognizance of the court, so that no determination of it would be necessary, and that had been done upon the footing that the Crown had agreed to pay to the claimants the value which the Crown themselves had placed upon the property, and that, too, entirely without prejudice to the position of the Crown or the claimants with regard to the question that would have required to be tried if the arrangement had not been made. The mode of doing it and giving effect to that arrangement had not been finally arrived at; but no mode would be adopted that would in any degree authorize me to say that there was any admission by the claimants that it was a valid forfeiture.'

The Messrs. Bravay made no concession which could be taken as a surrender of their right as French subjects to buy or to have built for them a vessel of any description in England. They did only what other private parties have often done, namely, consent to an arrangement rather than to continue an expensive and tedious litigation with the State, and it is hardly probable that the law officers of the Crown would have advised a settlement which resulted in a pecuniary profit to the claimants, if they really thought that Messrs. Bravay had infringed the terms of the Foreign Enlistment Act. It is fair and reasonable to assume that, having in remembrance the judgment of the Court of Exchequer in the '*Alexandra* Case,' and also that of the Vice-Admiralty Court of Nassau in respect to the *Oreto*, they had no hopes of obtaining a favourable verdict, and no expectation of proving that there had been 'a valid seizure for a valid cause of forfeiture.'

I am bound to say that as soon as it was decided to get out of the difficulty by buying the ships, the Admiralty conducted the operation in a perfectly fair and straightforward way. The ships were valued with scrupulous regard to their intrinsic worth, and with due reference to the state of the shipbuilding trade at the time, and as a mere commercial transaction the sale was satisfactory, the aggregate amount agreed to be paid by the Government being about £30,000 in excess of the original contract price of the two ships, which proves that they were good vessels of their kind, and that the work upon them had been faithfully executed. The whole of the purchase money did not of course revert to the Confederate Treasury, but only a part proportioned to the amount that had been paid on account; and although the circumstances which brought this pecuniary reinforcement to the funds of the Navy Department were most distressing, yet the relief came at a time when much work would have been necessarily abandoned, and some important contracts cancelled, if it had not been obtained. In the month of September,

1863, I had reported that the prospective wants of the Department were £705,300 in excess of the visible supply. Mr. Secretary Mallory had made every possible effort to meet the deficiency, but it had not been made good, the demands always increasing in a larger ratio than the means for meeting them. These matters of finance have, however, been dealt with and explained in another chapter.

The gratitude of the United States to Earl Russell for the seizure of the rams was even greater than the gratification Mr. Seward expressed for the prosecution of the *Alexandra.* As soon as the purpose of her Majesty's Government was known in Washington, Mr. Adams was instructed to thank Lord Russell, and to say that the President was gratified in being able to regard his conduct in the light of a sincere desire, on just principles, to maintain friendly relations with the United States. Mr. Adams concluded his letter of thanks in these words :—'I am therefore instructed to inform your lordship that the Government will hereafter hold itself obliged, with even more care than heretofore, to endeavour so to conduct its intercourse with Great Britain as that the war in which it is now unhappily involved may, whenever it may terminate, leave to neither nation any permanent cause of discontent.'*

The Government of Great Britain zealously fulfilled its share in accomplishing the purpose which Mr. Adams so ardently hoped would follow the seizure of the rams. Earl Russell applied the Foreign Enlistment Act so stringently with reference to the Confederate States, that it was very difficult to forward the most essential supplies, and while the drain of battle, and the lack of necessary comforts were thinning the ranks and wasting the

* Appendix to 'British Case,' vol. ii. p. 400.

strength of the armies in the field, and the difficulty of placing funds in Europe was daily increasing, the cheapest and most favourable market, that of England, was well nigh closed to the Confederacy, while the United States were permitted to buy and ship what they liked, without hindrance, and at the ordinary current prices.

I do not wish to overstate the case, but I say without hesitation, and without fear of contradiction, that the practice of stopping ordinary merchant steamers and detaining them for examination and inquiry, unless they were loading for a Northern port, drove the Confederate agents to such shifts in order to get their purchases out of England, that the cost of every rifle and every ounce of powder was greatly increased, irrespective of the high blockade rates for freight. A notable and distressing feature of this unequal treatment of the two belligerents was that the restrictive watchfulness practised over the weaker side became more cold and rigid as the disparity of strength became more and more manifest.

But while Earl Russell thus did all in his power to conciliate the United States, and to conduct his intercourse with them so that the termination of the war should 'leave to neither nation any permanent cause of discontent,' the Government at Washington did not act in the spirit of Mr. Adams's promise. No sooner was the war over than Mr. Seward began to collect complaints against Great Britain. He originated what are known as the '*Alabama* Claims.' He began and continued for several years an active, harassing, and sometimes angry correspondence with the British Foreign Office, and finally his successor haled her Majesty's Government before an International Court, with a result which all the world knows.

Anyone who cares to read 'The Case of the United States' in the Geneva Arbitration, will be struck with the harsh epithets and disparaging insinuations which are cast upon the Ministry which governed England during the war, and indeed upon British officials generally, and will think that the assurance given by Mr. Adams was forgotten as soon as the occasion which inspired it had served its purpose.

The Government of the United States did not exaggerate the importance of preventing the departure of the rams from Liverpool, and the passionate appeals, and strong asseverations of Mr. Adams are not surprising. He knew the formidable character of the ships, and foresaw the havoc they would work if they ever got into the hands of a competent Confederate officer. The defensive powers of the rams were quite up to the standard of the years 1861-63. They were cased over the vital parts with $4\frac{1}{2}$-inch armour upon twelve inches of teak backing, and an inner skin of $\frac{5}{8}$-inch iron plates. Each had two revolving turrets with $5\frac{1}{2}$-inch armour over twelve inches of teak. In each turret there would have been two guns of the best possible manufacture, mounted parallel to each other, and five feet from centre to centre. Calibre of gun, 9-inch rifled ; weight of projectile, about 220 pounds ; weight of gun, about twelve tons. If one of the rams had gone into smooth water, and had suffered a 'Monitor' to make deliberate practice at her with 15-inch shot at short range, as in the engagement between the *Weehawken* and the *Atlanta* in Warsaw Sound, no doubt in time her plates would have been loosened and the backing splintered ; but their power and speed was such that in open water, with room to manœuvre, I think they would have had no difficulty in running down any 'Monitor' then afloat, and I confidently believe that they would have broken up the blockade completely, and then perhaps they would have paid New York or Boston an unpleasant visit.

I have now given a full and accurate account of the formidable vessels '294' and '295,' from the first discussion of their plans to the time when they became part of the naval force of Great Britain. Those persons who permit their judgment to be swayed by political bias, who were unfriendly to the South during the war, and who have pledged themselves to the opinion that the Confederate Government should not have been allowed to get ships in England under any circumstances, may say that the foregoing confession of the ultimate ownership and purpose of the rams fully justified their seizure. But I think that those, on the other hand, who only wish to come to a right judgment after a dispassionate examination of the facts, will be brought to the conclusion that there was no valid reason for the interference of her Majesty's Government, and that the proceedings against the vessels prescribed by Earl Russell, and so rigidly enforced by the Customs authorities and by the naval commander at Liverpool, were not in accordance with the principles of international duty laid down for its practice by the Government itself, and that they went far beyond the purpose of the prohibitory clauses, and were in excess of the powers granted in the preventive clauses of the Neutrality Laws of Great Britain, as expounded by the Solicitor-General in Parliament, and defined by the judgment of the Court of Exchequer in the *Alexandra* case.

In forming an opinion with reference to Earl Russell's proceedings against the rams, it is clearly essential to consider, not what is known now, but what were the actual circumstances and the precise position of affairs at the time of the seizure; and it is equally important to bear in mind the statements made by leading members of the Government in the House of Commons in explanation of the Foreign Enlistment Act, and defining what each belligerent might do towards supplying its wants without infringing the statute. Without quoting again in full the principles of action laid down by the Government, I may for the present purpose merely remind the reader that the Prime Minister, Lord Palmerston, said that there was no difference in principle between supplying a belligerent with rifles or with ships that are to operate in war, and that on the mere ground of international law it was quite admissible to supply either of two belligerents not only with arms and cannon, but also with ships destined for warlike purposes; that the Solicitor-General said it was a great mistake to suppose that the Foreign Enlistment Act was meant to prohibit all commercial dealings in ships-of-war with belligerent countries, and that even the *Alabama*, though a ship-of-war, might have formed a legitimate article of merchandise, even if meant for the Confederate States; and that Earl Russell himself, in a letter to Mr. Adams, said that her Majesty's Government 'cannot interfere with commercial dealings between Britsih subjects and the so-styled Confederate States, whether the object of those dealings be money or contraband goods, or even ships adapted for warlike purposes.'

The letter from Earl Russell containing the above statement was read in Court by Sir Hugh Cairns, the leading counsel for the defendants in the trial of the *Alexandra*, and was commented upon by him as the opinion of a Minister of the Crown, and it probably had a good deal of weight, not in determining the 'direction' of the Lord Chief Baron, but in affecting the minds of the jury.

When the Messrs. Laird engaged as a purely commercial transaction to build the rams, the views of the Government were not fully and specifically known, and neither those gentlemen nor the Confederate agent had any other guide to the scope of the Foreign Enlistment Act than the opinions of their legal advisers. But the statements above referred to were made in the House of Commons, and the letter of Earl Russell was written, several months before the seizure of the rams. They were not merely the opinions of three eminent men upon an abstract question of international or municipal law, but they were the declarations of two responsible Ministers of the Crown, and of a chief law officer of the Government, in reference to a specific Act of Parliament, and must have been intended to lay down the principle upon which the act would be administered in the practice of their neutrality. When those statements of Ministers and of the Solicitor-General were followed by a judgment of the Court of Exchequer which fully confirmed their view of the municipal law, it can hardly be doubted that the Confederate Government was justified in thinking that their agents might supply all their wants in the ordinary commercial way, and that they might buy in the British markets and from British subjects, not only 'contraband goods,' but 'even ships adapted for warlike purposes,' provided there was no intention that in the port of Liverpool or in any other port (of the British dominions) the vessels should be, in the language of the Act of Parliament, 'either equipped, furnished, fitted out, or armed,' which the Lord Chief Baron in his summing up declared all meant the same thing, and referred exclusively to the warlike armament.

It has been alleged that while any ordinary ships,

even though well suited in structure and general arrangements for warlike purposes, might be legitimate objects of sale by British subjects to a belligerent, yet armour-cased vessels were fitted for hostile operations, and could attack and destroy an enemy immediately after leaving port, without being armed at all in the sense of being provided with guns, and therefore the privilege which might be permitted to trade in the former, would not be permissible with reference to the latter class. In reply to this I will call attention to the fact that the official statements previously quoted were made by Ministers, and the judgment of the court was rendered, when not only other armoured vessels had been built, and were building, but when the particular vessels in question, namely, those bought by Messrs. Bravay, were well-advanced in their construction, and that neither in the Ministerial statements nor in the judgment of the court was there any limitation to the broad and inclusive declaration, that 'even ships adapted for warlike purposes' were on a parity with gunpowder and saltpetre as articles of commercial traffic.

But there is something more than mere negative testimony to offer on this point. On the 5th of September, 1863, Mr. Adams wrote a very strong letter to Earl Russell, which certainly contained an ill-concealed threat of serious consequences if the rams were permitted to leave England.* Earl Russell sent a brief memorandum to Mr. Adams on the 8th of September:—'Lord Russell presents his compliments to Mr. Adams, and has the honour to inform him that instructions have been issued which will prevent the departure of the two

* 'British Case,' Appendix, vol. ii., pp. 352, 353.

ironclad vessels from Liverpool.'* Now it must be borne in mind that the letter of Mr. Adams, of September 5th, referred exclusively and specifically to the two rams, '294' and '295,' and Lord Russell's memorandum of the 8th had reference to them also. On the 11th of September, three days after, Earl Russell replied in full to Mr. Adams's letter of the 5th. There was no question now of a duplicate *Alabama*, or of any ordinary ship merely capable of being subsequently adapted to warlike purposes. Earl Russell was replying to a remonstrance against the departure of the two iron-cased rams alleged to be building for the Confederate Government, and he wrote thus:—

'With regard to the general duties of a neutral according to international law, the true doctrine has been laid down repeatedly by Presidents and judges of eminence of the United States, and that doctrine is, that a neutral may sell to either or both of two belligerent parties any implements or munitions of war which such belligerent may wish to purchase from the subjects of the neutral, *and it is difficult to find a reason why a ship that is to be used for warlike purposes is more an instrument or implement of war than cannon, muskets, swords, bayonets, gunpowder, and projectiles to be fired from cannon and muskets. A ship or a musket may be sold to one belligerent or the other, and only ceases to be neutral when the ship is owned, manned, and employed in war, and the musket is held by a soldier and used for the purpose of killing his enemy. In fact, the ship can never be expected to decide a war or a campaign, whereas the other things above mentioned may, by equipping a large army, enable the belligerent which acquires them to obtain decisive*

* 'British Case,' Appendix, vol. ii., p. 355.

*advantages in war.'** Earl Russell, in continuation, points out very forcibly that if the Confederates had been able to obtain some vessels and 'a limited supply of arms from the United Kingdom,' the Federal Government had obtained a far greater supply of warlike stores; and then he adds that her Majesty's Government had reasons to believe, although they could not prove, that agents of the Federal Government had been employed to engage emigrants to go to the United States for the purpose of entering into the military service of the Federal Government.

The linking together of a ship and so great a variety of contraband goods, as being equally articles of legitimate trade between neutrals and either of two belligerents, and the illustration of the inefficiency of a ship in comparison with arms to decide a campaign, which Earl Russell so forcibly employs in the above letter, are quite in harmony with the declarations previously made by himself, by Lord Palmerston, by the Solicitor-General, and with the judgment of the Court of Exchequer, on the right of a British subject to build and sell, and a belligerent to buy, an unarmed ship in England.

I think anyone reading the paragraphs of the letter I have quoted above, knowing that they were parts of a long argumentative reply to a demand for the seizure of the rams, would naturally expect that they were intended to lead up to and to justify a refusal; but in the last paragraph of the letter Earl Russell confirms the promise contained in his memorandum of September 8th, and says that the vessels will be detained 'until satisfactory evidence can be given as to their destination.'

For several months previous to the seizure of the rams

* See 'British Case,' Appendix, vol. ii., pp. 358—360.

the Foreign Office had been inundated with affidavits by Mr. Dudley, the Liverpool Consul. The law officers of the Crown had looked with distrust upon these Consular statements. They recognised probably the stereotyped form with which they had become unpleasantly familiar in the *Alexandra* case. They saw the names of Clarence R. Yonge and George Temple Chapman attached to some of them, and doubtless shrank from again bringing two such witnesses before a jury. At any rate, they reported several times that the 'depositions were insufficient,' that there was 'no evidence capable of being presented to a court of justice,' etc.

The last time the law officers were consulted before the seizure of the vessels appears to have been on the 19th-20th of August. The opinion is signed by Sir Roundell Palmer, who was then the Solicitor-General, now Lord Selborne and the Lord Chancellor of England. He alludes to the fresh affidavits that had been forwarded by Mr. Dudley, and concludes with the following final opinion :—'There is in fact no additional evidence, and we therefore continue to think that the interference of the Government, by seizure of these vessels or otherwise, would not be warranted by any of the depositions which have been brought to our notice.'*

I suppose it will be admitted that every Government has the right to determine the standard of its own neutrality, subject only to the requirements of international law. I mean, that if the municipal law does not confer the power necessary to comply with neutral duties as prescribed by international law, the statutes should be amended; but if the municipal law is stronger than the law of nations requires, the neutral is not bound to enforce it with full rigour.

* See 'British Case,' Appendix, vol. ii., pp. 337, 338.

It is well known that the United States complained bitterly because her Majesty's Government, so they alleged, were precipitate in acknowledging the Confederate States as belligerents. The reply was in effect that the United States had themselves both created and acknowledged the state of war, and that the British Government had only recognised a condition of affairs which already existed. The South could have urged a valid plea to belligerent rights, and the claim could hardly have been denied, but the chief Powers took the initiative, and acknowledged the existence of a *de facto* Government at Richmond, as soon as the President of the United States proclaimed a blockade of the Southern ports. This recognition did not, however, carry with it a diplomatic equality with foreign States, and the Confederate Government could not therefore communicate its views nor urge remonstrances in a direct official manner.

Great Britain laid down at a very early date the rules of neutrality by which she would be guided. It was manifest from the very beginning that those rules, even if administered with scrupulous impartiality, would give the United States an advantage, because of their open ports and their command of the sea. But the Confederate Government, perceiving the improbability of getting a modification of the rules, refrained from wrangling over them, and was content to use the opportunities of supplying the wants of the country to the best possible advantage. One of the chief requirements of the south was ships, not only for the purpose of cruising against the enemy, but to run the blockade.

If there had been anything in the municipal law of Great Britain which prohibited the purchase of an unarmed ship for any subsequent purpose whatever, or if the responsible Ministers of the Crown had stated specifically that there was a difference in principle between trading with a belligerent in arms and in ships, and that they would permit the one and forbid the other, the justice of the distinction would have been doubted, and the policy questioned, but both belligerents would at least have known what to expect. The odds against the Confederacy, great enough in all conscience at best, would have been somewhat increased, but the Southern people would have fought their battle with none the less spirit, even though with less chance of success. But the Foreign Enlistment Act (as it stood in 1861-65) did not forbid a British subject to build or sell a ship of any kind to any mortal man who could pay for her. This has been settled by the decision of a court of law, which has never been reversed, and there is not in the original definition of their neutral policy, nor in the subsequent statements of Ministers, any notice or hint that it was their purpose to draw the line at ships, and to set a ban upon that branch of trade alone. On the contrary, whether we examine the speeches of the Prime Minister and the Solicitor-General in Parliament, or the despatches of the Foreign Secretary, we find one uniform maxim, one fundamental rule of action, namely, that there is no difference in principle between selling a belligerent rifles and gunpowder or ships, and that her Majesty's Government cannot interfere with or forbid either.

The feeling of the Government on the above subject was never more plainly expressed than in Earl Russell's letter of September 11th, 1863, to Mr. Adams, in which his lordship not only reiterates the general proposition that muskets and ships may be dealt in alike, but with striking particularity he proceeds to specify a condition of affairs in which rifles and cannon, swords, bayonets and gunpowder, may be more useful to one belligerent than a ship to the other, and says that neither a ship nor a musket ceases to be neutral until it is in the possession of a belligerent and is about to be used by him against his enemy, and yet in that very letter he announces the purpose to seize the alleged Confederate vessels.

It appears from the printed documents that the vessels were seized by the order of her Majesty's Secretary of State for Foreign Affairs on his own authority as a Minister of the Crown. There was at that time 'no evidence capable of being presented to a court of justice;' the seizure was therefore an act of the State, an exercise of prerogative, and not a process of law. Earl Russell stated that the object of the seizure was to detain the ships until the Government could obtain satisfactory evidence of their destination. To get the evidence the Government took a great deal of trouble, and must have incurred no little expense. A special Commission was sent to Egypt to inquire whether the Viceroy, Ismail Pasha, had really ordered Messrs. Bravay to build two armour-cased vessels for him in Europe; and I may state at once that the Viceroy said he had not. This was all the evidence the Government ever did get, and no legal proceedings were ever taken against either the Messrs. Bravay or Messrs. Laird, except the filing of the 'information.' But was her Majesty's Government under any obligation to go to all this trouble and expense to inquire into the business relations of a French mercantile house and a foreign Government? Was it not perfectly legal for Messrs. Bravay, being French subjects, and their country at peace with both belligerents and with Great Britain, to contract for any ships they liked in

England ? and did it matter at all, as a question of law, what they intended to do with them after taking them away from Liverpool ? Is it to be understood that the precedent is now established that whenever Great Britain is a neutral in all future wars, the Government will undertake to compel every shipbuilder in the kingdom to report who he is working for, and will then require the person, even though a neutral foreigner, to prove what he is going to do with the ship ? If this is so, the Consuls of the belligerents will give her Majesty's Foreign Office more work than any ordinary staff can accomplish.

When the arrangements were made to sell the two rams to Messrs. Bravay, there was no necessity for manufacturing any plea of a pretended contract with the Viceroy of Egypt. It was well known both in Paris and in Alexandria, and it was known to the French Government, that the firm had been for years in business relations with the Egyptian Government, and that they had executed large contracts for the Viceroy in France. The letters from M. François Bravay respecting the commissions he had undertaken on account of the Viceroy, and the reply of the Paris house, quoted in a previous part of this chapter, were written months before any arrangement in respect to the rams at Liverpool was contemplated, and therefore could not have been prepared as a cover for that transaction. Indeed, at the date of those letters neither Mr. Slidell nor I knew anything whatever of Messrs. Bravay, and had never met any member of the firm. It is well known in Europe that his Highness Ismail Pasha, and his predecessor, Said Pasha, had very large and peculiar dealings with private persons in England and France, and that they both made efforts to add to their military and naval strength secretly, wishing for political reasons to avoid the interference or inquisitive supervision of the Sublime Porte.

When the Messrs. Laird were requested to sell the ships, they were open, of course, to all practicable offers, and they looked about for a purchaser, just as any other business men would have done under the same circumstances. They knew that the sale of the ships would involve the release of one contractor, with whose financial position they were satisfied, and the substitution of another, as to whose commercial credit they must be assured. Any ship-builder in England would have treated the matter in this way, and no other. When the Messrs. Bravay came forward to buy the ships, it is not probable that Messrs. Laird inquired particularly into the precise nature of their dealings with the Viceroy. It did not concern them to know whether the 'order' from the Egyptian Government was a specific contract in writing or not; I do not even know whether they asked anything about it. As prudent business men, they inquired into the financial position of the Messrs. Bravay, and, being satisfied with the security they could give for the payment of the two ships, they reported the offer and effected the sale. The whole transaction was carried out in a perfectly legal way, and the ships became the absolute property of the Messrs. Bravay. No process of law could have destroyed their title. Of this we were assured by eminent counsel. They made all subsequent payments, and when Her Majesty's Government called upon Messrs. Laird to say for whom they were building the ships, they replied 'For Messrs. A. Bravay and Co., No. 6, Rue de Londres, Paris.'

The Viceroy had refrained from making a specific

contract in writing for any ships 'for political reasons.' When brought to the ordeal of a formal diplomatic inquiry, he repudiated the transaction for the same reasons; but even though he thus denied the validity of the alleged commission to M. Bravay, how could that destroy the right of the Paris firm to the property which they held by a clear, indisputable title in England? If a neutral has the right to sell a rifle or a ship to a belligerent, and her Majesty's Ministers and the Court of Exchequer have both declared that he has, why may not a neutral buy from another neutral a rifle or a ship and sell either or both of them afterwards to a belligerent for a profit?

I think anyone who examines this case fairly upon the facts will be driven to acknowledge, even if he does not willingly admit, that in seizing the two rams at Birkenhead, and in bringing about a forced sale to the British Admiralty, Earl Russell departed from the rules of neutrality laid down by her Majesty's Government, from the principles often affirmed by himself, and from the judgment of a competent court, and that he applied the Foreign Enlistment Act, not merely to prevent the danger of hostile collision, or an infringement of law within the kingdom, which the Lord Chief Baron said was its intent, but so as to afford protection to a belligerent, which he distinctly said was not the intent.

I have not pretended to discuss this question with reference to international law as commonly understood, and I do not bring it forward as a matter of complaint on behalf of the late Confederate States. Arguments upon dead issues cannot change results or moderate past disappointments. My whole and only purpose in this narrative is to demonstrate that the Confederate Government, in the effort to supply its wants in England during the Civil War, acted with due circumspection, and endeavoured to conform to the laws of the realm and to the principles of neutrality as they were expounded by the highest constituted authorities in the kingdom.

My acquaintance with the Messrs. Bravay began and ended with the transaction described in this chapter. I have never seen a member of the firm since. Mr. Adams, in one of his strongly worded letters on the subject, speaks of M. Bravay as 'a French commercial adventurer, proved to have been capable of prevarication, if not of absolute falsehood.' As a matter of fact, M. Bravay was not placed in a position requiring him to prevaricate, and was certainly not tested to the extreme point insinuated by Mr. Adams. He exhibited proof of his large dealings with the Viceroy, and showed the correspondence with reference to the building of two ships, merely as evidence that he could undertake a large transaction. I think no one who was conversant with the circumstances would have doubted that he was telling the truth in the statement then made, and I have never heard of his making any other. The firm performed their agreement with Mr. Slidell and me with perfect good faith as regards all monetary transactions, and unhesitatingly waived the stipulated commission when the enterprise failed. The only way in which it could possibly be said that they misled us was in this respect, that they were very sanguine that the Viceroy would not deny the verbal order for the ships, and that even if he did, then, as French subjects, they could get the vessels out of England and take them to a French port. In these respects they failed both in their expectations and in their promises; but there was a political element in the transaction which helped to give them confidence and to mislead us; and there was another disappointment in store for the Confederate Government emanating from the same political source, which will be fully explained in another chapter.

END OF VOL. I.